Junior
Chronicle
of the 20th
Century

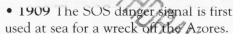

- **1906** Nichrome wire used as an element in electric fires for the first time.
- **1906** Women aged over 24 get the vote in Finland.
- **1906** San Francisco, USA, is razed to the ground by a violent earthquake and fire.
- **1907** New Zealand becomes independent from British rule.

- **1907** More than 1 million immigrants enter USA.
- **1907** First circus is set up by the US Ringling brothers.
- **1908** The first international football match is played in Austria.
- **1908** The first Model T Ford goes on sale in the USA.
- **1908** Two-year-old Pu Yi ascends the throne of China.

- **1909** The SOS danger signal is first used at sea for a wreck off the Azores.
- **1909** Curtis Model D pusher flies in first speed contest.

1910s

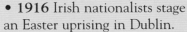

- **1916** Irish nationalists stage an Easter uprising in Dublin.
- **1916** One million Allied and German soldiers die in the Somme offensive in France.
- **1916** The Russian monk Gregory Rasputin is murdered by two relatives of the tsar.
- **1917** Tsar Nicholas II abdicates.

- **1917** US troops enter World War I on the side of the Allies.
- **1917** The Bolsheviks, led by Lenin, seize power in Russia.
- **1917** Mata Hari, the exotic dancer, is executed by the French for spying.
- **1918** In the Urals, the Russian royal family is murdered in a cellar.

- **1918** Led by Faisal and T E Lawrence, Arab forces capture Damascus, Syria.
- **1918** The Great War ends and peace comes to Europe.

1920s

- **1927** Duke Ellington begins playing at the Cotton Club.
- **1927** US pilot Charles Lindbergh flies non-stop across the Atlantic.
- **1927** The first "talkie", US film *The Jazz Singer*, stars Al Jolson.
- **1927** Tomb of Genghis Khan found.

- **1927** In China, Chiang Kai-shek crushes attempted coup by communists.
- **1927** Model A Ford is released on the market with a choice of four colours.
- **1928** Flying doctor service begins in Australia.
- **1929** St Valentine Day's massacre in Chicago, USA.

- **1929** Benito Mussolini's Fascist Party rigs an election in Italy and forms a government.
- **1929** USA Wall Street crash leads to world financial crisis.

1930s

- **1936** 200 out-of-work UK men go on the Jarrow hunger march.
- **1936** German troops march into the cities of the Rhineland.
- **1936** Edward VIII of the UK abdicates to marry a divorcee.
- **1936** France abandons the Gold Standard and prints money freely.

- **1937** *Marie Claire* magazine is launched in Paris, France.
- **1938** Austria is made a German province.
- **1938** Action Comics, with Superman, are launched.
- **1939** After the invasion of Poland, Britain and France declare war on Germany.

- **1939** Soviet Igor Sikorsky designs the first helicopter with rotor arms for lift.

1940s

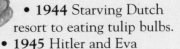

- **1944** Starving Dutch resort to eating tulip bulbs.
- **1945** Hitler and Eva Braun commit suicide in Berlin.
- **1945** Germany surrenders and Europe celebrates VE Day.
- **1945** After two atom bombs are dropped, Japan surrenders.
- **1946** The United Nations holds its first session.

- **1947** Marshall Plan offers aid to countries in western Europe.
- **1947** Dutch Jewish girl Anne Frank's war diary is published.
- **1947** US pilot Chuck Yeager flies faster than the speed of sound.
- **1948** Mahatma Gandhi is assassinated at prayers in India.
- **1948** Jewish leaders declare the new Jewish state of Israel.

- **1948** Birth-rate soars in a postwar baby boom.
- **1949** NATO (the North Atlantic Treaty Organization) is formed.

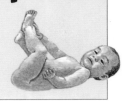

Junior
Chronicle
of the 20th
Century

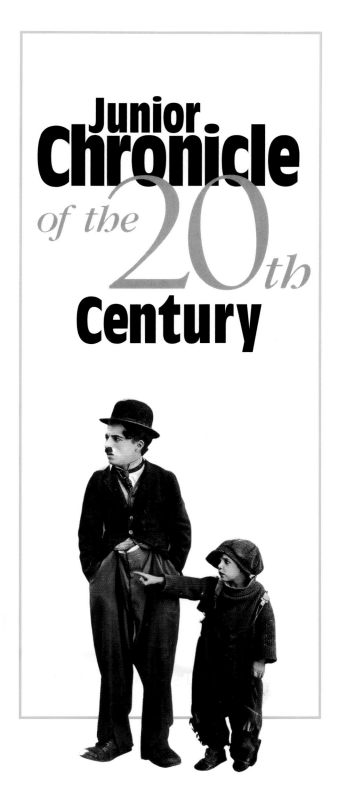

LONDON • NEW YORK • STUTTGART • MOSCOW • SYDNEY

A DORLING KINDERSLEY BOOK

Senior editors Bridget Hopkinson, Miranda Smith
Senior art editor Andrew Nash
Editors Susila Baybars, Laura Buller,
Julie Ferris, Melanie Halton, Helena Spiteri
Art editors Diane Klein, Sharon Spencer
Designers Goldberry Broad, Carlton Hibbert,
Joseph Hoyle, Susan St. Louis
Managing editors Gillian Denton, Linda Martin
Managing art editor Julia Harris
Production Charlotte Traill
Picture research Melissa Albany, Jo Carlill,
James Clarke, Kathy Lockley
Research Prue Grice, Sean Stancioff
DTP designer Nicola Studdart

Written by Simon Adams, Robin Cross,
Ann Kramer, Haydn Middleton, Sally Tagholm

First published in Great Britain in 1997
by Dorling Kindersley Limited,
9 Henrietta Street, London WC2E 8PS

A CIP catalogue record for this book is
available from the British Library.

909.82

ISBN 0751

356 131 6404

Colour reproduction by
Colourscan, Singapore
Printed in Italy by Mondadori

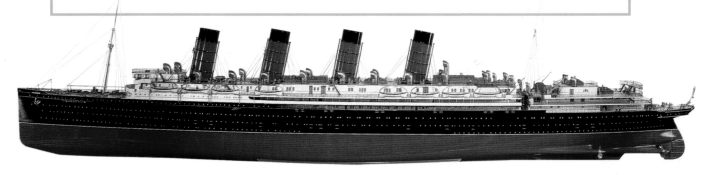

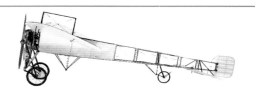

FOREWORD

The 20th century has been a century of unique change, exploration, discovery, and invention. JUNIOR CHRONICLE tells the story of an extraordinary century month by month, year by year. Lively news stories and dramatic images bring to life the historic events that have transformed the world, as well as lesser events of particular interest to younger readers.

The Wright brothers' first flight, Neil Armstrong's historic steps on the Moon, the splitting of the atom, the creation of anti-matter, television, satellites, two world wars, AIDS, and the struggle for democracy have all played a major part in defining the 20th century. So too have Disney cartoons, trend-setting fashions, musical innovations, and the microchip.

Throughout the book, special pages examine in depth topics such as life in the trenches in World War I, the Roaring Twenties, the Spanish Civil War, cinema, the Swinging Sixties, the Vietnam War, the end of the Cold War, and the impact of information technology. The world leaders, sport and movie stars, musicians, inventors and scientists, and even law-breakers who have made this century memorable have their own section in the back of the book. With its ground-breaking news stories, the JUNIOR CHRONICLE is a detailed diary of world events, presenting all the changes of this incredible century as they happened.

CONTENTS

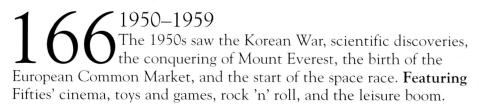

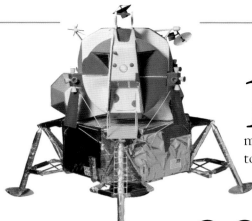

190 1960–1969
The "Swinging Sixties" was a decade of mini-skirts, flower power, pop music, the US civil rights movement, and China's cultural revolution. **Featuring** the race to the Moon, Sixties' culture, television, and peace and protest.

220 1970–1979
A decade of international terrorism, protest, political scandal, platform shoes, and punk music. **Featuring** the war in Vietnam, the feminist fight, sounds of the Seventies, and the microchip revolution.

250 1980–1989
Yuppies, AIDS, power dressing, gender bending, superpowers, and conservative politics defined the Eighties. **Featuring** Live Aid, minimalism, the "green" movement, and the end of the Cold War.

280 1990–1996
The Nineties saw the collapse of the Iron Curtain, ethnic conflicts, international co-operation, rave culture, and the "world wide web". **Featuring** the technological "global village", Nineties music, the end of apartheid, and hopes for the future.

CENTURY AT A GLANCE

304 Hollywood superstars

306 Scientists and inventors

308 Sporting heroes

310 World leaders

312 Music-makers

314 Law-breakers

316 British government and structure

318 British sport and culture

320 Index and acknowledgements

1900

Dawn of the century

1 JANUARY

After taking part in wild celebrations into the early hours of the morning, people woke up today to the dawn of a new century. In spite of concerns over the present course of events in the South African War and the actions of Boxer rebels in China, the general feeling is one of optimism since the state of world affairs is far rosier today than it was at the beginning of the 19th century. During the last 100 years there have been remarkable developments in communications and industry. Today there is every hope that, along with further progress in these and other important fields, the years that follow will bring peace and prosperity across the world.

Detail from a poster to celebrate the start of the 20th century

World Exhibition opens in Paris

14 APRIL

The president of France Émile Loubet today opened the World Exhibition in Paris, the biggest of its kind ever staged in Europe. The exhibition site covers 221 hectares (547 acres) along the Rue des Nations and the Quai d'Orsay. Among the sights on display are electrical illuminations in the Palace of Electricity (above) and the Hall of Illusions. In a pavilion dedicated to his sculpture, a new work by Auguste Rodin, *The Kiss*, is attracting great attention from art critics.

THE MAGIC OF OZ
The Wonderful Wizard of Oz, written by US author Frank Baum, is a new tale certain to enchant children. It tells of Dorothy, who is whisked away by a cyclone to the magical land of Oz.

JANUARY–JUNE

World Events	**JAN** The British army is defeated by Boers at the Battle of Spion Kop in the South African, or Boer, War.	**MAR** In India, millions of famine victims appeal for help from the UK government as their meagre food supplies run out.	**MAY** The South African town of Mafeking is relieved by British forces after a seven-month siege by Boer troops.	**JUN** Chinese rebels, the "Fists of Righteous Harmony" known as the Boxers, try to expel all Europeans from China.
Entertainment	**FEB** US college tennis star Dwight F Davis puts up a trophy for an international contest.	**MAR** New York University in the USA becomes the site for the Hall of Fame, set up for notable Americans.	**MAY** UK actress Lillie Langtry is a hit in the USA with the play *The Degenerates*.	**MAY** The second Olympic Games opens in Paris, France, and will run until late July.
Innovations	**FEB** US Eastman Kodak Co launches the Brownie Box camera priced at $1.	**WALL PAINTING, KNOSSOS** — **MAR** UK archaeologist Arthur Evans begins to unearth an ancient civilization at Knossos, Crete.	**APR** The world's first tape recorder, which uses magnetic wire, is demonstrated at the Paris Exhibition.	**BOX OF PLASTICINE** — **MAY** Commercial production of Plasticine modelling clay begins in an old flour mill at Bathampton, UK.

HARBUTT'S PLASTICINE
For Home Modelling
A Game! A Toy! An Occupation!

1900

The final whistle

Casey Jones in Engine 638

29 APRIL

Casey Jones, an American train driver, died today in an act of great heroism. Late in starting out from Memphis, Tennessee, Jones was pushing the *Cannon Ball Express* to its limits on the dangerous route to Canton, Mississippi. As he entered Vaughan, Mississippi, a stationary train forced him to slam on the brakes. Seeing that a collision was about to happen, he made his fireman jump out, but stayed himself to slow down the train and save many passengers' lives.

Lift off for Zeppelin

1 JULY

Count Ferdinand von Zeppelin's huge airship moved forwards, backwards, and sideways, before it rose off the ground and finally proved it could fly. The maiden flight took place over Lake Constance, Switzerland, and lasted for more than an hour. The airship contains 16 cells filled with hydrogen gas and is powered by two 16 hp engines.

Airship LZ1 rises above Lake Constance

Paris Métro opens

10 JULY

Paris today celebrates the opening of the Chemin-de-Fer Métropolitain de Paris, the underground railway Parisians have nicknamed "le Métro". Construction of the 10-km (6.25-mile) long railway began in 1898. Many of the stations are designed by the architect Hector Guimard, whose ornate wrought-iron designs are winning praise across the city.

Métro entrance of Guimard design

The latest tennis racquet has a grooved grip and fishtail handle

US victory in first Davis Cup

10 AUGUST

The US tennis team today won the first International Lawn Tennis Trophy, the Davis Cup, at the Longwood Cricket Club, Boston, Mass. The US team was leading Britain 3–0 in a five-match series when rain forced an early end to the contest.

JULY–DECEMBER

JUL Umberto I, the king of Italy, is shot four times by an anarchist at Monza, near Milan, and dies almost immediately.

AUG German philosopher Friedrich Nietzsche, noted for his concept of the "superman", dies at the age of 56.

AUG The first long-distance bus service is introduced on the 320-km (200-mile) journey from London to Leeds in the UK.

COCA-COLA

AUG Allied European forces, 10,000 strong, storm Peking in China to end the 56-day siege by Boxer rebels.

AUG Coca-Cola, in the form of a syrup, is first brought to Europe from the USA and is an immediate success.

SEP Italian explorer the Duke of Abruzzi comes closer to the North Pole than anyone before him.

NOV British forces step up hostilities in South Africa by opening concentration camps and setting light to Boer farms.

OCT Austrian psychiatrist Sigmund Freud publishes a groundbreaking book, *The Interpretation of Dreams*.

NOV Viennese scientist Dr Karl Landsteiner discovers and classifies three different blood types.

NOV Republican William McKinley wins a second term in the White House as president of the USA.

NOV Oscar Wilde, the notorious Irish playwright and wit, dies in exile in France at the age of 44.

SIGMUND FREUD

DEC German scientist Max Planck proposes that energy comes in atom-sized units.

1901

The birth of a nation

1 JANUARY

A new country was born this morning when the six British colonies in Australia joined together as an independent nation. The Commonwealth of Australia, as the new country is formally known, is today holding celebrations in Sydney that are expected to draw 50,000 people. A new government, led by Edmund Barton, has already been formed. One of its first tasks will be to agree on a site for the new capital city.

End of an era

Queen Victoria

22 JANUARY

After a short illness, Victoria, queen of Britain and empress of India, died today at Osborne, her seaside home on the Isle of Wight, surrounded by close members of her family. She was 81 years old. Victoria's reign lasted nearly 64 years, longer than any monarch before her. It was an age of expansion in which trade and industry flourished and the British Empire stretched to all four corners of the world.

High performance

31 MARCH

The German motor manufacturer Gottlieb Daimler today delivered a remarkable new car to Émil Jellinek, consul-general of the Austro-Hungarian Empire in Nice, France. The high-performance car, especially made for the consul-general and named Mercedes after his daughter (above left), is an improved version of a model designed by Daimler two years ago. The Mercedes is quite unlike the horse-drawn carriages that are still a common sight on our roads. The car has a 4-cylinder, 5.9-litre engine, giving it a top speed of 80 km/h (50 mph).

The new high-performance Mercedes

JANUARY–JUNE

World Events	**FEB** Leaders from around the world come to London, UK, to attend the state funeral of Queen Victoria.	**MAR** Students and workers stage riots in major Russian cities to protest against the new government regulations.	**MAY** In a confidential memorandum, the UK votes to uphold its policy of "splendid isolation" from events in Europe.	**JUN** A new constitution for Cuba is agreed that gives the US government almost total control over the island.
Entertainment	**JAN** Russian playwright Anton Chekhov's *Three Sisters* premieres in Moscow.	**JAN** Italian opera composer Giuseppe Verdi, best known for *Rigoletto*, dies at the age of 88.	**APR** French sculptor Auguste Rodin's new sculpture of Victor Hugo attracts criticism from art critics and patrons.	**MAY** French film producer Claude Grivolas invents a projector that makes three-dimensional pictures.
Innovations	**JAN** UK toy-maker Frank Hornby introduces Meccano, a self-assembly engineering toy. **MECCANO**	**MAR** The first diesel engine goes on show, demonstrated by the Diesel Motor Co near Manchester, UK.	**MAY** The world's first multi-storey car park, made up of seven levels, opens off Piccadilly, London, UK. **AUGUSTE RODIN**	**JUN** French physicist Henri Becquerel discovers small particles known as electrons inside atoms.

1901

Harlequin and his Companion *by Pablo Picasso*

Art world discovers new genius

24 JUNE

An exhibition by a Spanish artist is receiving much praise in Paris, France. Nineteen-year-old Pablo Picasso from Malaga in Spain set up a studio in Montmartre earlier this year, and has become known as "Le Petit Goya" because of his native Andalusian hat. Picasso's paintings show a remarkable range of subjects. Dancers of the Moulin Rouge, children, courtesans, and race meetings are among the subjects that fill the canvases of this talented painter.

US president dies

14 SEPTEMBER

United States president William McKinley died early this morning, eight days after he was shot by Polish anarchist Leon Czolgosz while opening an exhibition in Buffalo, New York. At first the president's wounds were not thought to be serious, but in the last few days his condition has deteriorated rapidly. Vice-President Theodore Roosevelt was tracked down in the Adirondack Mountains and brought hastily to Buffalo, but arrived a few hours after McKinley's death. He took the presidential oath of office this afternoon. At 42, he is the youngest United States president.

PING PONG CRAZE HITS HOME

Ping Pong fever is sweeping Europe and the United States this year as families convert their tables into indoor tennis courts. The game, originally known as Gossima, failed to catch on until its manufacturer changed its name to Ping Pong. The first tournament was held in December this year.

JULY–DECEMBER

SEP A peace protocol is drawn up and signed in Peking, China, formally ending the Boxer Rising.

AUG Irish athlete Peter O' Connor sets a new world long-jump record of 7.6 m (24 ft 11 in).

JUL German doctor Robert Koch states that the bubonic plague may have been due solely to rats.

LITHOGRAPH BY TOULOUSE-LAUTREC

SEP The Ashanti kingdom in Africa is annexed by the UK to the Gold Coast Colony.

SEP French painter Henri de Toulouse-Lautrec dies in Malrome, southern France, at the age of 36.

AUG A new US car company is founded in Detroit, Michigan, to produce Cadillac cars.

OCT Booker T Washington is the first black American to be invited to dine at the White House in Washington, USA.

OCT US yacht *Columbia* beats the UK *Shamrock II* in a very close finish to retain the America's Cup.

DEC US businessman King C Gillette invents the disposable razor, revolutionizing home grooming.

REVERSE OF NOBEL PRIZE MEDAL

DEC The first Nobel Prizes are awarded in Norway and Sweden to those who have acted for the benefit of humankind.

DEC Intrigue continues over the mystery author of *Claudine à Paris*, who is thought to be a woman.

DEC Italian inventor Guglielmo Marconi transmits the first radio signal across the Atlantic Ocean.

1902

Louis Tiffany's lamps are all the rage in modern homes

"Modern style" makes a splash

20 APRIL

An exciting new exhibition of "modern style" art, or "Art Nouveau" as it is known in France, opened today at the Société Nationale des Beaux-Arts in Paris. This decorative arts style has been developed by artists all over Europe for the past few years and is characterized by snake-like lines and patterns. It can be seen in many places, from the posters of Alphonse Mucha and the jewellery of René Lalique, to the design of the Métro stations in Paris and furnishings for the homes.

Méliès excels

1 MAY

A *Voyage to the Moon*, the latest film from French director Georges Méliès, has been made using sophisticated new techniques. Audiences will be spellbound at the special effects that run throughout this 13-minute production, which took three months to make and cost a record 10,000 francs. The plot, loosely based on a novel by Jules Verne, tells the story of six scientists who visit the moon and are captured by strange aliens.

The spacecraft lands in the eye of the moon

Mount Pelée erupts

8 MAY

Of the 30,000 inhabitants of St Pierre, the capital of the Caribbean island of Martinique, a drunk in jail was the only survivor when Mount Pelée erupted this morning. Shortly before 8 am the volcano threw out a cloud of glowing gas that engulfed the port within minutes. An eyewitness on a ship in the harbour stated that a "wave of fire was on us and over us like a lightning flash". Latest reports confirm that all the buildings in the town have been destroyed.

JANUARY–JUNE

World Events

JAN After crushing the Boxer Rising, the Chinese imperial court returns to the capital of Peking.

JAN The UK signs an alliance with Japan to safeguard both countries' interests in China and Korea.

APR Russian and Chinese officials sign an agreement in Peking to restore Manchuria to Chinese control.

JUN US Congress authorizes President Roosevelt to spend up to $40 million to build a canal across the Panama isthmus.

Entertainment

JAN Michigan beats Stanford in the first US college Rose Bowl football competition.

MAR UK author Conan Doyle publishes a new Holmes mystery, *The Hound of the Baskervilles*.

APR French film producer Charles Pathé opens a new film studio at Vincennes in Paris.

JUN Renault, the French car manufacturer, wins every prize in the first Paris–Vienna motor race.

Innovations

FEB US doctors prove that yellow fever is spread by a species of mosquito.

THE HOUND OF THE BASKERVILLES

FEB *Motor Cycling*, the world's first magazine for motorbike fanatics, goes on sale in the UK.

APR Cecil Rhodes' will provides funds for US, German, and UK citizens to study at Oxford University.

THOMAS EDISON

MAY US inventor Thomas Edison develops a new longer-lasting and lightweight type of electric battery.

1902

Boer War ends in South Africa

1 JUNE

Last night, in the Transvaal border town of Vereeniging, Boer leaders signed a peace treaty with Britain, finally ending the bitter conflict that has lasted for two years and seven months. The war started when the Boer states of the South African Republic, seeking to keep control of their rich goldfields, refused to give resident foreigners political rights. In signing the treaty, the Boers have agreed to meet the British terms: to lay down their weapons and recognize the British monarch as their sovereign. This bitter pill was made easier to swallow by the fact that the Boers will receive

£3 million from the British government to assist with the restocking and repairing of their farmlands. The treaty also promises that self-government will follow at a later date. These are such favourable terms that it is questionable who the real winner of the war is.

Birth of the "teddy"

18 NOVEMBER

A cartoon by Clifford Berryman in the *Washington Post* has sparked the idea for a new children's toy. The cartoon shows US president Theodore "Teddy" Roosevelt refusing to shoot a captive bear cub while on an unsuccessful bear hunt in Mississippi. Toy-makers are now eager to transform the cartoon bear into a toy made of brown plush with moveable arms and legs. The "teddy" bear, as it is affectionately being called, is certain to be popular as a mascot for the well-respected president and future sales predictions are high.

The new toy bear is called "teddy" after President Roosevelt's nickname

PETER RABBIT DEBUTS

A charming character appeared in children's literature this year. Written and illustrated by British writer Beatrix Potter, *The Tale of Peter Rabbit* tells of mischievous Peter's adventure in Mr McGregor's garden and introduces us to Peter's sisters, Flopsy, Mopsy, and Cottontail.

JULY–DECEMBER

JUL The celebrated 1,000-year-old Gothic belltower of St Mark's Cathedral in Venice, Italy, collapses during a safety inspection.

AUG French film director George Méliès makes a film based on the coronation of UK king Edward VII.

JUL German scientists patent the formula for barbituric acid, which is used to produce sleeping pills.

ST MARK'S BELLTOWER

AUG At the age of 60 and despite concerns of ill health, Edward VII is crowned king in Westminster Abbey, London, UK.

SEP Émile Zola, French author of *Germinal* and *L'Assommoir*, dies from suffocation at the age of 62.

AUG The first parcel mail is sent from the UK to the USA on the White Star ocean liner *Teutonic*.

OCT Russian exile Leon Trotsky escapes from Siberia and makes his way to London, UK, arriving at Vladimir Lenin's door.

OCT UK writer Rudyard Kipling publishes a collection of *Just So Stories* for children.

NOV J M Bacon becomes the first person to cross the Irish Sea in a hot-air balloon.

JUST SO STORIES

DEC A spectacular engineering feat, the Aswan Dam, is officially opened in Egypt.

NOV Sales of Italian tenor Enrico Caruso's first record reach one million copies.

DEC Major Ronald Ross is awarded the Nobel Prize for work on the causes of malaria.

1900 GERMAN ZEPPELIN
AIRSHIP *LZ1* FIRST LIFTS OFF

1909 FRENCH DEPERDUSSIN
MAKES SLEEK MONOPLANES

1909 MODEL-D PUSHER
WINS AIRSPEED CONTEST

PIONEERS OF AVIATION

FOR HUNDREDS OF YEARS inventors had been devising ways of flying through the air with the ease of a bird. Although balloons and airships had taken to the skies, it was not until a cold December day in 1903 that the Wright brothers made the first powered, sustained, and heavier-than-air flight. After that, aircraft technology progressed at a rapid rate and aviators crossed first the English Channel and then the Atlantic and Pacific oceans. In 1914 the onset of World War I created a demand for fast, agile fighter planes, and by 1918 the aeroplane had become a relatively sophisticated and reliable machine. The introduction of passenger flights between major cities in the 1920s confirmed that a new age of travel had arrived.

Twelve seconds of glory

Soon after 10.30 am, on 17 December 1903, Orville Wright took to the air above the beach at Kitty Hawk, North Carolina, in the United States. His first flight in *Flyer* lasted 12 seconds and covered 36 m (120 ft). By the fourth and final flight of the day, his brother Wilbur had covered 260 m (853 ft) in 59 seconds.

Blériot crosses the Channel

In July 1909, French aviator Louis Blériot became the first person to fly across the English Channel. He took off from Sangatte, France, and flew northwest to land at Dover Castle in England after a flight lasting 43 minutes. He had designed the Type XI monoplane with control wires to warp the wings and made it with strong, flexible woods. After his flight, Blériot became an international celebrity. More than 100 monoplanes were sold and he became the first large-scale aircraft manufacturer.

LOUIS
BLÉRIOT

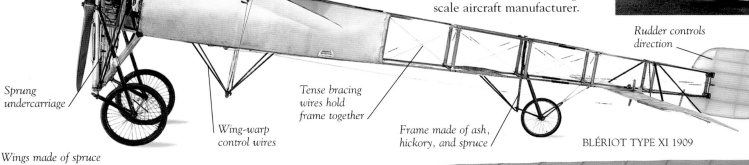

*Three-cylinder
Anzani engine*

*Sprung
undercarriage*

*Wing-warp
control wires*

*Tense bracing
wires hold
frame together*

*Frame made of ash,
hickory, and spruce*

*Rudder controls
direction*

BLÉRIOT TYPE XI 1909

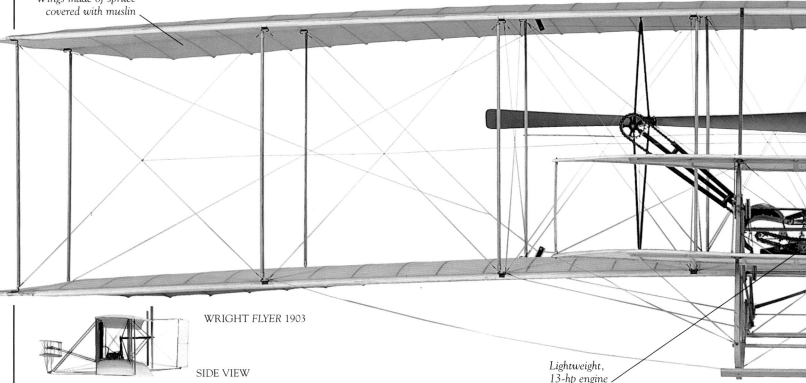

*Wings made of spruce
covered with muslin*

WRIGHT *FLYER* 1903

SIDE VIEW

*Lightweight,
13-hp engine*

1915 FOKKER TRIPLANE
IS MADE BY THE DUTCH

1917 GERMAN LVG CVl
IS DEVELOPED FOR WAR

1917 AGILE SOPWITH PUP TAKES
PART IN DRAMATIC "DOGFIGHTS"

Air shows

Displays of flying skills quickly became popular as bold young aviators demonstrated incredible feats above the heads of adoring crowds. Many became superstars – Louis Paulham earned more than one million francs from his flying exploits.

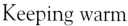

GOGGLES

Button-up cuffs to keep out the wind

FUR-LINED BOOTS

LEATHER FLYING JACKET

Keeping warm

Early aircraft gave little protection to the pilots, who sat in uncomfortable seats that were open to the elements. Wool-lined leather jackets, sheepskin-lined gloves and boots, windproof leather helmets, and goggles were all needed to keep out the cold.

GLOVES

Across the Atlantic

Piloting a Vickers-Vimy biplane, Captain John Alcock from Britain and US navigator Lieutenant Arthur Brown became the first people to fly non-stop across the Atlantic Ocean. They left Newfoundland on 15 June 1919, flying through fog and sleet storms to crash land in an Irish bog 16 hours 12 minutes later. They covered the 3,040 km (1,900 miles) at an average speed of 192 km/h (120 mph).

Female pilots

Women also put themselves in the record books. In 1930, Amy Johnson became the first woman to fly solo from Britain to Australia. Two years later, Amelia Earhart flew solo across the Atlantic Ocean.

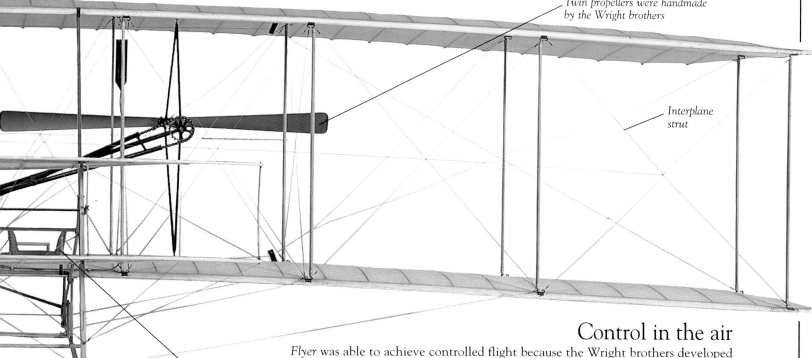

Twin propellers were handmade by the Wright brothers

Interplane strut

Harness for the pilot

Control in the air

Flyer was able to achieve controlled flight because the Wright brothers developed a way to warp, or twist, the wings. A taut cable connected the wings and allowed either side of the craft to be lifted so that it could fly level or make banked turns.

1903

Jewish victims of the Kishinev massacre

Massacre of Jews

16 APRIL

In an organized attack, or pogrom, that began two days ago, Russian peasants have murdered hundreds of Jews in Kishinev, southwestern Russia. The appalling slaughter is an act of revenge for the killing of a Christian boy. Local people suspect that both he, and a girl that went missing last week, were killed by Jews. Police are turning a blind eye while the Jewish population, which makes up almost half the 100,000 inhabitants of the town, is brutally attacked, and homes and businesses are set on fire and destroyed.

NEW LONDON NOVEL

The Call of the Wild is the story of a tame dog that returns to the wild after his master dies and leads a wolf pack. It is earning praise for its US author Jack London, who has based the tale on his experiences in Alaska.

Wild West is cinema success

15 MAY

A ten-minute film from US director Edwin S Porter is breaking new ground in film production. Called *The Great Train Robbery* it is set in the American West and the plot features cowboys and outlaws. The film is packed with action and suspense: a robbery, a horseback escape, and a chase by the local posse are punctuated with fist-fights and gunplay. Filming was done largely on location and clever editing gives the movie a realistic atmosphere not previously achieved. The highlight is when the chief outlaw turns towards the camera and fires his Colt revolver at point-blank range. The screen turns a bloody red, prompting screams from the audience! The formula has proved such a success that it seems certain we shall be seeing more films of this kind.

George Barnes, who plays the role of a gun-wielding outlaw

JANUARY–JUNE

World Events	**JAN** A coronation reception is held at Delhi to crown UK king Edward VII emperor of India.	**MAR** In an attempt to keep undesirables out, the USA imposes a $2 head tax on all immigrants entering the country.	**APR** In Holland, the Dutch government forces an end to the strike of railway and dock workers by calling in troops.	**JUN** The Serbian king and queen are murdered by rebellious army officers who burst into the Royal Palace in Belgrade.
Entertainment	**JAN** A musical production of *The Wonderful Wizard of Oz* opens on Broadway, New York, USA.	**MAR** A major French exhibition of modern art, including paintings by Matisse and Derain, opens.	**MAY** French painter Paul Gauguin, known for his Tahiti paintings, dies in the South Pacific at the age of 54.	**MAY** The first Paris–Madrid road race is abandoned when six die at Bordeaux, France, on the first day.
Innovations	**JAN** UK doctor Henry Smith perfects the operation for curing eye cataracts.	**FEB** US dentists propose that porcelain can replace gold or silver for filling teeth or making crowns.	**MAY** The first outdoor telephone kiosk, is installed in High Holborn, London, UK.	**JUN** The year-old Pepsi-Cola company registers its trade name "Pepsi-Cola" in the USA.

AN IMMIGRANT FAMILY

DETAIL FROM A GAUGUIN PAINTING

1903

Cyclist sweeps to victory

19 JULY

After 19 gruelling days in the saddle, Maurice Garin, a 32-year-old chimney sweep from France, today won the Tour de France cycle race. Cyclists started the six-stage race in Paris on 1 July and covered a distance of 2,428 km (1,509 miles), with stops at Lyon, Marseilles, Toulouse, Bordeaux, and Nantes. Garin finished in fine style, 2 hours 49 minutes ahead of his nearest rival, the unknown Louis Pothier, "the butcher of Sens". Of the original 60 entrants, only 21 finished the race, which was the brainchild of *Le Vélo* journalist Henri Desgrange. Over the past weeks, crowds have flocked to watch and cheer on the cyclists, and the Tour has been the talk of France. Organizers hope to make it an annual event in the future.

Maurice Garin speeds his way to victory on the latest make of racing bicycle

Woman wins the Nobel

10 DECEMBER

French scientist Marie Curie became the first woman to win a Nobel Prize when she was given the award for physics today. She shares the prize with her husband Pierre and colleague Henri Becquerel, in recognition of the work they have done to investigate the scientific mystery of what they are calling "radioactivity". Several years ago Polish-born Marie proved that it is always present in uranium atoms. She has been working on the phenomenon ever since.

Marie and Pierre Curie in their laboratory

Baseball battle

13 OCTOBER

Boston beat Pittsburgh 5–3 in the first World Series baseball competition in the United States. The new contest pits the winners of the National League against those of the American League in an end-of-season showdown. Match favourites Pittsburgh were generally outplayed by Boston and Patrick Dougherty hit two homers to ensure victory.

JULY–DECEMBER

AUG At its congress in the UK, the Russian Social Democratic Party splits into Mensheviks and Bolsheviks.

SEP Turks massacre 50,000 Bulgarian men, women, and children in an attempt to suppress the uprising in Macedonia.

OCT In the UK Emmeline Pankhurst founds the Women's Social and Political Union to campaign for women's right to vote.

DEC Japanese marines land at Mok-Pho in Korea, an act that will further increase tension in the area.

JUL The world's first powerboat race takes place in Cork Harbour, Ireland.

SEP *Kit Carson*, a Western film, opens in the USA, after *The Great Train Robbery*'s success.

NOV French impressionist landscape painter Camille Pissarro dies in Paris at the age of 73.

DEC UK cricketer R E Foster scores a record test innings of 287 runs against Australia.

JUL US president Roosevelt inaugurates a Pacific communications cable by sending a message around the world.

MODEL A FORD

JUL The US Ford Motor Co sells the first two-cylinder Model A to a physician in Detroit, Michigan, for $850.

NOV Dutch physiologist Willem Einthoven invents the electro-cardiograph to monitor heart contractions.

WRIGHT FLYER PROPELLER

DEC Orville and Wilbur Wright make the first powered flight in *Flyer* at Kitty Hawk, North Carolina, USA.

1904

The world visits St Louis

30 APRIL

One hundred years after President Thomas Jefferson purchased much of the US midwest from France, a world fair has opened in St Louis, Missouri, to mark the event.

The world's largest ferris wheel

Night raid stuns Russian fleet

10 FEBRUARY

Last night at Port Arthur, off the coast of Korea, Japanese torpedo boats carried out a surprise attack on the Russian fleet. A cruiser and two battleships have been severely damaged and there are claims by the Japanese that seven other warships in the area have been captured. Today in Tokyo, with the success of the raid confirmed, the emperor of Japan officially declared war on Russia. In the Russian capital of St Petersburg, the tsar, unprepared for such a turn of events, was enjoying an evening out at the opera. Officials waited until the end of the performance before telling him the news so as not to spoil his evening. The outbreak of war comes after months of tension in the Far East caused by Russian and Japanese rivalry over control of the Chinese province of Manchuria and over Korea. Within hours of the raid, 8,000 Japanese forces landed unopposed in Korea and began to march towards the capital, Seoul.

FANTASY OF ETERNAL YOUTH

Scottish dramatist J M Barrie has written *Peter Pan,* a new play in which Peter Pan and Tinkerbell take three children to Never-Never Land where they meet Captain Hook.

JANUARY–JUNE

World Events	**JAN** Russia sends warships to Korea, an indication that war with Japan is imminent.	**FEB** The British consul Roger Casement publishes an account of Belgian atrocities in the Congo.	**APR** UK and French governments sign the Entente Cordiale, resolving all their former disagreements.		**MAY** The steerage fare on ocean liners is cut to $10, increasing the number of immigrants entering the USA.
Entertainment	**FEB** Popular Italian tenor Enrico Caruso makes his first recording in the USA.	**FEB** Italian composer Giacomo Puccini's opera *Madame Butterfly* flops at its Milan premiere.	**MAY** Czech composer Antonin Dvorák, much of whose work has folk influences, dies aged 62.		**JUN** Jack White wins the Open Golf Championship in the UK with a low score of 296.
Innovations	**MAR** US *Daily Illustrated Mirror* is the first newspaper to carry colour photographs.	**MAR** Lucien Bull makes a major breakthrough in developing slow-motion photography in France.	**MAY** UK explorer Henry Morton Stanley, leader of many African expeditions, dies at the age of 63.		**JUN** The excavation of a remarkable Viking burial ship begins at Oseberg, Norway.

MADAME BUTTERFLY

ENTENTE CORDIALE

1904

The fair is attracting large crowds despite the sweltering heat. Sales of ice cream have soared since vendors came up with the idea of selling their wares in edible cone-shaped holders made of waffle pastry. Richard Blechtynden has also started a new craze, putting ice in his tea and selling it as a cold drink.

Rolls joins Royce

4 MAY

Charles Rolls and Henry Royce are all set to go into partnership. A provisional agreement has been made today in which Rolls, a London car dealer, will sell the cars made by Royce, a self-made engineer based in Manchester. The luxury cars will be sold under the name of Rolls-Royce, with the partnership aiming to build on the reputation for perfection already established by Royce over the past year.

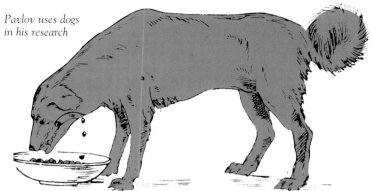

Pavlov uses dogs in his research

Behaviour can be learned!

10 DECEMBER

Russian physiologist Ivan Pavlov today received the Nobel Prize for his research into how the digestive system works. His experiments, which he carried out on dogs, have shown that nerve messages transmitted from the brain play a part in the digestion of our food. Scientists however are more excited by what Pavlov calls his "conditioned reflex" experiments, which may be of major importance for understanding how we learn. Pavlov has found that if a bell is rung each time a dog is fed it will eventually salivate when it hears the sound of a bell alone, even if no food is visible. If the same is true of humans, it suggests that kinds of behaviour can be learned, just like any other skill.

Railway crosses Siberia

25 SEPTEMBER

Thirteen years after plans were laid to build a railway across Russia to the Pacific coast, the Great Siberian Railway, a landmark in railroad engineering, is finally complete. The 7,371-km (4,607-mile) track stretches from the Ural mountains in the west to Vladivostock in the east. The Russian government hopes it will open up Siberia and boost trade with China and the Far East.

The railway has more than 1,000 stations

JULY–DECEMBER

SEP Helen Keller, who has been blind, deaf, and dumb since the age of two, graduates with honours in the USA.

JUL The third Olympic Games open in St Louis, Missouri, USA, and will run until the end of August.

JUL A Gobron-Brillié is the first car to travel over 160 km/h (100 mph) at Ostend, Belgium.

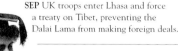

HELEN KELLER

SEP UK troops enter Lhasa and force a treaty on Tibet, preventing the Dalai Lama from making foreign deals.

JUL Russian dramatist and story-writer Anton Chekhov, known for *Uncle Vanya*, dies at the age of 44.

AUG SS *Victorian*, the first ocean-going turbine steamer, is launched in Belfast for the Irish Allan Line.

OCT The Russian fleet, on its way to fight Japan, fires on UK trawlers in the North Sea.

NOV Irish dramatist George Bernard Shaw's controversial new play, *John Bull's Other Island*, opens in the UK.

OCT UK inventor John Fleming creates a new electric diode valve, a breakthrough for radio technology.

NOV Theodore Roosevelt wins a four-year term as US president in his own right, after taking over from McKinley.

DEC French film pioneer Georges Méliès shoots a new special effects movie, *Voyage Beyond the Possible*.

OCT Germany is the first country to produce postcards that have pictures in natural colour.

PRESIDENT ROOSEVELT

19

1905

CONSERVATION
In 1889 ruthless hunting had reduced the 60 million bison roaming the US Great Plains to 85. The American Bison Society has helped increase numbers to 1,000.

Bloody Sunday riots in St Petersburg

22 JANUARY
Over 100 men, women, and children were shot dead and many more were wounded when Russian troops opened fire on demonstrators outside the Winter Palace in St Petersburg this afternoon. The demonstration of 300,000 workers, led by the radical priest Father Georgy Gapon, had marched through the Russian capital to petition Tsar Nicholas II for better working conditions. They were stopped outside the Winter Palace by lines of infantry backed by Cossack troops. As the workers attempted to move forward, the troops opened fire without warning on the unarmed crowd. The attack, which is already being called "Bloody Sunday", is likely to kindle the growing unrest against the Russian government and "Little Father" Tsar Nicholas II.

Sherlock Holmes returns

31 MARCH
If you thought that Sherlock Holmes had died falling off a precipice at the Reichenbach Falls with his arch enemy Moriarty, be prepared for a surprise, for Sherlock Holmes is alive and back at work again. Holmes' many fans refused to accept his death,

Holmes, wearing a deerstalker hat, is accompanied by Watson

so British author Sir Arthur Conan Doyle brought his detective-hero back to life. Today the new stories from the *Strand* magazine are published in a single volume, *The Return of Sherlock Holmes*. However, as the London *Daily Telegraph* reports, perhaps "realization is not up to expectation".

JANUARY–JUNE

World Events	**JAN** The Russian garrison at Port Arthur falls to the Japanese after a seven-month siege.	**MAR** The 200,000-strong Russian army is defeated by the Japanese at Mukden, a key point for control of Manchuria.	**APR** More than 10,000 people die in an earthquake that hits the province of Lahore in northeastern India.	**JUN** The Norwegian parliament refuses to recognize the Swedish king and declares its independence.
Entertainment	**JAN** Baroness Emmuska Orczy's *The Scarlet Pimpernel* is published in the UK.	**MAR** Jules Verne, French science fiction writer of *20,000 Leagues Under The Sea*, dies at the age of 77.	**MAY** Dutch-born oriental dancer Mata Hari wins much praise after her debut appearance in Paris, France.	**JUN** A group of Expressionist artists form in Germany, and take the name "Die Brücke" ("The Bridge").
Innovations	**JAN** Henri Oedenkoven of Belgium founds the first vegetarian organization.	**FEB** The first Rotary Club is founded in Chicago, USA, to promote high standards of practice in business.	**APR** French psychologist Alfred Binet develops a way of testing the brain on its ability to reason.	**APR** The world's first mobile public library service is set up in Washington County, USA.

20,000 LEAGUES UNDER THE SEA

EARTHQUAKE IN INDIA

1905

Japan set for victory

28 MAY

The Russian fleet suffered a devastating defeat today in the Straits of Tsushima between Korea and Japan. This, following losses at Port Arthur and Mukden earlier this year, finally dashes all Russian hopes of defeating Japan in the year-long war for control of Manchuria and Korea. The 38-strong Russian fleet entered the strait at 1.30 pm, but within hours their formation was wrecked and all but three ships had been sunk, disabled, or captured. The victorious Japanese, on the other hand, lost only three of their boats.

Potemkin crew stage mutiny

27 JUNE

Anchored off the Black Sea port of Odessa, sailors on the Russian battleship *Potemkin* staged a mutiny after a sailor complained about bad food and was shot by a lieutenant. The crew promptly set upon their superiors throwing the commander and several officers overboard and raising the red flag of revolution. In

Odessa the authorities, already battling with civil unrest, must now cope with an all-out strike in sympathy.

The Open Window *by Henri Matisse*

Paris shocked by "wild beasts"

1 OCTOBER

The annual exhibition at the Salon d'Automne in Paris features a new group of artists who have turned their backs on traditional techniques and use primary colours straight from the tube. The result is bold bright canvases that are so startling that art critic Louis Vauxcelles has called the group "Les Fauves" – the "wild beasts" – a name they have readily adopted. Henri Matisse from northern France is the originator of this group of brash young artists, which includes Georges Braque, André Derain, Maurice de Vlaminck, and Raoul Dufy.

JULY–DECEMBER

SEP France, assured of UK support, agrees to call a conference with Germany to discuss their intentions in Morocco.

JUL US tennis player May Sutton becomes the first non-Briton to win the Wimbledon ladies' singles title.

JUL The world's first artificial textile yarn – rayon – starts commercial production in Europe.

ALBERT EINSTEIN

SEP US President Roosevelt organizes the signing of a treaty in New Hampshire, USA, to end the Russo-Japanese war.

NOV The first nickelodeon, a cinema that shows a programme of short films for 5 cents, opens in Pittsburgh, USA.

JUL German physicist Albert Einstein proposes the idea that time and motion are relative.

OCT In a new manifesto Tsar Nicholas II promises Russians limited civil rights and an elected parliament, the Duma.

DEC Russian choreographer Michael Fokine writes a dance, *The Dying Swan*, for ballerina Anna Pavlova.

DEC The recently produced one-arm bandit slot machines are a great success in San Francisco, USA.

FRANZ LEHÁR'S MERRY WIDOW

OCT In the UK, vote campaigners Emmeline Pankhurst and Annie Kenney are sent to prison for assault.

DEC Hungarian composer Franz Lehár's operetta *The Merry Widow* premieres in Vienna, Austria.

DEC German doctor Robert Koch receives the Nobel Prize for identifying the tuberculosis germ.

LIFE IN THE NEW CENTURY

DURING THE EARLY YEARS OF THE 20TH CENTURY, life in the home was remarkably changed by one phenomenon – electricity. Although it was known about in the 1700s, it was nearly 200 years before electricity made its impact on everyday life. The application of a power source to appliances such as washing machines and vacuum cleaners removed much of the hard work from domestic labour and led to cleaner, warmer, and brighter houses. Electricity also saved time, releasing people from housework so that they could enjoy their leisure hours. The invention of the gramophone meant that musicians were no longer needed to play music in the home. It also provided a new form of entertainment for people who had previously spent time sewing, reading, and drawing.

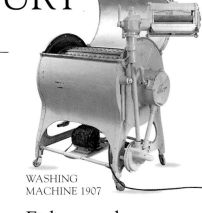

WASHING MACHINE 1907

All lit up

Electricity was supplied to many houses in Europe in the early 1900s, enabling householders to replace their oil lamps and candles with electric lights.

Fisher washer

No invention eased the burden of housework more than Alva Fisher's electric washing machine of 1907. Clothes were washed in a drum driven by an electric motor. The drum's rotation reversed occasionally so that the clothes did not tangle up in a big knot.

ELECTRIC COOKER 1912

Cook electric

Gas cookers were already in use when the first electric-powered oven was manufactured, so the producers advertised the safety and economy of the new stove.

Tea's made

The first automatic tea-maker was a bizarre-looking contraption, operated by a number of levers and springs. It is doubtful whether it actually saved any time!

Steam from kettle activates tea-maker

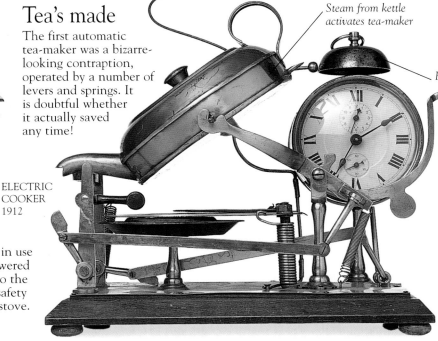

Bell sounds when tea is ready

AUTOMATIC TEA-MAKER 1904

Bellow power

This early cleaner needed two people to operate it – one to work the bellows, and another to move the device around. In 1908 mass-produced electric cleaners, designed by William Hoover, first appeared in the United States.

A pressing business

The first electric arc irons were highly dangerous, as they required an electric spark to leap between two carbon rods to generate heat. Safer irons, which worked by heating up an element within the body of the iron, appeared a few years later.

Insulated wooden handle

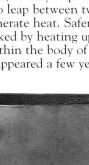

DAISY VACUUM CLEANER 1901

Hand-powered bellows create a vacuum to suck up dirt

Heavy cast-iron base to press fabric

ELECTRIC ARC IRON c 1885

BROWNIE BOX CAMERA 1900

Snap happy

Photography came within the reach of the entire population with the introduction of the Brownie Box camera. The camera, which went on sale in the United States in 1900, cost only $1, encouraging amateur photographers to record everything from portraits to sporting events.

Connecting up

Early telephone exchanges were manual. An operator answered your call, took your number and the number you wanted to be connected to, and plugged in your line wire to complete the appropriate electrical circuit.

Mouthpiece

Earpiece

CANDLESTICK TELEPHONE 1912

Getting in touch

Scottish-born Alexander Graham Bell invented the telephone in 1876, revolutionizing communications. At the turn of the century most middle-class homes had a telephone.

Horn amplifies sound

GRAMOPHONE EARLY 1900s

Music in the home

Thomas Edison invented a phonograph in 1877 that could both record and play back sounds stored on a piece of tinfoil wrapped around a rotating drum, but its sound quality was poor. Emile Berliner improved on this system by developing a flat-disc record player, or gramophone, in 1888. By the early 1900s pieces of music up to four minutes long could be played in homes for the first time without any musicians being present!

Needle rests in groove and vibrates from side to side as disc revolves

Flat disc made of shellac sits on turntable

The development of radio

In 1901, Italian Guglielmo Marconi sent the first radio message across the Atlantic Ocean. Regular broadcasts began in the USA in 1907, and by the 1920s national companies were broadcasting popular entertainment.

1906

San Francisco razed to the ground

19 APRIL

At 5.16 yesterday morning, the US city of San Francisco was shaken to its very roots when a violent earthquake struck. Five more shocks followed. Stone buildings shook and their foundations split, roads buckled, and the wharfs in the port warped and shattered. At least 1,000 people are feared dead, but this number is sure to rise as rescue teams begin to sift through the piles of rubble. Those who could fled the city on trains and ferries. Last night, parks and squares were full as people slept outdoors, afraid to go back to their houses in case another quake struck. Most of the severe damage, however, was caused by the fire that followed the quake.

Temporary business establishments on Market Street

Dreadnought outclasses all rivals

10 FEBRUARY

The biggest and fastest battleship in the world, HMS *Dreadnought*, was launched in Britain by King Edward VII today. The revolutionary ship, which took just four months to build, surpasses its rivals in naval firepower – it has ten 30-cm (12-inch) guns on each side, eight of which can fire at the same time. Experts believe that the new *Dreadnought* will make all competitors obsolete.

JANUARY–JUNE

World Events	**JAN** The Liberal Party achieves a landslide victory in the UK general election.	**FEB** The Japanese government announces its intention to double the size of its navy within three years.	**MAR** At the Spanish seaport of Algeciras, a conference decides to give Spain and France joint control over Morocco.	**MAY** The first Duma, an elected parliament that was formed to advise the tsar and his ministers, meets in St Petersburg, Russia.
Entertainment	**JAN** US dancer Isadora Duncan is banned from performing in Germany.	**MAR** England beats France 35–8 in the first international rugby contest, held in Paris.	**APR** The Olympic Games are held in Athens, Greece, rekindling enthusiasm for the Olympic ideal.	**MAY** Norwegian playwright Henrik Ibsen, author of *Ghosts* and *Hedda Gabler*, dies at the age of 78.
Innovations	**JAN** A car takes only 28.2 seconds to travel 1.6 km (1 mile) in USA.	**THE LATEST RUGBY BALL** — **FEB** US businessman William K Kellogg forms a company to market his corn flake breakfast cereal.	**APR** French physicist Pierre Curie, winner of the Nobel Prize in 1903, dies in a road accident at the age of 46.	**HENRIK IBSEN** — **JUN** The world's largest and fastest ocean liner, Cunard's *Lusitania*, is launched in Glasgow, Scotland.

1906

Looking east on Sacramento Street

Swept along by strong winds, it raged from the business to the residential districts, engulfing the flimsy wooden buildings in its path. It will cost about $250 million to rebuild the city.

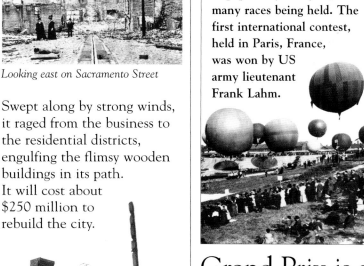

A LOT OF HOT AIR

Hot-air ballooning has grown in popularity this year, with many races being held. The first international contest, held in Paris, France, was won by US army lieutenant Frank Lahm.

Cézanne dies

22 OCTOBER

One of the world's greatest painters, Paul Cézanne, died today at his family house in Aix-en-Provence, France. He was 67. As a young artist Cézanne was identified with the Impressionists, but in his later work he was more interested in portraying the solidity and permanence of objects. Through his still-lifes and landscape paintings, he has greatly influenced the new generation of artists, including Pablo Picasso.

Self-portrait by Paul Cézanne

Grand Prix is grand success

27 JUNE

The world's first Grand Prix motor race finished today at Le Mans, France. The 1,250-km (780-mile) race was organized by the Automobile Club de France and took place over two days. The competitors raced around 12 laps of a 104-km (65-mile) triangular course. The winner, Hungarian driver Ferenc Szisz, drove his 90-hp, 13-litre Renault at an average speed of 100 km/h (63 mph). His winning time of 12 hours 14 minutes started from when he got behind the wheel and included stoppages for tyre changes, which he carried out himself. The Le Mans race attracted crowds of spectators and will almost certainly become an annual event.

The winner Szisz at full speed

Pictures move!

31 OCTOBER

The first animated cartoon, *Humorous Phases of Funny Faces*, has been produced by British designer John Stuart Blackton. The film, made using stop-frame photography, shows a man blowing cigar smoke on a woman, which makes her vanish.

JULY–DECEMBER

JUL Major Dreyfus is declared innocent of treason by the French government after an 11-year fight to clear his name.

JUL UK tennis ace H L Doherty wins the Wimbledon men's singles title for the fifth year running.

AUG Canadian surgeons perform kidney operations on animals to prove that transplants are possible for people.

LAWRENCE DOHERTY

JUL The Duma, dissolved by the Russian government, meets in Finland and calls on Russians to refuse to pay their taxes.

AUG Film companies worldwide set up studios in New York, establishing it as the undisputed US film centre.

OCT The permanent wave (perm), a costly and time-consuming process, is shown to UK hairdressers.

SEP Following the resignation of Cuba's president, the USA imposes a provisional government there until order is restored.

NOV George Bernard Shaw's *The Doctor's Dilemma*, containing the Irish playwright's first death scene, premieres in London, UK.

OCT German professor Arthur Korn transmits the first picture by telegraph, the culmination of several years' work.

A RADIO DIODE

DEC The UK grants self-government to the Transvaal and Orange River Colonies in southern Africa.

DEC Gabel's "Automatic Entertainer", the world's first jukebox, is a great success after its launch in the USA.

DEC The first known radio broadcast is made in the USA by R A Fessenden, who transmits a poem and a talk.

TOWARDS A NEW LIFE

ONE OF THE GREATEST MIGRATIONS in human history took place during the 19th and early 20th centuries, when millions of people fled poverty and persecution in their homelands and travelled to the United States. The immigrants came from South and Central America, Europe, and eastern Asia, attracted by the opportunity to begin a new life in a new country. At first they were welcomed with open arms, but as their numbers grew many US citizens feared that the huge influx would reduce the country to anarchy. Restrictions were gradually placed on immigrants until, in 1921, a Quota Law was passed limiting the numbers allowed to enter. Between 1892 and 1954, the immigration centre on Ellis Island processed more than 12 million immigrants. Today, half of the 255 million people in the USA can trace their roots back to Ellis Island.

Across the Atlantic Ocean

Immigrants came to the United States by passenger liner. Because many were poor, they could only afford to travel by third, or steerage, class. Conditions on board were cramped – hundreds of families lived below deck in dormitories with only bunks to sleep on. In 1904 the reduction of the steerage class fare to $10 made the journey affordable for even the poorest immigrants.

ELLIS ISLAND IMMIGRATION CENTRE

Arrival at Ellis Island

On arrival in the United States, immigrants were processed on Ellis Island in New York Harbour. The immigration centre contained dormitories, a medical examination room, and the Great Hall, where immigrants waited to receive their entrance papers. The centre finally closed in 1954. After years of neglect it has now been restored and is regarded as a national monument.

AN IMMIGRANT FAMILY LOOKS ASHORE FROM ELLIS ISLAND

A new life

Many immigrants found fame and fortune in the United States. In 1912, British-born actor Charlie Chaplin arrived on tour as part of a music hall revue. Within a few years he became the most famous film actor in the world.

The melting-pot

Until 1890 most immigrants came from northwestern Europe, particularly Germany, Ireland, and Britain. After 1890 a new wave of people arrived from Italy, Austro-Hungary, and Russia. At first, the immigrant groups lived and mixed only with their friends and families, but gradually they mingled together, creating a vast melting-pot of cultures and religions.

Waiting to be let in

In the Great Hall, immigrants stood in long lines, waiting for an interview with officials in the Registry Room. Providing they were of sound mind and body and were not criminals they were given papers allowing them to settle in the United States. Only two out of every 100 people were refused admittance to the USA.

PEOPLE QUEUE UP IN THE GREAT HALL

A warm welcome

The Statue of Liberty, which stands on an island neighbouring Ellis Island, was the first thing many immigrants would have seen. On the base of the statue are the words of a poem by Emma Lazarus: "Give me your tired, your poor, Your huddled masses yearning to breathe free." It is recognized as a symbol of freedom throughout the world.

DOCTOR EXAMINES IMMIGRANT CHILDREN

THE STATUE OF LIBERTY

Seven rays represent seven seas and seven continents

Open wide!

All immigrants were given a health check to make sure they were not carrying any contagious diseases. If they were healthy, they received a card signifying a clean bill of health; unhealthy immigrants could be sent back to their homeland.

Ticket to ride

On Ellis Island immigrants could buy railway tickets at a special discount to enable them to travel to their new homes in the United States. From New York they took the train to cities as far away as Chicago, Illinois, and some even made it to San Francisco, California, on the west coast.

IMMIGRANTS WAIT FOR A TRAIN TO A NEW LIFE

A SPECIAL DISCOUNT RAIL TICKET FOR IMMIGRANTS

1907

Indians demand rights

22 MARCH

In South Africa Indian-born lawyer Mohandas Gandhi has said he will start a campaign of "Satyagraha", or civil non-violent disobedience, against the Transvaal government. He is protesting at the recently passed Asiatic Law Amendment Ordinance bill, the effects of which will come into force on 1 July. The new law will require all Indian residents in South Africa to have their fingerprints taken, after which they will receive a certificate of registration, which they will be obliged to carry with them at all times. If they fail to do this, the

Indians could face loss of residence, a fine, or even deportation. Mr Gandhi, who qualified as a barrister in Britain, has been resident in South Africa since 1893. He is objecting to the bill on the grounds that it constitutes racial discrimination against the large Indian community living in the country.

ANIMALS ON DISPLAY

A new type of zoo opened in Hamburg this year, inspired by the vision of German animal trainer Carl Hagenbeck. Angry at the caged conditions most animals were kept in, he purchased a site on the outskirts of Hamburg and created a zoo that gave the animals freedom to wander around, while providing protection for spectators.

Picasso's new style causes uproar

31 MARCH

A startling new painting by Spanish-born artist Pablo Picasso has shocked the art world. Opinions are divided on the bizarre canvas, entitled *Les Demoiselles d'Avignon*, that is on show at his studio in France. The picture is vast – almost 2.5 m (8 ft) square – and features five naked women. Rumour has it that they are prostitutes. Whoever they are, their portraits are far from flattering, with their savage, masklike heads and dislocated bodies. Fellow artist Georges Braque is horrified, accusing Picasso of "drinking turpentine and spitting fire". But some critics are excited by this bold new approach to portraiture, finding in it influences of the work of the late Cézanne.

Les Demoiselles d'Avignon *by Pablo Picasso*

JANUARY–JUNE

World Events	JAN A huge earthquake devastates the Jamaican capital of Kingston and kills 700–800 people.	JAN At a lavish ceremony Mohammad Ali Mirza is crowned Shah of Persia in the Royal Palace of Teheran.	APR Plans to construct a tunnel under the English Channel are withdrawn due to fears about defence.	JUN In Russia, Tsar Nicholas II dissolves the second Duma, or parliament, accusing some deputies of treason.
Entertainment	JAN UK music halls fall quiet as artists strike for better pay.	JAN The premiere of *The Playboy of the Western World* in Dublin, Ireland, provokes riots.	MAR The world's first model-aircraft competition takes place at Crystal Palace, London, UK.	MAY The world's first 24-hour motor race, the Endurance Derby, is held in Philadelphia, USA.
Innovations	JAN The US Hurley Machine Corps prepare to sell electric washing machines. A RADIO RECEIVER	FEB The De Forest Radio Telephone Co makes the first regular experimental radio broadcasts in New York, USA.	APR In Paris, French doctors announce the discovery of a serum that can be used to cure dysentery. AUGUSTE AND HENRI LUMIÈRE	JUN The pioneering Lumière brothers claim a breakthrough in developing colour photography.

1907

Special place for motor race

6 JULY

The world's first purpose-built motor-racing track is now open at Brooklands, southern Britain. The track, which is 4.45 km (2.77 miles) long, is covered with a thin layer of concrete. Modelled on the design of a horse-racing track, it is oval in shape, and the corners bank steeply at each end, enabling the cars to take them at speed. At today's opening meeting, British driver J E Hutton won the Montague Cup in a Mercedes.

British boys taught outdoor skills

29 JULY

Four days ago Sir Robert Baden-Powell, the Boer War hero, took 20 boys to camp on Brownsea Island in Poole Harbour, southern Britain. While there, the boys learned outdoor skills and basic first aid. Baden-Powell's purpose was to introduce British boys to the discipline and duty he had seen in the army scouts. The camp was a great success, and today Baden-Powell officially set up the "boy scout" organization in London.

The boy scouts wear a distinctive uniform

New Zealand gains its independence

26 SEPTEMBER

The British colony of New Zealand, situated in the southwestern Pacific Ocean, became independent this morning after 67 years of British rule. New Zealand has had self-government for many years now, and has a long tradition of equal rights for its citizens. In 1893 it was the first country in the world to give women the vote and was among the first countries to introduce social security benefits and pensions. It also has an excellent public health service. From today it will become an independent dominion within the British Empire.

Government buildings in the capital of Wellington

Vertical takeoff a reality at last

13 NOVEMBER

French bicycle-maker Paul Cornu flew straight into the record books today as his motor-driven helicopter rose vertically into the air above a field near Lisieux, Normandy. Cornu's craft is powered by two motor-driven propellers, or rotors, which push the craft vertically up off the ground. Although the craft rose only 0.3 m (1 ft) today, Cornu hopes to win the 50,000-franc prize on offer to the first Frenchman who completes an aerial circuit of 1 km (0.6 miles).

Cornu's helicopter

JULY–DECEMBER

JUL Riots start in the Korean capital of Seoul after the Japanese insist on the abdication of the Korean emperor.

JUL The first of the *Zeigfeld Follies*, a spectacular music and dancing show, is performed in New York, USA.

AUG The Singer Building in New York, USA, although incomplete, is the tallest building in the world.

EDVARD GRIEG

JUL Germany, Austria, and Italy renew the Triple Alliance for another six years, despite reservations from Italy.

SEP Norwegian composer Edvard Grieg, famous for his *Peer Gynt* suite, dies at the age of 64.

SEP USS *Virginia* and *Connecticut* are the first naval vessels to be equipped with radio-telephones.

AUG French gunships stage a two-day bombardment on Casablanca, Morocco, following anti-European hostilities.

NOV *The Count of Monte Cristo* is shot in Los Angeles, establishing the city as a major US film location.

OCT The *Lusitania* breaks the record for crossing the North Atlantic and takes the prestigious Blue Riband.

THE LUSITANIA

DEC The USA's "Great White Fleet" of 16 battleships leaves on a world tour to show off US strength.

DEC Rudyard Kipling, UK author of *The Jungle Book*, wins the Nobel Prize for Literature.

DEC The world's first circus, set up by the Ringling Brothers, has a successful year in the USA.

1908

Gold medallist disqualified

Stewards help Pietri, with his legs folding beneath him, to cross the finishing-line

JUMPING JUKEBOX
An advanced version of the jukebox invented in 1906, the hexaphone plays a selection of tunes recorded on cylinders.

30 JULY

Italian athlete Dorando Pietri today received a gold cup from Queen Alexandra of Britain as an acknowledgement for his valiant failure to win the Olympic marathon. Pietri had dominated the race from its start at Windsor and led throughout the 41-km (26-mile) course. As he entered the White City stadium in London for the final leg of the race, he took a wrong turning, stumbled four or five times, and fell. He received medical attention and a helping hand from race stewards as, half-conscious, he crossed the finishing-line. Sadly, he was disqualified for receiving assistance and first prize was awarded to runner-up John Hayes of the United States.

New motor car for the masses

12 AUGUST

The first Model T Ford went on sale in the United States today priced at $850, the fulfilment of Henry Ford's promise to "build a car for the multitude". The car is made of a tough but lightweight steel alloy, and is built using the revolutionary assembly line technique that the Ford Motor Co hopes will mass-produce 18,000 cars a year.

The Model T is the sturdiest car on the market

JANUARY–JUNE

World Events	**FEB** King Carlos I of Portugal and his heir are assassinated in Lisbon, in the wake of a failed revolution.	**FEB** Emmeline Pankhurst, leading campaigner in the UK suffrage movement, complains about the conditions of prison life.	**MAY** The Franco-British exhibition opens in London, UK, with the White City stadium as its centrepiece.	**JUN** 200,000 people gather in Hyde Park, London, UK, in support of the women's suffrage movement.
Entertainment	**JAN** Austrian composer and conductor Gustav Mahler makes his US debut in New York.	**FEB** The US film industry heads west, attracted by cheap labour and the climate and scenery of southern California.	**MAY** French artist Claude Monet destroys many of his paintings, believing them to be unsatisfactory.	**JUN** Russian composer Nikolai Rimsky-Korsakov, noted for *Scheherazade*, dies at the age of 64.
Innovations	**FEB** Dutch scientists succeed in producing a form of solid helium for the first time.	**BELL OF THE MAURETANIA** **MAR** The UK Cunard liner the *Mauretania* sets a record Atlantic crossing time of 5 days 5 mins.	**MAY** Commercial quantities of crude oil are first struck in Persia, in the Middle East, at Masjid-i-Sulaiman.	 **DEMONSTRATION IN HYDE PARK** **JUN** The first international football contest is played in Vienna, with England beating Austria 6–1.

1908

Badger's winter stores

Fantasy written for children

31 OCTOBER

Kenneth Grahame, a secretary in the Bank of England, has proved to be one of this year's most unlikely authors. *The Wind in the Willows*, published earlier this month, tells a story about the exciting adventures of Badger, Ratty, Toad, Mole, and other creatures who live around the river bank. This enchanting tale is certain to entertain children and adults alike for many years to come.

Toddler ascends Chinese throne

2 DECEMBER

Following the death of Emperor Kuang-Hsu, Hsuan T'ung, or Pu Yi, has ascended to the imperial throne of China. It will be many years before he is able to rule the country himself, so in the mean time his father Prince Chun will control the nation as regent. This is the will of Tsu-Hsi, the former dowager empress, who in recent years has exercised considerable influence in China. After her suspicious death there were rumours that the royal dynasty may be on the verge of collapse, to be replaced by a republican government.

Two-year-old Emperor Pu Yi stands next to his father Prince Chun and his younger brother

Street scene in Messina showing earthquake wreckage

Earthquake in Italy

28 DECEMBER

Messina, the second largest city in Sicily, was struck early this morning by the most violent earthquake ever recorded in Europe. Of the city's 150,000 inhabitants, it is estimated that more than half have died in the disaster, with many more still trapped under the debris. The damage that the quake has caused is widespread. The city of Messina, its surrounding villages, and the nearby towns in Calabria, the toe of mainland Italy, have all suffered from the devastating effects of its force. Many fine ancient Italian buildings have been reduced to rubble. Eyewitness reports say that the earthquake caused a tidal wave that surged across the Straits of Messina, engulfing the city of Reggio and several other nearby ports. An international rescue operation is being organized, but it will be days before the precise damage and death toll are known and the process of rebuilding can begin.

JULY–DECEMBER

JUL A revolt staged by the Young Turk movement forces Sultan Abdul Hamid II to restore Turkey's constitution.

JUL US author Joel Chandler Harris, creator of Uncle Remus and Br'er Rabbit, dies at the age of 60.

SEP In Germany the scientist Hermann Minkowski defines time as the "fourth dimension".

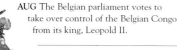

BR'ER RABBIT

AUG The Belgian parliament votes to take over control of the Belgian Congo from its king, Leopold II.

AUG UK cricketer W G Grace plays his final first-class game at the end of an eminent 43-year career.

SEP US aircraft pioneer Orville Wright sets a new flight record, staying airborne for 70 minutes.

OCT Austria-Hungary annexes the Balkan states of Bosnia and Herzegovina by decree, and with the approval of Russia.

DEC Texan boxer Jack Johnson becomes the first black American to win the world heavyweight boxing championship.

NOV German physicist Albert Einstein presents his quantum theory of light at a Switzerland conference.

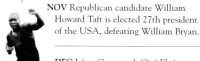

JACK JOHNSON

NOV Republican candidate William Howard Taft is elected 27th president of the USA, defeating William Bryan.

DEC Léon Gaumont's Cité Elgé, advertised as the world's largest film studio, is completed in Paris, France.

DEC Ernest Rutherford from the UK wins the Nobel Prize for his work on radioactivity and the atom.

1900 *HAMBURG-AMERIKA*
LINE LAUNCH *DEUTSCHLAND*

1907 *MAURETANIA BEGINS*
22-YEAR "BLUE RIBAND" REIGN

1911 *OLYMPIC IS WORLD'S*
LARGEST AND LONGEST SHIP

THE GREAT OCEAN LINERS

FLAG OF THE WHITE
STAR SHIPPING LINE

BETWEEN THE ERAS of the slow but beautiful sailing ships of the 1800s and the sleek, fast jet planes of the 1950s, the only way to travel across the seas was by ocean liner. Driven by powerful steam turbines, these floating palaces carried thousands of passengers. They were called liners because they worked regular routes, or lines. Competition between the different shipping companies was fierce, as each tried to carry more passengers more quickly across the ocean and earn the prestigious "Blue Riband" for the fastest North Atlantic crossing. Throughout the heyday of liner travel, the Cunard Line, based in Liverpool, Britain, led the way in the building of record-breaking ships, including the *Mauretania* in 1907 and the *Queen Mary* in 1936.

ADVERTISING POSTER
FOR THE CUNARD LINE

Battling for supremacy

Cunard, White Star, the North German Lloyd Line, Hamburg-Amerika, and the smaller lines all battled for supremacy on the all-important North Atlantic route. They built liners that were bigger, faster, and more luxurious than their competitors in order to attract custom.

Luxury living

For first-class passengers, life on board an ocean liner was like being in a luxury hotel. There were many ballrooms, dining rooms, smoking rooms, and lounges which were lavishly furnished and decorated with gilt mirrors and wood panelling.

DINING ROOM OF WHITE STAR'S *BRITANNIC*

Cunard's leading lady

The *Mauretania*, affectionately nicknamed "The Grand Old Lady of the Atlantic", made 538 crossings in a career lasting 28 years. On board there was accommodation for 560 first-class, 475 second-class, and 1,300 third-class passengers. They were looked after by 376 staff, while a crew of 366 ran the ship.

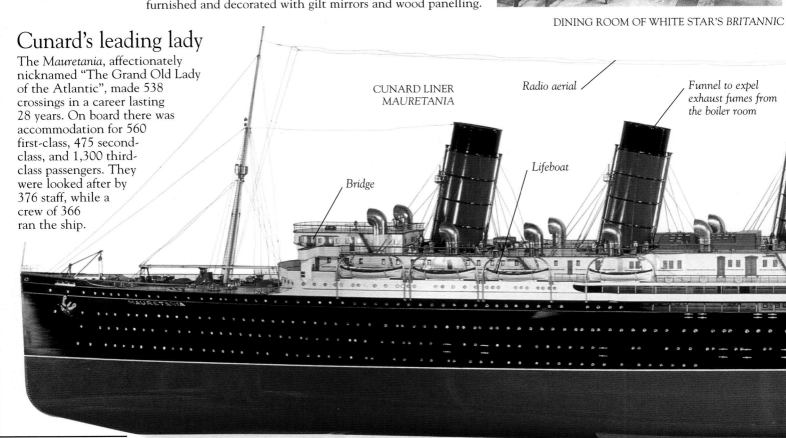

CUNARD LINER
MAURETANIA

Radio aerial

Funnel to expel exhaust fumes from the boiler room

Lifeboat

Bridge

1912 *TITANIC* SINKS AFTER
HITTING AN ICEBERG

1913 GERMAN *IMPERATOR*
RIVALS BRITISH LINERS

1914 CUNARD BEGINS A WEEKLY
LIVERPOOL–NEW YORK SERVICE

Swimming at sea

In 1911, the *Olympic*, built by the White Star Line, became the first ocean liner to have an outside swimming pool. Also on board were indoor pools, saunas, and deck games such as shuffleboard and quoits, a ring-tossing game. The liners of later years had at least one cinema.

BY THE 1930s OUTDOOR POOLS WERE A COMMON FEATURE ON OCEAN LINERS

CUNARD FLAG

Promenade deck

Garden lounge

First-class restaurant

CROSS-SECTION OF THE *AQUITANIA*

Third-class restaurant

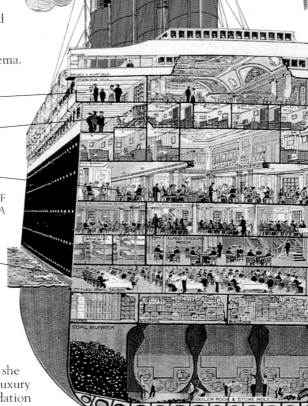

The loss of the *Titanic*

The *Titanic*, the sister ship of the *Olympic*, departed on her maiden voyage on 10 April 1912, but tragedy struck after four days when she hit an iceberg and sank. The wreck was discovered 73 years later in 1985, and divers began salvage work.

The super-liner

Cunard launched the impressive *Aquitania* in 1914, some years after the new generation of super-liners in 1907. Although she was no record-breaker, she offered a superb degree of luxury in her first-class accommodation and immediately became popular.

Coal bunker

Boiler room and stoke-hole

Love afloat

A long voyage provided the perfect opportunity for couples to get to know each other better, and many a romance blossomed on board.

First-class music and lounge room

First-class smoking room

Baggage crane

Second-class lounge

Bridge for docking

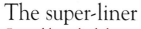

1909

Souvenir postcard featuring Charles Pathé holding a newsreel camera

News is broadcast to cinema audiences

31 MARCH

The pioneering French film producers Émile and Charles Pathé have now started to film the news. Beginning this week, the latest events from around the world will be shown once a week as part of the film programme at their cinema in Paris. Entitled *Pathé Faits Divers* and edited by Albert Gaveau, the newsreel will act as a witness to current events. In order to achieve this, the Pathé brothers have sent an army of cameramen to every continent of the globe to search out the week's important and sensational stories. The newsreel, which is intended for general distribution, will soon be shown in other countries.

Ballets Russes take Paris by storm

20 MAY

A new dance company, the Ballets Russes, headed by Russian impresario Sergei Diaghilev, has caused a sensation in Paris. Last night's premiere in the Théâtre Châtelet was met with rapturous applause. Performing Polovtsian dances from *Prince Igor* and *Les Sylphides*, the troupe, led by Vaslav Nijinsky and Anna Pavlova, electrified audiences as they displayed Mikhail Fokine's daring choreography, which combined music, drama, and painting. But it was Nijinsky who stole the limelight as he defied gravity in his leaps across the stage. One critic has described him as having "the power of youth, drunk with rhythm, terrifying in his muscular energy". During their stay, the company will aim to show a full repertoire of their talents.

A star is born

10 JUNE

All eyes in the film industry are on a 16-year-old girl from Canada. Toronto-born Mary Pickford had performed on Broadway in New York for two years when her acting talent was spotted by the film director D W Griffith. Following her screen debut in *The Violin-Maker of Cremona* at the beginning of the year, he has now offered her a part in his next film, *Her First Biscuits*. It is expected that her career will go from one hit film to the next.

JANUARY–JUNE

World Events	**MAR** Hand-picked by Roosevelt, William Howard Taft is inaugurated 27th president of the USA.	**MAR** The "Great Powers" urge Serbia to cease waging war with Austria-Hungary over control of Bosnia and Herzegovina.	**APR** Young Turks overthrow the sultan of Turkey and replace him with his brother, who assumes the title Mohammed V.	**APR** UK chancellor David Lloyd George raises taxes on the rich to pay for pensions in the "People's Budget".
Entertainment	**FEB** Italian poet Filippo Tommaso Marinetti publishes *The Futurist Manifesto* in Paris.	**MAR** J M Synge, Irish playwright of the notorious *The Playboy of the Western World*, dies at the age of 37.	**APR** A memorial to the UK poets Keats and Shelley is opened by the Spanish Steps in Rome, Italy.	**JUN** King Edward VII opens the Victoria and Albert Museum in South Kensington, London, UK.
Innovations	**JAN** UK astronomers report that they might have sighted a ninth new planet. **SOUTH POLE EXPLORERS**	**JAN** In Antarctica Ernest Shackleton leads a UK expedition nearer to the South Pole than ever before.	**MAY** Bacteriologist Paul Ehrlich produces the world's first successful anti-syphilis drug in Germany.  **DAVID LLOYD GEORGE**	**JUN** The SOS danger signal is first used at sea when SS *Slavonia* is wrecked off the Azores.

1909

Peary's North Pole conquest confirmed

21 DECEMBER

US naval commander Robert Peary has been officially declared the first person to reach the North Pole. A committee appointed by Copenhagen University in Denmark made the decision today after rejecting evidence supplied by Dr Frederick Cook from New York who has also made this claim. The controversy that started earlier this year, after Peary claimed that he reached the Pole first on 6 April, should now end. Peary set sail from the USA on board the *Theodore Roosevelt* in July 1908 and established a base camp at Cape Columbia. He left the camp the following

Near the North Pole, Henson (centre) and the team of Eskimos

March and crossed 145 km (90 miles) of mountainous terrain before making the 36-day trek across the frozen Arctic Ocean to the Pole itself. On this, his third attempt to reach the North Pole, Peary was accompanied by four Eskimos and Matthew Henson, his chief assistant since his first expedition to the Arctic in 1891.

Peary with the husky dogs he used to pull the sledges carrying his supplies

BUILDING IN STEEL

"Steel is the epic of this age," pronounced US architect Frank Lloyd Wright this year, and new buildings across the world are proving him right. In Barcelona, Spain, Antonio Gaudí has designed the Casa Milá apartment building. It looks as if it is quarried from solid stone, but in fact it is supported by a hidden steel structure.

JULY–DECEMBER

JUL The shah of Persia Mohammad Ali is deposed in favour of his 12-year-old brother, Ahmed Mirza.

JUL Aristide Briand takes over the office of prime minister of France on the resignation of premier Georges Clemenceau.

NOV The "People's Budget" is defeated in the House of Lords, creating a major constitutional crisis in the UK.

DEC The Union of South Africa under Louis Botha is proclaimed independent by royal declaration in the UK.

JUL At 41, UK tennis player Arthur Gore is the oldest man to win the singles title at Wimbledon.

AUG The US Simplified Spelling Board publishes a dictionary of 3,261 difficult words.

NOV Russian composer Sergei Rachmaninov premieres his third piano concerto in New York, USA.

DEC US architect Frank Lloyd Wright completes the acclaimed Robie House in Chicago, USA.

JUL French aviator Louis Blériot is the first person to fly across the English Channel, taking 37 minutes.

BLÉRIOT ARRIVES AT DOVER, UK

SEP German psychologists Sigmund Freud and Carl Jung tour the USA, lecturing on psychoanalysis.

DEC US chemist Leo Baekeland prepares to market his newly invented synthetic plastic – "Bakelite".

LOUIS BOTHA

DEC Italian Guglielmo Marconi shares the Nobel Prize for physics with K F Braun from Germany.

1910

Second death

21 APRIL

The well-loved US novelist and humorist Mark Twain died today at the age of 74. Twain was reported to have died once before, forcing him

Huckleberry Finn catches a rabbit

to send a cable to the Associated Press stating that "the report of my death was an exaggeration". This time there is no mistake. Born Samuel Langhorne Clemens, Twain began life as a river pilot. He took his pen name "mark twain" from a river call meaning "two fathoms". His novels *Tom Sawyer* and *The Adventures of Huckleberry Finn* will almost certainly become children's classics.

Black rights group founded

1 MAY

The National Association for the Advancement of Colored People (NAACP) officially came into being in the United States today. It is formed from a group of liberals and radicals who came together last year after the anti-black riots. The new group hopes to bring an end to racial discrimination, using education and litigation to get its message across. It will be distributing informative pamphlets and is planning to publish a journal containing the work of black authors and artists later this year.

NAACP co-founder W Du Bois

The sight of the comet in the night sky causes amazement and alarm

Shooting star in near miss

16 MAY

Halley's Comet is about to pass very close to the Earth. Some people are terrified, convinced that the comet will release poisonous gases into Earth's atmosphere. Others are planning comet parties to celebrate. The comet is of particular interest to scientists, who will use the event, which occurs only once every 75 years, to increase their astronomical knowledge.

South Africa unites

31 MAY

The Union of South Africa, declared independent by a royal proclamation last December, became a self-governing dominion of the British Empire today. The new country unites the British colonies of the Cape and Natal with the former Boer countries of Transvaal and the Orange River. The new government will be headed by Louis Botha,

who led the defeated Boer army nine years ago. But it hopes to put memories of the Boer War behind it, as Botha strives to achieve unification.

Transvaal

Orange River · Natal

Cape Colony

INDIAN OCEAN

□ British   □ Boer

Map showing the united provinces of South Africa

JANUARY–JUNE

World Events	**FEB** Greece, led by Cretan-born Eleutherios Venizélos, clashes with Turkey over control of Crete.	**FEB** The Chinese army occupies Lhasa, Tibet, forcing the Tibetan spiritual leader, the Dalai Lama, to flee Tibet for India.	**FEB** Boutros Pasha Gahli, the first Egyptian prime minister under UK rule, is shot dead by a nationalist fanatic.	**MAY** The UK king Edward VII dies at the age of 68 after a nine-year reign; he is succeeded by his son George.
Entertainment	**MAR** *In Old California* is the first film to be made in the Hollywood area, USA.	**MAR** A US banker pays £103,000 for a Franz Hal painting, the largest sum ever paid for any work of art.	**MAR** The first *Frankenstein* film, starring Charles Ogle, is made by the Edison studio in New York, USA.	**JUN** A new season of the popular Ballets Russes opens in France with Igor Stravinsky's *The Firebird*.
Innovations	**FEB** An X-ray machine guides a surgeon to remove a nail from the lung of a boy in the USA. **BARONESS DE LAROCHE**	**MAR** French aristocrat Baroness de Laroche becomes the first woman to be granted a pilot's licence.	**JUN** UK explorer Captain Robert Scott sets out from England for the South Pole on the ship *Terra Nova*. **TERRA NOVA**	**JUN** The first aerial reconnaissance mission is made by two pilots from the French army around Vincennes.

1910

Ethel Le Neve is led down the ship's gangway, with Crippen following

IT TAKES TWO TO TANGO

Tango fever has swept across the United States and Europe this year as couples take to the dance floor to perform the latest complicated steps. The original, intimate and sexy dance came from the slums and backstreets of Argentina during the 19th century. Today, in a more restrained form, it is all the rage among fashionable young people on both sides of the Atlantic.

Radio used to catch criminal

31 JULY

Dr Hawley Harvey Crippen, wanted for the brutal murder of his wife at their home in London, Britain, was arrested at sea today thanks to the use of ship-to-shore radio. Crippen disappeared from London on 9 July, fleeing to Belgium with his mistress, 27-year-old Ethel Le Neve. Then, posing as Mr Robinson and son, the couple boarded the SS *Montrose*, bound for Quebec in Canada. The ship's captain, noticing the couple's odd behaviour – he spotted the "men" holding hands as well as other things that did not add up – radioed back to Britain with his suspicions. Crippen will be brought back to face trial for murder in his home country.

Portugal overthrows its king

4 OCTOBER

In a well-planned coup, republican revolutionaries have overthrown the Portuguese monarchy. The 20-year-old king, Manuel II, who came to the throne after the assassination of his father and brother, has fled to Gibraltar. The revolution comes after a decade of discontent about royal extravagance in the face of widespread poverty. Last night, hostilities broke out in the capital Lisbon. Sailors joined in and shelled strategic points from ships on the River Tagus. This morning most of the fighting had ceased and cries of "long live the republic" were heard as victorious soldiers and sailors marched through the city.

JULY–DECEMBER

AUG UK founder of nursing Florence Nightingale, also known as the "Lady of the Lamp", dies at the age of 90.

JUL Former US heavyweight boxing champion Jack Johnson takes the title from current holder Jim Jeffries.

AUG The first 13-km (8-mile) stretch of the Panama Canal is opened at its eastern end near the Caribbean.

FLORENCE NIGHTINGALE

AUG Following its victory over Russia in Manchuria, Japan formally annexes the strategically important Korea.

SEP Self-taught French painter Henri Rousseau, who created bold, dream-like canvases, dies at the age of 66.

SEP The French aviator M. Tabuteau makes the first flight across the Pyrenees mountain range.

SEP Louis Botha loses his seat in South Africa's first parliamentary elections, but his Nationalist Party wins by a safe majority.

NOV The work of Post-impressionist painters, including Picasso, Matisse, and Gauguin, is shown in the UK.

SEP Pioneering French physicist and Nobel Prize winner Marie Curie isolates pure radium for the first time.

OCT Dr Hawley Crippen, brought back to the UK from Canada to face trial for murder, is sentenced to death.

NOV Russian novelist Leo Tolstoy, author of *War and Peace* and *Anna Karenina*, dies at the age of 82.

LEO TOLSTOY

DEC The first neon lighting, developed by Georges Claude, is used at the Paris Motor Show.

1911

Mexican dictator surrenders

25 MAY

The Mexican dictator Porfirio Díaz was forced to resign from office today after almost 31 years in power. He has carried out his brutal rule by ruthlessly eliminating any opposition. His bold efforts to transform Mexico's economy were unfortunately achieved at the expense of the peasants, who have become slaves to a few rich landowners. Such actions have bred discontent, but the real trouble started last year when Francisco Madero stood against him for the position of president. Rather than risk a contest, Díaz had Madero arrested and imprisoned, but he was released on bail and escaped to the USA. From there,

Former president Porfirio Díaz

aided by rebel forces led by Zapata in the north and Pancho Villa in the south, he organized the uprising to oust Díaz. As the provisional president, Madero has the difficult task of governing this unruly and unhappy country.

Inca city discovered

24 JULY

High in the Andes, US archaeologist Hiram Bingham today discovered the ruins of Machu Picchu, the last great capital of the ancient Inca civilization. Bingham was on an expedition near Cuzco in Peru. He followed an Indian guide through the jungle and up sheer cliffs before he came upon the city on a flat piece of land nestled between two towering peaks. The site has long been known to Peruvians, but its camouflaged location has kept it a secret from Europeans for centuries. The discovery of the ruined city is of great importance to knowledge of Peruvian history. Archaeologists will be able to find out more about the Inca civilization, which disappeared soon after the Spanish conquest of South America in the middle of the 16th century.

THE SECRET GARDEN

British author Frances Hodgson Burnett has written one of the most popular children's novels of the year. *The Secret Garden* tells the story of Mary, an orphan who is sent to live in the gloomy mansion of her uncle. She is wretched and disagreeable until she discovers a garden hidden behind a wall, that opens her eyes to the world around her.

JANUARY–JUNE

World Events

MAR As trouble brews in Mexico, President Taft sends 30,000 US troops to guard the border territory.

MAR The UK announces plans to build five more *Dreadnought* battleships for the Royal Navy in response to German naval expansion.

APR Following an appeal from the sultan of Morocco, France sends troops to protect Europeans in both Casablanca and Fez.

APR US troops intervene in the Mexican civil war, crossing the Rio Grande and fighting the rebel forces led by Francisco Madero.

Entertainment

JAN Richard Strauss' opera *Der Rosenkavalier* debuts in Dresden, Germany.

FEB *A Tale of Two Cities*, based on the novel by Charles Dickens, is produced as a film in the USA.

MAY Austrian composer and conductor Gustav Mahler dies at the age of 50.

MAY The first Indianapolis 500 road race is won by US racing driver Ray Harroun.

STRAUSS'S DER ROSENKAVALIER

Innovations

JAN The Académie des Sciences in France refuses membership to Marie Curie.

MAR Clocks in France are put back 9 mins 21 secs to join the world on Greenwich Mean Time.

MAY The White Star shipping line launches the SS *Titanic*, the largest vessel afloat, in Belfast, Ireland.

RAY HARROUN IN MARMON WASP

MAY The first ocean liner to have an outside swimming pool is the White Star's SS *Olympic*.

1911

Mona missing

22 AUGUST

Last night da Vinci's *Mona Lisa* was stolen from the Louvre, the premier art gallery in Paris, France. Today the astonished curators are wondering why any thief would be foolish enough to steal the painting, as the world-famous picture could never be re-sold. Now that it has vanished, police must solve a crime as enigmatic as the *Mona Lisa*'s smile itself.

The Mona Lisa, painted 400 years ago by Leonardo da Vinci, is today viewed as a masterpiece

The hidden city of Machu Picchu, high up in the Andes mountains

Imperial regime abolished in China

29 DECEMBER

Dr Sun Yat-sen was elected president of a newly declared republic of China today, so bringing to an end more than 2,000 years of Chinese imperial history. This turn of events comes as a result of the nationalist uprising that started in central China in October. Sun Yat-sen, the leader of the revolution, has been an active reformer for many years. As leader of the nationalist Kuomintang Party, he has campaigned to bring an end to the 300-year rule of the corrupt Manchu dynasty and to establish a stable government in China. His support has grown rapidly in recent years, as imperial rule has become increasingly dictatorial and of a conservative nature. It is still too early to know what the future government of China will be like, but one thing is sure, China has seen its last emperor.

Sun Yat-sen and his wife

JULY–DECEMBER

JUL Germany sends the gunboat *Panther* to the Moroccan port of Agadir, provoking a crisis with France.

SEP The first Channel crossing for 36 years is made by UK swimmer Thomas Burgess.

JUL The first windscreen wipers, a rubber device operated by a piece of string, are fitted to a Benz.

AIRMAIL ARRIVES AT WINDSOR

SEP Peter Stolypin, the hard-line Russian prime minister, dies after he is shot while attending the opera at Kiev.

SEP French poet and art critic Guillaume Apollinaire is arrested for stealing the *Mona Lisa*.

SEP A two-week experimental airmail service is set up between Hendon and Windsor in the UK.

OCT Pu Yi, the five-year-old emperor of China, surrenders his power and agrees to grant a constitution.

DEC "The Blue Rider" group of artists led by Kandinsky and Franz Marc has its first show in Munich, Germany.

DEC French physicist Marie Curie wins an unprecedented second Nobel Prize for her scientific research.

ALEXANDER'S RAGTIME BAND

NOV The crisis at Agadir in North Africa ends as Germany accepts French control in Morocco.

DEC *Alexander's Ragtime Band*, a tune by US songwriter Irving Berlin, is the hit of the year.

DEC Norwegian explorer Roald Amundsen becomes the first man to reach the South Pole.

19 OCTOBER 1911 AMUNDSEN
LEAVES BASE AT FRAMHEIM

1 NOVEMBER 1911 SCOTT
LEAVES BASE AT CAPE EVANS

14 DECEMBER 1911 AMUNDS
REACHES SOUTH POLE

THE RACE TO THE SOUTH POLE

IN 1911, THE CONQUEST OF THE SOUTH POLE was the one of the few remaining challenges left for explorers. Two years before, Robert Peary of the United States reached the North Pole, and the race was now on to penetrate the frozen continent of Antarctica. Late in 1911, two teams of explorers set out across the ice and snow in search of this ultimate goal. One team, led by Norwegian Arctic explorer Roald Amundsen, was well organized and properly equipped for the extreme conditions. The other, a British team led by Captain Robert Scott, concentrated on scientific research and underestimated the physical difficulties of reaching the Pole. The different approaches decided the victors.

MODEL OF THE *FRAM*

Amundsen sails south

Amundsen's ship, the *Fram*, was purpose-built to resist the crushing pressure of ice, a danger when sailing in Antarctic waters. He set off from Norway in June 1910 and sailed south across the Atlantic Ocean, arriving at the Antarctic in January 1911. He anchored at the Bay of Whales in the Ross Sea where he wintered with eight companions and 116 dogs.

The route to the Pole

The closest Amundsen and Scott could get to the Pole by boat was by way of the Ross Sea. They set up base camps on opposite sides of the Ross Ice Shelf at Framheim and Cape Evans. From there they went on foot across the Ross Ice Shelf and over the Trans-antarctic Mountains to the Antarctic plateau and the geographic Pole at 90° south.

South Pole

Amundsen's route

Scott's route

Scott's last camp

Framheim

Cape Evans

Ross Sea

ANTARCTICA

WISTING

HASSEL

AMUNDSEN

BJAALAND

HANSEN

A team of experts

As well as being experienced navigators, the four men who accompanied Amundsen were chosen for their expertise in various fields; dog-handling, sledge-driving, skiing, and whale harpooning. The team were used to the bitter climate of Norway and were well prepared for the snow and cold they encountered in the Antarctic.

Winter at Framheim

Amundsen spent the Antarctic winter at base camp, where he prepared for the gruelling final stage of the expedition. He arranged several trips along the planned route and established depots in which to store supplies of food and fuel. He trained the dog teams, and reduced the sledge loads to a minimum.

Scientific exploration

Scott and his team placed great emphasis on scientific discovery. They attached a milometer to the back of one of their sledges to record the distance they travelled, and took daily weather readings. Their return journey was severely hindered by more than 15 kg (35 lb) of geological specimens, which they had collected en route.

17 JANUARY 1912 SCOTT
REACHES SOUTH POLE

JANUARY 1912 AMUNDSEN
RETURNS FROM POLE A HERO

MARCH 1912 SCOTT'S TEAM
PERISHES BEFORE REACHING SAFETY

HORSES PULL THE SLEDGES
ON SCOTT'S EXPEDITION

Scott's expedition

Scott used motorized sledges and horses as well as huskies for transport – not a wise decision. The motor sledges broke down, and the horses died of exposure as frozen sweat encrusted on their bodies, leaving the men to pull the sledges. Scott arranged for some of his team to turn back as they progressed, so that he was only accompanied by four – Wilson, Oates, Bowers, and Evans – to the Pole itself.

SNOWSHOE
WORN BY OATES

SNOWSHOE
WORN BY A HORSE

SCOTT'S TEAM

First to the Pole

After crossing more than 3,200 km (2,000 miles) of snow and ice, Amundsen and his team reached the South Pole in fine, sunny weather on 14 December 1911. There they raised the Norwegian flag and rested for a few days, before returning safely to base camp after just 96 days.

Amundsen relied entirely on huskies to pull his sledges

Huskies sweat through their noses

A tragic failure

Scott and his team reached the South Pole on 17 January 1912, only to discover evidence that their Norwegian rivals had beaten them to it. Sadly, they began the long trek home. The party was suffering from frostbite, fatigue, and lack of food. The onset of severe blizzards was the final blow and all five men died, three of them – Scott, Wilson, and Bowers – only a short distance from a food dump.

Thick coat enables husky to survive freezing weather

AMUNDSEN PLACES
THE NORWEGIAN FLAG
AT THE SOUTH POLE

1912

Leap into the unknown

1 MARCH

Albert Berry made history today when he parachuted to the ground after jumping out of a biplane. The dramatic event took place at 457 m (1,500 ft) over Jefferson Barracks, Missouri, United States. Berry plummeted some 122 m (400 ft) before his parachute opened. But his jump went without a hitch, and he landed safely on the parade ground as planned.

Singer in screen breakthrough

9 MARCH

After the flop of *Tosca* a few years ago, Sarah Bernhardt is

Leading lady Sarah Bernhardt

once again winning critical acclaim for her "golden bell" voice and superb acting. The French tragic actress is already established as a great stage performer on both sides of the Atlantic. Now, at the age of 68, she is also a screen success. Bernhardt plays the leading role in *La Dame aux Camélias*, made last year in Paris by Henri Pouctal and Paul Capellani. She is currently filming another title role, *Queen Elizabeth*, due for release later this year.

"Unsinkable" ship in iceberg disaster

A few survivors watch the great ship go down

15 APRIL

Early this morning White Star's great SS *Titanic* hit an iceberg and sank, in one of the greatest disasters ever to happen at sea. Over 1,500 of its 2,224 passengers and crew are thought to have perished in the icy waters of the North Atlantic. The *Titanic* was launched last year in Belfast, Ireland. It was the biggest and most luxurious ocean liner in the world, and the pride of the White Star fleet. It was also believed to be unsinkable, as the hull was fitted with 16 watertight compartments, enabling it to stay afloat, even if two of them flooded. But its maiden voyage was also to be its last. Four days into its journey from Southampton, Britain, to New York, United States, the ship was speeding through

World Events	**FEB** China is officially declared a republic, with Yuan Shi-kai as its leader.	**MAY** In the House of Commons, the UK government passes a bill to grant Home Rule to Ireland.	**MAY** Italy bombards the entrance to the Turkish Dardanelles and occupies the Greek island of Rhodes.	**MAY** The first issue of the Bolshevik newspaper *Pravda*, meaning "truth", is published in St Petersburg, Russia.
Entertainment	**FEB** England beats Australia 4–1 in a five-match cricket series to regain the Ashes.	**MAR** In the UK, the boat race between Oxford and Cambridge has to be re-run as both boats sink.	**MAY** *Prélude à 'Après Midi d'un Faune*, a ballet choreographed by Nijinsky, causes controversy in France.	**MAY** The expressionist "Blue Rider Group" puts on a second exhibition of paintings in Munich, Germany.
Innovations	**JAN** In France, Professor Dastre pioneers a cornea graft to restore lost eyesight.	 **ROBERT FALCON SCOTT** **MAR** Captain Scott and his UK team finally reach the South Pole, but perish on their return journey.	**APR** Major new discoveries are made at the Roman town of Pompeii, Italy, as more excavations are carried out.	 **NIJINSKY'S NEW BALLET** **JUN** Races are timed electronically for the first time at the 5th Olympic Games in Stockholm, Sweden.

1912

an icefield off Newfoundland, hoping to win the sought-after "Blue Riband" prize for the fastest Atlantic crossing, when it collided with a large iceberg, which ripped through the starboard side. A 91-m (300-ft) gash opened up, and the ship tilted forward and slowly slid beneath the waves. In only three hours it had disappeared. Passengers made frantic attempts to get on deck and board the lifeboats, but relatively few of them were successful. There have been suggestions that there were, in fact, too few lifeboats to accommodate all the people on board and that some were sent off only half full. The first ship on the scene, the *Carpathia*, took the 700 survivors to Halifax, Nova Scotia. A full inquiry will be set up shortly to answer questions about this tragic affair.

A lifeboat heads for the Carpathia, *the first ship on the scene*

Royal Pavlova

3 JULY

The first Royal Command Performance was held last night in Britain. Russian ballet dancer Anna Pavlova topped the bill and performed her dramatic "Dying Swan" routine to great acclaim.

Pavlova simulates the beating of a swan's wings

The Keystone Kops on the beat

Keystone hits the funny bone

23 SEPTEMBER

The newly formed Keystone Pictures Corporation releases its first two pictures today in Hollywood, United States. *Cohen Collects a Debt* and *The Water Nymph* are the first productions of Mack Sennett's company of "popular fun-makers", most notable of whom is the stunning Mabel Normand. Future weekly releases will feature a team of accident-prone policemen known as the Keystone Kops.

DOUBLE GOLD

US athlete Jim Thorpe was the star of this year's Olympic Games in Stockholm, Sweden, winning two gold medals. He won the pentathlon, but caused a sensation in the decathlon with a world-record score of 8,412.955 points. The Swedish king, expressing his admiration, said, "Sir, you are the greatest athlete in the world." Thorpe replied, "Thanks, king".

JULY–DECEMBER

SEP In Ireland 471,414 Protestants sign a "solemn covenant" pledging themselves to resist the imposition of Irish Home Rule.

SEP French Cubist artist George Braque creates his first picture entitled *Fruit Dish and Glass* using a paper collage technique.

AUG French doctor Gaston Odin claims that he has isolated and cultivated a microbe of cancer.

OLIVER TWIST

SEP A conflict between Bulgaria and Turkey heats up in the Balkans, causing Greece, Serbia, and Bulgaria to mobilize troops.

DEC The first UK feature film, *Oliver Twist*, which is directed by Cecil Hepworth, opens in London.

SEP Electrical loudspeakers are used for the first time in public at the Olympic Theatre in Chicago, USA.

OCT The Balkan league – Greece, Serbia, Bulgaria, and Montenegro – launch a major offensive against Turkey.

DEC The first ice show, *Flirting at St Moritz*, starring Charlotte Oelschlagel, opens in Germany.

DEC German geologist Alfred Wegener outlines his theory on how today's continents have formed.

PILTDOWN MAN

OCT Turkey, preoccupied with the Balkan threat, signs a peace treaty at Ouchy, Switzerland, to end its war with Italy.

DEC *It's a Long Way to Tipperary*, a song by UK duo Jack Judge and Harry Williams, is a smash hit.

DEC The skull of the Piltdown Man, believed to be 50,000 years old, is found in Sussex, UK.

VOTES FOR WOMEN

WSPU EMBLEM SHOWS A YOUNG WOMAN CARRYING THE BANNER OF FREEDOM

THE ISSUE OF WOMEN'S SUFFRAGE was not new. Although women in New Zealand achieved their aim in 1893, in most countries campaigning continued for much longer. In Britain, the Women's Social and Political Union (WSPU), founded by Emmeline Pankhurst in 1903, staged a notorious and influential campaign that attracted thousands of supporters. They fought for the vote with "Deeds, not Words" in a war against the UK government that became increasingly fierce and bitter. The women, nicknamed "suffragettes", adopted militant direct action tactics that included heckling, mass demonstrations, and stunts. During World War I, with the men away fighting, women all over Europe finally won some recognition, doing everything the men had from driving ambulances to factory work.

Arrested!

On 18 November 1910, 300 suffragettes marched peacefully on the House of Commons in London. Police arrived on the scene, and in a struggle lasting more than six hours the women were violently attacked, something which only made them more militant. British women finally achieved their goal, the right to vote, in 1918.

Quite at ease

In 1906, Finnish women became the first in Europe to receive the vote. The following year, 19 had seats in parliament. *The Times* in London reported that all "appeared quite at ease".

Military precision

The WSPU was organized along military lines. Emmeline Pankhurst inspired the "troops", while her eldest daughter Christabel led them. Like soldiers, suffragettes followed orders without question and were prepared to go to any lengths, even to die, for their cause.

CHRISTABEL (LEFT) AND EMMELINE PANKHURST

US WOMEN DEMONSTRATE FOR THE RIGHT TO VOTE

"Votes for women" sash in suffragette colours

US women's fight for the vote had support in every state

 1923 BENITO MUSSOLINI GIVES
WOMEN THE VOTE IN ITALY
 1934 TURKISH WOMEN ARE GIVEN THE
VOTE AS PART OF MODERNIZING REFORMS
 1971 WOMEN IN SWITZERLAND ARE
THE LAST IN EUROPE TO GAIN THE VOTE

DETAIL FROM
A VOTES FOR
WOMEN COVER

Women's suffrage in Asia

Women all over Asia campaigned for the right to vote. The Women's Indian Association raised the issue in 1917, but the vote was not given universally until 1949, two years after Indian independence. Japanese women started campaigning in the 1920s, but had to wait until 1945 before they could vote. In China, women's right to vote came as part of the new communist regime.

Spreading the word

The WSPU knew how to get their message across. They set up a publishing company, the Woman's Press, and produced their own newspapers, *Votes for Women* and the more militant *Suffragette*. On street corners suffragettes gave pamphlets to passers-by.

Behind bars

Between 1906 and 1914, thousands of suffragettes were arrested in Britain, and many were imprisoned. Some went on hunger strike. The government, worried that women would die and become martyrs, introduced force feeding, a brutal torture that caused a public outcry.

FORCE FEEDING
EQUIPMENT

SUFFRAGETTES WORE COARSE
CALICO CLOTHING IN PRISON

Playing cat and mouse

In 1913, the British government introduced what became known as the "Cat and Mouse Act". Like a cat that plays with a mouse rather than kills it, the authorities released seriously ill hunger strikers from prison, but re-arrested them as they recovered.

Women often wore white dresses on demonstrations

OREGON   ILLINOIS

BUTTONS DECORATED
WITH WHITE, GREEN,
AND PURPLE

TRICOLOUR
ROSETTE WAS
WORN ON
EVERY MARCH

Suffrage in the States

As elsewhere, women's suffrage in the United States was a long, hard struggle, seen by some as a diversion to the main campaign for black rights. At first campaigning was on a state-by-state basis, but in 1890 it began to be fought on a federal level. Tactics varied from gentle persuasion to militancy, until the campaign achieved victory across the country in 1920.

Colours of suffrage

Green for life, purple for honour, and white for purity were the colours of the WSPU, and supporters wore them with pride. Fashion houses and department stores were quick to design appropriately coloured clothing and merchandise.

1913

Stravinsky with leading dancer Nijinsky

Grand Central's grand opening

2 FEBRUARY

Grand Central Station, New York City's impressive new railway terminus, opened for business today. Situated in central Manhattan, it is the largest railway station in the world, with 48 tracks. The steel-framed building, which is covered with granite and marble, was designed by the US architects Warren and Wetmore. It is a fine example of the Beaux Arts style which dominates many of today's public buildings. Sculptures of the Roman gods Mercury, Hercules, and Minerva crown the entrance, and the interior is dominated by a high-vaulted ceiling, painted with more than 2,500 stars.

THE ZIP FASTENER

Swedish inventor Gideon Sundback has made a new kind of fastener – the zip – to be used for clothing. His idea of mounting metal teeth onto parallel tapes was patented this April. It will be ready for manufacture next year.

The riot of spring

30 MAY

The premiere of Russian composer Igor Stravinsky's ballet *The Rite of Spring* was met with boos and whistles last night in Paris. The audience was unprepared for the dissonant and pounding rhythms of the music and Vaslav Nijinsky's fierce choreography, performed by the Ballets Russes.

Martyr at the Derby

4 JUNE

High drama occurred today at the Derby, an annual horse race held in Britain at Epsom. In the middle of the race a woman rushed onto the racetrack and grabbed at the reins of Anmer, the king's horse. Both horse and rider were brought down by her action. The jockey suffered slight injuries; the woman, who has been identified as Emily Davison, was knocked out and is unlikely to regain consciousness. Miss Davison is a suffragette and is now being hailed as a martyr by fellow campaigners.

Emily Davison brings down the king's horse

JANUARY– JUNE

World Events

JAN In China, 300 Chinese troops are killed in a single night during a raid across the border by Tibetans.

FEB In Mexico, right-wing army commander Victoriano Huerta seizes power from President Madéro and has him killed.

MAY A peace treaty is signed in London, UK, bringing an end to the first Balkan War between Turkey and the Balkan States.

JUN The second Balkan War begins as Bulgaria turns on its former allies, and attacks Serbia and Greece.

Entertainment

JAN US athlete Jim Thorpe is stripped of his Olympic medals for once competing as a professional.

JIM THORPE

FEB The first international exhibition of modern art, featuring Van Gogh and Cézanne, opens in New York, USA.

JUN US comic actor Roscoe "Fatty" Arbuckle makes his film debut in two of the new Keystone comedies.

JUN Ladies and Mixed Doubles matches are first held at the UK Wimbledon Tennis Championships.

Innovations

FEB A relief party recovers the bodies of the unsuccessful UK South Pole expedition team.

MAR The first bull-nosed Morris Oxford is made at the Oxford car factory in Cowley, UK.

APR Professor Behring announces the development of a new serum for diphtheria in Berlin, Germany.

WOOLWORTH BUILDING

APR The 241-m (791-ft) Woolworth Building, the world's tallest building, is completed in New York, USA.

1913

Ford's revolutionary assembly line rolls

If all goes well, 250,000 Model T cars will be built next year

7 OCTOBER

US car manufacturer Henry Ford today started an industrial revolution at his Highland Park factory in Michigan by introducing the assembly line. Cars will no longer be put together from scratch in one place by skilled workers. Instead, a 76-m (249-ft) long conveyer belt will move the partially assembled cars along the factory floor, allowing teams of unskilled men to work on one particular part before it moves on to the next team. Ford estimates that this new process will reduce the assembly time of a car to no more than six hours, resulting in a huge increase in output and, most importantly for the consumer, a big drop in price.

Blast links two oceans

10 OCTOBER

With a push of a button, the last remaining piece of rock between the Atlantic and Pacific oceans in Central America was removed. Over 6,437 km (4,000 miles) away in Washington DC, US president Woodrow Wilson set off the blast of dynamite.

This dramatic gesture brings the long-running Panama Canal project very near to completion. Hero of the day was Colonel George Goethals, chief engineer on the project since 1907. After final building work, the canal will be ready for the first ships to sail through it next year.

JULY–DECEMBER

AUG In the Balkans, Bulgaria agrees to a peace settlement, although it is forced to give up most of its newly gained land.

SEP The recently renovated and refurbished Gaumont Picture Palace reopens for business in Paris, France.

GAUMONT PICTURE PALACE

AUG Russian aviator Lt Peter Nesterov performs the first loop-the-loop, a spectacular aeroplane stunt.

SEP The Irish Home Rule Bill is passed by the UK parliament, but Irish Ulster Unionists prepare to oppose it.

NOV UK comic actor Charlie Chaplin makes his film debut in the USA in *Making a Living*.

AUG Stainless steel, an alloy of steel and chromium that does not rust, is first cast in Sheffield, UK.

NOV Yuan Shi-kai, elected president of the Chinese Republic last month, dismisses the parliament and sets up a dictatorship.

DEC The first crossword puzzle is printed in the *New York World* weekend supplement in the USA.

SEP German inventor Rudolf Diesel, who created the revolutionary diesel engine, dies at the age of 55.

THE FIRST CROSSWORD

NOV Mexican rebels led by Pancho Villa prepare to move on Mexico City and besiege right-wing President Huerta.

DEC The *Mona Lisa*, stolen from the Louvre in 1911, is recovered in Florence, Italy.

OCT The world's first oil-driven battleship, HMS *Queen Elizabeth*, is launched in Portsmouth, UK.

1914

Austrian Archduke assassinated

28 JUNE

Archduke Franz Ferdinand, the heir to the Austrian throne, and his wife were assassinated today during an official visit to the Bosnian capital of Sarajevo. The assassin Gavrilo Princip, who is a Bosnian Serb, ran out from the crowd and fired two shots at the couple with a Browning pistol. Both victims died almost immediately from their wounds. It appears that the assassination was part of a carefully laid plot. Earlier in the day the couple had had a narrow escape when a bomb was thrown at their car, but the Archduke knocked it away, injuring people in the following car. It is unclear who might be responsible for the attack, but there are suspicions that it may be Serbia, which opposes the Austrian rule in Bosnia. If this is true, Austria can be expected to take the strongest possible action in response.

War breaks out in Europe

Kitchener poster summons volunteers

4 AUGUST

Europe is at war! After two weeks of high tension across the Continent, all the major powers are now embroiled in conflict. France, Russia, and Britain stand on one side, facing Germany and Austria-Hungary on the other. The headlong rush into war was triggered by the assassination of Franz Ferdinand in June. On 23 July, Austria issued Serbia with an ultimatum, requesting that they collaborate to find those responsible for the plot.

Archduke Franz Ferdinand and his wife in Sarajevo

Serbia refused, and five days later Austria declared war and invaded. Russia rushed to defend its ally Serbia, while Germany came to the aid of its ally Austria. On 3 August Germany declared war on France and invaded Belgium. Britain, pledged to defend Belgian neutrality, entered the conflict today, declaring war on Germany. Opinion is divided on how long the war might last. The commander of the British Expeditionary Force Sir John French thinks it will be over by Christmas, but secretary of state for war Lord Kitchener believes that it could be much longer.

JANUARY– JUNE

World Events	**FEB** Northern Ireland appears on the brink of civil war as Protestants violently resist Home Rule.	**MAR** The editor of *Le Figaro* is shot dead by the French finance minister's wife for planning to slur her husband's name.	**APR** A 3,000-strong force of US marines intervenes in the Mexican civil war and seizes the port of Vera Cruz.	**JUN** The assassination of Archduke Franz Ferdinand leads to growing tension between Austria and Serbia.
Entertainment	**FEB** *The Word, the Flesh, and the Devil* is the world's first feature film to be shot in colour.	**MAR** Seven US newspapers, including the *New York Times*, issue newspaper colour supplements for the first time.	**APR** The bad language in Irish playwright George Bernard Shaw's *Pygmalion* causes much controversy.	**JUN** Wyndham Lewis publishes *Blast*, the manifesto of the futurist Vorticist art movement, in London, UK.
Innovations	**JAN** The US Ford Motor Co introduces the $5 working day for all its employees.	**FEB** UK explorer Campbell Beasley discovers the remains of three Inca cities hidden in the jungles of Peru.	**MAY** UK explorer Ernest Shackleton leaves the UK for a major three-year exploration of Antarctica.	**JUN** At Hamburg, Kaiser Wilhelm II launches the German-built *Bismarck*, the world's largest ship.

INCA VASE

PYGMALION

1914

Russians routed on Eastern Front

Russian prisoners-of-war

31 AUGUST

After four days of heavy fighting at Tannenberg on the Polish-German border, the Russian Second Army led by General Samsonov has suffered a terrible defeat at the hands of the Germans. According to eyewitness accounts, the battle was very one-sided, with the Russian cavalry proving no match for the heavily armed and well-organized German infantry. It is estimated that more than 100,000 Russian soldiers have been taken prisoner. The defeat is being taken well by Russian authorities, who have already achieved a chain of successes and made inroads into German territory. However, it will change the shape of the campaign on the Eastern Front.

THE TRAMP Dressed in a baggy suit with a battered hat and holding a cane, UK-born actor Charlie Chaplin has launched a new star. His first appearance dressed as the Tramp in the film *Kid Auto Races at Venice* has captured the hearts of US audiences.

Paris saved from German attack

10 SEPTEMBER

The German attempt to knock France quickly out of the war ground to a halt today after six days of fighting on the River Marne in northeastern France. The German plan, devised by General von Schlieffen, was to make a headlong sweep through Belgium and around the north of Paris, avoiding the heavily armed forts along the common Franco-German border. At first the bold attempt at a knockout blow against the French capital seemed to be succeeding. Within days of occupying Luxembourg and invading Belgium, the German army was moving quickly through France, but a decisive French counter-offensive with fresh troops has finally halted the

French soldiers in action

advance. The German army is now in retreat and is digging itself in in deep trenches along the River Aisne, 40 km (25 miles) to the north. The fighting – the first major engagement in western Europe between the warring sides – is thought to have resulted in as many as 500,000 casualties.

Truce halts war for Christmas

25 DECEMBER

Along a small section of the Western Front south of Messines, Belgium, soldiers from both sides of the war celebrated Christmas together. They exchanged gifts of cigars and jam and some are rumoured to have played a game of football.

JULY–DECEMBER

JUL Austria delivers an ultimatum to Serbia containing such humiliating demands that it makes war almost inevitable.

AUG 72-year-old Sam Lucas becomes the first black actor to star in a US feature film – *Uncle Tom's Cabin*.

AUG Electrically controlled lights for directing traffic are introduced in Cleveland, Ohio, USA.

PETROGRAD

SEP The Russian government changes the name of their capital city to Petrograd because St Petersburg sounds too German.

SEP German painter Auguste Macke and French novelist Henri Alain-Fournier are both killed in battle.

AUG The Panama Canal, joining the north Atlantic and south Pacific oceans, is finally completed.

OCT In the "Race to the Sea" Germany and the Allies wage battles through northern France in an attempt to outflank each other.

DEC US cartoonist John Gruelle paints a face on his daughter's faceless rag doll, so inventing the Raggedy Ann Doll.

OCT Russian manufacturer Sikorsky experiments with the design of a multi-engined heavy bomber.

TRENCH SPADE

NOV Stalemate is reached – a line of war trenches now stretches from the English Channel to the border of Switzerland.

DEC Among the new books published this year is *Dubliners*, a collection of short stories by Irish writer James Joyce.

OCT The US Eastman Kodak Co announces the invention of a colour photographic process.

JUNE 1914 ASSASSINATION OF
ARCHDUKE FRANZ FERDINAND

SEPTEMBER 1914 ALLIES STOP
THE GERMAN ADVANCE AT MARNE

MAY 1915 SS *LUSITANIA* SUNK
BY A GERMAN SUBMARINE

TRENCH WARFARE

WHEN WAR BROKE OUT IN 1914, the battles between German and Allied soldiers were fought using heavy artillery and machine guns. It soon became clear that the best means of defence in such attacks was to pick up a spade and dig a hole. Lines of trenches evolved, complex webs made up of front line, communication, support, and reserve trenches, gun pits and listening posts. At the rear were dugouts used as living quarters and stores. The front was fortified with barbed wire and watched over by armed sentries. Many men spent the entire war in these cramped, muddy ditches. As well as suffering from the cold and the rain, the horrors the men had to deal with included rats, lice, and lack of hygiene.

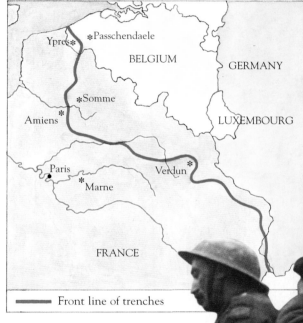

Front line of trenches

Eyeholes 0.3 m (1 ft) below the line of vision

GERMAN
ARTILLERY
OBSERVATION
INSTRUMENT

The Western Front

Within the first three months of war, the German and Allied armies had created a fixed line of trenches that stretched from the English Channel to the Swiss border. It was stalemate. Over the next four years many bloody battles (as starred right) were fought to try to break the deadlock, but the front line held, shifting no more than 16 km (10 miles) in either direction until the final months of the war in 1918.

Look out

Snipers would ruthlessly gun down any soldiers who put their heads over the top or climbed out of their trenches. During attacks, observation instruments were used to get a 3-D vision of fire over the battleground. At other times soldiers used trench periscopes, nicknamed "donkeys' ears" because of their shape, to observe what was happening in relative safety.

Poison gas

In an attempt to break the stalemate, German armies first used chlorine gas at Ypres in April 1915. A swirling cloud of thick greenish-yellow vapour drifted over the Allied lines, blinding the soldiers and causing the loss of 5,000 lives. Both sides swiftly developed the use of phosgene and mustard gas, causing choking, vomiting, and gut rot. Gas attacks became hated and feared by all soldiers in the war.

BRITISH TROOPS
SUFFERING FROM
THE BLINDING
EFFECTS OF GAS

Communications

Troops in the trenches needed to be able to communicate quickly with their officers and each other. In order to relate what was going on in different sections of the line, field telephones, like this German "feld fernsprecher", were located both in the dugouts and at the observation posts, and connected by a telephone wire. Radios, runners, dogs, and even pigeons were also used to convey messages.

Rats spread disease through the trenches

NOVEMBER 1916 ONE MILLION DIE
AFTER FOUR-MONTH SOMME OFFENSIVE

APRIL 1917 US TROOPS ENTER THE
WAR ON THE SIDE OF THE ALLIES

NOVEMBER 1918 END OF THE
GREAT WAR, ALLIES VICTORIOUS

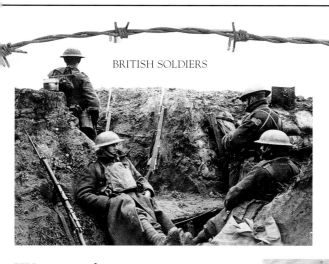

BRITISH SOLDIERS

Weaponry

The main weapons used at the front were machine guns, artillery shells, and, after 1916, tanks. Individual soldiers were equipped with a rifle, grenades for knocking out the enemy at close quarters, and clubs and knives for one-to-one combat. During an assault, soldiers used wire-cutters to cut through any wire that had not been destroyed in the initial artillery barrage.

GERMAN
CLUB

BRITISH
MILLS
BOMB

FRENCH
TRENCH
KNIFE

Waiting for action

Fighting did not take place every day on the Western Front, and some sections of line could often be quiet for months at a time. The biggest enemy the soldiers then encountered was boredom. The men would sit for hours in cramped, unhygienic conditions, with little to look forward to except the next meal. While they waited for their next orders, writing to or receiving letters from home were favoured activities.

LETTERS
HOME FROM A
BRITISH SOLDIER

GERMAN
STICK
GRENADE

BRITISH
WIRE-
CUTTERS

Illustrations helped to convey what war was like

1915

Outrage at epic movie premiere

3 MARCH

There were demonstrations outside the Liberty Theatre in New York today at the premiere of *The Birth of a Nation*, the new film by US director D W Griffith. Black activists, angry at the film's distorted view of black history and the Civil War, are trying to have the film banned. The activists are offended in particular by the idealized portrayal of the Ku Klux Klan and the scenes of black-faced white actors committing racial atrocities. The film, which runs for 180 minutes, was also shown to President Wilson at a private viewing held at the White House. "It is like writing history with lightning," he said after. "And my only regret is that it is all so terribly true."

SS *Lusitania* sunk

8 MAY

The sinking of the British liner SS *Lusitania* by German torpedoes off the coast of Ireland yesterday afternoon was met with outrage by the US public. The *Lusitania* had almost completed its North Atlantic crossing from New York to Liverpool when a German submarine struck without warning at 2.12 pm. It was hit by two torpedoes and sank within 21 minutes. Of the 1,978 passengers, 500 to 600 have survived the ordeal. Among the 1,400 men, women, and children who drowned are 128 US citizens, including prominent people and close friends of President Wilson. The US State Department said it viewed the sinking "most seriously", while the former president Theodore Roosevelt condemned it as an "act of piracy". Commentators are wondering what effect the sinking of the *Lusitania* will have on the United States' policy of neutrality.

Nurse executed on spy charge

12 OCTOBER

British nurse Edith Cavell was shot for treason today by a German firing squad in the Belgian capital of Brussels. Miss Cavell, who had run a school for nurses in the city since 1906, continued to work when war broke out last year and treated the sick and injured of all nations in the conflict. Despite the respect she had gained for her work from both warring sides, she was arrested on 5 August and charged with harbouring Belgians who were eligible to fight, and with helping British and French soldiers escape to safety across the Dutch border.

Nurse Edith Cavell and her dogs

JANUARY–JUNE

World Events	**JAN** German Zeppelin airships begin a bombing campaign against the UK by attacking ports on the east coast.	**FEB** Germany begins submarine warfare against the UK to try and frighten away neutral shipping and destroy the UK's economy.	**APR** Allied forces land on the Gallipoli Peninsula in Turkey in an attempt to force an entrance through to the Black Sea.	**MAY** Italy leaves the Triple Alliance with Germany and Austria and enters the war on the side of the Allies.
Entertainment	**FEB** In Berlin, it is decided to abandon plans to stage next year's Olympic Games in Germany.	**FEB** French actress Sarah Bernhardt has her right leg amputated following a fall during a performance of *La Tosca*.	**APR** Jess Willard, the US "Great White Hope", wins the world heavyweight boxing title, defeating Jack Johnson.	**APR** UK war poet and romantic hero Rupert Brooke dies in Greece from blood poisoning at the age of 28.
Innovations	**JAN** The first transcontinental telephone call is made between New York and San Francisco.	**JAN** Germans carry out the first-ever gas attack in warfare against Russian troops at Bolimov on the Eastern Front.	**APR** The first anti-chlorine gas masks are issued to UK troops in the second Battle of Ypres, France.	**JUN** The first 3-D films, developed by E S Porter and W E Wadell, are shown in New York City, USA.

ZEPPELIN BOMB

GAS MASK

1915

Women's work boosts war effort

10 NOVEMBER

Last March the British government appealed for women to sign up for work in factories in order to free men to fight. The thousands of women who volunteered are now achieving excellent results. One survey suggests that productivity has risen two and a half times. The initially wary factory foremen acknowledge that women's energy, punctuality, and willingness make them more than ideal substitutes for their male counterparts. Most women are involved in producing vital munitions, working up to 12 hours a day 7 days a week to ensure that the troops have enough arms.

Women workers in a shell factory

SHELL-SHOCKED

Long-range shells filled with gas or pieces of shrapnel have introduced a terrifying new dimension to warfare this year. Fired from behind the safety of enemy lines, the shells can inflict great damage on frontline troops sheltering in their trenches.

Allies retreat from Gallipoli shore

20 DECEMBER

After eight months of futile fighting, Allied forces retreated from the Gallipoli Peninsula in western Turkey last night. Under cover of darkness, troops from Britain, New Zealand, and Australia slipped away, leaving the peninsula in the hands of its Turkish rulers. More than 25,000 troops have been killed in the fighting, with more than 76,000 wounded, 96,000 admitted to hospital, and at least 13,000 missing. Commentators are calling the Allied withdrawal the biggest setback of the war so far.

The ill-fated expedition to Gallipoli was originally designed to force a passage through the Dardanelles strait into the Black Sea, and so open up a route to supply Russia with much-needed weapons. It was intended that this would knock Turkey out of the war. Also, by threatening Austria and Germany from the east through the Balkans, this would break the deadlock in western Europe. The strategic peninsula that overlooks the Dardanelles was first bombarded in February this year. An Allied naval assault in March failed when six ships were sunk in an unidentified minefield. The troops finally went ashore on 25 April, but by then the element of surprise was lost and the Turks had reinforced their positions. Despite some successes, the Allies remained pinned down on the beaches and were unable to capture the peninsula. The Australian and New Zealand troops have displayed great acts of heroism, but the cost of the fighting has proved to be too great, hence the instruction to withdraw. No lives were lost in this final retreat.

Medal given to Turkish troops

JULY–DECEMBER

SEP The autumn offensive opens on the Western Front, with French troops under the command of General Joffré.

JUL The first tourist car is admitted into Yellowstone National Park in northwestern Wyoming, USA.

OCT UK ships begin to tow a torpedo-shaped device from their bows in order to disarm mines.

GENERAL JOFFRE

SEP Tsar Nicholas II takes control of the army following the fall of the key Russian stronghold at Brest-Livotsk.

OCT US baseball team the Boston Red Sox purchase pitcher Babe Ruth from the Baltimore Orioles.

NOV An *AB-2* flying boat of the US navy is the first plane to be launched by catapult from a ship.

SEP Bulgaria enters the war on the side of Germany and Austria and moves its forces eastwards towards Serbia.

OCT William G Grace, the UK's greatest player of test cricket and figurehead, dies at the age of 67.

DEC As the production line continues to roll, the US Ford Motor Co produces its one-millionth motor car.

W G GRACE

DEC Sir John French is replaced as commander-in-chief of the UK forces by Sir Douglas Haig.

DEC Among the best-selling novels published this year was *The 39 Steps* by Scottish writer John Buchan.

DEC The general theory of relativity published by German-born physicist Albert Einstein causes controversy.

1916

Assault on French at Verdun

21 FEBRUARY
At exactly 7.15 this morning, German guns opened fire without warning at French positions around the fort of Verdun. During the course of the day more than a million shells fell as the Germans began their push at French defences in this key sector of the Western Front. As the German infantry advanced behind their artillery, the French retaliated with machine gun fire. As yet it is unclear whether the German aim is to engage a large part of the French army in a lengthy battle of attrition, or to break through their lines.

The bulk of French troops are being kept away from the front line to minimize losses. However, they are suffering from an earlier decision by General Joffré who, thinking that the Germans would strike further north at Champagne, has reduced defences at Verdun.

Pancho Villa and some of his bandits

US pursues Mexican rebel

15 MARCH
A force of 4,000 US soldiers, led by Brigadier-General John Pershing, crossed the border of Mexico today in pursuit of Mexican rebel leader Pancho Villa. They will join 5,000 men who are already looking for the bandit. Villa is responsible for the deaths of 18 US mining engineers who were removed from a train near Chihuahua and shot on 16 January. He also gave the order to kill 19 inhabitants of Columbus, New Mexico, on 9 March. The reason for these attacks is open to debate, but some reports say that Pancho Villa is hoping to draw the United States into the Mexican civil war and expose the weakness of Mexico's government.

JANUARY–MARCH

World Events	**JAN** Austro-Hungarian forces attack Montenegro and quickly overrun the small Balkan country.	**JAN** The last Allied troops leave the Gallipoli Peninsula in Turkey after they fail in their attempt to take it over.	**FEB** For the fifth time, the Italian army tries to break through the Austro-Hungarian lines at the Isonzo River.	**MAR** The first president of the Chinese Republic, Yuan Shi-kai, dies, leaving China without a clear political leader.
Entertainment	**FEB** US author Henry James, who wrote *The Portrait of a Lady*, dies at the age of 72.	**FEB** A group of artists, creators of a new art movement called "Dada", meet in Zurich, Switzerland.	**FEB** The first in a new cartoon series, *Krazy Kat and Ignatz Mouse Discuss the Letter G*, is shown in New York, USA.	**MAR** Handsome US actor Douglas Fairbanks makes a popular film debut in *The Habit of Happiness*.
Innovations	**JAN** As war continues, sugar rationing is introduced in the London area, UK.	**DADA POSTER BY KURT SCHWITTERS** **FEB** The first UK fighter squadron goes into operation in St Omer, northern France.	**FEB** Air-to-ground radio is first demonstrated by a UK military pilot to Lord Kitchener in France.	 **DOUGLAS FAIRBANKS** **MAR** The Austrian War Dog Institute begins to train dogs, which will be used to guide blind people.

1916

WOMEN AT WAR

As men are drafted into armies to fight at the front line, women all over Europe are playing an increasingly important part in the war. Factories, farms, and even public transportation are now being run by women workers, without whose contribution many vital services would otherwise grind to a halt.

Devastated corner of Sackville Street, Dublin

Rebels stage Easter Rising in Dublin

24 APRIL

In what appears to be a pre-arranged uprising, Irish nationalists in Dublin started a full-scale rebellion against British rule this morning, Easter Monday. The rebels, led by Patrick Pearse of the Irish Republican Brotherhood and trade union leader James Connolly of Sinn Féin, seized the General Post Office on Sackville Street in the centre of the city, and declared Ireland to be an independent republic. Other buildings across Dublin have been occupied, but attempts to seize Dublin Castle, the headquarters of British rule in Ireland, and an arsenal in Phoenix Park have failed. Fighting has broken out between republicans and British troops as both sides struggle to take control of key positions in the city. To cope with the worsening situation, Britain has called in reinforcements from other parts of Ireland.

Sea battle at Jutland

31 MAY

In what is being dubbed "the greatest naval battle ever waged", British and German *Dreadnought* battleships clashed at Jutland off the coast of Denmark today. A conflict between the fleets has been brewing for some time, with the Germans eager to break the long-standing Allied blockade off their coast. The outcome of the battle, however, is not clear, with both sides claiming victory. Although the German fleet was the first to retreat, the British fleet suffered greater losses in both ships and men. The test will be whether the German High Seas Fleet will venture out of port again to face the firepower of the British Grand Fleet. Meanwhile, the Allied blockade remains in place.

APRIL–JUNE

APR President Wilson threatens to break US diplomatic relations with Germany if it continues submarine warfare.

APR The International Olympic Committee cancels the Olympic Games until the war is over.

APR The first major airlift of supplies is conducted by UK pilots to a besieged garrison at Kut al-Imara, Iraq.

UK CLOCKS ADVANCE

MAY UK general Sir John Maxwell orders the execution of the rebels involved in the Easter Rising.

APR Two French girls who are accused of murder state that their crime was inspired by a film.

MAY Clocks go forward by one hour as a daylight-saving plan to help the war effort is introduced in the UK.

JUN Russian armies commanded by General Alexei Brusilov make huge advances into Austria-Hungary on the Eastern Front.

MAY Norman Rockwell designs the cover for the first edition of the Philadelphia *Saturday Evening Post*.

JUN US timber magnate William Boeing tests his newly designed aeroplane in Washington DC.

RUSSIAN GENERAL ALEXEI BRUSILOV

JUN UK war minister Lord Kitchener is killed when HMS *Hampshire* is sunk by a German mine off the Orkney Islands.

JUN The final episode of *The Vampires* series is shown in France starring the beautiful Musidora.

JUN The US Bell Telephone Co demonstrates an open-air public address system on Staten Island.

1916

Carnage as Somme campaign opens

British Pals battalion badge

1 JULY
At 7.30 this morning, the artillery barrage against German lines that has lasted for seven days came to an end. Five minutes later, thousands of Allied troops advanced, only to be mown down by enemy gunfire. This evening, 57,470 Allied and 8,000 German soldiers are lying dead or injured in "no-man's land". The attack on German lines near the River Somme in northern France has temporarily ground to a halt amid the worst scenes of slaughter the war has seen. In this long-prepared-for offensive, the troops attacked on a 32-km (20-mile) front, but the army was not at full strength. The 25 British divisions were mostly made up of Pals battalions, who are enthusiastic but inexperienced volunteers, and the French army only provided 11, rather than the 40 divisions it had promised, because most of its men were still fighting at Verdun. The main problem was that the Germans held the high ground surrounding the river, so much of the advance was uphill. In addition to this, the heavily fortified German lines were left relatively unscathed by the initial bombardment. The battle plan, devised by British Field Marshal Haig, called for a massive push against the German front line in order to break the stalemate and lead to a speedy victory in the war.

He calculated that the Allies would advance about 4 km (2.5 miles) by the end of the first day. He had not reckoned on the strength of the German fortifications, nor that they would retreat into second-line bunkers and ride out the bombardment. As the unwitting Allied soldiers climbed out of their trenches this morning, they were not met with the light resistance they had expected, but with a savage hail of gunfire. Loaded down with more than 30 kg (65 lb) of equipment, the soldiers could only progress at a slow walk, making each one an easy target for the German gunners. A truce at midday allowed some of the dead and wounded to be carried away from the battlefield. Tonight the British army must reflect on this terrible result.

German machine gun on trench mount

JULY–SEPTEMBER

World Events	**AUG** Former UK diplomat Roger Casement is executed for trying to smuggle arms to Irish rebels.	**AUG** Kaiser Wilhelm II appoints Paul von Hindenburg, victor of the Battle of Tannenburg, his chief of general staff.	**AUG** Romania joins the Allies and invades Austria-Hungary; Germany declares war on Romania; Turkey declares war on Russia.	**SEP** The Owen-Keating Labour Law, to diminish the appalling conditions of child labour, is passed in the USA.
Entertainment	**JUL** French symbolist painter of dreamlike images Odilon Redon dies at the age of 76.	**AUG** *Chu Chin Chow* premieres at Her Majesty's Theatre in London and is popular with UK troops.	**AUG** Spanish artist Picasso begins designing scenery for *Parade*, a new ballet for Diaghilev's Ballets Russes.	**SEP** The USA premiere of D W Griffith's epic film *Intolerance* starring Lillian Gish receives rave reviews.
Innovations	**JUL** The US Coca-Cola Co introduces a contoured bottle to make imitations difficult.	**JUL** The German U-boat UC7 becomes the first submarine to be sunk by depth charges.	**AUG** The US Ford Motor Co announces the launch of a touring car, at the incredibly low price of $250.	**SEP** False eyelashes are worn for the first time by US actress Seena Owen in D W Griffith's *Intolerance*.

PAUL VON HINDENBURG

US ACTRESS LILLIAN GISH

1916

NURSES AT THE FRONT

The unsung heroes of the war are the nurses who tend the injured. Often operating under extreme danger, they venture into "no-man's land", the ground between the front lines, to rescue the wounded. Sometimes they carry out minor surgery on the spot before the casualty can be moved to safety.

Tanks set to revolutionize war

15 SEPTEMBER

The British army revealed its latest weapon today: the tank. Built in the strictest secrecy, this armoured vehicle can roll over difficult terrain and withstand all but the most powerful artillery. This morning a fleet of 32 tanks was deployed on the Somme and within two hours had pushed back the front line 11 km (7 miles). German machine gunners scattered in their path and more than 2,000 were taken prisoner.

British Mark I *tank*

Mad monk murdered in Russia

30 DECEMBER

The Russian monk Gregory Rasputin was murdered today by two relatives of Tsar Nicholas II. Rasputin was

Rasputin, the so-called "miracle worker"

lured to the home of Prince Yussupov where he was shot and bludgeoned to death, before being dumped in the River Neva. The monk first came to St Petersburg in 1905. Despite his background he became a confidant of the tsarina as he was able to stop the bleeding of her haemophiliac son. With the tsar at the Eastern Front, Rasputin took advantage of his position to influence the tsarina in political decisions. He has been made to pay for his ambition.

OCTOBER–DECEMBER

NOV On the Western Front the Battle of the Somme ends, having caused a total of more than one million deaths.

NOV US author and adventurer Jack London, who wrote *Call of the Wild*, dies of alcoholism at the age of 40.

NOV US-born inventor of the machine gun Hiram Mixam dies at the age of 76.

NOV Franz Josef, who ruled the 17 nationalities of the Austro-Hungarian empire for 68 years, dies at the age of 86.

DEC French Impressionist artist Claude Monet began work this year on a series of murals, *Waterlilies*.

DEC US earth scientist Albert Michelson determines that the earth has a molten core.

EMPEROR FRANZ JOSEF

DEC David Lloyd George becomes UK prime minister in place of Herbert Asquith and forms a new war cabinet of five men.

DEC The Nobel Prize for Literature is awarded to Swedish poet Carl Gustav; no other prizes are awarded.

DEC Fortune cookies, produced this year by the Hong Kong Noodle Co in Los Angeles, USA, prove popular.

DAVID LLOYD GEORGE

DEC Continuing stalemate in the trenches on the Western Front makes for the third and bleakest Christmas of the war.

DEC *The Planets* orchestral suite is completed this year by UK composer Gustav Holst.

DEC Cutex, the first liquid nail polish, is introduced this year in the USA by Notham Warren.

1917

US counters submarine threat

26 FEBRUARY

Congress agreed today that US ships could be armed to defend themselves against any attacks by German submarines. This latest move follows the announcement by Germany on 1 February that any ships found trading in Allied waters would be sunk without warning. Two days later the United States broke off diplomatic relations with Germany. Yet, despite these events, US congressmen are still reluctant to sanction war.

MESSENGER PIGEONS

In an ingenious attempt to communicate with troops in the front line, the Allies are using messenger pigeons. More than half a million specially trained birds are being parachuted into France. They then fly back to England carrying vital messages. Some even work as spies – reconnaissance pigeons carry tiny cameras that photograph enemy defences.

US "doughboys" land in France

27 JUNE

Following the United States' declaration of war against Germany on 6 April, the first US troop ships arrived off the French coast at dawn today. The landing site had been kept a secret, but by the time the troops, nicknamed "doughboys", lined up on parade on French soil, a huge crowd had gathered to welcome them ashore. Commanded by Major General John "Black Jack" Pershing, a veteran of wars in the Philippines and Mexico, these troops are the first of many thousands that will soon be pouring into France to help the Allied war

Recruitment poster for the US navy

effort. The deployment of US troops on the Western Front will give a huge boost to the war-weary Allies. With the help of US resources, there is new hope that the fortunes of war will turn in their favour.

JANUARY–JUNE

World Events	**MAR** As discontent grows among the Russian peoples, Tsar Nicholas II abdicates.	**APR** Bolshevik leader Lenin returns from exile in Switzerland to Russia, travelling with German assistance.	**APR** US president Woodrow Wilson declares war on Germany in order "to save democracy", and prepares to send troops to Europe.	**JUN** German planes make the first bombing raid on London, UK – a 15-minute attack on the East End kills 100 and injures 400 people.
Entertainment	**FEB** The musical *Oh, Boy!* premieres at the Princess Theatre, New York, USA.	**MAR** US New Orleans group the Original Dixieland Jazz Band make the first jazz recording.	**APR** *The Butcher Boy* is filmed in the USA, featuring talented new actor Buster Keaton.	**MAY** French poet G Apollinaire describes Picasso's costumes for the ballet *Parade* as "Surrealist".
Innovations	**JAN** German scientists Hahn and Meitner discover the element proactium.	 **FIRST JAZZ RECORD**	**MAY** The first international airmail service begins operating between Italy and Albania.	**MAY** The world's first airmail stamps are issued in Italy for use on the air service between Rome and Turin.	**GERMAN** *LVG CV1* **BOMBER PLANE** **JUN** US communications company AT & T introduces the world's first telex service for United Press.

1917

Chaim Weizmann

Allies capture Passchendaele

6 NOVEMBER

After months of fighting, the bomb-blasted remains of the village of Passchendaele, Belgium, are finally in Allied hands. The third Battle of Ypres began over three months ago on 31 July, when British and French troops began bombarding the nearby ridge. In the initial offensive more than four million rounds were fired by 3,000 British guns – by far the heaviest bombardment made yet – in an attempt to break through German lines. However, as was the case at the Somme last year, more attention was paid to the initial artillery bombardment than to the land over which the soldiers were required to fight. The front line at Ypres was a disastrous place from which to attack as it was surrounded on three sides by the German army. In addition, dreadful weather has plagued the attack from the start, turning the battlefield into a sea of mud. Today's small victory has been achieved once again at a terrible price – more than 400,000 Allied lives have been lost and very little ground has been gained in return. It is expected that the British generals will call a halt to the attack in the next few days.

British stretcher-bearers struggle in mud near the Belgian village of Passchendaele

Jews promised new homeland

9 NOVEMBER

A week ago British foreign secretary Arthur Balfour promised the Jewish people full support in establishing a homeland in Palestine. The British war cabinet is now hoping that the declaration will encourage members of the Zionist movement, led by Dr Chaim Weizmann, to fully support the Allied war effort.

JULY–DECEMBER

JUL Lenin flees Russia after a Bolshevik uprising is crushed by the new Russian government led by Alexander Kerensky.

JUL A group of Dutch artists led by Piet Mondrian get together to publish *De Stijl*, a small modern art magazine.

AUG UK commander Edwin Dunning is the first pilot to land his plane on a moving ship, HMS *Furious*.

MATA HARI

OCT Italian troops are heavily defeated by German and Austro-Hungarian troops at Caporetto in northeastern Italy.

OCT Mata Hari, the Dutch dancer sentenced to death for spying for the Germans, is executed in Paris, France.

NOV At the Battle of Cambrai, the Germans use mustard gas for the first time, causing heavy Allied casualties.

NOV Having returned to Russia in October, Lenin leads a Bolshevik coup and seizes power from Kerensky.

NOV French sculptor Auguste Rodin, best known for his controversial work *The Kiss*, dies at the age of 77.

DEC UK physicist Charles Glover Barkla wins the Nobel Prize for Physics for his work on x-rays.

VLADIMIR ILYICH LENIN

DEC The fall of Jerusalem in Palestine to UK forces marks the climax of a 14-month offensive against the Turks.

DEC The first Pulitzer Prizes for literature, journalism, and music are awarded in the USA.

DEC Argentine Don Frederico Valle produces the world's first full-length cartoon feature film.

THE RUSSIAN REVOLUTION

IN 1917 A REVOLUTION TOOK PLACE in Russia that was to affect the entire world. The old order, led by Tsar Nicholas II, was overthrown, to be replaced first by the provisional government and then by a Bolshevik government. Led by Lenin, this government set about changing Russian society along communist lines. It took all private property into state control and gave the land to the peasants to farm. The world's first communist nation had to fight for its life as opponents inside the country, armed by foreign governments, tried to overthrow it. After three years of vicious civil war, the communists gained complete control of the country and in 1922 the country gained a new name – the USSR (Union of Soviet Socialist Republics). The revolution had succeeded.

On the boil

There was a dramatic rise in revolutionary feeling throughout Russia in the early 1900s. Many political parties campaigned to get rid of the powerful Russian nobility so that they could construct a fairer society.

The royal family

Tsar Nicholas II lived in great luxury in Petrograd and ruled over a vast empire. However, he was a weak leader who stifled all attempts at reforming the government of Russia.

The first revolution

When food riots broke out in March 1917, the Russian army, disillusioned with the tsar, took the side of the people. Without the support of the army, Nicholas II had no choice but to abdicate and the provisional government, run by members of the middle class, took control. Unfortunately it too failed to tackle the country's social and economic problems.

KERENSKY, LEADER OF THE PROVISIONAL GOVERNMENT FROM JULY 1917

Russia at war

In 1914 Russia sided with France and Britain in WWI. After initial successes, poor organization, bad leadership, low morale, and food shortages led to defeats. By 1917 the army was on the point of collapse.

The power of Rasputin

Grigori Rasputin exercised considerable influence over the Russian royal family. When Nicholas II took control of the armed forces in 1915, it was Rasputin who dominated the civil government. He was assassinated in 1916 by jealous rivals.

THE *AURORA* FIRES FROM THE RIVER NEVA

STATUES OF LENIN WERE ERECTED IN EVERY TOWN AND CITY OF THE SOVIET UNION

The Bolshevik revolution

On the night of 7 November 1917, the Bolsheviks, led by Lenin, staged an armed coup in Petrograd. In a many-pronged attack, they captured all the bridges and public buildings, and surrounded, shelled, and seized control of the Winter Palace. Two days later, Lenin officially announced the end of the provisional government.

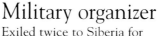

LEON TROTSKY, A KEY PLAYER IN THE RUSSIAN REVOLUTION

Military organizer

Exiled twice to Siberia for revolutionary activity, Leon Trotsky worked alongside Lenin towards communism. A brilliant military organizer, he trained the workers and set up the Red Army to defend the revolution in the civil war.

The new order

Following the revolution, the Bolsheviks began to transform Russia into the world's first communist state. They set about fulfilling their promise of "Peace, Bread, and Land", but opposition to the new regime plunged the country into civil war. The Red Army fought against the opposing "White" armies for three years before a victory was achieved and communism allowed to flourish.

HAMMER AND SICKLE, EMBLEM OF THE SOVIET UNION

Power for the people

Lenin's Communist Party, the Bolsheviks, wanted a people's revolution in which the masses at the bottom of the social order would rise up against the middle classes and the nobility.

The man behind the revolution

The driving force behind the Russian Revolution, Lenin spent much of his youth in exile in Europe. He studied the work of Karl Marx, who believed that a government should be based on equality, and planned a revolutionary takeover of Russia. In March 1917, Lenin was living in Switzerland, but after the uprising he returned to Petrograd in April. He rallied support among the peasants with rousing speeches, and demanded the overthrow of the provisional government. Despite opposition from some members of his own Bolshevik Party, he organized the successful revolution and became leader of a communist Russia.

1918

Cartoon of US president Woodrow Wilson

Germans attack Western Front

Wilson outlines terms for peace

8 JANUARY
In a speech to Congress today, President Wilson outlined US war aims and put forward 14 points for a post-war peace. These include ensuring absolute freedom of navigation on the seas, the removal of all trade barriers, and a reduction in arms to the lowest point "consistent with domestic safety". It is proposed among the various territorial details listed that Germany should evacuate the territory it has occupied, the people of Austria-Hungary should gain their independence, and that Poland should finally be recognized as an independent state with access to the sea.

31 MARCH
Ten days ago the German army launched a huge offensive on the Allied front line between Arras and La Fère in France. Now its soldiers, reinforced by troops from the Eastern Front, who have come to France following the Russian withdrawal from the war, have advanced more than 64 km (40 miles). They have taken 80,000 Allied prisoners. Commanded by General von Ludendorff, the attack has used entirely new tactics. The German artillery first launched a short, powerful bombardment of high explosives and gas and smoke shells. Then shock troops were sent to probe for any weak spots in the Allied front line rather than making

German sub-machine gun

the usual infantry charge. The plan is to achieve a speedy victory before the bulk of US troops reaches the front line. The operation has been successful so far, with the Allies hastily retreating towards Paris in confusion.

JANUARY–MARCH

World Events	**JAN** The Bolsheviks establish the Red Army in Russia to defend the revolution.	**MAR** Russia signs the peace treaty of Brest-Litovsk with Germany and Austria-Hungary, and leaves WWI.	**MAR** Following the terms of the peace treaty Germany and Turkey gain large regions of western and southern Russia.	**MAR** The Russian government moves its capital city from Petrograd to Moscow to keep away from the war zones.
Entertainment	**JAN** A major new exhibition of paintings by Matisse and Picasso opens in Paris, France.	**FEB** Austrian artist Gustav Klimt, who painted in the Art Nouveau style, dies at the age of 55.	**FEB** US composer George Gershwin's new song *Swanee* is sung in public for the first time in New York, USA.	**MAR** French composer Claude Debussy, who wrote *Prélude à l'après midi d'un faune*, dies at the age of 55.
Innovations	**JAN** In Germany, engineers begin the construction of the first all-metal aeroplane.	**MAR** Trials for the new Browning light machine gun are conducted successfully in New Jersey, USA.	**MAR** The world's first regular airmail service is set up between cities in Austria-Hungary.	**MAR** US manufacturer Henry Ford turns out the first mass-produced tractors at the rate of 80 per day.

***THE KISS* BY GUSTAV KLIMT**

CLAUDE DEBUSSY

1918

PLAYING SOLDIERS

While the adults fight a real war in the trenches of Europe, their children are enacting battles in the safety of their homes. Playing with tin soldiers is a popular game, but the difference is that unlike some real soldiers, tin ones will fight another day.

"Red Baron" shot down in flames

22 APRIL

The "Red Baron" is dead! Germany's most famous fighter pilot, Baron Manfred von Richthofen, was shot down and killed over the battlefields of northern France yesterday. The "Red Baron", nicknamed after his red Fokker triplane, is said to have destroyed an astonishing 80 Allied aircraft in less than two years. His successes were matched by the deadly marksmen in his squadron, Richthofen's Circus, who carried out his tactics of waiting for the enemy plane to fly towards them before returning fire. His flying skills have earned him great respect, and his funeral, held today at the site of his death, was conducted with full military honours.

German fighter pilot the "Red Baron"

Long-range weapon "Big Bertha" bombs Paris

26 JUNE

Despite its huge range and crude targeting, "Big Bertha" is once again raining down destruction on the people of Paris, France. More than 800 people have already been killed by this vast howitzer, thought to be located nearly 100 km (63 miles) away behind German lines. "Big Bertha", named after the wife of its manufacturer Gustave Krupp, fires 800-kg (1,764-lb) shells from its 42-cm (16.5-in) long muzzle. The heavy bombardment of the French capital began over three months ago on 23 March, but it took some time to find out from where the gun was being fired. The task was difficult as the Germans moved "Big Bertha" around at night on railway tracks so that it could easily be hidden from any Allied reconnaissance. The gun was eventually located by means of aerial photography.

"Big Bertha", also known as the Paris gun

APR The Allies agree that US troops will fight as a single army under the command of US General Pershing.

APR Charlie Chaplin's new film *A Dog's Life*, the first under his million-dollar contract, opens in the USA.

APR The UK sets up the Royal Air Force (RAF) in order to fight an effective air war against Germany.

ELMO LINCOLN AS TARZAN

APR Romania signs a peace treaty with Germany and Austria-Hungary in exchange for land in Russia.

APR US actor Elmo Lincoln stars in a screen version of Edgar Rice Burroughs' novel *Tarzan of the Apes*.

APR The first battle fought by opposing tanks takes place at Villers Brétonneaux in France.

JUN Austro-Hungarian forces make a further attack on Italian lines in northeastern Italy, but are repulsed.

MAY Vera Kholodnaya, the "queen of the Russian screen", stars in two films that premiere in Moscow.

MAY The first airmail service between Washington and New York in the USA is established.

RUSSIAN ACTRESS VERA KHOLODNAYA

JUN Civil war rages in Russia as the Red Army struggles against opposing White Russians.

MAY D W Griffith leads the US film industry's effort to help the war by selling bonds.

JUN A playing speed for records of 78 revolutions per minute is becoming standardized.

1918

Tsar murdered

16 JULY

Nicholas II the former tsar of Russia was murdered with his family in the Urals mountain town of Ekaterinburg today. Approaching White armies had frightened the Bolshevik locals, who shot the royal family in the cellar of the house where they were being detained.

Decisive conflict at Amiens

8 AUGUST

In the words of German general Erich von Ludendorff it has been "a black day for the German army". This morning 20 Allied divisions, which included British, Canadian, Australian, US, and French troops, went into action on the Western Front near Amiens. Increasing numbers of tanks and planes are being used in the attack, as the face of warfare changes. By the end of the day the Germans had been pushed back 8 km (5 miles) to the lines they occupied before their successful offensive last spring. The beleaguered German soldiers surrendered without a struggle, many only too relieved to get out of the front line of fire.

Allied forces go over the top in the momentous thrust against the German army

JULY–SEPTEMBER

World Events	**JUL** Fighting under one supreme command, the Allies halt the German advance in the second Battle of Marne.	**JUL** French commander General Foch leads the Allies in a major offensive on the Western Front using a new tactic of elastic defence.	**SEP** Allied forces capture the Hindenburg Line, the most fortified German trenches, and begin their advance into Belgium.	**SEP** Spanish influenza sweeps through Europe, causing millions of deaths despite efforts made by organizations like the Red Cross.
Entertainment	**JUL** Baseball is declared non-essential under the US "Work or Fight" law.	**SEP** US stage actress Mae West wows Broadway in *Sometime*, in which she introduces the "shimmy" dance.	**SEP** The work of Gerard Manley Hopkins, a celebrated UK poet and Jesuit priest, is published posthumously.	**SEP** Russian composer Igor Stravinsky's ballet *A Soldier's Tale* is first performed in Lausanne, Switzerland.
Innovations	**JUL** In the USA Henry Ford launches the first *Eagle* boat, a type of fast submarine-chaser.	**HELMET WORN BY GERMANS** **AUG** "Par avion" ("by air") airmail stickers are first used in the transport of mail by the French civil air service.	**AUG** The German army uses the 13-mm (0.5-in) *T-Gewehr 18* anti-tank weapon for the first time. **RED CROSS NURSE**	**SEP** The world's largest reflecting telescope, housed at Mount Wilson, California, USA, begins to operate.

1918

Lawrence of Arabia

Arabs triumph

1 OCTOBER

Arab forces are celebrating today after capturing the ancient city of Damascus in Syria. Led by the Arab prince Feisal and advised by Major Lawrence, a young British officer known as Lawrence of Arabia, Arab armies have been in open revolt against Turkish rule since June 1916. The opposing forces used guerrilla tactics as they fought their way through the barren wastes of the Arabian desert on camels. Today's victory, following the British capture of Jerusalem last December, confirms the Arab liberation from the Ottoman Empire.

Peace in Europe as war ends

11 NOVEMBER

At 11 am on the eleventh day of the eleventh month of the year, the guns of war have fallen silent across Europe. After more than four years of bitter fighting, the German leaders have finally admitted defeat and signed an armistice with the Allies. The truce, signed at dawn in a railway carriage in the forest of Compiègne in northern France, brings to an end one of the most bitter conflicts in the history of the world.

Deaths count the real cost of war

30 NOVEMBER

As the year draws to a close, the world is beginning to count the cost of the Great War, which ended earlier this month. No-one will ever know exactly how many people lost their lives in the fighting, but it is thought to be in excess of ten million, a number greater than in any other single conflict in history. A whole generation of young men from all classes and walks of life has been lost to many nations.

WAR ART

Artists on both sides of the conflict have drawn on their war experiences to produce some controversial and disturbing paintings. The young British artist Paul Nash's painting of the devastated Flanders landscape (above) is entitled, ironically, *We Are Making a New World.*

OCTOBER–DECEMBER

OCT Italian forces achieve a major victory against Austro-Hungarian forces at Vittorio Veneto; Austria-Hungary sues for peace.

OCT The Austro-Hungarian empire, led by Emperor Karl, begins to break up as Czechoslovakia declares itself a republic.

OCT In the shadow of defeat, and with many of its allies already withdrawn from the conflict, Germany appeals for an armistice.

NOV The kingdom of the Serbs, Croats, and Slovenes is created out of former Austrian and independent nations.

OCT Following the success of the film *Tarzan of the Apes, The Romance of Tarzan* is released in New York, USA.

NOV UK war poet Wilfred Owen is killed in action at the age of 25, just a week before the war ends.

NOV French Surrealist poet and art critic Guillaume Apollinaire dies at the age of 38.

DEC A film version of the opera *Carmen* starring Pola Negri is released in Germany.

OCT The world's first propaganda broadcast incites German civilians to remove their government.

WILFRED OWEN

DEC The world's first three-colour traffic lights are introduced in New York City, USA.

DEC Two German scientists win Nobel Prizes, Max Planck for physics and Fritz Haber for chemistry.

FILM VERSION OF CARMEN

DEC Electric clocks are sold commercially by Henry Ellis Warren in Massachusetts, USA.

1919

"Red Rosa" is murdered

15 JANUARY

Four days ago an uprising by communist "Spartacists" in Berlin was crushed by the German government. Today Karl Liebknecht and "Red Rosa" Luxemburg, the leaders of the revolt, were murdered and their bodies thrown into a canal. Their calls for the formation of a socialist republic had stood little chance of success, but they are still being hailed as martyrs.

Rosa Luxemburg

Bauhaus reforms art education

12 APRIL

A revolutionary new school of art has been founded by the German architect Walter Gropius in the city of Weimar. The aim of the Bauhaus school is to combine the visual arts with architecture, and to teach the students design and craft skills that are suited to the modern industrial age. Tutors include the notable artists Wassily Kandinsky and Paul Klee.

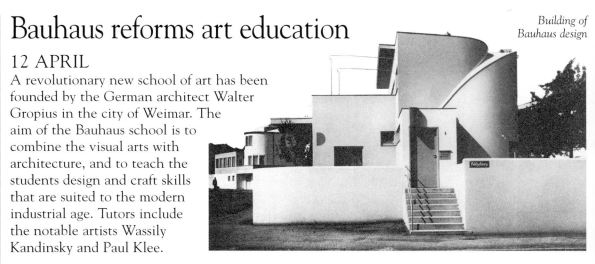
Building of Bauhaus design

Crowds massacred in Amritsar

13 APRIL

At least 500 people were killed and 1,500 injured when British troops opened fire on demonstrators in the northern Indian city of Amritsar today. All over the country Indian people have been protesting at the new security laws, but events came to a head when Brigadier General Dyer called out his troops to restore peace. He gave the order to fire into the crowd without warning, an act that resulted in chaos. Today's massacre will do little to reduce the current strong anti-British feeling.

Amritsar's Golden Temple, most sacred to Indian Sikhs

JANUARY–JUNE

World Events	**JAN** The Sinn Féin MPs elected to the UK parliament meet at an unofficial Irish parliament in Dublin.	**FEB** At the French peace conference in Versailles, 27 nations agree to US president Wilson's proposal for a League of Nations.	**MAR** Italian socialist Benito Mussolini founds a new political party, the "Fasci d'Italiani di Combattimento", in Italy.	**APR** Éamon de Valera, known as "Dev" to his followers, is elected president of the Irish parliament, the Dáil.
Entertainment	**MAR** The anti-war film *J'accuse* by French director Abel Gance premieres in Paris, France.	**APR** Jazz arrives in Europe when the Original Dixieland Jazz Band makes its debut in London, UK.	**JUN** US actress Lillian Gish stars in *True Heart Susie*, in which she plays a naïve country girl.	**JUN** The first photomontage is begun by artists George Grosz and John Heartfield in Germany.
Innovations	**JAN** UK scientist Ernest Rutherford is the first to split the atom, the smallest particle.	**ERNEST RUTHERFORD** **MAR** UK scientists, watching the eclipse of the sun, confirm Einstein's theory of relativity.	**MAY** Charles Strite of Minnesota, USA, patents his latest invention, the pop-up electric toaster.	**JOHN ALCOCK AND ARTHUR BROWN** **JUN** UK John Alcock and US Arthur Brown are the first pilots to fly nonstop across the Atlantic.

1919

Stars form own film company

17 APRIL

Four of Hollywood's biggest stars, Douglas Fairbanks, Charlie Chaplin, Mary Pickford, and D W Griffith, have formed a company, United Artists in America. They hope to control more of the profits from their work, and share in its distribution.

Tide turns for Red Army in Russian civil war

21 OCTOBER

After nearly two years of civil war in Russia, the Bolshevik Red Army is making gains on its "White" opponents for the first time. White armies, led by Alexander Kolchak and Anton Deniken, have been progressing rapidly on both eastern and southern fronts, but this has stretched them too far. Leon Trotsky, leader of the disciplined and highly motivated Red Army, seized his chance. In the past weeks he has taken the upper hand, and his troops are now on the offensive on all fronts.

Peace agreement at Versailles

28 JUNE

At ten minutes to four this afternoon two grim-faced German delegates signed a peace treaty in the Palace of Versailles outside Paris, France. The Great War has officially come to an end. The treaty has been drawn up by the Allies following six months of negotiations. The terms it proposes are so harsh that the German chancellor and his cabinet resigned at first rather than agree to sign it. But the Allied threat of military occupation forced their national assembly to concede meekly. The French are protesting that the terms are too lenient, but British prime minister Lloyd George fears that the stage has been set for another world war.

FELIX THE CAT

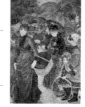

A new cartoon character made his appearance this year. Felix the Cat, a perky and indestructible character devised by the Australian cartoonist Pat Sullivan, is delighting everyone who sees his antics on the screen.

JULY–DECEMBER

AUG Following the death of Louis Botha, General Jan Smuts becomes the new prime minister of South Africa at the age of 49.

JUL US boxer Jack Dempsey beats Jess Willard in three rounds in the world heavyweight championship.

SEP The first intercontinental airline service begins regular flights between Europe and North Africa.

GENERAL JAN SMUTS

NOV The US Senate rejects the Versailles peace treaty, a setback for President Wilson who has been campaigning strongly for it.

JUL French tennis player Suzanne Lenglen wins the ladies' singles at the first postwar Wimbledon, UK.

SEP US aviator Roland Rohlfs sets a flight altitude record of 10,550 m (34,610 ft) in a Curtiss *Wasp*.

DEC US-born Nancy Astor is the first female MP to sit in the House of Commons in London, UK.

SEP The world's first film school, the State School of Cinematography, opens in Moscow, Russia.

DEC Trailer caravans make their first appearance at the annual motor show at Olympia in London, UK.

LES PARAPLUIES BY RENOIR

DEC UK prime minister Lloyd George puts forward a proposal to divide Ireland into two states.

DEC French Impressionist painter Auguste Renoir dies in Cannes, France, at the age of 78.

DEC Belgian doctor Jules Bordet wins the Nobel Prize for Medicine for his work on immunology.

1920

Yankees scoop baseball "Babe" for $125,000

5 JANUARY

US baseball history was made today when the New York Yankees signed Babe Ruth for $125,000 – the largest signing-on fee that has ever been paid. Twenty-four-year-old Babe Ruth, whose real name is George Herman Ruth, began his professional baseball career in 1914, playing for the Baltimore Orioles, but transferred soon after to the Boston Red Sox. A left-handed pitcher, Babe quickly made a name for himself as a remarkable player. Out of 158 games for Boston, he achieved a pitching record of 89 victories and 46 losses. He has recently become known for regularly

Babe Ruth in action

scoring home runs and will join the New York Yankees as a hitter. His great batting ability and colourful personality are sure to attract many supporters.

DADAISTS SHOCK ART WORLD

Art and protest are coming together in a new movement called Dadaism. Taking the motto "destruction is also creation", the Dadaists have set out to shock the conventional art world. In the US, Marcel Duchamp has exhibited a urinal signed R Mutt; in Cologne, Max Ernst and Jean Arp invited visitors to smash their paintings.

Alcohol banned in United States

16 JANUARY

The United States goes dry today as Prohibition officially comes into force. Last night the long-time anti-alcohol campaigner, evangelist William "Billy" Sunday, along with 10,000 followers, marked the start of an alcohol-free new year by holding a mock funeral for John Barleycorn, the spirit of malt liquor. No doubt "mourners" marked his passing with glasses full of fizzy pop rather than bourbon.

"Mourners" dance around John Barleycorn's coffin

Garvey calls for black rights

1 AUGUST

A national conference of the Universal Negro Improvement Association (UNIA), initiated by black nationalist leader Marcus Garvey, opened in New York, USA, today. Jamaican-born Garvey founded the UNIA in 1914 "to promote race pride" among black people. His aim is to create a black empire in Africa, free of white interference, because he believes black Americans cannot achieve full rights in the United States. Inspiring speeches made in his "Back to Africa" campaign and his newspaper *Negro World* have already earned him considerable support.

JANUARY–JUNE

World Events	**JAN** The newly formed League of Nations, consisting of 29 countries, holds its first meeting in Paris, France.	**MAR** The Kapp putsch, a coup to seize Berlin, Germany, collapses as conspirators fail to secure the support of the army.	**APR** The newly formed extremist National Socialist (Nazi) Party in Germany adopts the swastika as its symbol.	**JUN** The Treaty of Trianon, which reduces the size of Hungary and ends the Austro-Hungarian empire, is signed.
Entertainment	**JAN** Controversial Italian artist Amadeo Modigliani dies in Paris, France at the age of 35.	**MAR** A screen adaptation of Robert Louis Stevenson's novel *Treasure Island* is released in Hollywood, USA.	**MAR** US screen stars Mary Pickford and Douglas Fairbanks marry in Los Angeles, USA.	**JUN** In the UK, opera singer Nellie Melba broadcasts a concert of songs that includes *Home Sweet Home*.
Innovations	**JAN** The Good Humor bar, a chocolate ice cream on a stick, is made in the USA.	**FEB** The first colour cartoon film, *The Debut of Thomas Kat*, uses paintings on transparent celluloid.	**FEB** US explorer Robert Peary, who was the first person to reach the North Pole, dies at the age of 64.	**APR** KLM, the national airline of the Netherlands, operates a scheduled service from Amsterdam to the UK.

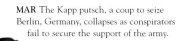

TREASURE ISLAND

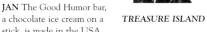

NAZI PARTY SYMBOL

1920

Election results heard on radio

2 NOVEMBER

Several hundred US families tuned in on home-made radio receivers today to hear that Republican W G Harding has won the presidential election. The announcement marks the start of regular weekly broadcasts by Westinghouse from their Pittsburgh radio station. It is expected that interest in radio sets will now soar.

Headphones are used for listening to today's radio broadcasts

Dublin suffers "Bloody Sunday"

21 NOVEMBER

Violence in Ireland reached new levels today as 14 British army officers and officials were killed in Dublin after dawn raids by the Irish Republican Army (IRA). In the afternoon the notoriously brutal British special force, the Black and Tans, retaliated by firing into a crowd of local people at the Croke Park football ground. Twelve people were killed, and 60 others were injured. The shocking events of today's "Bloody Sunday" come as the culmination of several months of increasing violence in Ireland. Last December the British government declared its intention to divide the country into two regions. The decision was met with outrage by the nationalist Sinn Féin party. Since then a battle using guerrilla tactics has been waged between British troops and the IRA, led by Michael Collins. With the situation in Ireland becoming increasingly difficult to resolve, more British troops are expected in an attempt to impose order.

Black and Tan auxiliaries, named after the colour of their uniforms, stop and search a member of the Sinn Féin

---

JULY–DECEMBER

AUG After more than 50 years of campaigning, US women gain the vote as Congress passes the 19th amendment to the constitution.

AUG The seventh Olympic Games opens in Antwerp, Belgium, after a gap of eight years due to World War I.

JUL The Southern California Telephone Co sets up a public radio telephone service in the USA.

US SUFFRAGETTE

SEP Nationalist Mohandas Gandhi launches a peaceful non-cooperation movement in India against the UK.

SEP Margaret Gorman is crowned the first Miss America beauty queen in Atlantic City, USA.

OCT The ministry of transport in the UK instructs motorists to raise their right arm to indicate stopping.

NOV Civil war ends in Russia as the Red Army led by Leon Trotsky achieves victory for the communist Bolsheviks.

DEC Mamie Smith is the first black American singer to make a record, *Crazy Blues*, which is a smash hit.

NOV The first electrical recording is made by UK inventors L Guest and H Merriman in London, UK.

LEON TROTSKY

DEC The UK parliament passes an act to set up separate parliaments in northern and southern Ireland.

DEC UK author Agatha Christie introduces detective Hercule Poirot in *The Mysterious Affair at Styles*.

DEC Retired US army officer John T Thompson patents his sub-machine gun – the "Tommy" gun.

1921

New child star

6 FEBRUARY

Tears and laughter greeted Charlie Chaplin's first full-length film, *The Kid*, which opened in the US today. A clever blend of humour and pathos, the film stars British actor Chaplin in his famous tramp role. He befriends an endearing little waif, played by talented child actor five-year-old Jackie Coogan.

Charlie Chaplin

Jackie Coogan

Communist party forms in China

1 JULY

Only four years after the Russian Revolution, a communist party has formed in China. As yet it has only 57 members, most of whom are students who have studied Karl Marx and believe that China's problems can only be solved by revolution. Their first meeting was held last month at a girls' school in Shanghai where, amid lively debate, they called for the overthrow of the wealthy "capitalist class". The fledgling party believes that this is the only way to overcome China's poverty and unwelcome foreign interference. Among those who attended was a young primary school teacher named

Young radicals Lin Bao and Mao (right)

Mao Zedong. He believes that Russian communism can be adapted to the needs of China. Whether he and his followers succeed in their aims remains to be seen.

SCREEN HEART-THROB

Women everywhere are swooning over Rudolph Valentino. He first appeared as an Argentine gigolo turned war hero in *The Four Horsemen of the Apocalypse* (right). But his smouldering-eyed performance in the title role of *The Sheik* will confirm his status as a sex symbol.

JANUARY–JUNE

World Events	JAN Wartime Allies fix German war debts at 132 million gold marks, to be paid over 42 years.	JAN Greece defies the League of Nations and declares war on Turkey, launching an offensive into Anatolia.	MAR Bolsheviks under Trotsky put down a mutiny of Russian sailors at Kronstadt as the Russian economy collapses.	JUN UK king George V opens the new parliament in Belfast, Northern Ireland; James Craig is prime minister.
Entertainment	JAN *This Side of Paradise* by US writer F Scott Fitzgerald continues to sell strongly.	APR The world's first radio sports commentary is made for a boxing match in the USA.	MAY Amid concerns over morality, a $10 fine for women who wear short skirts is issued in Chicago, USA.	MAY The first international athletics meeting for women opens in Monte Carlo, France.
Innovations	MAR Marie Stopes opens the first birth control clinic in the UK, despite much opposition. **CHANEL N0 5 PERFUME**	MAY "Coco" Chanel launches her *Chanel No 5* perfume in France on the 5th day of the 5th month.	MAY The Ford Motor Co in Detroit, USA, mass-produces a record 4,072 cars in one day. **A MODERN WOMAN**	JUN The world's largest airship, the R-38, built in the UK for the US navy, makes its maiden flight.

1921

Fight attracts bumper crowds

2 JULY

Boxing proved to be lucrative show business today. In a specially built stadium in New Jersey, US heavyweight champion Jack Dempsey took on French challenger Georges Carpentier, and defeated him in just ten minutes. Advance publicity attracted more than 80,000 spectators, and drew $1.7 million in gate money.

Dempsey and Carpentier slug it out in front of huge crowds

Sacco and Vanzetti – not guilty?

14 JULY

In a stormy sea of controversy, a US jury today found two Italians – Nicola Sacco and Bartolomeo Vanzetti – guilty of a crime that took place last year. The pair allegedly murdered two men at a Massachusetts shoe factory and stole the $16,000 payroll. Vague accounts from witnesses led to their arrest. Although they were armed at the time and admitted to lying in their early statements to the police, they flatly deny that they carried out the robbery.

In fact, none of the stolen money can be traced to them. However, the fact that they are self-confessed anarchists, opposed to all forms of government, weighed heavily against them in the trial.

Sacco (left) and Vanzetti in handcuffs

Famine in Russia

4 AUGUST

Famine is devastating Russia. At least 18 million Russians are said to be starving, with the situation made worse by outbreaks of cholera and typhus. The immediate cause was a severe drought that destroyed the harvest. However, the revolution and subsequent civil war has also had a disastrous effect on the country's economy. Last March, in an attempt to combat this, Russian leader Lenin brought in the "New Economic Policy", which re-introduced limited private enterprise in place of state planning. A retreat from the communist way of thought, the policy has faced much criticism, and has failed to help the famine, forcing Lenin to appeal for aid to the international community.

Russian peasants queue for soup

JULY–DECEMBER

JUL Muslim Berbers under Abdel Krim attack and destroy the Spanish army at Anual in northern Morocco.

AUG In Italy 50,000 mourners attend the funeral of opera singer Enrico Caruso, who died at the age of 48.

JUL Canadians F Banting and C Best extract insulin from the pancreas, which they hope can be used to cure diabetes. **BOTTLE OF INSULIN**

NOV Indians in Bombay burn clothing on a massive bonfire to campaign against the import of foreign cloth.

SEP Fans mob Charlie Chaplin as he arrives in London, UK, on his first visit to his native country in nine years.

SEP The world's first motorway, the Avus Autobahn in Berlin, Germany, opens exclusively to motor traffic.

NOV Italian blackshirt Benito Mussolini declares himself "Il Duce", or leader, of the National Fascist Party.

NOV US dancer Isadora Duncan opens a dance school in Moscow, Russia, and dances for the communist nation.

NOV The British Legion holds a memorial day for those who died in WWI; paper poppies are sold. **BENITO MUSSOLINI**

DEC The Catholic counties of southern Ireland become the Irish Free State; Northern Ireland remains in the UK.

DEC A male nude wrestling scene in UK novelist D H Lawrence's *Women in Love* causes controversy.

DEC Sales of fried potato slices, introduced by E Wise as a snack food, continue to rise in the USA.

1922

Vampire movie terrifies crowds

5 MARCH

Blood curdled at the German premiere of *Nosferatu* as Bram Stoker's 1897 novel *Dracula* hit the screen. The film stars Max Schreck as a sinister Count Orlock (Dracula), complete with long fingernails and cavernous eyes. Strange camera angles and eerie images are used to terrifying effect by German director Fredrich Murnau.

Nosferatu – *a masterpiece of German Expressionism*

ISADORA BANNED

Isadora Duncan is not only renowned for her dancing. Her outrageous actions have got her booed off stage and banned from appearing in Boston, United States.

Barrier broken

9 JULY

A staggering new world record was set today when 18-year-old Johnny Weissmuller, from Chicago, USA, swam 100 m (328 ft) in a remarkable 58.6 seconds. The Austrian-born young man is the first person to break the up-to-now elusive one-minute barrier.

Michael Collins in Free State army uniform

Irish leader shot dead

22 AUGUST

Irish nationalist Michael Collins was killed today by a ricocheting bullet from a republican ambush in his native town of Cork. Collins, who was prime minister and co-founder of the Dáil Eireann, Ireland's provisional government, came to prominence in the Easter Rising of 1916. He went on to lead the republicans in the guerrilla campaign that forced the British to sue for peace in 1921. Although a convinced republican, Collins supported the treaty that set up the Irish Free State in 1921, a move that angered many other republicans. In January, Collins' colleague Éamon de Valera rejected the treaty and resigned from the Dáil. Collins' shooting follows the untimely death of Arthur Griffith, president of the Dáil. With only two of its four original supporters now remaining, the treaty is now in jeopardy. General Richard Mulcahy, chief of staff for the Free State army, referring to Collins' "strength, bravery, and unfinished work", has called for calm.

JANUARY–JUNE

World Events	**JAN** In Russia, an estimated 33 million people face starvation as famine spreads through the Volga.	**MAR** Indian nationalist Mohandas Gandhi is sentenced to six years' imprisonment following anti-UK demonstrations.	**APR** In the Irish Free State, republicans seize Kilmainham jail in Dublin in a new wave of anti-treaty insurrection.	**JUN** UK mountaineers climb to within 975 m (3,200 ft) of the top of Everest, the world's highest mountain.
Entertainment	**FEB** A new magazine, *The Reader's Digest*, is launched in New York, USA.	**FEB** *Ulysses*, the controversial new novel by Irish writer James Joyce is published in Paris, France.	**APR** *Robin Hood*, the latest film starring Douglas Fairbanks, astounds US audiences with its exciting technical innovations.	**MAY** The US magazine *Vanity Fair* coins the term "flapper" to describe brazen young women in society.
Innovations	**JAN** In Canada, Leonard Thompson is the first diabetic to be treated with insulin.	*READER'S DIGEST EMBLEM* **FEB** French physicist Marie Curie, co-discoverer of radium, is elected to the Académie des Sciences in Paris.	**MAY** A US teenager named George Frost installs a wireless in his Model T Ford, so creating the first car radio.	**JUN** US scientists claim that the Sun produces a vitamin "D" in the body, which prevents the disease rickets.

A "FLAPPER"

1922

Fascists march on Rome

Mussolini is summoned to Rome after the success of the Fascists' march

30 OCTOBER

The leader of the Fascist Party Benito Mussolini – "Il Duce" to his followers – became the undisputed leader of Italy today. This follows a symbolic march on Rome two days ago by some 30,000 of his followers, who all wore the distinctive black shirts of the Fascist movement. Mussolini himself, who has built up a large following through his nationalism and strong anti-communist stand, did not actually take part in the march, but stayed in Milan awaiting its outcome. When the Fascists arrived in Rome, their presence was so strong that King Victor Emmanuel, fearing all-out civil war, sent for Mussolini and asked him to take up the post of prime minister. There can be little doubt now that the stage is set for Mussolini to take up absolute powers.

Reuters news hits the airwaves

15 NOVEMBER

This is the news. Yesterday evening at 6 pm, and again at 9 pm, news was broadcast from a room in Marconi House in London, Britain. The material was provided by Reuters News Agency and it was read by Arthur Burrows. Most listeners heard the broadcast through personal headphones, but some fixed loudspeakers to their radio sets. A mixture of news, music, and talks will now be available every day.

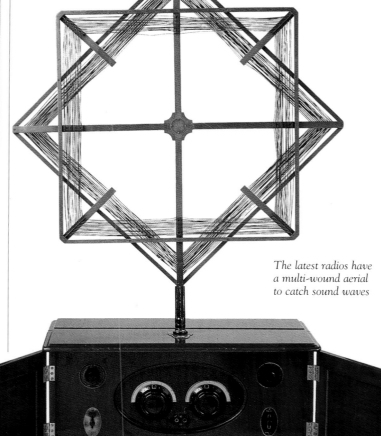

The latest radios have a multi-wound aerial to catch sound waves

JULY–DECEMBER

AUG. Turkey launches an offensive against Greece at the Battle of Afyon to recover land lost in World War I.

JUL Walter Hagen is the first US golfer to win the British Open at Sandwich, UK.

AUG Alexander Graham Bell, the Scottish inventor of the telephone, dies at the age of 75.

A GERMAN BANKNOTE

AUG The German mark goes into free fall, with its value dropping from 162 to 7,000 against the US dollar.

SEP The first 3-D feature film, *The Power of Love*, premieres in the USA.

AUG US pilot James Doolittle makes the first coast-to-coast flight, taking less than 24 hours.

NOV After a 30-year search, UK archaeologists uncover the tomb of Tutankhamun near Luxor, Egypt.

OCT Marie Lloyd, a popular singer and dancer of the UK music hall, dies at the age of 52.

OCT UK social reformer George Cadbury, who made his fortune from chocolate, dies aged 83.

TUTANKHAMUN'S TREASURE

DEC Russia is officially renamed the Union of the Soviet Socialist Republics (USSR).

DEC Huge acclaim greets US explorer Robert Flaherty's *Nanook of the North*, the first film documentary.

DEC Danish physicist Niels Bohr is awarded the Nobel Prize for his work on the structure of the atom.

THE TOMB OF TUTANKHAMUN

ON THE AFTERNOON OF 26 NOVEMBER 1922, in a remote Egyptian valley, one of the most amazing archaeological discoveries of the 20th century was made. Egyptologist Howard Carter, having cleared a passageway of debris, came to a sealed doorway covered with oval insignia bearing the name of Tutankhamun. He carefully removed some of the stones and peered inside. "Can you see anything?" asked his patron, Lord Carnarvon. "Yes, wonderful things," he replied. In front of him were thousands of objects, glinting with gold. Although robbers had stolen a large amount of the jewellery from the tomb soon after the pharaoh was buried, the majority of its contents, and most importantly the coffins containing the mummy, remained untouched. The splendour of the discovery, aided by extensive press coverage, created an international sensation. Overnight Tutankhamun became a household name, and his tomb a yardstick by which all archaeological finds were measured.

The Valley of the Kings

Situated in hills on the west bank of the River Nile, the valley was the final resting-place for many of the Egyptian pharaohs. For this reason it was a popular hunting-ground for archaeologists and by the 1920s most of the tombs had been plundered. The tomb of Tutankhamun remained undisturbed until the 1920s as all record of his existence had been lost.

Carnarvon

Carter

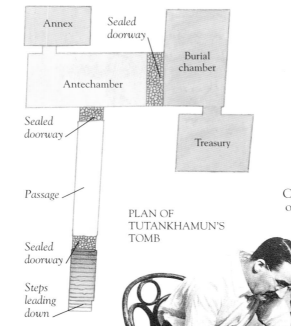

Annex

Sealed doorway

Burial chamber

Antechamber

Sealed doorway

Treasury

Passage

PLAN OF TUTANKHAMUN'S TOMB

Sealed doorway

Steps leading down

The lordly patron

Lord Carnarvon from Britain had been fascinated by Egypt ever since he spent a winter there recovering from a car accident. He was rich enough to pursue his interest by employing Howard Carter as his personal archaeologist.

Painstaking work

Carter and his small team of archaeologists carried out their work inside the tomb with extreme care. Each object was recorded and photographed before it was removed, and many individual pieces were carefully treated to protect them from decay. It was three years before the mummy was unwrapped and it took ten years to clear the tomb.

CARTER REMOVES BLACK RESIN COVERING THE INNERMOST COFFIN

The mummy lay in a nest of three coffins

STATUE OF ISIS, MADE OF GILDED WOOD, ADORNS THE CANOPIC SHRINE

1923 THE ENTRANCE TO THE
BURIAL CHAMBER IS UNBLOCKED

1924 THE LID OF TUTANKHAMUN'S
SARCOPHAGUS IS FINALLY RAISED

1925 THE WRAPPINGS ARE REMOVED
FROM TUTANKHAMUN'S MUMMY

Vulture's head symbolized sovereignty over Upper Egypt

Eyes of quartz and obsidian

Cobra symbolized sovereignty over Lower Egypt

Blue glass stripes imitate lapis lazuli

Clearing out

The entire contents of the tomb had to be moved to the Cairo Museum. A railway track was built down to the banks of the Nile, where the treasures were loaded onto a steamer for the seven-day trip down the river.

LION GODDESS FROM ONE OF THE RITUAL COUCHES

FIRST VIEW OF THE ANTECHAMBER

A gigantic game of spillikins

The rooms of the tomb were piled high from floor to ceiling with priceless objects. Ritual couches, statues, clothes, thrones, a large bed, jewellery, weapons, alabaster caskets, and musical instruments all lay in a jumbled heap, having been put there to accompany the pharaoh in his afterlife. It was a difficult task to remove one object without risking damage to others.

The face of Tutankhamun

Inside a quartzite sarcophagus, covered with a heavy lid of granite, were three coffins, each one fitting snugly inside the other. The smallest coffin was made of solid gold and contained the mummy of Tutankhamun, his face and shoulders covered with a mask of solid gold, semi-precious stones, and blue glass. An outstanding example of metalwork, this is one of the greatest treasures found in the tomb.

LORD CARNARVON

Death certificate

Cut-throat razor for shaving

The boy king

Tutankhamun was only seven years old when he ascended the throne of Egypt in about 1333 BC. It is probable that he was the son of the pharaoh Akhenaten and his wife Kiya. The young pharaoh died suddenly at the age of 17 in 1323 BC.

The death curse

On one of the walls of the tomb an inscription stated that uncovering the tomb of the pharaoh would cause death. Four months after discovering the tomb, Lord Carnarvon died from pneumonia. He took the top off a mosquito bite while shaving with a cut-throat razor and this caused a fatal blood infection.

1923

Bessie not blue

16 FEBRUARY

Bessie Smith, a talented new singer on the US jazz scene, makes her first recording, *Downhearted Blues*, in New York today. Originally from Chattanooga, Tennessee, 29-year-old Bessie has been making a name for herself as the "empress of jazz" in honky-tonk bars. Today she is using her rich blues voice and impeccable rhythm into a recording that is sure to be a smash success.

Lenglen makes it five in a row

6 JULY

The crowds roared with delight when popular French tennis star Suzanne Lenglen defeated Kathleen McKane to win the ladies' singles at Wimbledon today – for the fifth consecutive year. Lenglen, who is coached by her father, started playing tennis at the age of 12. She won the women's hard-court championship at the age of 15, and five years later, in 1919, won the ladies' singles for the first time. An Olympic gold medallist, Lenglen not only plays tennis brilliantly but also sets new fashions with her daring style of tennis dress.

Lenglen sporting her new loose-fitting dress

Bessie Smith, the hot new talent on the music scene

Quake razes Tokyo

6 SEPTEMBER

The worst earthquake ever to have rocked Japan destroyed the cities of Tokyo and Yokohama nearly a week ago. Relief workers estimate that 300,000 people have died, thousands from the initial impact. The raging fires and flooding that followed the quake have made a further 2.5 million homeless. Today the scene is one of chaos. More than one million refugees are trying to make their way out of Tokyo, while those who remain behind face severe food shortages and must survive on a handful of rice a day. Cholera is spreading as there is only ditch-water to drink. Despite all this, the work of reconstruction has begun.

MODEL RAILWAY

Any child can now be "chief engineer of their own railway" with a Hornby train set. Made in Britain, these miniature trains can be powered by electricity or steam. Extra carriages, stations, and signals are also available.

JANUARY–JUNE

World Events — MAR The salt tax is restored in India, a move that will affect many families already living in an impoverished state.	APR Prince Albert, Duke of York, marries fashionable commoner Lady Elizabeth Bowes-Lyon at Westminster Abbey, UK.	APR Lord Carnarvon dies from an insect bite at the Tutankhamun dig in Egypt, causing rumours that the tomb is cursed.	JUN The Ku Klux Klan, the racist US secret society founded after the civil war, claims that it now has one million members.
Entertainment — FEB French designer "Coco" Chanel says even sweaters can be chic.	MAR The first issue of *Time*, a weekly news magazine, goes on sale in the USA.	APR More than 600,000 attend the opening of the Yankee Stadium in New York, USA.	MAY Frenchmen R Leonard and A Lagache win the first 24-hour Le Mans motor race.
Innovations — FEB German physicist Wilhelm Roentgen, who invented X-rays, dies in Munich.	**ROYAL WEDDING SOUVENIR TIN** — MAR The first special shopping centre opens in the USA with 150 stores and parking for 5,500 cars.	APR US World War I veteran Colonel Jacob Schick patents the first practical electric shaver.	**1923 RACING CAR** — MAY US astronomer E P Hubble demonstrates that there are other star systems outside the Milky Way.

1923 RACING CAR

1923

Republic of Turkey formed

29 OCTOBER

General Mustapha Kemal today declared Turkey a republic, with himself as its president. Kemal has already proved himself a brilliant soldier and diplomat as leader of the Turkish nationalist movement. With military

expertise, he successfully drove out the Greek forces occupying Anatolia, and helped secure the Treaty of Lausanne which ended the conflict and guaranteed Turkey's border. Kemal, moving the capital city from Constantinople to Ankara, ends the centuries-old power of the sultans. He is aiming to turn the new Republic of Turkey into a modern state.

Conspirators Ludendorff and Hitler

Hitler fails with beer-hall putsch

12 NOVEMBER

Politics and farce came together in Germany when Adolf Hitler and General Erich von Ludendorff were arrested for attempting to overthrow the Bavarian government. Their so-called "beer-hall putsch" took place four days ago in Munich when Hitler, who is head of the extreme Nazi Party, burst into a beer-hall with armed supporters, declaring that "the national revolution has begun". With help from Ludendorff, Hitler seized the city government, but failed to follow up his success. The next day he fled the city after being fired on by local police.

The mark collapses

20 NOVEMBER

The German mark is not worth the paper it is printed on. As inflation spirals out of control, a loaf of bread costs more than 200 billion marks. The collapse of the economy began in August 1922 when the Allies, at a conference in Britain, did not agree to allow Germany to postpone payment of war debts. It worsened in January when French and Belgian troops entered the Ruhr, the centre of German industry, to pressure for repayment. The country is now in financial chaos as savings are wiped out and public discontent grows. In an attempt to restore financial order, the Reichsbank has today introduced a new currency, the Rentenmark.

German children use bundles of the worthless currency as building bricks

---

JULY–DECEMBER

JUL A ceremony marks the creation of the USSR, consisting of Russia, Ukraine, Transcausia, and White Russia.

AUG US boxer Jack Dempsey retains the world heavyweight title in a dramatic 15-round bout.

JUL Soviet airline Aeroflot begins operations with a six-passenger flight from Moscow to Nizhny Novgorod.

NEW EMBLEM OF THE USSR

SEP After a bloodless coup, Miguel Primo de Rivera assumes control in Spain and suspends the Spanish parliament.

SEP US film actor Lon Chaney gains acclaim as Quasimodo in *The Hunchback of Notre Dame*.

OCT A planetarium, for viewing the solar system, opens at the Deutsche Museum in Munich, Germany.

OCT The UK agrees to make the African country of Southern Rhodesia a self-governing UK colony.

OCT *Running Wild* opens in New York; its catchy song, *Charleston*, launches a new US dance craze.

NOV Further treasures from the tomb of Tutankhamun in Egypt are found in the burial chamber.

TUTANKHAMUN'S SARCOPHAGUS

DEC In Mexico, Adolfo de la Huerta leads an unsuccessful revolt against the government.

DEC US film producer Cecil B De Mille finishes his biblical epic *The Ten Commandments*.

DEC Soviet Vladimir Zworykin introduces his iconoscope, a device to transmit pictures.

1924

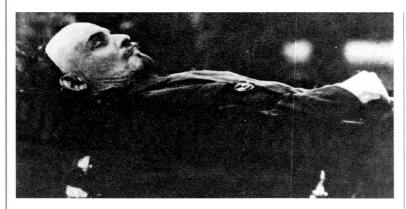

Father of USSR dies

21 JANUARY

Soviet leader Vladimir Ilyich Ulyanov, better known as Lenin, died today at the age of 54. Lenin was born into a politically active middle-class family in Simbirsk – his older brother was executed for attempting to assassinate Tsar Alexander III. Lenin qualified in law but, influenced by the works of theorist Karl Marx, he gave it up to work towards establishing communism in his native Russia. He spent many years in forced exile, but returned to Petrograd in 1917 to lead his Bolshevik Party to victory in a dramatic coup, earning himself the title "father of the Russian Revolution". Lenin's death leaves a serious power vacuum. His possible successors include Leon Trotsky, leader of the Red Army, and Joseph Stalin, general secretary of the Communist Party.

TABLE FOOTBALL

If the thought of running up and down a full-sized football pitch is far too exhausting, why not try table football. The new game from France, otherwise known as "match de foot", is played on a green baize with players made of lead.

Fun and games in the snow

4 FEBRUARY

The first winter "Olympics" finished today at Chamonix in the French Alps. With the beautiful Mount Blanc as a backdrop, this new festival of winter sports lasted for a week and attracted competitors (mostly men, as only figure-skating was open to women) from 18 nations. There have been several top performers, among them the 29-year-old Norwegian Thorleif Haug, who won the 18-km (11-mile) and 50-km (31-mile) cross-country races, as well as a bronze medal in ski-jumping, and the Finn Clas Thunberg who skated off with three gold medals, a silver, and a bronze. The idea of a winter games was controversial. Although the International Olympic Committee finally gave their approval to hold the event, they still denied use of the "Olympic" name.

The Canadian ice hockey team waits to compete against the United States

JANUARY–JUNE

World Events	**JAN** The first UK Labour government comes to power with Ramsay MacDonald as prime minister.	**FEB** UK archaeologist Howard Carter lifts the lid on Tutankhamun's stone coffin, revealing a golden effigy.	**APR** Nazi leader Adolf Hitler is jailed for his part in the failed "beer-hall putsch" in Munich, Germany.	**JUN** UK climber George Mallory dies in an attempt to climbed Mount Everest because "it is there".
Entertainment	**MAR** A beautiful Swedish actress, 18-year-old Greta Garbo, makes her film debut.	**MAR** Walt Disney makes *Alice's Wonderland*, the first in a series of cartoons, in Hollywood, USA.	**MAY** UK author E Nesbit, who wrote *The Railway Children* and other popular stories, dies at the age of 85.	**JUN** Sales soar of *A Passage to India*, by UK author E M Forster, a book that explores Anglo-Indian tensions.
Innovations	**FEB** Countdown pips precede the broadcast of a new regular time signal by the BBC in the UK.	**IMPERIAL AIRWAYS** **MAR** Based in Croydon, Imperial Airways, the UK's first national airline, takes to the air with a fleet of 13 planes.	**APR** Crossword mania hits the USA after Simon and Schuster publishes the first book of crossword puzzles.	**ADOLF HITLER BEHIND BARS** **JUN** The UK and Australia are the first countries to communicate by wireless as opposed to the telegraph.

1924

Studios merge

16 MARCH

A massive new film studio is formed in Hollywood. Metro-Goldwyn-Mayer (MGM) brings together three smaller US studios: Goldwyn Pictures, Metro Pictures, and Louis B Mayer's company.

In cold blood

31 MAY

In a crime that has shocked the United States, two boys from millionaire families have confessed to murdering a young neighbour for "thrills". Nathan Leopold and Richard Loeb, both 19 years old and successful university students, have described how they cold-bloodedly kidnapped and strangled 14-year-old Bobby Franks ten days ago and then demanded a $2,000 ransom from his parents. The two students have told police that they had wanted to murder someone for a long time. Their shocked parents have hired leading lawyer Clarence Darrow to defend them, and have said that the pair will plead not guilty on account of emotional illness.

Rinty is a natural performer in front of the camera and is capable of all kinds of stunts

Nathan Leopold (left) and Richard Loeb

New canine star hits the screen

1 SEPTEMBER

Cinema audiences are applauding an unlikely new film star – a German Shepherd dog named Rin Tin Tin. The dog was discovered as a puppy by US army lieutenant Lee Duncan, who found him in a trench during World War I. Duncan took the dog, affectionately known as Rinty, back to the United States and trained him for the movies. Rinty first appeared in *The Man from Hell's River* and is currently starring in *Find Your Man*. Already as popular as some human stars of the screen, this dog's future movie career is assured.

JULY–DECEMBER

AUG France and Belgium agree to withdraw their troops from the Ruhr within a year as Germany promises to pay off war debts.

SEP Indian nationalist Mohandas Gandhi goes on hunger strike in protest against the rioting between Muslims and Hindus.

OCT The League of Nations adopts the Geneva Protocol for settling international disputes peacefully rather than by war.

OCT The "Zinoviev Letter" is published, in which the USSR supposedly urges the UK to start a revolution.

JUL Athlete Paavo Nurmi, the "Flying Finn", wins a record five gold medals at the eighth Olympic Games in Paris.

AUG A US comic strip featuring little orphan Annie, her dog, and her doll appears in the *New York Daily News*.

OCT Deadpan US comedian Buster Keaton scores an immediate hit with his latest film, *The Navigator*.

NOV Italian opera composer Giacomo Puccini dies at the age of 66, leaving *Turandot* incomplete.

AUG US pilots L Smith and E Nelson complete the first round-the-world flight, starting and finishing in Seattle.

MOHANDAS GANDHI

SEP The first intercity motorway, the 48-km (30-mile) long Milano–Varuse Autostrada, opens in Italy.

NOV The new "fonofilm" process of creating sound on film is used to film a speech by US President Coolidge.

BUSTER KEATON

DEC People in the USA can now blow their noses on Kleenex disposable paper hankies.

THE ROARING TWENTIES

THE 1920S BEGAN WITH A BANG, as a war-weary world turned to enjoyment with a vengeance. The United States, which had emerged as a leading power after World War I, set the trend, influencing fashion, music, and even food. A new leisure industry sprang up and there were major breakthroughs in recording, cinema, and radio. Social attitudes were more relaxed, and young people rejected convention to follow free and daring lifestyles. Women in particular embraced a new freedom. They wore shorter skirts, cropped their hair, and danced brazenly in public. Jazz too had arrived; its syncopated sounds and rhythms permeated the clubs and dance halls of Chicago, New York, Paris, and London and gave the name "Jazz Age" to the era. However, as the Twenties roared on, the economy began to weaken. In 1929, the Wall Street Crash in New York, USA, brought days of carefree living to an abrupt end.

Jazz-age icons

Zelda and F Scott Fitzgerald enjoyed a fast-living life of drinking and partying. A US writer, Fitzgerald called the era the "Jazz Age", and his novels *This Side of Paradise* and *The Great Gatsby* describe what it was like to be young and fashionable in the 1920s.

Jumpin' jazz

Black musicians had been playing jazz in the southern US states for many years, but as the recording industry grew jazz musicians went north to Chicago and New York to make money. From there the exciting African-style rhythms moved across to Europe, in particular to Paris and London.

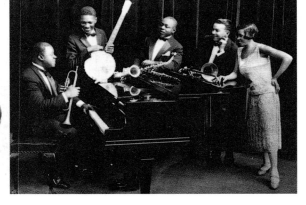

Give me five

One of the greatest and most influential jazz musicians in the 1920s was Louis Armstrong. In 1922 he teamed up with Joe "King" Oliver and together they created imaginative music that came to define New Orleans jazz. Later, with his band the Hot Fives, Armstrong thrilled audiences with his brilliant trumpet solos and virtuoso "scat" singing.

THE RAW SOUND OF THE SAXOPHONE WAS A FEATURE OF JAZZ MUSIC

Rhapsody in Blue

In 1924 George Gershwin made his name as a composer with *Rhapsody in Blue,* "an experiment in modern music". Gershwin called it "a musical kaleidoscope of America", and its popularity swept the world. Gershwin's brilliant career, which included scores for *An American in Paris* and *Porgy and Bess,* lasted well into the 1930s.

Strapped shoes

1924 BIX BEIDERBECKE
FORMS *THE WOLVERINES*

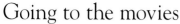

1927 DUKE ELLINGTON BEGINS
PLAYING AT THE COTTON CLUB

1927 AL JOLSON STARS IN *THE
JAZZ SINGER*, THE FIRST "TALKIE"

Going to the movies

Cinema came of age in the 1920s. Great directors continued to produce silent masterpieces until, in 1927, *The Jazz Singer* synchronized pictures with sound. Cinema-going became a weekly habit, and stars such as Mary Pickford, Greta Garbo, and the sultry-eyed Rudolph Valentino became heart-throbs and fashion leaders for a new mass audience.

RUDOLPH
VALENTINO
IN *THE SHEIK*

FRENCH FASHION
DESIGNER "COCO"
CHANEL IN TYPICAL
CHANEL SUIT

The new woman

The role women had played in World War I, and the fact that many could now vote, shattered the concept of frail femininity. The 1920s saw the emergence of the liberated "new woman" who favoured an active lifestyle. This attitude was reflected in the clothing of the time. "Coco" Chanel created a new style of clothes for these women: stark, yet stylish outlines, and knitted jackets and jumpers influenced a generation and beyond.

*Powder
and rouge*

*Cloche hat to
cover bobbed or
shingled hair*

*Cupid-bow mouth
painted with
scarlet lipstick*

*Lowered
waistline*

*Short skirt for freedom
of movement*

*Silk
stockings*

Doing the "Charleston"

Many new dances, such as the "Lindy hop" and the "Black bottom", began in the United States. They had their roots in the off-beat rhythms of African music, which had travelled through the black communities. Among them, the "Charleston" was the leading craze. The dancers moved frenetically, turning in their toes, kicking out their legs, and swinging their arms.

Flappers

Freedom was the theme of the 1920s and it was reflected in the new fashions, which were highly daring and much criticized by the establishment. This was the age of the flapper – the young woman who wore make-up, smoked in public, and danced and drank unchaperoned at cocktail parties and nightclubs.

STYLISH HEELED
SHOES FOR
EVENING WEAR

1925

Theory of evolution in the dock

25 MAY

US biology teacher John Scopes has been arrested – for teaching evolution. His hearing will start in July in Dayton, Tennessee. Scopes, in teaching Darwin's theory that humans are evolved from apes, has gone against the Bible's account of the Creation. Christian fundamentalists in the state have recently introduced a law that makes this illegal. The case, already nicknamed the "Monkey Trial", is attracting media attention. Civil rights lawyer Clarence Darrow will conduct the defence and William Bryan, who has crusaded against evolution, will act for the prosecution. The judge is not allowing anyone to put forward scientific evidence.

John Scopes – the teacher at the centre of the evolution row

Art Deco tea set by potter Clarice Cliff

Home Cubism

30 APRIL

There are millions of visitors flocking to the Exposition Internationale des Arts Décoratifs in Paris, France. Architecture, interior design, and high fashion all appear in the distinctive bold colouring and geometrical shapes of Art Deco – a style that some people have described as Cubism domesticated. Among the exhibits are brilliant textiles by painter Raoul Dufy and beautiful gowns by "Coco" Chanel.

Ban on skilled jobs for blacks

29 JUNE

Racial segregation at work has officially come into force in South Africa. Today a bill was passed that bans black South Africans from doing skilled jobs in all industries. The first law along these lines, the Mines and Works Act, was passed in 1911 and blacks were forced to do badly paid, unskilled work. Demand for the policy increased and in 1922 white mine workers in the Witwatersrand gold fields staged a strike against the use of black workers. In a violent conflict more than 200 lives were lost. The law passed today will finally make the widely practiced colour bar legal. It is one of the first measures introduced by the pact government, the recent coalition between the Afrikaaner National Party, which does not want to maintain ties with Britain or share power with blacks, and the Labour Party, which consists mainly of white urban workers. At the same time, Afrikaans, the Dutch-based dialect, has been made the official language of South Africa to help ensure white supremacy in the country.

JANUARY–JUNE

World Events	**JAN** Following Lenin's death, Joseph Stalin makes moves to become the supreme head of the USSR.	**MAR** Chiang Kai-shek becomes leader of the nationalist Kuomintang, following the death of Chinese premier Sun Yat-sen.	**APR** The Australian government promises low-interest loans for settlers to encourage Britons to emigrate.	**MAY** In Italy, Catholic bishops condemn the "scandalous" women's fashions and ban bare-legged women from churches.
Entertainment	**FEB** In the USA, the *New Yorker*, a weekly magazine with stories and social comment, goes on sale.	**MAR** As the US crossword craze grows, the Chicago Health Department says that crosswords are good for your health.	**JUN** Charlie Chaplin's *The Gold Rush*, which has taken longer than a year to make, premieres in Hollywood, USA.	**JUN** UK playwright Noel Coward's *Hay Fever* opens in London's West End. It is his third play to be staged this year.
Innovations	**JAN** Canadian Arthur Sicard develops the snowblower, a machine for clearing snow.	**FEB** London zoo announces it will install lighting to cheer up the animals during thick UK fogs.	**APR** In-flight movies get off the ground when UK Imperial Airways shows *The Lost World* during a flight.	**JUN** The Chrysler motor company is founded in Detroit, USA, and produces a six-cylinder $1,500 luxury car.

CHIANG KAI-SHEK

 UK EMIGRANT

1925

Klan marches on Washington, but rain stops demonstration

8 AUGUST

More than 40,000 members of the United States' most notorious secret society, the racist Ku Klux Klan, staged a major demonstration in the capital city of Washington today. The Klansmen wore their sinister attire of white robes and conical hoods, and waved US flags. The march ended at the foot of the Washington Memorial, where the planned ceremony and cross-burning was cancelled due to heavy rain. The Klan, which today boasts a large membership of some four million, was founded in 1866 in Tennessee. It conducted a reign of terror against freed black slaves, with strange rituals, midnight rites, lynchings, and whippings that struck fear into the southern states, until the society was outlawed in 1871. However, in 1915, the Klan re-formed, and today actively crusades against black Americans, Jews, Catholics, and evolutionary Darwinism in its campaign for an all-white Protestant United States. The Klan has entered politics, and last year helped to prevent Catholic Democrat Al Smith from holding office. Today, even the fearsome Klan was powerless against the driving rain.

Ghoul-like members of the Ku Klux Klan march through Washington DC

Great *Potemkin*

21 DECEMBER

The *Battleship Potemkin*, the creation of Soviet director Sergei Eisenstein, premiered tonight in Moscow. The film, made to commemorate the 1905 Russian Revolution, tells of the mutiny that took place at the port of Odessa. Critics are raving about the film's stunning ten-minute sequence on the Odessa steps, in which clever editing and camera angles are used to show soldiers carrying out a seemingly endless massacre of innocent civilians.

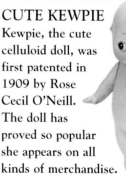

CUTE KEWPIE
Kewpie, the cute celluloid doll, was first patented in 1909 by Rose Cecil O'Neill. The doll has proved so popular she appears on all kinds of merchandise.

JULY–DECEMBER

JUL US teacher John Scopes, on trial for teaching Darwin's theory of evolution, is found guilty and fined $100.

JUL While in prison, German dictator Adolf Hitler publishes *Mein Kampf*, promoting Nazism and attacking Jews.

DEC The Locarno Conference finalizes post-World War I treaties and defines Franco-German and Belgo-German borders.

DEC Reza Khan, who has ruled Persia since 1921, is declared shah and vows to modernize his country.

SEP "Big Bill" Tilden, the USA's most popular tennis player, leads his country to a sixth Davis Cup win.

SEP The latest US dance craze, the outrageous "Charleston", takes Europe by storm.

OCT Black US dancer Josephine Baker enchants Paris, France, with her performance in *La Revue Nègre*.

DEC *The Great Gatsby*, published this year by US author F Scott Fitzgerald, receives great acclaim.

JUL The first successful insulin treatment is performed in Europe at Guys Hospital in London, UK.

CHARLESTON DANCERS

SEP In the Italian capital of Rome, the city's first underground railway line opens for business.

DEC The 35-mm miniature Leica camera, developed in Germany by E Leitz, revolutionizes photography.

JOSEPHINE BAKER

DEC The first-ever motel opens in San Luis Obispo, California, USA, with room for 160 guests.

1926

Seeing by radio

27 JANUARY

Scottish inventor John Logie Baird has created a system for transmitting moving images via airwaves called a televisor. Members of the Royal Society in Britain applauded at its first public demonstration in London. Later, a similar display was given to members of the scientific press. Baird transmitted the faces of two ventriloquist dolls with a beam of light and, using a photoelectric cell, changed the light into electricity. The electric signals were sent to a receiver that reversed the image. As yet the images flicker and are not as good as those in the cinema, but Baird has proved that the concept of television is possible. Perhaps one day it will be as popular as radio.

Baird's televisor

General strike hits Britain

12 MAY

The first general strike in Britain's history is over. It began when mine owners, threatened by foreign competition, proposed to cut the miners' wages and lengthen the working day. The miners refused, and went on strike, adopting the slogan "Not a penny off the pay, not a minute on the day". The Trades Union Congress (TUC) called for a general strike in their support and some three million workers – dockers, printers, railwaymen, building workers, and iron and steel workers – responded. On 4 May nearly half of Britain's workforce stayed at home. But the government retaliated. It used soldiers and middle-class volunteers to keep food supplies moving and to provide some public transport. On the radio and in its own newspaper, *The British Gazette*, it put its case to the public. Seeing that the strike was not only failing in its aim to paralyse the country but that it could also be seen as illegal, the TUC called it off today leaving the miners to fight on alone.

JANUARY–JUNE

World Events	**JAN** Abdul Aziz ibn Saud becomes king of Hejaz, changing the name of the region to Saudi Arabia.	**MAR** Irish republican Éamon de Valera resigns as leader of the Sinn Féin, and founds the Fianna Fáil ("soldiers of destiny").	**APR** At least 100 die in savage riots as fighting breaks out again between Muslims and Hindus in Calcutta, India.	**MAY** Polish nationalist and soldier Jozef Pilsudski marches on Warsaw with army units and seizes power in Poland.
Entertainment	**FEB** French tennis champion Suzanne Lenglen announces her retirement from singles play.	**MAR** In the USA, Douglas Fairbanks stars in *The Black Pirate*, the first full-length film to use two-tone colour.	**MAY** US comic star Buster Keaton's latest film, *The General*, the story of a runaway train, thrills audiences across the world.	**JUN** US golfer Bobby Jones wins the prestigious US Open golf tournament, the first amateur to do so since 1897.
Innovations	**JAN** France's Pasteur Institute announces the discovery of an anti-tetanus serum.	**MAR** US physicist Robert Goddard launches the first liquid fuel-propelled rocket in Massachusetts, USA.	**MAY** Two US aviators, Richard Byrd and Floyd Bennett, make the first ever aeroplane flight over the North Pole.	**JUN** The first electric pop-up toaster is produced by the McGraw Electric Co in the USA and goes on sale for $13.50.

GODDARD'S LIQUID ROCKET

BOBBY JONES

1926

Record swim

6 AUGUST
Nineteen-year-old Gertrude Ederle from the United States today became the first woman to swim the English Channel. She battled against currents, winds, and cold to swim the 56 km (35 miles) from France to Britain in 14 hours and 31 minutes – two hours faster than the current record held by a man. On arrival Ederle said, "It had to be done, and I did it."

THE COTTON CLUB

US black music, art, and literature is flourishing in New York. Young white audiences are flocking to Harlem's Cotton Club, a new nightspot, to see African-style revues and hear the latest jazz sounds.

The bear with little brain

14 OCTOBER
A delightful little bear has entered children's literature – Winnie-the-Pooh, or Pooh for short. Created by British author A A Milne and beautifully drawn by E H Shepard, Pooh appears today in his first full-length book. Other characters in the stories include Christopher Robin (Milne's son) and a host of the boy's nursery friends – Piglet, Tigger, Eeyore, Kanga, and Roo.

Christopher Robin pulls on his boots, helped by Winnie-the-Pooh

New emperor for Japan

Hirohito ascends the throne of Japan on the death of his father Emperor Yoshihito

25 DECEMBER
Japan has a new emperor, a position in the country that is considered divine. Twenty-five-year-old Hirohito will take over from his father Yoshihito who died today after a long illness. Yoshihito had ruled Japan for 14 years. Hirohito has been carrying out imperial duties for the past five years, so being the new head of state will not be totally daunting. In 1921, although still young, he was proclaimed regent because his father was seriously ill and incapable of "paying further attention to his state duties". At this time Hirohito successfully completed an important world tour, the first member of the Japanese imperial family to do so. However, despite coming to the throne today, his coronation – when he will take his place on the "August Heavenly Throne" and become a living god – will not take place for a few years.

JULY–DECEMBER

SEP Brazil resigns in protest and Spain threatens to leave as Germany is finally admitted to the League of Nations.

AUG Thousands of devoted women fans mourn the death of US screen heart-throb Rudolph Valentino, who was only 31.

AUG In the USA, Warner Bros develops "Vitaphone", a movie sound system that synchronizes all kinds of sounds.

HARRY HOUDINI

SEP Nationalist Kuomintang forces under Chiang Kai-shek capture Hangkow and begin the unification of China.

OCT US escape artist Harry Houdini dies from a burst appendix following a stomach injury incurred during a stunt.

SEP The pioneering Ford Motor Co introduces a 5-day week and an 8-hour day for their workers in Detroit, USA.

NOV In Italy the Pope says Mussolini must have divine protection to survive four assassination attempts in one year.

DEC The Bauhaus school of design moves to a site especially designed by Gropius at Dessau, Germany.

DEC US natural historians discover traces of what could be the earliest human ancestors in Outer Mongolia.

WATERLILY POND BY MONET

NOV Hunger and poverty force UK miners to accept wage cuts and to return to work after their seven-month strike.

DEC French artist Claude Monet, a leader of the Impressionist movement, dies at the age of 66.

DEC The popularity of the wireless grows with more than 2 million homes in the UK having radios.

TWENTIES TRANSPORT

FAMILY OUTING TO THE SEASIDE

THE 1920s SAW A HUGE INCREASE IN TRANSPORT with more people than ever before on the move. All over the world railway networks expanded and passenger airlines introduced scheduled flights, but the most remarkable developments were in motoring. For the rich there were stunningly beautiful, handcrafted touring cars such as Lagondas or Bentleys. For those who were less well off, the decade saw the rise of the cheap, mass-produced car. Private car ownership became widespread, particularly in the United States. But by the end of the 1920s Britain and France were also producing affordable cars. The age of mass motoring had arrived.

Low-cost cars not only brought a new freedom to their owners, they also affected the infrastructure of the country. There was a demand for new roads and the building of new houses began on the outskirts of main cities.

FIAT WAS ITALY'S LEADING CAR PRODUCER

Finding the way

Motoring became a major leisure activity during the 1920s. People took drives in the countryside, but lack of road signs often caused problems. Sales of road maps and other essential accessories soared.

SET OF ROAD MAPS IN LEATHER INDEX CASE

Makes and marques

In 1920 there were hundreds of small producers making handcrafted cars. Each one had a unique marque, or badge. However, as mass production made cars cheaper, the smaller companies were taken over or put out of business by the large-scale manufacturers.

BUGATTI MADE SUPERB STYLISH CARS

BUGATTIS ON THE RACE TRACK

Built for speed

Although speed on the road was discouraged, speed on the track was a different matter. In May 1923 the first Le Mans 24-hour motor race took place in France, and ushered in an era of fast cars and a new sport – motor racing. The powerful new sports cars, which included the Duesenberg, Bentley, Alfa Romeo, and Bugatti, were fitted with huge engines and could exceed 160 km/h (100 mph), but they were expensive. Only the wealthy could afford to compete in motor races, but for others it was a sensational spectator sport.

Running board

1927 1ST- OR 2ND-CLASS
SEATS OFFERED ON PLANES

1928 A LONG-DISTANCE BUS
SERVICE OPERATES IN USA

1930 STEAM TRAINS GIVE WAY
TO DIESEL AND ELECTRIC

Taking to the air

After World War I pilots were employed in civil aviation, and the 1920s saw a steady growth in scheduled air services. Flying was surprisingly safe, but it was expensive and often uncomfortable. French airlines tried to ease the discomfort of flying by providing elaborate five-course meals and wine. In 1931 United Airlines recruited air hostesses to serve meals and assist passengers.

AIR HOSTESSES ON UNITED AIRLINES

A quick hop

In 1933, as increasing numbers of people began to travel by air, the twin-engined Boeing 247 was launched. It could carry up to ten passengers over a distance of 965 km (600 miles) in four hours. Its advanced features included an all-metal skin, and wheels that could be pulled up once airborne.

Great Scot!

Although local rail lines were being electrified, the great mainline trains were largely still pulled by steam engines. Far from being an outdated mode of transport, they were constantly being improved and were capable of travelling at terrific speed. One of the great trains of the decade was the coal-burning *Flying Scotsman*. In 1928, equipped with a walk-through tender so that crews could be changed at high speed, it began regular services between London and Edinburgh, taking about eight hours to cover the 640 km (400 miles) across Britain.

THE *FLYING SCOTSMAN*

Windscreen

Cars for all

In 1908, United States manufacturer Henry Ford applied mass-production techniques in his factories and launched the first cheap, popular car – the Model T. With its simple four-cylinder engine, push-pedal gear, four seats, and cape hood, it was the first "family" car. It was ugly but it was cheap, and the US public rushed to buy it. Car owners had the freedom to travel wherever they wanted, whenever they wanted. Family outings became part of everyday life, and people could live some distance from their workplace.

THE MODEL T FORD,
THE FIRST AFFORDABLE
"FAMILY" CAR

SLEEPING COMPARTMENT
OF AN EXPRESS TRAIN

Sleeping through the journey

In the 1920s most people travelled long distances by rail and even the moderately wealthy could travel in a good degree of comfort. The glamorous *Orient Express* was the height of luxury, but the smaller trains also had sleeping compartments and dining cars, which offered excellent food in elegant surroundings.

1927

Land speed record smashed

29 MARCH

British racing driver Major Henry Segrave achieved a land speed record today of 328.041 km/h (203.841 mph) in his Sunbeam *Mystery*. Only six weeks ago Malcolm Campbell set what seemed to be an unbeatable record – 281.439 km/h (174.883 mph) – in the British-made *Bluebird*, but Segrave has convincingly smashed it. Campbell praised his rival for an "excellent feat", but says he already has a new, faster car and is now confident that he can regain the record. It seems that the speed race is set to continue.

Future vision

10 JANUARY

Austrian director Fritz Lang's latest film, *Metropolis*, has been hailed as a masterpiece after its premiere in Germany. Set in the year 2000, it uses special effects to create a gigantic city ruled by machines. The plot focuses on the exploited workers, who stage a rebellion incited by a beautiful but evil robot that is ultimately destroyed.

Lindbergh first to fly Atlantic solo

21 MAY

Waiting crowds of over 100,000 people at St Bourget near Paris, France, cheered as United States pilot Charles A Lindbergh completed his non-stop Atlantic flight. Lindbergh is not the first pilot to achieve this feat, but he will go down in history as he is the first to do it solo. The 26-year-old departed from Roosevelt Field in New York, USA, yesterday. His single-engined monoplane, *Spirit of St Louis,* was so laden with fuel it barely cleared the runway. Buffeted by wind and rain, the little craft at times came within 3 m (10 ft) of the waves. Lindbergh, weary from lack of sleep, kept going by munching on sandwiches. He finally landed at 10.24 this evening, having flown the 5,793 km (3,600 miles) in 33½ hours. The handsome midwesterner is already being hailed as a national hero.

Charles Lindbergh – dashing in his flying gear

JANUARY–JUNE

World Events	**FEB** An uprising against the military dictatorship of Antonio Carmona is crushed in Lisbon, Portugal.	**MAR** In China, nationalist troops led by Chiang Kai-shek defeat the warlords and capture the rich port of Shanghai.	**APR** Chiang Kai-shek sets his troops against the communist trade unions and prepares to set up a new government.	**MAY** The UK and USSR sever diplomatic relations when Soviet trade delegates are accused of spying.
Entertainment	**FEB** Clara Bow becomes known as the "It" girl after playing a flapper in the US film *It*.	**FEB** French audiences are stunned by a recital by US violinist Yehudi Menuhin, aged 10.	**MAY** In the UK, the number of hairdressers soars as women flock to have their hair fashionably "bobbed".	**MAY** In the UK, snooker player Joe Davis wins the first ever world professional snooker championship.
Innovations	**JAN** A telephone service is set up between the UK and the USA.	**JAN** The first underwater colour photograph is published in US *National Geographic* magazine.	**MAR** Archaeologists in Iraq find what they claim is a 5,000-year-old manicure set on the site of the ancient city of Ur.	**MAY** Wireless listeners around the world hear the latest news and cricket scores live from London, UK.

YEHUDI MENUHIN

THE "BOB" HAIRCUT

1927

Vienna burns as riots rock the city

16 JULY

The Austrian capital Vienna burned today as riots spread through the city. Economic hardship and post-war difficulties have caused

Troops set up a blockade using whatever material is at hand

called for a general strike, and workers took to the streets. When soldiers mutinied in their support, the opposition called for Chancellor Ignaz Seipel's resignation. However,

tension to build up between the supporters of the socialist government and the Nazis who want to make Austria part of Germany. Problems came to a head yesterday when charges against three Nazis, for the murder of two communists, were dropped. The socialist press called for retribution, labour leaders

Seipel appealed to the right-wing provinces for help, and troops entered Vienna, where they clashed violently with rioters. At present, 12,000 troops and police are patrolling the debris-strewn streets of the city and order is being restored while the authorities appeal for peaceful discussions.

Crowds stunned as pictures "talk"

6 OCTOBER

US cinema audiences went wild as they heard the first live speech in a feature-length movie – and not only words, but songs as well. The film *The Jazz Singer* which has been produced by Warner Bros, who last year developed the Vitaphone, a new system which records synchronized music and speech. The film stars the talented Al Jolson, who plays the son of a Jewish cantor, torn between a life in the synagogue and one singing on Broadway, New York. Although the sound is slightly

Al Jolson in The Jazz Singer

indistinct, it does appear that Jolson is speaking directly to the audience. He performs four sequences of dialogue and song in what is, for the most part, a silent movie. At today's premiere in New York, the atmosphere in the cinema was electric when he began singing *Toot, Toot, Tootsie Goodbye*, and as he uttered the prophetic words "you ain't heard nothin' yet" the audience stood up and cheered. Some even climbed onto their seats with excitement. It is clear that the "talkies" have arrived; actors with squeaky voices had better watch out!

TARKA THE OTTER

Children everywhere will love the new book by British author Henry Williamson. Entitled *Tarka the Otter*, it narrates in faithfully observed detail the life of a Devon otter, describing all the events and the landscape of the surrounding countryside through the eyes of the otter itself.

JULY–DECEMBER

JUL Kevin O'Higgins, vice-president of the Irish Free State, is shot dead fuelling fears of furthur civil war in Ireland.

JUL The love affair between John Gilbert and Swedish film star Greta Garbo boosts box-office takings.

JUL In the UK Christopher Stone is the first ever radio DJ to broadcast a programme of selected records.

GARBO AND GILBERT

AUG In the USA, Italian-born anarchists Sacco and Vanzetti die in the electric chair, despite worldwide protests.

SEP US dancer Isadora Duncan dies at the age of 49 when she is accidentally strangled by her scarf.

AUG Vets in France say they have developed a vaccine for distemper, a life-threatening disease among dogs.

NOV In USSR, Joseph Stalin continues to remove opposition, and expels rival Leon Trotsky from the Communist Party.

DEC US jazz composer and pianist Duke Ellington opens at the Cotton Club, the famous Harlem nightclub.

OCT Soviet archaeologist Peter Koslov discovers the 700-year-old tomb of Genghis Khan in China.

JOSEPH STALIN

DEC An attempted coup by communists in Canton is crushed by Chiang Kai-shek's troops and 600 are executed.

DEC *Show Boat*, a musical by US composers Hammerstein and Kern, opens on Broadway, New York.

DEC The new Model A Ford, a successor to the Model T, rolls off the production line in the USA.

1928

Woman claims to be a Romanov

6 FEBRUARY

Ten years ago the Russian royal family was murdered during the country's turbulent civil war. Now a woman has arrived in the United States claiming to be Anastasia Romanov, the youngest daughter of Tsar Nicholas II. Mrs Chaikovsky, as she is now called, says she managed to survive the massacre of her family because she was shielded from the bullets by one of her sisters. Mr Gleb Botkin, son of the former tsar's doctor, has confirmed her identity and says they were childhood friends.

Mrs Anastasia Chaikovsky

Mrs Chaikovsky is not the first to claim to be a Romanov, but whether or not her story is true remains to be seen.

Australian doctors take to the air

15 MAY

A flying doctor service has been set up in Queensland, Australia, where there are only ten local doctors for an area of 647,450 square km (250,000 square miles). The doctors, who can be contacted by Morse radio, will be flown to patients in a de-Havilland aeroplane provided by the Queensland and Northern Territory Aerial Service (QANTAS).

Chinese nationalist army enters Peking

8 JUNE

Nationalist forces, led by General Chiang Kai-shek, entered the Chinese capital city of Peking yesterday. In the streets, student supporters cheered and waved flags. The arrival of Chiang's troops marks the end of the civil war. It also brings hope that China may be unified under one government for the first

In 1926, his Kuomintang army, which included communists, set out on the "Northern Expedition" to drive out the warlords. By March last year, after a series of successes, Chiang's army was in control of the key port of Shanghai and the whole of China south of the Yangtze River. In December, after an attempted coup by the

time since 1916, when power passed to the warlords. Chiang Kai-shek, a former military commander, took control of the Nationalist Party three years ago on the death of Sun Yat-sen.

communists, Chiang turned on them, brutally expelling them from the Kuomintang. Now that he has successfully taken control of Peking, Chiang may be regarded as the effective ruler of China.

JANUARY–JUNE

World Events	**JAN** In USSR, Joseph Stalin exiles all key opposition figures, including Leon Trotsky, Lenin's right-hand man.	**APR** In China, nationalist troops launch a major offensive, with the ultimate aim of capturing the capital of Peking.	**MAY** The long struggle of UK suffragettes comes to an end as the voting age for women drops to 21, the same as for men.	**MAY** In the USA, stock market prices plummet on Wall Street as more shares than ever before change hands in a day.
Entertainment	**JAN** Thomas Hardy, the UK author of *Jude the Obscure*, dies at the age of 87.	**MAR** Cloche hats are the latest headgear fashion for flappers on both sides of the Atlantic Ocean.	**MAY** The 9th Olympic Games, held in Amsterdam, Holland, attracts competitors from 46 countries.	**JUN** *The Jazz Singer*, the first "talkie", is shown in Paris, France, and creates a stir in the European film industry.
Innovations	**FEB** The world's first fully air-conditioned office block opens in San Antonio, Texas, USA.	**CLOCHE HAT** **MAY** The rail service from London to Edinburgh, UK, on the *Flying Scotsman* reaches 112 km/h (70 mph).	**JUN** Norwegian explorer Roald Amundsen, who was first to reach the South Pole, goes missing in the Arctic. **ROALD AMUNDSEN**	**JUN** US aviator Amelia Earhart is the first woman to cross the Atlantic Ocean by air, as a passenger.

1928

Penicillin discovered

30 SEPTEMBER
Scottish doctor and bacteriologist Alexander Fleming has made one of the most remarkable medical discoveries – completely by chance. While he was on holiday he left a dish of the *staphylococcus* bacteria, which causes infection in humans, lying around in his laboratory. When he returned three weeks later, he noticed a *penicillium notatum* mould, which often grows on stale bread,

had contaminated the dish. The area around the mould however, was free of bacteria, suggesting that its presence had stopped bacterial growth. Fleming's next task is to isolate the active chemical present in *penicillium*, which may take some years. But he has discovered that it does not harm human white blood cells, so is hopeful that it may eventually be used to treat human bacterial infections.

Alexander Fleming in his laboratory at St Mary's Hospital, London, UK

Mouse set for stardom

18 NOVEMBER
The first animated cartoon with sound, *Steamboat Willie*, opened at New York's Colony Theatre today, and launched a new star – Mickey Mouse. The joint creation of US animators Walt Disney and Ub Iwerks, Mickey has previously appeared in two silent films, but with little success. Disney's masterstroke was to give the mouse a voice (his own) and use sound as part of the humour. Today, the comical mouse was an instant success. No doubt he will win many fans.

New star Mickey Mouse at the helm in Steamboat Willie

JULY–DECEMBER

AUG The Kellogg-Briand pact, officially abolishing all war, is signed by 15 nations at the French foreign ministry in Paris.

JUL The jazz term "boogie woogie" is coined when Clarence "Pine Top" records *Pine Top Boogie Woogie*.

JUL The first commercially available TV set, made by the Daven Co, goes on sale in the USA priced at $75.

BERTOLT BRECHT

SEP The regent of Ethiopia, Ras Tafari, stages a palace coup forcing the Empress Zauditu to abdicate, and seizes power.

AUG German playwright Bertolt Brecht's *The Threepenny Opera* opens in Berlin, with music by Kurt Weill.

AUG UK car manufacturers Morris Motors launch a new model, the Morris Minor, in the UK.

OCT Soviet leader Joseph Stalin introduces his first economic five-year plan to industrialize the USSR.

NOV French composer Joseph Ravel's *Boléro*, which is inspired by a Spanish folk tune, premieres in Paris, France.

SEP The iron lung, developed last year by US physicist Philip Drinker, is used for the first time in the USA.

HERBERT HOOVER

NOV Republican Herbert Hoover is elected US president with a landslide victory over Democrat Al Smith.

DEC US composer George Gershwin's *An American in Paris* opens with Gershwin at the piano.

DEC Hungarian biochemist Albert Szent-Györgyi manages to isolate vitamin C.

1929

Bonjour Tintin

10 JANUARY

Belgian cartoonist George Remi, also known as Hergé, has created a new cartoon character – Tintin, the boy detective. His adventures appear in *Le Petit Vingtième*, the children's section of the *Vingtième Siècle* newspaper.

Massacre of the mob

The Academy Award – a figure on a reel of film

Hollywood awards its best

Clara Bow with Richard Arlen and Charles "Buddy" Rogers in Wings

Thompson sub-machine gun – the gangsters' favourite

14 FEBRUARY

Valentine's Day brought bullets, not roses, to seven US gangsters who were gunned down in Chicago this morning. The men, who were all members of George "Bugs" Moran's North Side gang, were lured to a warehouse by the prospect of a first-rate liquor deal. Shortly after they arrived, a Cadillac disguised as a police car pulled up for what appeared to be a routine inspection. Lined up against the wall, the men were suddenly mown down by two men firing sub-machine guns and finished off by another two with pistols. The police believe the killing is the work of Al "Scarface" Capone, king of the Chicago underworld and deadly rival of Moran. Gang warfare for control of the lucrative trade in illegal alcohol has been common in Chicago since 1920 when Prohibition was introduced. A massacre on today's scale, however, is unprecedented.

17 MAY

A banquet was held in Hollywood last night for the first award ceremony of the US movie industry. The Academy of Motion Picture Arts and Sciences, founded by Louis B Mayer of MGM, voted William Wellman's war film, *Wings*, best picture of 1927–28. A special award was given to Warner Brothers for the pioneering talkie, *The Jazz Singer*. The gold-plated statuettes were presented by popular actor Douglas Fairbanks, the president of the Academy. A total of 13 awards were given to various films, actors, and technicians.

THE DAWN OF THE TELEVISION AGE

As the decade is ending a new medium – television – has begun to appear. After a period of experimentation, in October this year the British Broadcasting Company began to televise a daily programme of shows. But as yet few people have TV sets on which to watch them!

JANUARY–JUNE

World Events	**JAN** Wyatt Earp, former US peace officer of Dodge City, Kansas, dies at the age of 80 – with his boots off.	**MAR** Benito Mussolini's Fascist Party wins a rigged election and forms Italy's first fascist government.	**MAY** In Berlin, Germany, 15 people die when street fighting breaks out between communist demonstrators and police.	**JUN** Allied forces put forward the Young Plan, a concessionary deal that rejigs and reduces German war repayments.
Entertainment	**FEB** UK society beauty Lillie Langtry, the "Jersey Lily", dies in her Riviera home at the age of 74.	**FEB** MGM's *Broadway Melody*, the world's first all-singing, all-dancing musical, breaks US box office records.	**APR** *Un Chien Andalou*, the first Surrealist film, is made by Spanish director Louis Buñuel.	**MAY** The four Marx Brothers make their hilarious and zany US film debut in *The Cocoanuts*.
Innovations	**FEB** The first individually packaged frozen food goes on sale in Toronto, Canada.	**MAR** The UK introduces a long-distance airmail service, delivering to India, Egypt, Pakistan, and Iraq.	**MAY** German scientist Hans Berger develops a new device to measure the brain's electrical activity.	**JUN** The first colour television image is demonstrated in the Bell Laboratories, New York, USA.

A REHEARSAL FOR BROADWAY MELODY

UN CHIEN ANDALOU

1929

Popeye makes his debit

Crowds gather in Lakehurst for the arrival of the Graf Zeppelin

Popeye the Sailor Man, spinach in hand

1 JULY

The newest cartoon character to appear in a comic strip is one-eyed, spinach-eating Popeye the Sailor Man. Popeye is the creation of US strip cartoonist Elzie Crisler Segar. The son of a house-painter, Segar took a course in cartoon design and went to Chicago to work on *Charlie Chaplin's Comic Capers*. His first creation was Barry the Boob for the *Chicago Herald*. Moving to New York, he started up his own comic strip, *Thimble Theater*. Today it features big-hearted Popeye, together with his corncob pipe – and several cans of spinach.

Zeppelin airship circles the world

29 AUGUST

The German-built airship *Graf Zeppelin* landed in Lakehurst, New Jersey, United States, today, having circled the world. Its creator Dr Hugo Eckener piloted the airship, which carried a crew of 37 and had 16 passengers. The giant airship made just three stops during its 31,200-km (19,500-mile) journey – in Germany, Japan, and Los Angeles. The historic trip, which is another first for aviation, took 21 days, seven hours, and 26 minutes.

Wall Street crashes

US stockbrokers struggle with a tangled mass of ticker tape

24 OCTOBER

The New York Stock Exchange has collapsed with terrified investors selling more than 13 million shares in one day. Today's crash started last Saturday when a wave of panic resulted in share prices plummeting.

Intervention by some major banks restored confidence, but it was only temporary. Prices continued to slide, and today the crash was complete. The causes are complex, but much has to do with the United States' postwar boom. The economy has grown rapidly, and millions of people have invested to make quick profits. During the last two or three years, however, the economy has slowed down, and experts have indicated that some stocks were vastly overpriced. This created a crisis of confidence. Banks called in loans, and those who borrowed to buy shares started to sell rapidly. After today's events millions face financial ruin, not only in the United States but in countries all over the world.

JULY–DECEMBER

JUL Border clashes between Chinese and Soviet troops, following the rupture of trade relations, bring fresh fears of war.

AUG Great Soviet impresario Sergei Diaghilev, founder of the Ballets Russes, dies suddenly in Italy at the age of 57.

JUL The German liner SS *Bremen* crosses the Atlantic Ocean in a record time of 4 days, 14 hrs, and 30 mins.

SERGEI DIAGHILEV

AUG In Jerusalem, Palestine, 113 Jews are killed as fighting breaks out between Arabs and Jews over access to the Wailing Wall.

AUG German novelist Erich Marie Remarque's *All Quiet on the Western Front* evokes the horrors of trench warfare.

SEP In the UK, traffic lights are standardized: red for stop, green for go, and amber to warn of change.

OCT The kingdom of the Serbs, Croats, and Slovenes is renamed Yugoslavia under the dictatorship of King Alexander.

NOV The first exhibition by Spanish Surrealist artist Salvador Dali opens in France.

OCT London crowds stared upwards as the R-101, the world's biggest airship, flew over the UK capital.

AIRSHIP R-101

NOV Following New York's stock market crash last month, economic depression deepens worldwide.

DEC German author Thomas Mann wins the Nobel Prize for *The Magic Mountain*.

NOV US navy commander Richard Byrd makes the first flight over the Antarctic continent.

THE GANGSTER ERA

THE ARRIVAL OF PROHIBITION in 1920 sparked off an unprecedented wave of crime, making it as much a feature of 1920s United States as the Charleston. Bootlegging – the making, selling, and transportation of illegal alcohol – was highly profitable, and Chicago, nicknamed "the wickedest city in the world", became the centre of its trade. Rival gangs battled it out for control of this multi-million-dollar industry, while police were bought off, and corruption spread upwards through city hall. Speakeasies, illegal bars where respectable citizens rubbed shoulders with gangsters, and stills for producing illegal alcohol were widely available. But by 1933 the public, sick of violence and rotgut alcohol, demanded change. Prohibition was repealed and gangsters were forced to look elsewhere for easy money.

Illegal drinking

Alcohol was carried in hip flasks and consumed in the illegal speakeasy bars. In New York, where there had been 15,000 legal bars, there were soon 32,000 speakeasies, with names like "Chez Florence" or "Frankie and Johnny's". Some were disguised as ice-cream parlours, others were jazz-filled basement dives where customers needed passwords to enter.

WOMEN DRINK ALCOHOL FROM HIP FLASKS

A new era of clean living

Prohibition – banning the manufacture, sale, and drinking of alcohol – was enforced through the Volstead Act on 17 January 1920. It was hailed as the start of an era of clear thinking and clean living. In fact, it created big business for corrupt gangsters.

Fedora hat

Flamboyant suit

Double-barrelled shotgun

ARMED HENCHMEN STAND BESIDE THEIR SPECIALLY ADAPTED CAR

Spats

Bonnie and Clyde

Bonnie Parker and Clyde Barrow had a short but bloody criminal career. They robbed banks and petrol stations, and committed some 12 murders in southwestern United States. They were gunned down by Texas rangers in 1934.

The kings of vice

Prohibition created ideal conditions for crime to flourish. In 1920 "Diamond" Jim Colosimo was boss of the Chicago underworld, but Johnny Torrio had Colosimo shot and took over his empire. He split Chicago into sections and set about organizing the city's criminals into an efficient force of professional bootleggers. They smuggled alcohol from abroad, took over breweries, and produced rotgut alcohol, which they sold at huge profits. The gangsters ruled the city like feudal overlords, bribing police and city officials, and living like millionaires. Gang warfare was common; rivals were blasted to death or "taken for a ride", their murders usually followed by lavish funerals.

1929 ST VALENTINE'S DAY
MASSACRE IN CHICAGO

1931 CAPONE IS ARRESTED AND
IMPRISONED FOR TAX EVASION

1933 VOLSTEAD ACT IS REPEALED –
PROHIBITION COMES TO AN END

C28169

*Violin case
hides gun*

Sawn-off shotgun

Gun power

Gunfire was a commonplace
sound on the street, as gangsters
used firepower to defend their
profits. The Thompson "tommy" sub-
machine gun was favoured for mass
executions otherwise, gangsters used sawn-off
shotguns or bombs. At least 2,500 gangsters
and federal agents were killed during Prohibition.

"Scarface" Capone

Al "Scarface" Capone was the undisputed head of the
Chicago gangsters. Brought up in New York, Capone went
to Chicago in 1920 to work for gang leader Johnny Torrio.
Capone learned quickly. By 1925 Torrio had faded into the
background, and Capone controlled the city's crime in
his own way. Ruthlessly brutal, he was said to have been
responsible for over 400 murders. His dealings secured him
an annual income of over $20 million and allowed him to
lead a flamboyant lifestyle. He drove a $30,000 bullet-
proof armoured Cadillac and wore expensive clothes.

Celluloid gangsters

Gangsterism became something of a
cult. Small boys mimicked mobsters
and there was a spate of gangster
films. *Little Caesar* starring Edward
G Robinson set the pattern in
1930, and *The Public Enemy*, which
launched James Cagney as a screen
gangster, was released a year later.

JAMES CAGNEY AND
JEAN HARLOW STAR
IN *THE PUBLIC ENEMY*

*Slots for
gun barrels*

*Getaway
driver*

*Steel-armoured
body*

A CRATE OF
CAPTURED LIQUOR
IS UNLOADED

422-000

Law and order

In 1924 J Edgar Hoover
became director of the
Federal Bureau of
Investigation (FBI) and
began to wage war against the
bootleggers. Federal agents raided
speakeasies and intercepted
illegal alcohol, but most of
the time they were powerless
against the unruly lawlessness.

1930

Stalin's new state farms

Soviet propaganda poster promoting Stalin's new collective farms

5 JANUARY

Soviet leader Joseph Stalin today declared that all farmland in the Soviet Union will be "collectively owned" by the people. Commentators believe there will be chaos throughout the countryside as plans are made to combine millions of small farms into large, state-owned units. Stalin has sent thousands of special agents to oversee the operation and has threatened to seize land if people refuse to co-operate. The peasants will now be expected to work on the vast new state farms for a wage instead of farming their own land. Stalin believes his new measures will soon double the Soviet Union's agricultural output and strengthen party control.

STYLE OF THE TIME
With its sleek, curved shape, this elegant Zephyr clock epitomizes the style of Art Deco that is currently at the forefront of modern design.

New planet

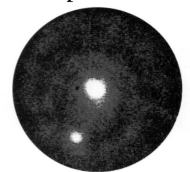

18 FEBRUARY

US astronomer Clyde Tombaugh has sighted a new planet in our solar system. It is named Pluto after the Greek god of the underworld.

Garbo talks

14 MARCH

Fans of silent screen star Greta Garbo have finally heard her speak. In her new film *Anna Christie*, Garbo's first words are uttered in a deep, husky voice, "Gif me a visky – and don't be stingy, baby." It appears that Garbo will be successful in making the transition from silent films to the "talkies".

JANUARY–JUNE

World Events	**FEB** In Spain, riots follow the fall of military dictator General Primo de Rivéra.	**MAR** US gangster Al Capone is released from prison after serving nine months for tax evasion.	**APR** The USA, UK, France, Italy, and Japan agree to cut naval fleets to control the arms race.	**MAY** French troops leave the Rhineland five years before the date set in the postwar Versailles treaty.
Entertainment	**JAN** In Sydney, Australian cricketer Donald Bradman scores a record 452 runs.	**FEB** *The Maltese Falcon* by US crime writer Dashiell Hammett is published to wide acclaim.	**MAY** The US anti-war film *All Quiet on the Western Front*, directed by Lewis Milestone, opens.	**JUN** The first newsreel theatre opens on Shaftesbury Avenue in the UK's capital London.
Innovations	**JAN** A picture telegraphy service between the UK and Germany opens.	**MAR** Nylon is discovered by Wallace Carrothers of the Du Pont Company in the USA.	**APR** UK actress Peggy O'Neil is the first person to be interviewed on television.	**JUN** The world's first air hostess, Ellen Church, starts work for United Airlines, USA.

DONALD BRADMAN

ALL QUIET ON THE WESTERN FRONT

1930

Gandhi's salt march

Mahatma Gandhi on his great march across India

6 APRIL

Mohandas Gandhi, known as "Mahatma" ("great soul"), reached the coast at Dandi today after a 380-km (238-mile) march across India. This is in protest about the tax on salt imposed on Indians by their British rulers – a tax that Gandhi believes is unfair. At Dandi, in defiance of the British authorities, he symbolically picked up a piece of natural salt from the mud flats as the crowds called out, "Hail deliverer."

The champ retires

17 NOVEMBER

US golfer Bobby Jones today retired from competition. He has run out of golfers to beat! In a single year, 28-year-old Jones has completed the supposedly impossible grand slam – the United States Open and Amateur, and the British Open and Amateur.

Grand slam golf champion Bobby Jones

Solo flight feat

Amy Johnson waves to the crowds

24 APRIL

Amy Johnson arrived in Darwin today after flying solo from Britain to Australia. She is the first woman ever to do so. The British woman's epic 16,000-km (10,000-mile) flight halfway round the world began only 19 days ago. At one stage she was forced to make an emergency landing on the island of Java in Indonesia and use sticking plaster to mend the wings of her *Gipsy Moth* aircraft. Amy, who is 27 years old, made her journey with only 100 hours flying experience. She left Britain practically unnoticed, but will return an international heroine.

JULY–DECEMBER

JUL Mackenzie King resigns as Canadian prime minister and is succeeded by Richard B Bennet.

JUL Uruguay wins football's first World Cup in Montevideo, beating Argentina 4–2.

JUL The skull of a man who lived a million years ago has been found in China.

THE FIRST WORLD CUP

JUL Following a liberal revolt in Brazil, Dr Getulio Vargas is installed as temporary president.

SEP William Van Alen's Art Deco skyscraper, the Chrysler Building, is completed in New York, USA.

SEP Dutch chemist P J W Debye uses x-rays to investigate the structure of molecules.

NOV In north Africa, Ras Tafari is crowned "king of kings" and becomes Emperor Haile Selassie of Abyssinia.

OCT US studio MGM releases the film *Billy the Kid* in the new "Realife" widescreen process.

OCT US company Birds Eye perfect their quick-freezing method and frozen peas go on sale.

EMPEROR HAILE SELASSIE

DEC US president Herbert Hoover asks Congress for $150 million to help the unemployed.

DEC The Youth Hostel Association (YHA) is formed in England and Wales.

DEC Acrylic plastics (Perspex) are invented in the UK and the USA.

1931

New republic for Spain

14 APRIL

After seven years of authoritarian rule, King Alfonso XIII has abdicated and Spain has declared itself a republic. King Alfonso's abdication was inevitable after the victory of the Republican Party in the recent elections, as well as the resignation of Spain's military dictator, General Miguel Primo de Rivera. It was made clear that if the king did not step down, civil war would erupt. While the republicans celebrate in Madrid, the Spanish royal family are on their way to exile in Britain.

Stratospheric record

Piccard and Kipfer land their balloon in the Austrian Tyrol

27 MAY

The Swiss physicist Auguste Piccard and fellow scientist Paul Kipfer have become the first men to reach the Earth's stratosphere. They took off in a huge hydrogen-filled balloon from the town of Augsburg in Germany, and rose a staggering 15,281 m (50,135 ft) into the stratosphere. Their adventure ended when they landed safely on a glacier in the high Austrian Tyrol. An airtight gondola (passenger compartment), designed by Piccard, enabled them to survive the low air density and intense cold at such extreme height. The purpose of the journey was to study the sun's cosmic rays.

Al Capone

"Scarface" jailed again

17 OCTOBER

Al "Scarface" Capone has been jailed again, this time for income tax fraud. The gangster, whose crime empire has dominated Chicago since the 1920s, has been given a stiff 11-year sentence. He must also pay a staggering $137,328 in back taxes. The investigation was led by Eliot Ness, a 28-year-old justice department agent.

A monster hit

21 NOVEMBER

Hollywood is certainly enjoying a horror boom at the moment. *Dracula* was an immediate success earlier this year, and today's release of James Whale's horror film *Frankenstein* is certain to pull in massive audiences. Boris Karloff stars as the poor, bewildered monster in this tragic fantasy horror.

JANUARY–DECEMBER

World Events	JAN Pierre Laval becomes the new prime minister of France.	MAY President Hoover opens the 381-m (1,250-ft) high Empire State Building in New York, USA.	MAY Soviet leader Stalin announces the second five-year plan for the introduction of state-owned farms.	JUL The Benguella Katanga, the first trans-African railway, opens in southern Africa, spanning the continent from east to west.
Entertainment	JAN Soviet ballerina Anna Pavlova, famous for her "Dying Swan", dies aged 49.	FEB Hungarian-born Béla Lugosi stars as the vampire in Tod Browning's US film *Dracula*.	MAY *Public Enemy*, a tough gangster movie starring James Cagney, causes a sensation in Hollywood, USA.	SEP The children's book *The Story of Babar* by Cécile de Brunhoff is an instant best-seller in Europe.
Innovations	MAR Electric razors are manufactured by Schick Inc in Connecticut, USA.	MAR US engineer Harold Edgerton invents the first electronic re-usable camera flash.	MAY Thousands of people flock to visit the world's first open zoo at Whipsnade in the UK.	JUL Central Ice Co installs the first ice-vending machine in Los Angeles, USA.

PRIMA BALLERINA ANNA PAVLOVA

BABAR

1932

Broadcasting House in London

BBC finds a new home

1 MAY

The British Broadcasting Corporation, known as the BBC, has moved to new London headquarters. The spectacular new home of radio and television looms like a liner under its radio masts. A plaque inside the entrance to this national institution bears the motto "Nation Shall Speak Peace Unto Nation".

Bolivia and Paraguay at war

15 JUNE

Full-scale war has erupted between the Latin American countries of Bolivia and Paraguay over the Gran Chaco, which is a large, densely forested, low-lying plain bordering the two countries. Paraguay has invested millions of dollars in the Gran Chaco to raise cattle and "quebracho", a hard wood that is used for tanning leather. Income from these goods has become a vital ingredient in the survival of Paraguay's weak economy. Landlocked Bolivia, on the other hand, needs access to the Gran Chaco in order to trade overseas. Bolivia, with a population that is three times the size of Paraguay and an army trained by German mercenaries, seems set to win the war.

ELECTRIC GUITAR
American musician Adolph Rickenbacker has introduced a new guitar that ampliflies sound electronically. Popular music may never sound the same again.

Roosevelt's "New Deal"

8 NOVEMBER

Franklin D Roosevelt, the Democrat candidate for the US presidency, has won a landslide victory over the Republican president Herbert Hoover. Roosevelt scooped all but six of the 48 states and gained a majority of over seven million in the popular vote. The campaign has been full of optimism. He has promised a "New Deal", a complete programme of reforms scheduled to be put into effect over the next few years. Above all, he has promised that when he is president "No American will starve".

Roosevelt wins landslide victory

JANUARY–DECEMBER

FEB Japanese troops create the puppet state of Manchuko, securing their control over Manchuria.

MAR After nine years of construction, the Sydney Harbour Bridge opens in Australia.

MAY US aviator Amelia Earhart becomes the first woman to fly solo across the Atlantic ocean.

OCT German physicist Albert Einstein dates the age of the earth at an amazing ten billion years.

MAY US film producer Walt Disney releases *Flowers and Trees*, the first film in three-strip Technicolor.

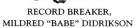

AUG US Mildred Didrikson is the most successful track-and-field athlete at the Olympic Games.

OCT US Jean Harlow and Clark Gable star in film *Red Dust*, a romance set in a rubber plantation.

NOV UK author John Galsworthy wins the Nobel Prize for his Forsyte novels.

JAN The Sukkur Dam, the largest irrigation project in the world, opens in India.

RECORD BREAKER, MILDRED "BABE" DIDRIKSON

MAR US scientists announce the development of the first vaccine against yellow fever.

MAR The UK's *Times Weekly Edition* is the first newspaper to feature colour photographs.

THE EARTH IS DATED

AUG US food manufacturer Forrest Mars launches a nougat, caramel, and chocolate Mars Bar.

THE GREAT DEPRESSION

By 1925 IT SEEMED THAT THE UPHEAVALS of World War I were over and that a new era of peace and economic stability had arrived. This illusion was shattered in 1929 with the crash of the New York Stock Exchange. It was the beginning of an economic depression that was to affect the whole world throughout the following decade. For several years the price of staple products such as wheat, rubber, and sugar had been falling. This made it very difficult for countries exporting these commodities. Their national incomes dropped and they could not afford to buy goods manufactured in Europe and the United States. All over the world exports fell, factory production slowed down and, before long, millions of jobs disappeared. In industrialized countries up to a quarter of the workforce was out of work. Full recovery did not come about until the build-up to World War II, when the world's major economies employed all their resources to meet the needs of the war effort.

COFFEE

SUGAR BEET

GERMAN PROPAGANDA POSTER

Our last hope

Recession and unemployment led many people to support extreme right-wing parties such as Hitler's Nationalist Socialist Workers' (Nazi) Party in Germany, which they hoped would pull them out of poverty.

Falling prices

Sugar beet and coffee were just two staple products that suffered steeply falling prices from the mid-1920s. The effect on the countries that exported them was disastrous. Coffee made up 75 per cent of Brazil's exports. The collapse of the market led to a civil war lasting three months and the dictatorship of unpopular President Getulio Vargas.

Living on the breadline

Long lines of unemployed people queuing for food were a common sight in large cities. With little or no public welfare provisions, hundreds of starving people had no alternative but to queue for free soup provided by private charities. Millions found themselves in absolute poverty, often having to choose between fuel to stop them from freezing and food to stop them from starving. Families lost their homes and were forced onto the streets. Young people delayed marriage until prospects improved, which led to a massive drop in the birthrate.

Apples for sale

Professional people were hit just as badly by the Depression as everyone else. It was a common sight to see ex-businessmen lining the streets of large cities selling apples or farm produce to make a little money for food, fuel, and clothing.

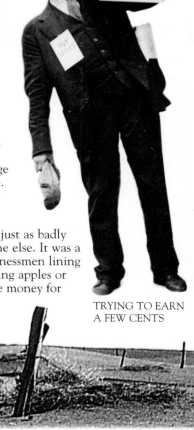

TRYING TO EARN A FEW CENTS

Economic miracle

In the 1930s Stalin introduced a series of five-year plans to boost the production of coal and steel. They transformed the Soviet Union from a backward agricultural society into a major industrial power. But many workers were used as slave labour, with little reward for their efforts.

Dry, dust-covered fields

1931 140,000 MINERS LOSE
THEIR JOBS IN CHILE

1936 IN THE UK, 200 OUT-OF-WORK MEN
FORM THE JARROW HUNGER CRUSADE

1936 FRANCE ABANDONS THE GOLD
STANDARD AND PRINTS MONEY FREELY

FRENCH STRIKERS DEMAND
WORK OR BREAD

PRESIDENT ROOSEVELT MEETS THE FARMERS

Economic growth in the USA

When Franklin D Roosevelt was elected
president in 1932 he offered the US people a
"New Deal" – a series of rescue programmes to
stimulate the economy and to bring work to the
unemployed. Among them was the Agricultural
Adjustment Act of 1933, which gave farmers
government subsidies in return for limiting
the output of their produce.

In protest

Strikes, hunger marches, and riots occurred frequently during
the Depression. In France, widespread strikes paralysed industrial
production. This resulted in a period of great political unrest
which led to the 1936 election of France's first socialist prime
minister, Léon Blum, at the head of the Popular Front. His
government made many promises to striking workers, including
a 40-hour week and a minimum wage. But these reforms proved
too expensive and Blum was forced to resign the following year.

A POVERTY-STRICKEN MIGRANT
WORKER WITH HER CHILDREN

Midwest dust bowl

In 1935 a series of catastrophic dust storms swept across the American
midwest, causing a terrible trail of destruction. High winds blew clouds
of dust over fields and
farms, destroying millions
of dollars' worth of crops
and suffocating herds of
cattle. Thousands of
farmers were ruined
and forced to leave
their homes behind
them in search of
work and a new life.
Many went west
to to find work
fruit-picking in
the orchards
of California.

*Abandoned
farmhouse in
the midwest*

1933

Hitler is chancellor

Adolf Hitler, the new German chancellor

30 JANUARY

Adolf Hitler has been appointed chancellor of Germany by President von Hindenburg. The 44-year-old leader of the Nazi Party has come to power at a time when Germany's democratic system faces virtual collapse. In recent weeks, the country has come to the brink of civil war, with members of the

Nazi Party and the German communists fighting vicious street battles. Although support for the Nazis seemed to be fading, a series of backroom intrigues has led to Hitler being awarded the chancellorship. Apart from Hitler himself, the 11-strong German cabinet has only two other Nazis in it. The rest are right-wing nationalists.

Reichstag on fire

Flames lick the dome of the Reichstag

28 FEBRUARY

A mysterious fire has gutted Berlin's Reichstag, the building that houses the German parliament. The new chancellor, Adolf Hitler, has accused the communists of starting the fire and has used this to persuade President von Hindenburg to sign a decree suspending all freedom of speech and assembly.

King Kong brings the latest in special-effects technology to the screen

Monkey trouble

2 MARCH

Fay Wray's new leading man is tall, dark, and menacing – he is a giant gorilla called King Kong. Captured on

Skull Island, Kong is taken to New York where he escapes. Although he seems huge on the screen, in real life Kong is a tiny articulated model, given life by Willis O'Brien's clever "stop-go" animation.

AIR FRANCE

The air transport industry is continuing to grow. The latest major international airline to emerge is Air France. It formed in August after the merger of four air transport companies and the purchase of Compagnie Générale Aéropostale.

JANUARY–JUNE

World Events	**JAN** The Spanish government authorizes martial law as revolutionary forces grow.	**MAR** F D Roosevelt is sworn in as the 32nd US president, declaring "The only thing we have to fear is fear itself".	**MAR** In Germany, the Enabling Act allows Hitler rather than the president to rule by decree.	**MAY** Women vote for the first time in South Africa; the results lead to a coalition between Hertzog and Smuts.
Entertainment	**JAN** René Clair's latest film *Quatorze Juillet (14 July)*, is released in Paris, France.	**MAR** Lloyd Bacon's US musical film *42nd Street* starring Ginger Rogers and Warner Baxter is released.	**JUN** Hollywood star Charlie Chaplin marries actress Paulette Goddard in a secret ceremony in Los Angeles, USA.	**JUN** Italian Primo Carnera defeats Jack Sharkey to win the world heavyweight boxing title in New York, USA.
Innovations	**FEB** The first speaking clock service opens in the Paris telephone area.	**APR** Four Britons make the first flight over Mount Everest in a Westland Wallace biplane.	**APR** Sir Frederick Henry Royce, co-founder of the UK motor-car company Rolls-Royce, dies.	**JUN** The first drive-in cinema, the Camden Automobile Theatre, opens in New Jersey, USA.

QUATORZE JUILLET

PRIMO CARNERA

1933

Dictator rules

22 MARCH

Portugal's new constitution, passed today, gives António de Oliveira Salazar's single-party government the right to suspend all individual civil liberties.

Champ again

8 JULY

In a thrilling final at the tennis championships at Wimbledon, in the UK, the reigning women's champion American Helen Wills Moody has beaten the popular British challenger Dorothy Round 6–4, 6–8, 6–3. For the crowd watching on a blazing hot summer day, the tension on Centre Court was almost unbearable. It is the sixth time in the last seven years that Helen Wills Moody has won this sought-after title.

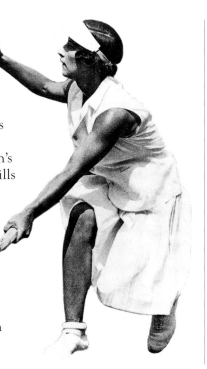

Dietrich sets trend for menswear

21 MAY

German film star Marlene Dietrich, who moved to Hollywood in 1931, has created a fashion sensation. She appears in a scene in the new Paramount movie *Morocco* wearing a man's top hat and tails. Even off the set the languid Marlene is frequently seen in men's trousers and suits, and arrived in France today wearing a brown suit, coat, beret, and red necktie. "I am at heart a gentleman," the film star said when interviewed. The Dietrich look – "Dietrickery" – has caught on and women are flocking to buy similar outfits.

Hollywood star Marlene Dietrich

JULY–DECEMBER

AUG Indian activist Mahatma Gandhi is released from a prison hospital in Poona, emaciated after a five-day hunger strike.

JUL The opera *Arabella* by Richard Strauss premieres in Germany.

RICHARD STRAUSS' OPERA ARABELLA

JUL US pilot Roscoe Turner flies from New York to Los Angeles in a record time of 11 hours 30 mins.

SEP The Shroud of Turin, a linen cloth believed to be the burial shroud of Jesus, is shown to a crowd of 25,000 people in Italy.

SEP Fred Perry is the first UK tennis player to win the US Open since 1903.

OCT The German post office opens the first "telex" service between Berlin and Hamburg.

OCT Hitler announces in Berlin that Germany is withdrawing from the League of Nations.

NOV In the USA, the film version of Louisa May Alcott's novel *Little Women* is released.

OCT More than 9,000 Arabs riot in protest against Jewish emigration to Palestine.

LITTLE WOMEN

DEC The USA says farewell to Prohibition, as Utah becomes the last state to ratify the 21st Amendment.

DEC Fred Astaire and Ginger Rogers star together in the US film *Flying Down to Rio*.

DEC Imperial Airways and Indian Trans-Continental start a London-Singapore service.

1934

Japan appoints Pu-Yi as puppet emperor

1 MARCH

Pu-Yi, once known as the boy emperor of China, has been installed as the puppet emperor of the Chinese province of Manchuria, conquered by the Japanese. He is the apparent ruler, but it is the Japanese who are actually in control of Manchuria and have re-named the Chinese province Manchukuo. Some spectacular celebrations have taken place in the capital city of Hsinking to mark the grand occasion. Lama priests and painted geishas mingled with medal-wearing soldiers and members of the Mongol cavalry, while delegations of Chinese nobles paid homage to their new emperor.

Pu-Yi, puppet emperor of Manchukuo

Italy triumphs

10 JUNE

In front of a beaming Benito Mussolini, the Italian football team snatched a late goal to beat Czechoslovakia 2–1 in the World Cup Final. The team was guided by their brilliant manager, Vittorio Pozzo.

"Nessie" rises

8 AUGUST

Public excitement at reported sightings of a monster in Loch Ness, Scotland, has increased since the publication of a remarkable photograph taken by a British surgeon. Can this really be "Nessie"?

The elusive monster?

Prison on Alcatraz

18 AUGUST

Alcatraz prison, built on a large rock in the middle of San Francisco Bay off the coast of California in the United States, opened today as a federal penitentiary. In the past the island has housed a giant fortress and a lighthouse that was specially built to guard San Francisco. Raised on the foundations of the fortress, the "escape-proof" prison will house only the most dangerous criminals.

JANUARY–JUNE

World Events	**FEB** French prime minister Edouard Daladier is forced to resign following two days of major riots in Paris.	**MAY** In Canada, Oliva and Elzire Dionne become the proud parents of the first set of quintuplets to survive birth.	**MAY** The US gangster couple Clyde Barrow and Bonnie Parker are shot dead by police in an ambush in Louisiana, USA.	**JUN** Hitler arrests and executes the leaders of the German Storm Troopers (SA) in the "Night of the Long Knives".
Entertainment	**FEB** Noel Coward's play *Conversation Piece* opens in London, UK.	**FEB** *It Happened One Night*, a comedy starring Clark Gable, is a box-office hit.	**JUN** Walt Disney's Donald Duck makes his first appearance in the cartoon *The Little Wise Hen*.	**JUN** US film thriller *The Thin Man*, based on Dashiel Hammett's best-selling novel, is released.
Innovations	**FEB** In Germany, Deutsche Lufthansa introduces the first transatlantic airmail service.	**DRIVING TESTS INTRODUCED** **MAR** The Automobile Association introduces the first voluntary driving tests in the UK.	**MAR** The first practical radar test is carried out by Dr Rudolph Kuhold in Germany.	**CAT'S-EYE ROAD STUDS** **APR** UK inventor Percy Shaw revolutionizes road safety with his cat's-eye road studs.

1934

MARY POPPINS
British author P L Travers has just published a novel about a "perfect" nanny who delights her young charges with her special brand of magic.

Audiences get a kick out of Ethel!

21 NOVEMBER
Anything Goes, a new musical comedy, opened at New York's Alvin Theatre in the United States today. The story by P G Wodehouse and Guy Bolton follows the romantic adventures of a group of passengers on board a luxury transatlantic liner. Ethel Merman and William Caxton excel in the leading roles, and the show features a wealth of irresistible lyrics and melodies composed by that maestro of US popular music, Cole Porter. The musical includes the catchy hit songs *You're the Top*, *All Through the Night*, and *I Get a Kick out of You*.

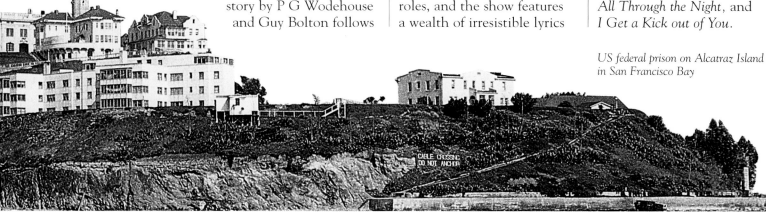

US federal prison on Alcatraz Island in San Francisco Bay

JULY–DECEMBER

JUL Chancellor Englebert Dollfuss is assassinated in an attempted Nazi coup in Austria.

JUL UK tennis players Fred Perry and Dorothy Round win the singles titles at Wimbledon, UK.

AUG In the UK, Elizabeth Cowell is the first woman to make a live television broadcast for the BBC.

CHANCELLOR DOLLFUSS

OCT In China, the First Front Army begins a "Long March" after breaking out of a nationalist blockade.

SEP German actress Marlene Dietrich plays Russia's Catherine the Great in the US film *The Scarlet Empress*.

AUG US explorers Barton and Beebe navigate a bathyscaphe to a record 3,028 ft (922 m) below sea level.

OCT King Alexander of Yugoslavia and French foreign minister Louis Barthou are assassinated by a Croatian nationalist in France.

NOV In Germany, Leni Rienfenstahl causes a sensation with her film-documentary *Triumph of the Will*.

AUG In the USA, Chrysler introduce the first car with a curved one-piece windscreen.

AVIATOR RAYMOND DELOTTE

DEC Secret trials begin in the USSR after the assassination of Josef Stalin's chief aide Sergei Kirov.

NOV Italian playwright Luigi Pirandello is awarded the Nobel Prize for Literature.

DEC French aviator Raymond Delotte sets a new speed record of 505 km/h (316 mph).

1935

Oscar for Shirley

27 FEBRUARY

A miniature Oscar has been awarded to seven-year-old actress Shirley Temple at the Academy Awards ceremony in Hollywood for her "outstanding contribution" to the movies. The singing and dancing

child star made her film debut three years ago in *Red-Haired Alibi*. Following her recent success in *Little Miss Marker*, this curly haired, dimple-cheeked cherub is now Hollywood's favourite star. "It is a splendid thing," commented President Roosevelt, "For 15 cents, an American can go to a movie and look at the smiling face of a baby and forget his troubles."

Shirley Temple curtsies to her fans

Lavish decor in station

Moscow metro

15 MAY

The Moscow metro began a regular service at 7am this morning. This new network is certainly the most impressive underground rail system in the world. Each of the 104 stations is decorated in a different style, many of them resembling palace halls with their marble panels, chandeliers, stained glass, and great wealth of paintings. The building of all these new stations was carried out under the direction of Nikita Khrushchev, the Communist Party chief.

TWIN DOLLS

Rag dolls are enjoying a new wave of popularity at the moment. These felt and velvet twins are manufactured by the Chad Valley toy company in the United Kingdom.

German Jews deprived

15 SEPTEMBER

Hitler's Nuremberg decrees have deprived 600,000 Jews of their German citizenship and banned them from a long list of jobs including teaching and journalism. Existing marriages between Jews and non-Jews have been rendered illegal and couples who will not divorce are subject to imprisonment.

Star symbolizes hatred of Jews

JANUARY–JUNE

World Events

FEB Turkish women win the vote and participate in a parliamentary election for the first time.

MAR King Prajadhipok of Siam gives up the throne to his nine-year-old nephew Ananda Mahidol.

MAY UK soldier and writer T E Lawrence (Lawrence of Arabia) dies after five days in a coma following a motorcycle crash.

JUN Bolivia and Paraguay sign an armistice to end their three-year dispute over the Chaco region.

Entertainment

JAN The USSR holds its first annual international film festival in Moscow.

MAR *Becky Sharpe* is the first film to use the "three strip" Technicolor method perfected by Herbert Kalmus.

APR The film *Les Misérables*, based on Victor Hugo's successful novel about the French Revolution, premieres in the USA.

JUN Alfred Hitchcock's new thriller, *The 39 Steps*, set in the Scottish Highlands, premieres in London, UK.

Innovations

JAN The first canned beer is introduced by Kreuger beer in New Jersey, USA.

PHYSICIST ROBERT WATSON-WATT

FEB Physicist Robert Watson-Watt builds the first practical radar equipment for detecting aircraft.

FEB Y-fronts manufactured by Cooper underwear go on sale in Chicago in the USA.

THE NORMANDIE

MAY France's luxurious liner, the *Normandie*, travels from Le Havre to New York on her maiden voyage.

1935

L'AFRICA
È IL
CONTINENTE
DI DOMANI

LAVORO PER L'EUROPA
RESA DALL'ASSE
PADRONA DEI SUOI DESTINI

Poster depicting Italy ploughing its way through the African continent

Italy invades Abyssinia

3 OCTOBER
The expected Italian invasion of the north African kingdom of Abyssinia has begun. After several months of border clashes, two armies from the Italian colonies of Eritrea and Italian Somaliland have advanced into Abyssinia. Emperor Haile Selassie's army of Abyssinian tribesmen, armed with spears and ancient muskets, stand no chance against the strength of the Italian troops supported as they are by tanks and bombers.

Mao's march ends

20 OCTOBER
After 12 long months of marching, fighting, and terrible suffering, the Chinese communist First Front Army, led by Mao Zedong, has reached relative safety in the Shaanxi Province. The communists began their 9,600-km (6,000-mile) journey across southwestern China when the nationalist government launched a fierce campaign against their bases in the Kiangsi Province. Although pursued by nationalist troops, the marchers' worst battles were with nature. Only 10,000 of the original 100,000 who set off survived the ordeal.

Mao Zedong, leader of the Chinese Communist Party

First flight of Hawker Hurricane

6 NOVEMBER
A new British fighter aircraft has made its maiden flight. It will be the first Royal Air Force (RAF) fighter with a top speed of over 480 km/h (300 mph) and the first to be armed with eight machine guns.

The Hawker Hurricane on its maiden flight

JULY–DECEMBER

AUG In the USA, the Social Security Act is passed, introducing welfare for the sick, old, and unemployed.

OCT George Gershwin's *Porgy and Bess*, the first all-black musical, opens in New York, USA.

JUL In the UK, the first paperback novel, *Ariel* by André Maurois, is published by Penguin Books.

PARKING METER

AUG Riots break out in the French cities of Paris, Le Havre, and Brest in protest over unemployment.

NOV Clark Gable stars as the dashing Fletcher Christian in the US film adventure *Mutiny on the Bounty*.

JUL The world's first 150 parking meters are installed in the streets of Oklahoma City, USA.

NOV Mackenzie King is appointed prime minister of Canada following the victory of the Liberal Party.

NOV The Marx Brothers star in their first US comedy film for MGM, *A Night at the Opera*.

JUL The first modern opinion poll, conducted on car ownership, is published in the USA.

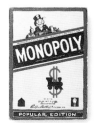

MONOPOLY GAME

NOV King George II of Greece is returned to the throne after spending 12 years in exile.

DEC Monopoly, a popular new board game, goes on sale in the USA, priced at $2.50.

NOV The US *New York Times* is the first newspaper to store back issues on microfilm.

ARCHITECTURE OF THE THIRTIES

THE BAUHAUS

THE 1930S WAS A DECADE of exciting changes in building design. Steel, glass, and reinforced concrete were used in new ways to create some remarkable constructions. Two distinct styles emerged. Art Deco, influenced by Egyptian, Aztec, and Chinese architecture featured striking geometric motifs to create a heightened sense of drama. Some of New York's most extravagant skyscrapers, such as the Chrysler Building and the Empire State Building, were designed in the Art Deco style. The International Style was much less ornate. It emerged from the German Bauhaus movement and relied upon clean, simple lines. The aim of the International Style architects was to create "machines for living" – buildings that were spacious, functional, and economical.

Le Corbusier

Charles-Édouard Jeanneret, known as Le Corbusier (French slang for "the crow"), was one of the greatest architects of the International Style.

International villa

Designed by Le Corbusier in 1931, the Villa Savoye in Poissy, France, is a perfect example of the International Style. It has a geometric shape, white concrete walls, a flat roof, and a long line of windows to give a sense of light and space inside. The whole building is supported by stilts, creating the impression that the villa is growing out of the landscape. Inside, concrete screens divide the living quarters and a ramp rises through the centre of the house to the terraces on the upper floor.

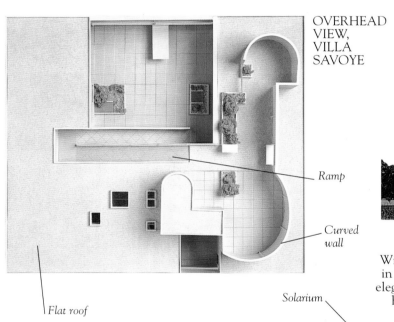

OVERHEAD VIEW, VILLA SAVOYE

Ramp

Curved wall

Flat roof

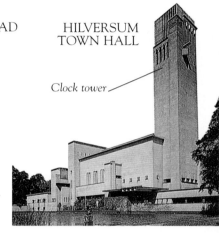

HILVERSUM TOWN HALL

Clock tower

Town hall

Willem Dudok designed this town hall in the Netherlands. Its plain walls and elegant windows show the influence on him of De Stijl ("The Style") artists.

Solarium

Cement rendered wall of lightweight slabs

Terrace

Sliding pane of glass

FRONT VIEW, VILLA SAVOYE

Garages on the ground floor

Reinforced concrete stilts support the structure

Ornate tower

The Chrysler Building in New York has been described as "a jewel" of the Art Deco period. Designed by the architect William Van Alen, it stands 319 m (1,047 ft) tall. Its elegant and cathedral-like exterior is ornately decorated with bold features like the eagle gargoyles on each corner of the sixty-first floor. The interior has lavish details such as lift doors elegantly inlaid with cherry wood and brass.

Sparkling stainless steel spire

Semi-circular sunbursts, a typical feature of Art Deco

Tower is made of white glazed brick

CHRYSLER BUILDING

CHRYSLER BUILDING SPIRE

Projecting eagle gargoyle

CHRYSLER BUILDING DETAIL

Clean living

In contrast to the cluttered rooms of the 1900s, interiors in the 1930s emphasized clean lines and new materials such as Bakelite.

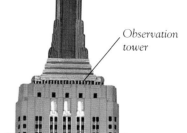

Skyscraper

By the 1930s construction techniques had greatly improved. Higher-grade steel girders and safer passenger lifts allowed architects to build higher and higher. When the 381-m (1,250-ft) Empire State Building was erected in New York in 1931 it was the tallest building in the world. It has 102 storeys, 73 lifts, and 1,860 steps. Its construction was so well planned that it only took a record 15 months to complete.

Scalloped masthead

Circular lantern

Observation tower

Light industry

The Hoover Building in London, UK, was designed by the firm Wallis, Gilbert & Partners. With its white walls, metal-framed windows, and stripped corners and cornices, it is considered to be one of the most distinguished examples of British Art Deco.

HOOVER BUILDING

Doorway detail

Elaborate tiling above the doorway of the Hoover Building is influenced by the buildings of ancient Egypt.

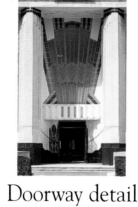

Windows are trimmed with aluminium and nickel

Limestone and granite facing

Fan-like decoration

SYDNEY HARBOUR BRIDGE

Masterpiece in design

Sydney Harbour Bridge, known for its characteristic shape on the Sydney skyline, is Australia's greatest engineering feat. At 1,650 m (5,413 ft) it is the longest single-span bridge in the world. It opened in March 1932, after nine years of construction.

Flat roof

Stepped cornice

Ground floor entrance

EMPIRE STATE BUILDING

1936

Machine mania

5 FEBRUARY

The film *Modern Times* throws Charlie Chaplin's famous tramp character into the modern world. The Tramp gets a job on an assembly line, causes chaos, and ends up in jail. The film pokes fun at the manic nature of factory life, but it also has a serious side, exposing the hardships encountered by factory workers. Chaplin intended to make *Modern Times* his first film with sound, but could not decide what voice to give the Tramp. In the end, all we hear is a strange little nonsense song.

A PEOPLE'S CAR

The first "people's car" is in the early stages of design in Germany, and Volkswagen expect to go into production soon. Hitler hopes that the car will put the nation on wheels and do for Germany what Ford did for the United States.

Germans enter the Rhineland

Local crowds salute the German troops as they march into the cities of the Rhineland

7 MARCH

At dawn today, in defiance of the Treaty of Versailles and on the orders of Adolf Hitler, German troops marched into the cities of the Rhineland. The region was lost by Germany to France at the end of World War I. Hitler's move was a gamble. because no-one knew how the French were going to react. Hitler's own generals advised him against taking such a risk and General Werner von Blomberg, minister of war, gave orders for the troops to be withdrawn the minute the French and British showed signs of response. French politicians want to take military action, but the generals are pleading for restraint. The British have told the French to do nothing until Hitler's action has been given "full consideration". No-one is calling Hitler's bluff. He has proposed a new treaty that guarantees peace for the next 25 years, and the British are taking this as evidence of peaceful intent. According to one newspaper, he has "merely re-occupied his own backyard".

JANUARY–JUNE

World Events	**JAN** The UK mourns the death of King George V, who is succeeded to the throne by Edward Prince of Wales.	**MAY** Sixteen-year-old Crown Prince Farouk, the eldest son of King Fuad, is proclaimed king of Egypt after his father's death.	**MAY** Italian fascist leader Mussolini claims the rebirth of an empire with the annexation of Abyssinia.	**JUN** Léon Blum, leader of the Socialist Party, wins the election to become prime minister of France.
Entertainment	**JAN** UK author and poet Rudyard Kipling dies at the age of 70.	**FEB** Charles Boyer and Danielle Darrieux star in the French film *Mayerling*, a tragic love story.	**APR** In the USA, baseball player Joe Di Maggio plays his first competitive game with the New York Yankees.	**MAY** US film stars Gary Cooper and Jean Arthur star in Frank Capra's thought-provoking comedy *Mr Deeds Goes to Town*.
Innovations	**JAN** German scientists Dr Jaeger and Dr Espig produce the first synthetic emerald.	**APR** In the UK, *Supermarine Spitfire I*, the RAF's new weapon, has its maiden flight.	**MAY** In Germany, Rudolph Opitz flies the twin-engined Messerschmitt *Bf 110* fighter for the first time.	**MAY** Gatwick, the first airport with covered walkways leading to the aircraft, opens in the UK.

MAYERLING

JOE DI MAGGIO

1936

The official poster of the Olympics

Sour Olympics

16 AUGUST

The Berlin Olympic Games closed today with a host of outstanding records set by athletes from 49 competing nations. However, this great sporting occasion has left a bitter taste in many people's mouths. Although the games were organized by Germany to a high standard, Hitler transformed the event into a gigantic propaganda exercise to glorify the Nazi regime. The games were awarded to Berlin before Hitler came to power. Once his dictatorial and racist policies became known, there were a number of moves, particularly in the

United States, to organize a boycott. The Nazi regime actively promotes the Aryan race – white people of non-Jewish descent. So, when the undisputed star of the Games was the US black athlete Jesse Owens, Hitler was so angry that he refused publicly to congratulate this fine young man. Owens won gold medals in two sprint events, the long jump – setting a staggering Olympic record of 8.06 m (26.4 ft) – and the relay. When the crowds rose to salute Owens on his final victory, Hitler could contain himself no longer and stormed out of the Olympic stadium in a furious rage.

Jesse Owens shatters the long jump world record

King quits for love

11 DECEMBER

Edward VIII has abdicated the throne of Britain. He is going to marry twice-divorced American Wallis Simpson against the advice of the British government and the Church of England. The king made his abdication speech from Windsor Castle in a radio broadcast that sent shock waves across a stunned nation. Although the king has many supporters in parliament and among the

press barons, there is an overwhelming feeling that the British people will not accept Mrs Simpson as their queen. The king will be succeeded by his younger brother Albert George.

The king and Mrs Simpson on holiday last summer in Yugoslavia

JULY–DECEMBER

JUL Civil war erupts in Spain when General Franco heads an army rebellion against the republican government.

JUL UK film tycoon J Arthur Rank establishes a Hollywood-style studio at Pinewood in London, UK.

JUL The giant German airship *Hindenburg* crosses the Atlantic in a record time of 46 hours.

CIVIL WAR IN SPAIN

AUG Soviet premier Stalin has 16 political opponents, two of them his former comrades, executed for treason.

AUG The BBC makes its first television broadcast from Alexandra Palace, London, in the UK.

SEP UK aviator Beryl Markham is the first woman to cross the Atlantic solo from east to west.

OCT In the UK, 200 unemployed men "march against starvation" on the Jarrow Crusade across England.

NOV Nadia Boulanger is the first woman to conduct the London Philharmonic Orchestra in the UK.

OCT The $120-million Hoover Dam opens on the Colorado River in the USA.

LIFE MAGAZINE

NOV In the USA, Roosevelt becomes the first president to win a second four-year-term since 1914.

NOV *Life*, a new photo-magazine featuring news and human interest stories, is launched in the USA.

OCT US airline Pan Am starts the first trans-pacific service from San Francisco to the Philippines.

1937

Margot's debut

Margot Fonteyn with stage mask

19 JANUARY

An 18-year-old ballerina has made a sensational debut in *Giselle* at Sadler's Wells theatre in London, Britain. Margot Fonteyn, whose real name is Peggy Hookham, will become the prima ballerina at Sadler's Wells, a post left vacant since the departure of Alicia Markova two years ago.

Fonteyn steps into Markova's shoes

Pride of Germany in flames

6 MAY

The airship *Hindenburg* exploded in a ball of flames today as it approached Lakehurst Field, New Jersey, in the United States, after a routine transatlantic flight from Frankfurt, Germany The ship was destroyed in less than a minute, and 35 of the 97 passengers and crew on board are dead. Since its maiden flight in 1936, the *Hindenburg* has become a symbol of Nazi Germany. It was the world's largest airship, longer than any battleship and capable of carrying 70 passengers across the Atlantic in luxury. The *Hindenburg*'s arrival at Lakehurst was delayed by a thunderstorm, and when it approached the landing tower, eyewitnesses saw a sudden flash on top of the airship. Within ten seconds the craft was ablaze. Sabotage is suspected but a more likely explanation is that, following the storm, static electricity in the air ignited hydrogen leaking from the craft's gasbags.

The cover of a German magazine shows the horrors of the explosion

George VI crowned

12 MAY

On the day that had originally been chosen for the coronation of Edward VIII, George VI and Queen Elizabeth were crowned in Westminster Abbey in London, Britain. A million well-wishers lined the streets to watch the procession, and millions more listened to the ceremony on their radios.

The new royal family

JANUARY–JUNE

World Events	**JAN** Major floods in the midwest of the USA leave millions homeless and destitute.	**JAN** Thirteen Bolshevik leaders are sentenced to death for conspiring with Trotsky to overthrow Stalin.	**APR** The German air force, fighting for Franco in the Spanish Civil War, carries out a massive air raid on the town of Guernica.	**JUN** Former king of the UK, Edward, Duke of Windsor, marries Wallis Simpson at the Château de Candé in France.
Entertainment	**APR** Rodgers and Hart's musical *Babes in Arms* opens in the USA.	**APR** Sabu, a former stable boy in India, stars in the film *Elephant Boy*.	**APR** US film studio Warner Brothers releases cartoon *Porky's Duck Hunt*, with Daffy Duck.	**MAY** US writer Margaret Mitchell wins the Pulitzer Prize for her best-selling novel *Gone With the Wind*.
Innovations	**JAN** Turk Sabiha Gokchen is the first woman to fly on a combat mission.	**JAN** UK aviator Jean Batten wins the Britannia Trophy following her solo flight from the UK to New Zealand.	**APR** UK engineer and ex-pilot Frank Whittle builds the first prototype jet engine.	**JUN** The first colour news photograph, of the *Hindenburg* in flames, is published in the USA.

ELEPHANT BOY

FRANK WHITTLE'S JET ENGINE

1937

Golden span

27 MAY

Some 200,000 people have crossed the Golden Gate Bridge today in celebration of one of the greatest engineering marvels to be built this century. The longest suspension bridge in the world spans 11 km (7 miles) across San Francisco Bay in the United States.

PARIS EXPOSITION

Funfairs, pavilions, and arcades are attracting millions of visitors to the Paris Expo in France. The monumental stone towers of Germany and the Soviet Union are proving to be the most popular structures.

Japan provokes war with China

7 JULY

War has broken out between China and Japan after Japanese troops on a military exercise in the state of Manchukuo opened fire on a Chinese patrol just outside the Chinese capital, Peking. The Japanese claim they were provoked, but it is probable that they set up the incident as an excuse to attack China.

A fairytale success

Snow White sings to the woodland animals

21 DECEMBER

Today is the premiere of Walt Disney's long-awaited *Snow White and the Seven Dwarfs*. Disney hit the road to fame and fortune back in 1928 with his Silly Symphony cartoons, starring the loveable Mickey Mouse. *Snow White and the Seven Dwarfs* is the first feature-length animation in three-strip Technicolor. The film is an enormous financial and artistic gamble for Disney. It cost a staggering $1.5 million to produce, and took a large team of artists and animators over four years to complete.

It is a musical fantasy based on the popular Brothers Grimm fairytale about Snow White, her friends the seven dwarfs, and an evil queen. As well as the extraordinary, new visual techniques, the film features some unforgettable songs including *Some Day My Prince Will Come*, *Whistle While You Work*, and *Hi-Ho, Hi-Ho, It's Off To Work We Go*, which are certain to be big hits with both young and old. Walt Disney plans to follow *Snow White* with more feature-length animations which he will base on other popular children's stories.

JULY–DECEMBER

JUL The UK government announces proposals to partition Palestine to end the conflict between Jews and Arabs.

JUL George Gershwin, composer of *Rhapsody in Blue*, dies in the USA from a brain tumour, aged 39.

JUL Nestlé introduce the Milky Bar, a white chocolate bar made from cocoa butter, milk, and sugar.

US COMPOSER GEORGE GERSHWIN

JUL Irish prime minister Éamon de Valera is re-elected for a second term with a majority of 69 seats.

SEP US singer Bessie Smith, known as the "empress of blues", dies in a car accident in Memphis, aged 43.

SEP In Germany, the first national prizes are awarded to Nazi artists and scientists.

JUL US aviator Amelia Earhart disappears over the Pacific on the last leg of her round-the-world flight.

NOV A play based on John Steinbeck's novel *Of Mice and Men* opens on Broadway, New York, USA.

OCT The first major car show opens at the new Earls Court Exhibition Centre in London, UK.

AVIATOR AMELIA EARHART

NOV In northern Spain, 6,000 republican forces surrender to General Franco's nationalist army at Gijon.

DEC The musical comedy *Me and My Girl* opens at the Victoria Palace theatre in London, UK.

NOV J Armand Bombardier designs the first snowmobile in Quebec, Canada.

THE SPANISH CIVIL WAR

IN 1931 THE SPANISH MONARCHY was overthrown and King Alfonso XIII went into exile. A republican government was elected which introduced socialist policies to limit the power of the wealthy ruling élite, the church, and the army. In 1936 the army rose up against the new government. General Francisco Franco emerged as the leader of the army rebels, who became known as the nationalists. In the bloody civil war that followed Franco received military aid from both Germany and Italy. The republicans were supported by the USSR and an International Brigade of volunteers from various countries. By the end of 1936 Franco's nationalists troops had seized almost half of Spain, but the war dragged on for another three years before the republican resistance finally collapsed.

General Franco

The nationalist leader General Franco was declared chief of the Spanish State in 1936. Although not a brilliant general, Franco was extremely ruthless and, supported by the fascists in Spain, Germany, and Italy, he eventually led the nationalists to victory.

Rebels with a cause

The republican forces were less well trained and equipped than the nationalists, who were mostly professional soldiers. The republican ranks were swelled by regiments of the International Brigade, an army of idealistic young Europeans and Americans who saw the Spanish Civil War as the first great struggle of democracy against fascism.

REPUBLICAN SOLDIERS

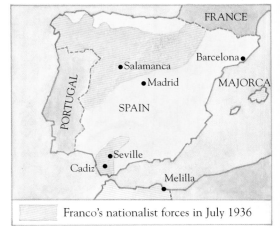

Franco's nationalist forces in July 1936

Nationalist-held territory

In the summer of 1936 the nationalists took over much of western Spain. They gradually overcame republican resistance by gaining control of most of Spain's coastline and cutting off their supply lines.

REPUBLICAN POLITICAL CARTOON

Taunting the enemy

This republican propaganda poster shows caricatures of Franco's main supporters: a fat bishop represents the church, and one of the generals who supported the nationalists is seen armed with a toy cannon. The monocled banker in the stern wears a swastika badge, symbol of Nazi Germany. He holds a bag of money which represents aid from Germany.

GERMAN JUNKERS AIRCRAFT OVER MADRID

Raid on Madrid

Germany and Italy supplied Franco with most of his air force. The German contingent was called the Condor Legion and operated from the nationalist-held island of Majorca, attacking republican strongholds like Madrid and Barcelona.

A country in ruins

After three years of bitter fighting, and the massacre of thousands of civilians by both sides, Spain was a devastated land. Industry and agriculture were in ruins and millions were on the verge of starvation. About 750,000 people died in the Spanish Civil War.

CHILDREN SIT IN THE RUINS OF MADRID

PISTOL USED BY REPUBLICAN FORCES

Detachable butt

Pistol can deliver a short burst of automatic fire

A writer's war

Many poets and writers were drawn to the struggle in Spain. The British writer George Orwell fought as a volunteer on the republican side. He wrote about his experiences in *Homage to Catalonia*, which paints a vivid picture of the grim conditions in the front line.

GEORGE ORWELL

Call to arms

This pistol is the kind of weapon that was used by the republican forces. They were never as well equipped as their nationalist opponents and were always short of ammunition. For them it was a war of ancient rifles and jamming machine guns. In one battle, artillery shells had to be rushed to the republican front line straight from the factory that made them. Their fighter aircraft were often too slow to catch the nationalist bombers that were carrying out air raids on republican-held cities.

Hollywood heroes

This scene from the movie *For Whom the Bell Tolls* (1943) shows a motley band of republican soldiers. The film was adapted from the best-selling novel by US writer Ernest Hemingway who covered the war as a journalist. His sympathies were strongly on the side of the republicans.

Picasso painting protests against war

On 26 April 1937 the German Condor Legion carried out a heavy bombing raid on the town of Guernica in the Basque region of Spain. The centre of the town was completely destroyed and nearly 1,700 people were killed. In his painting *Guernica*, Spanish artist Pablo Picasso depicted the agony and terror of the helpless citizens as the bombs fell around them.

1938

A celebration of French history

9 FEBRUARY

Director Jean Renoir has just released *La Marseillaise*, a remarkable documentary-style film telling the story of the French Revolution. Resisting the temptation to deal with the leading figures of the period, Renoir has instead chosen to contrast the lives of ordinary people and the aristocracy. The film follows the fortunes of a group of revolutionary volunteers who leave their humble homes in the city of Marseilles and march the long route to Paris in protest over the corrupt monarchy of Louis XVI.

Lise Delamare (centre) plays the French queen Marie Antoinette

Propaganda poster depicts Hitler as ruler of Austria

Hitler claims Austria

14 MARCH

Adolf Hitler has made Austria into a province of Germany. The Austrian-born dictator drove through the streets of Vienna, the capital city of his native land, in a spectacular procession led by tanks and field guns. Wearing the same brown uniform as his storm troopers, Hitler stood upright in his open car and gave the Nazi salute to the ecstatic crowds that came to greet him. Later in the evening Hitler appeared on his hotel balcony and proudly told the Austrian people, "The German nation will never again be rent apart."

New hero of Sherwood

12 MAY

Warner Brothers have just released *The Adventures of Robin Hood* starring Errol Flynn as the legendary hero of Sherwood Forest. The swashbuckling adventure has a superb cast, including Olivia de Havilland as the beautiful Maid Marian. The film is shot in three-strip Technicolor and cost a lavish $2 million to produce. It features some superb sets and boasts a record number of action stunts for a film, including Robin Hood's duel to the death with the hissable villain Sir Guy of Gisbourne.

JANUARY–MARCH

World Events	**JAN** Austrian psychiatrist Sigmund Freud moves to the UK after being persecuted by the Nazis.	**JAN** Mikhail Kalinin wins an election in the USSR to become president of the country's supreme ruling body.	**JAN** The dominion of Australia celebrates the 150th anniversary of European settlement.	**FEB** King Carol of Romania ousts the elected premier Octavian Goga and becomes dictator.
Entertainment	**JAN** US jazz musician Benny Goodman plays to a sell-out audience at Carnegie Hall.	**FEB** US child star Tommy Kelly stars in the film *The Adventures of Tom Sawyer*, based on Mark Twain's novel.	**MAR** In the UK, BBC radio broadcast the first comedy series *Bandwagon*, starring Arthur Askey.	**MAR** Cary Grant and Katharine Hepburn star in the US screwball film comedy, *Bringing Up Baby*.
Innovations	**FEB** US chemical company E I du Pont manufacture nylon bristles for toothbrushes.	**FEB** The first purpose-built air-raid shelter for the use of the general public is opened in the UK.	**FEB** UK engineer John Logie Baird demonstrates the first high-definition colour TV in the UK.	**MAR** Low-voltage fluorescent lights go on sale in major department stores in the USA, priced at $1.50 and $2.00.

PSYCHIATRIST SIGMUND FREUD

AUSTRALIAN KOALA BEARS

1938

Bombs keep falling

8 JUNE

For ten days and nights Japanese bombers have been mercilessly bombing the defenceless Chinese city of Canton. Thousands of people are dead and countless others injured. Entire areas of the city have been reduced to great piles of rubble. Air-raid warnings no longer work, and when the sound of a fresh swarm of the Japanese bombers is heard soldiers and police run through the streets shouting, "They are coming." There are so many false alarms that the city is being kept in a state of agonizing suspense. Power stations have been destroyed and there is no electricity, not even in the hospitals. The only light people have is that of the blazing oil refineries and the many fires burning all over the city. The Japanese have made it perfectly clear that they are determined to bomb Canton into submission. Nationalist leader General Chiang Kai-shek has no more fighters left to defend the city. Japan has control of most of China's coastline, as well as most of the major cities, railways, and large parts of China's interior, making it very difficult for China to receive weapons and ammunition. But still the brave people of Canton refuse to surrender.

Authorities search for survivors after a bombing raid

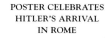

HITLER YOUTH

The spectacular Nuremberg Rally is held every September in Germany. It is the high point of the year for members of the Hitler Youth, who proudly show off their military-style training in front of their leader, the Führer.

Knockout!

22 JUNE

Joe Louis, the brilliant 24-year-old US boxer, has taken revenge on Max Schmeling, the reigning German champion. Schmeling knocked out the young Louis two years ago, but, at Yankee Stadium in New York City, Louis' amazing punching power demolished his challenger in the fourth round.

APRIL–JUNE

APR France's first socialist prime minister Léon Blum is forced to resign following the defeat of his radical budget.

APR *The Adventures of Marco Polo* is released in Hollywood, USA, with Gary Cooper in the title role.

APR US chemist Roy J Plunkett accidentally finds a new non-stick substance and calls it teflon.

POSTER CELEBRATES HITLER'S ARRIVAL IN ROME

MAY Adolf Hitler and Benito Mussolini meet in Rome, Italy, and pledge lasting friendship in a grand ceremony.

JUN US writer John P Marquand wins the Pulitzer Prize for fiction for his novel *The Late George Apley*.

APR New York is the first state to pass a law requiring medical tests for US marriage licences.

JUN US president Franklin D Roosevelt signs the Labor Standards Act introducing a minimum wage of 25 cents an hour.

JUN Italy wins its second consecutive football World Cup, by beating the Hungarians 4–2 in Paris, France.

APR Two US companies begin production of fluorescent lamps, available in seven colours.

CHANCELLOR KURT VON SCHUSCHNIGG

JUN Kurt von Schuschnigg, the last chancellor of pre-Nazi Austria is tried and sentenced for treason.

JUN *Action Comics* featuring a new action-hero called Superman is launched in New York, USA.

JUN The first television serial, a comedy called *Vine Street*, is broadcast in Los Angeles, USA.

1938

Mallard sets new world speed record

3 JULY

A British locomotive has set a new world speed record for steam engines of 203 km/h (127 mph). *Mallard*, a streamlined Gresley A4 Pacific, achieved the record while pulling a special train, including a speed-recording car, down a gradient on the main line between Grantham and Peterborough. British engineer Sir Nigel Gresley, who designed *Mallard*, was on board to record the speed. The locomotive maintained a speed of 193 km/h (121 mph) for over 8 km (5 miles), beating the previous British record – 183 km/h (114 mph) – set by *Coronation Scot*.

Mallard, the fastest locomotive in the world

Around the world in three days

14 JULY

The dashing multi-millionaire Howard Hughes has flown around the world in his specially built Lockheed 14 Electra. By keeping his stopovers to a minimum, Hughes circumnavigated the northern hemisphere in the remarkable time of three days, 19 hours, and 8 minutes – almost half the time it took fellow US pilot Wiley Post four years ago. After landing the plane in front of 25,000 cheering fans at New York's Floyd Bennet Field in the United States, Howard Hughes declared, "Any one of the airline pilots of this nation could have done the same thing."

"Peace for our time"

30 SEPTEMBER

There will be no war over Czechoslovakia. Germany, Britain, and France have agreed to give Hitler Czech Sudetenland at a conference held in Munich. They hope that by appeasing the Nazis war will be averted. Back in Britain today, Prime Minister Neville Chamberlain proudly told the nation, "I believe it is peace for our time."

Chamberlain displays new peace accord

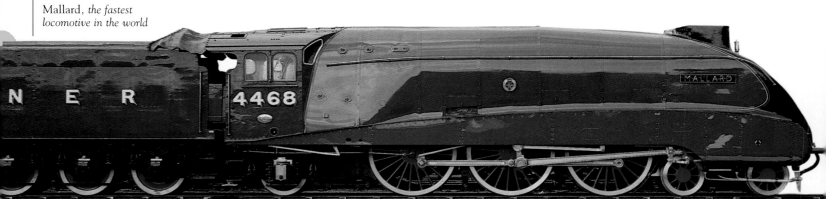

NER 4468   MALLARD

JULY–SEPTEMBER

World Events	AUG Celebrations are held in the Netherlands to mark Queen Wilhelmina's 40-year reign.	AUG Germans living in the Czech territory of the Sudetenland hold mass rallies demanding union with Germany.	JUL A peace treaty is agreed between Paraguay and Bolivia, ending their six-year dispute over claims to the Chaco region.	AUG German pilot Kurt Henke flies non-stop from Berlin, Germany, to New York, USA, in a record time of 24 hours 36 mins.
Entertainment	JUL US tennis player Helen Wills Moody wins her eighth Wimbledon singles victory.	JUL French actress Danielle Darrieux stars in her first US film *The Rage of Hollywood*, with Douglas Fairbanks Jr.	AUG UK cricketer Len Hutton scores a record 363 runs in a test match against Australia in London, UK.	SEP Alfred Hitchcock's latest mystery thriller, *The Lady Vanishes*, is released in the UK.
Innovations	JUL The first children's zoo opens in Regents Park, London, in the UK.	JUL The first experimental television transmissions are broadcast in the USSR.	AUG The UK's BBC transmit a feature-length film on TV, *The Student of Prague*, a German film with subtitles.	SEP Long-lasting nylon-bristled toothbrushes are marketed for the first time in the USA.

QUEEN WILHELMINA

KURT HENKE

1938

Awesome Orson causes hysteria

30 OCTOBER
Orson Welles, the talented 23-year-old actor and producer, has thrown the population of the United States into mass hysteria with his sensational radio broadcast of H G Wells' science fiction thriller, *The War of the Worlds*.

The radio play simulated a news broadcast, with bulletins and on-the-spot coverage of Martians "as high as skyscrapers" landing in New Jersey. It sounded so realistic that around one million listeners actually believed there was a Martian invasion. Welles claims to be astounded by the uproar. All this chaos certainly demonstrates the power of broadcasting.

Orson Wells broadcasts War of the Worlds *to the public*

Local residents laugh at the damage caused to Jewish shops

The night of broken glass

10 NOVEMBER
Last night, the German Jewish community was subjected to unprecedented violence. More than 7,000 Jewish-owned shops were broken into and looted, synagogues were burned to the ground, and hundreds of Jews were beaten in the streets. German propaganda minister Dr Josef Goebbels claims the violence was sparked by the assassination of a German diplomat by a Jewish student in Paris. But it is clear that the rampage of destruction was organized by the Nazi Party itself. Because of the piles of broken glass left lying in the streets after the looting of the shops, this tragic event is already being called "Kristallnacht," or "Crystal Night".

Fisherman discovers a "living fossil"

22 NOVEMBER
A fisherman made an extraordinary catch today. While fishing from his boat near the Comoros Islands, off the coast of east Africa, he reeled in a live coelacanth fish. Fossil coelacanths have been found in the past and dated back some 400 million years, but scientific experts were convinced the fish became extinct around 70 million years ago. Remarkably, the species has remained virtually unchanged from its original form. It is a bony fish with a distinctive fleshy three-lobed tail and flipper-like fins. It was Professor Smith, an ichthyologist from South Africa, who first identified the living coelacanth. He is offering a generous reward of £100 to anyone who can find a second living specimen.

Fossil coelacanth

The living coelacanth

OCTOBER–DECEMBER

OCT Czech president Edward Bënes resigns in protest over the German occupation of the Sudetenland.

NOV Eighteen synagogues are destroyed by Nazi firebomb attacks in Vienna, the capital city of Austria.

NOV Adolf Hitler decorates US aviator Charles Lindbergh with the German Service Cross.

DEC The UK government unveils the "National Register", stating what people will do in time of war.

SEP *The Corn Is Green*, a play about a Welsh pit boy who wins a place at university, opens in the UK.

OCT *Picture Post*, a new illustrated news magazine, is launched by Edward Hulton in the UK.

DEC Soviet film director Sergei Eisenstein produces *Alexander Nevsky*, his first film with sound.

DEC UK actor Leslie Howard stars in the film *Pygmalion*, based on G B Shaw's play.

OCT The first successful flexible drinking straw is designed by US entrepreneur Joseph Friedman.

PICTURE POST

OCT US physicist and lawyer Chester Carlson makes the first successful photocopy with his xerox machine.

DEC The first drink-driving test, the Drunkometer, is used by police in Indianapolis, US.

ALEXANDER NEVSKY

DEC Boeing's *Supermarine*, the first pressurized airliner, makes its maiden flight in the USA.

HIGH LIFE IN THE THIRTIES

IT IS EASY TO SEE THE 1930s as the decade of the Depression, with sweeping unemployment, the rise of the dictators, and the drift towards war, poverty, and homelessness. But for the more fortunate sectors of society, such as those born into money, and film and radio stars, it was an age of glamour, beauty, and style. Fashion changed dramatically, and new feminine styles were celebrated by challenging young designers such as Elsa Schiaparelli and Mainbocher (the favourite designer of the Duchess of Windsor). Hollywood too became enormously influential in setting styles – not only for women but also for men. Theatres and cinemas sprang up everywhere and people flocked to see musicals. If you could not live the lives of the rich and famous, you could read about them in one of the many new celebrity magazines that were becoming increasingly popular. Or you could pick up a newspaper to follow the leisurely pursuits of royalty and the aristocracy in the society columns.

An evening at the theatre

Theatre thrived in the 1930s. British stars Noel Coward and Gertrude Lawrence starred in several sparkling comedies, such as *Cavalcade* and *Private Lives*, which had a high society setting. Coward wrote the plays and the pencil-thin Lawrence dazzled audiences in her elegant costumes.

The golden age of the musical

Musicals experienced a golden age in the 1930s. US composers such as Irving Berlin, George Gershwin, and Cole Porter wrote the songs for a number of successful shows. Popular shows of the day, including the synchronized dance group the Rockettes, were staged at New York's lavish Radio City Music Hall in the USA. Situated in the Rockefeller Center, Radio City was the largest theatre in the world.

THE ROCKETTES PERFORMING AT RADIO CITY MUSIC HALL

Travelling in style

For the rich and famous the 1930s was the era of "grand routier", or "grand touring". In Europe, the wealthy drove their luxury cars to fashionable bathing spots such as Nice in the French Riviera. Magnificent cars including Mercedes, Lagondas, and Bentleys were often exclusively designed to meet their owners' particular requirements, with special fittings such as drinks cabinets. Wealthy female celebrities, including actress Marlene Dietrich, even went as far as to have their cars painted to match the colours of their favourite outfits.

Glamorous "gems"

Costume jewellery was considered a cheap imitation before French designer Coco Chanel transformed it into an art form. She poured scorn on people who bought gems simply to flaunt their wealth, and set about designing her own "fake" jewellery. Chanel made her fakes as stunning and sought-after as the real thing. Alongside slinky evening bags, costume jewellery became an essential fashion accessory to complement the elegant evening gowns of the 1930s.

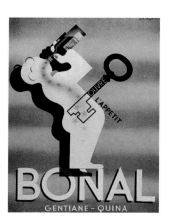

A new look

Commercial art and design flourished in the 1930s. Vast sums of money were spent on colourful and sophisticated advertisements to promote all kinds of products. This innovative poster by A M Cassandre is designed to promote a popular French alcoholic drink.

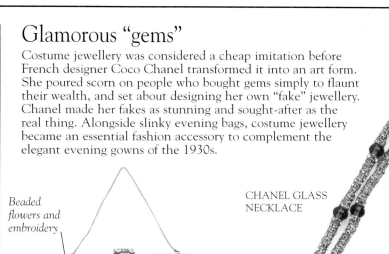

Beaded flowers and embroidery

Garden path design

CHANEL GLASS NECKLACE

Glass beads

EVENING BAG

Celebrity couple

Nowhere seemed more glamorous in the Thirties than Hollywood, the American film capital of the world. The sophisticated costumes worn by screen idols set fashion trends for women all over the world. The acting couple William Powell and Myrna Loy were considered to be among the most stylish in the business.

EVENING COAT WITH FUR TRIMMING

Haute couture

High fashion gradually changed from the boyish designs of the 1920s to a more feminine and elegant look in the 1930s. French designer Coco Chanel remained a popular choice, but she was challenged by Italian designer Elsa Schiaparelli. Famous for introducing "shocking pink" evening wear, Schiaparelli was influenced by the artist Salvador Dali.

EVENING DRESS BY ELSA SCHIAPARELLI

1939

Uranium atom split in half

German physicist Otto Hahn

28 JANUARY

German physicist Otto Hahn and his colleague Fritz Strassmann have made a discovery of great scientific potential. Through their experiments, the two men have discovered that when uranium atoms are bombarded with neutrons they split in half, releasing more neutrons, and producing huge amounts of energy. The released neutrons cause the uranium atoms to split, releasing more energy and more neutrons. Otto Hahn has called this continuing process "nuclear fission". His work raises the possibility of harnessing energy to build a weapon of colossal destructive power.

Hitler's troops march into Prague

Prague is invaded

15 MARCH

Adolf Hitler took the Czech Sudetenland six months ago – now he has swallowed up the rest of Czechoslovakia. Hitler entered Prague, the Czech capital, today, and installed himself in the Hradzin Castle, the ancient palace of the kings of Bohemia. The way the German army has been received by the people of Prague is, however, in striking contrast to the tremendous welcome given to them in the Sudetenland and in Austria. In Prague, the crowds wept and courageously sang the national anthem as they were forced to salute the Nazis.

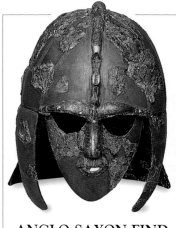

ANGLO-SAXON FIND
An Anglo-Saxon burial boat has been discovered during an archaeological dig at Sutton Hoo in Britain. The boat was filled with gold, silver, and weapons, and is the most significant find this century.

Western hero

22 MARCH

Since its release on 2 March, *Stagecoach* has attracted so many people to the box office that John Wayne, who has only appeared in low-budget films until now, has become an instant success.

JANUARY–MARCH

World Events	**JAN** The Irish Republican Army (IRA) begin a major bombing campaign aimed at cities in the UK.	**FEB** The UK government decide that Palestine should not become a Jewish state, but an independent Arab-Jewish state.	**MAR** In the Vatican City in Rome, Cardinal Eugenio Pacella is elected Pope Pius XII on his 63rd birthday.	**MAR** The Spanish Civil War ends as nationalist leader General Franco takes control of Madrid.
Entertainment	**JAN** W B Yeats, Irish poet, dramatist, and Nobel prize-winner, dies aged 73.	**FEB** US actor Spencer Tracy wins an Academy Award for Best Actor for his role as Father Flanagan in *Boys' Town*.	**MAR** In Durban, South Africa, a cricket test match against England is declared a draw after ten days.	**MAR** Hollywood film stars Clark Gable and Carole Lombard marry in Kingman, Arizona, USA.
Innovations	**JAN** Anderson air-raid shelters are erected by the inhabitants of Islington, London, UK.	**FEB** The first washing machine is demonstrated at the Industrial Fair held in London in the UK.	**MAR** The launch of instant coffee in the UK by Swiss company Nestlé is a huge hit with the public.	**MAR** The UK Interplanetary Society conclude a two-year study for landing men on the Moon.

IRISH POET W B YEATS

POPE PIUS XII

1939

Three-year-old inherits throne

4 APRIL

Iraq is in mourning following the sudden death of King Ghazi in a car crash. Officials in the country suspect a plot by the British, who still maintain important air bases in Iraq. King Ghazi has been succeeded by his son, three-year-old Amir Faisal. The boy's uncle, Amir Abdul Ilah, has been appointed regent, but the real power in Iraq lies in the hands of the reforming prime minister General Nuri.

Amir Faisal, the new king of Iraq

New York views the future

30 APRIL

At 3.12 pm today, President Franklin D Roosevelt opened the New York World Fair in the United States. Sixty nations and 1,300 businesses are exhibiting the latest in technological wonders. The most impressive structures are the Trylon, a 213-m (699-ft) tall tower, and the Perisphere, a 60-m (197-ft) giant sphere showing a futuristic film set in the year 2036.

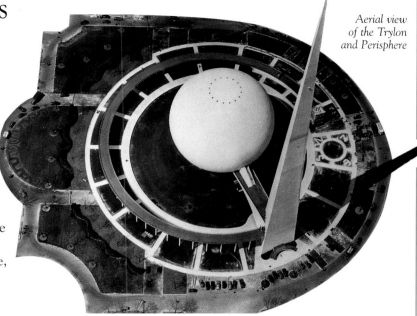

Aerial view of the Trylon and Perisphere

Across the Atlantic in style

The Boeing 314A Dixie Clipper flying boat

28 JUNE

The world's first scheduled transatlantic passenger flights began today when Pan America's Boeing 314A *Dixie Clipper* flying boat took off from Manhasset Bay at Port Washington in the United States. It is carrying 22 passengers to the city of Marseilles in southern France.

The first passengers have paid an amazing $675 for a roundtrip ticket on the 45-hour 52-minute flight, which includes a 22-hour stopover in the Azores in Spain. They are travelling in the lap of luxury – the flying boat is equipped with dining rooms and staterooms that are worthy of an ocean liner. This is the first air service to cross the Atlantic since the 1937 *Hindenburg* disaster killed 35 people and halted Germany's airship flights.

APRIL–JUNE

APR King Zog of Albania flees his country when Italian troops capture Tiranë, the capital city.

APR UK actor Laurence Olivier stars in the film *Wuthering Heights*, based on Emily Brontë's classic novel.

APR German aviator Fritz Wendel sets a new air speed record of 768 km/h (480 mph) in a Messerschmitt jet.

KING ZOG OF ALBANIA

APR At the New York World Fair in the USA, Franklin D Roosevelt is the first president to be televised.

APR US black contralto Marian Anderson sings in front of 75,000 people at the Lincoln Memorial, USA.

APR Swiss chemist Paul Hermann Müller confirms the bug-killing properties of the chemical DDT.

APR Adolf Hitler tears up the 1934 Anglo-German naval treaty and denounces the mutual assistance pact with Poland.

MAY Batman, created by 18-year-old US artist Bob Kane, makes his first appearance in *Detective Comics*.

APR Kodak introduces the first colour film at the New York World Fair in the USA.

MAY Robert Menzies, aged only 44, succeeds Joseph Lyons as the new prime minister of Australia.

MAY US baseball star Lou Gehrig retires after 2,130 consecutive games with the New York Yankees.

ROBERT MENZIES

MAY The first regular North Atlantic airmail service is inaugurated between the USA and Portugal.

1939

Jazz king is *In the Mood*

1 AUGUST

The rich saxophone sound of the Glenn Miller Band has scored a huge hit in the United States with its latest recording, the swinging riff tune, *In the Mood*. Thirty-five-year-old Miller is now established as one of the United States' most popular band leaders. He began his career in 1926 playing the trombone with Ben Pollack's band, before playing for others, most notably Tommy Dorsey and Ray Noble. His own group of musicians, the Glenn Miller Band, is famous for its popular orchestrated dance music. He achieves the distinctive sound by blending the playing of a clarinet with a quartet of saxophones.

Off to see the wizard!

17 AUGUST

Tonight is the Hollywood premiere of a new film, *The Wizard of Oz*, a magical $3 million Technicolor musical fantasy, starring a bright new actress, 17-year-old Judy Garland. The story follows the dream adventures of Dorothy (played by Garland), who is carried away by a twister to the magical land of the Munchkins, where she meets a scarecrow, a tin man, and a cowardly lion.

Dorothy meets the scarecrow on the yellow brick road

British children evacuate cities

Young evacuees arrive in the countryside

31 AUGUST

As the prospect of war with Germany draws nearer, one-and-a-half million British children are being evacuated out of large cities and into safer areas in the countryside or small towns which are less likely to be targets of air-raids. The children, who are being accompanied by their schoolteachers, are only allowed to carry one spare set of clothing and a gas mask. Buses have been taken off their usual routes to carry the children to train stations. Billeting officers are receiving the "townie" children and intoducing them to their new host families. But there are already some problems. Often, the evacuees are bewildered and unprepared for such new experiences. Many of them have never seen cows, sheep, or even fields before. Some have never slept in a bed, or learnt how to use a knife and fork. Some middle-class hosts are shocked by the unkempt and filthy condition of some of the children from city slums, and do not seem to know how to handle their charges.

JULY–SEPTEMBER

World Events JUL UK member of parliament Winston Churchill calls for a military alliance between the UK and the USSR.	AUG The USSR shocks the rest of Europe by signing a non-aggression pact with Germany.	SEP US president Franklin D Roosevelt announces that the USA will remain neutral in the European war.	SEP Stained-glass windows are removed from Notre Dame Cathedral for fear of air-raids in Paris, France.
Entertainment SEPT In the UK, the BBC TV service is suspended at the outbreak of war.	SEP UK actor Basil Rathbone stars as Sherlock Holmes in the film *The Hound of the Baskervilles*.	SEP In the UK, ENSA, an entertainment organization for the armed forces, is formed.	SEP US author John Steinbeck's outstanding novel *The Grapes of Wrath* is published in the USA.
Innovations AUG Airborne interception radar is installed in UK aircraft to locate the enemy.	**NAZI SOVIET PACT** AUG The first aeroplane powered by a jet engine, the Heinkel *He-178*, is demonstrated in Germany.	SEP UK company ICI starts the regular production of a new chemical material called polythene.	 **NOTRE DAME WINDOW** SEP The first game of American football is televised by NBC in New York in the USA.

1939

German tanks advance into Poland

Poland is invaded

1 SEPTEMBER

Hitler has invaded Poland. The invasion began when the Luftwaffe, the German air force, led by Junkers *Ju52* dive-bombers, launched a massive attack on Polish airfields, communication centres, and the entire railway system. Columns of fast-moving German tanks raced ahead of the Polish infantry cutting supply lines and spreading mass panic and terror. It is the first time the Germans have used their revolutionary "Blitzkrieg", or "lightning war", tactics that are aimed at taking the enemy by surprise.

War is declared

3 SEPTEMBER

At 11.15 this morning, the British prime minister Neville Chamberlain informed an anxious nation that Britain is at war with Germany. Yesterday the British government had issued Adolf Hitler with an ultimatum demanding he withdraw all German forces from Poland. Hitler failed to reply and, consequently Britain declared war. Some hours later, the French ultimatum ran out, and at 5 pm France also declared war. The Allies of 1914 find themselves once again united in a war against oppression. Only a few minutes after the prime minister's radio broadcast the first air-raid sirens wailed in London. It proved a false alarm, but it is a warning of the terrible destruction that may follow.

Finnish troops camouflaged in the snow

Winter war in Finland

30 NOVEMBER

The Soviet Union has invaded Finland. This comes after the Finns refused to surrender Karelia, an area of land bordering the outskirts of the Soviet city of Leningrad. Over a million Red Army soldiers have been deployed on a massive attack across the frozen waters that divide Finland from the Soviet Union. The Finns only have a handful of tanks and aircraft, but their ski patrols are well trained for warfare conducted in the snow. In contrast, the Red Army does not have the equipment to be able to function in the freezing Arctic temperatures.

OCTOBER–DECEMBER

OCT Over 150,000 UK troops are moved to France to strengthen the French troops against any German attack.

DEC *The Black Swan*, a new pirate film starring Tyrone Power, premieres in Hollywood, USA.

SEP Birds Eye introduce the first US pre-cooked frozen meals, chicken fricassée and steak.

GONE WITH THE WIND

NOV In Munich, Germany, Adolf Hitler narrowly escapes a bomb explosion that kills seven high-ranking Nazis.

DEC *Gone With the Wind*, the most eagerly awaited film of the year, is released in the USA.

DEC In the US General Electric launches the first refrigerator with a freezer compartment.

NOV Magnetic mines laid by German submarines sink 60,000 tons of UK shipping off the east coast of England.

DEC In London, UK, the Royal Opera House is turned into a dance-hall to entertain the public during blackouts.

DEC The first propeller torpedo boats are manufactured for the Finnish navy by Higgins Industries Inc in the USA.

NYLON STOCKINGS

DEC The German battleship *Graf Spee* is sunk in Montevideo, Uruguay, after a fierce battle with UK cruisers.

DEC *We'll Hang Out the Washing on the Siegfried Line* is the most popular hit song of the year in the UK.

DEC In the USA, nylon stockings go on sale for the first time, at a price of $1.15 a pair.

1940

Epic film wins nine Oscars

29 FEBRUARY

Producer David O Selznick's spectacular American Civil War epic *Gone With The Wind* has swept all before it at the Academy Awards ceremony in Los Angeles in the United States. The film won nine Oscars, including best picture. The warmest welcome of the night went to actress Hattie McDaniel, who won the Oscar for best supporting actress for her performance as Scarlett's faithful servant. She is the first black person to win an Academy Award. However, racial prejudice is still so strong in Hollywood that permission was needed for McDaniel to sit at David O Selznick's table during the Awards ceremony.

Hattie McDaniel with her Oscar for best supporting actress

Holland and Belgium invaded

10 MAY

Hitler's foreign minister Joachim von Ribbentrop today informed Dutch and Belgian envoys that German armed forces had crossed the borders of their countries. Holland and Belgium have been taken by surprise by the German invasion and are

Devastation left by the German forces as they travelled through France

expected to surrender any day, in spite of requests to the Allies for support. The vital Belgian fortress of Eben Emael has already fallen after a daring assault by German airborne troops, and German tanks are pouring through the forests of the Ardennes on France's border with Belgium. Following the Nazi invasion of Denmark and Norway on 9 April 1940, Hitler now appears intent on taking the Blitzkrieg, or "lightning war", to the Netherlands.

WURLITZER

In US cafes, bars, and restaurants jukeboxes like this ornate Wurlitzer are becoming increasingly popular. A coin in the slot will play any song the user chooses.

JANUARY–APRIL

World Events			
JAN Seventy people are dying every day, mainly from starvation, in the Warsaw Jewish ghetto in Poland.	JAN For the first time since 1918, the UK introduces food rationing. Butter, sugar, ham, and bacon are now in short supply.	FEB The five-year-old new Dalai Lama is installed as the fourteenth spiritual leader of the Tibetan Buddhists.	APR Six people are killed by the explosion of an Irish Republican Army (IRA) land mine at Dublin Castle in Ireland's capital.

Entertainment			
JAN The US film version of John Steinbeck's novel *The Grapes of Wrath* is a triumph.	FEB US cartoonists Joe Barbera and William Hanna create a new cat and mouse team, *Tom and Jerry*.	FEB Walt Disney releases *Pinocchio*, his second full-length US feature film, based on the Italian story by Collodi.	FEB US film stars Mae West and W C Fields star in the Hollywood comedy *My Little Chickadee*.

Innovations			
JAN A UK company makes an electrical cable that can detonate magnetic mines. **THE GRAPES OF WRATH**	MAR The UK passenger liner *Queen Elizabeth* completes her secret maiden voyage.	MAR A new census puts the population of the USA at 131 million, with the average age 28. **THE DALAI LAMA OF TIBET**	APR US explorer Richard Byrd's current expedition to Antarctica charts previously unknown areas.

1940

Allied forces flee Dunkirk

4 JUNE

The evacuation of Dunkirk, codenamed Operation Dynamo, is complete. The operation, launched on 26 May, was an emergency measure to rescue the Allied soldiers retreating from a powerful German advance. Following their invasion of Holland last month, the unstoppable German troops crossed the River Meuse and swept northward to the Channel, cutting off the British expeditionary force from their French allies. A week later the Germans had reached the Channel coast, and the Allies fled to the port of Dunkirk. There, under constant bombardment from German guns and aircraft, the warships of the British Royal Navy and an armada of "little ships" sailed by civilians have rescued nearly 300,000 British, French, and Belgian soldiers from the beaches. However, many men have been left behind facing certain death or captivity, and some 200 ships and their crews, including naval warships, have been lost.

Soldiers struggle to reach safety off the beach at Dunkirk

French forces surrender

22 JUNE

France has surrendered to Germany. Today, at the town of Compiègne, the French delegation has agreed to cease fighting. Adolf Hitler forced them to sign the armistice in the same railway carriage in which the Germans surrendered in November 1918 at the end of World War I. In front of news cameras, the German dictator danced a jig. After the guns fell silent around Dunkirk, French resistance quickly collapsed, and, on 14 June, German troops marched into Paris. Only days later the French government fled south to Bordeaux. The Nazi swastika flag now flies from the Eiffel Tower in the capital city of Paris and the northern half of France faces an uncertain future under German occupation.

MAY–AUGUST

MAY Following Neville Chamberlain's resignation, Winston Churchill becomes the UK's prime minister.

MAY UK fascist leader Sir Oswald Mosley is interned under a new law allowing for the arrest of "suspected persons".

JUN General Charles de Gaulle broadcasts to France via the UK's BBC, "The flame of the French Resistance must not go out."

AUG Exiled Bolshevik leader Leon Trotsky is assassinated with an ice pick by Ramon Mercader in Mexico City.

JUN Paul Klee, German artist and teacher at the influential Bauhaus school, dies aged 61.

JUL In the UK, artists Stanley Spencer and Paul Nash are officially appointed to record the events of the war.

JUL The UK government advises women to conserve wood by choosing flat-heeled shoes instead of high heels.

AUG US star Bing Crosby's new country and western record *San Antonio Rose* is a massive hit.

MAY The first automatic swing doors are installed in a New York restaurant in the USA.

WINSTON CHURCHILL

JUN UK scientists discover that German bombers are guided to their targets by following radio beams.

JUL German scientist Albert Einstein states that no theory can provides a logical basis for physics.

CHARLES DE GAULLE

AUG Penicillin is developed for medical use at Radcliffe Infirmary, Oxford, in the UK.

1940

German air-raids in "Battle of Britain"

7 SEPTEMBER

Britain's capital city has experienced its first major air raid since the Battle of Britain began on 10 July. Hundreds of the German bombers, escorted by deadly swarms of fighters, left their French bases and arrived over London very early this morning. The heaviest attacks were suffered by the docklands of London's East End and the fighter airfields in the Thames Valley. Unknown to the Germans, the Royal Air Force (RAF) had advance warning that the Luftwaffe (the German airforce) were fast approaching because of the radar system that has been in operation throughout the war. According to a spokesperson at the air ministry, the Luftwaffe has lost 99 planes in this raid, and the RAF only 22. In July, Hermann Goering, commander of the Luftwaffe, sent German planes to attack British ports and shipping in the Channel, the narrow band of sea between England and France. In August, Goering switched his strategy and daily sent 1,000 planes across the Channel to bomb RAF bases and British radar installations. The attacks today suggest that for all Goering's boasts and tactical changes, he has failed to soften British defences and bring the country to its knees.

German fighter plane approaches the white cliffs of Dover on the southern coast of Britain

Boys find ancient treasure trove

12 SEPTEMBER

Four French schoolboys have discovered a cave full of prehistoric paintings. While out hunting rabbits near a village in the Dordogne their

dog disappeared down a hole. Climbing down after it, the boys found a cave with walls covered by magnificent paintings of animal hunting scenes. One wall showed a bison and a rhinoceros, on another there was a beautiful unicorn-like creature.

Some of the animals pictured are now extinct or no longer native to Europe. Archaeologists have dated the paintings to around 15,000–13,000 BC.

SEPTEMBER–DECEMBER

World Events	**SEP** Japan signs a ten-year military pact, allying itself with both Germany and Italy.	**SEP** The "Dig for Victory" campaign is introduced in the UK to encourage families to grow their own vegetables.	**NOV** US president Franklin D Roosevelt is re-elected for a third term in a landslide victory.	**NOV** The Germans bomb the UK city of Coventry, destroying the cathedral and killing 568 people.
Entertainment	**OCT** Princess Elizabeth makes her first radio broadcast to child evacuees in the UK.	**OCT** The first "Smellie" feature film with flower and food odours is shown in New York, USA.	**NOV** Walt Disney's new musical animation film *Fantasia* is released in Hollywood, USA.	**DEC** Charlie Chaplin's satirical comedy about Hitler, *The Great Dictator*, is released in the USA.
Innovations	**OCT** The US army carries out its first experiments with night photography.	**OCT** Motorized bicycles are used for the first time by women in the UK forces.	**OCT** Engineer Karl Pabst designs the first lightweight military-style Jeep for use by the US army.	**DEC** In the USA, Colonel Sanders formulates his special recipe for Kentucky Fried Chicken.

PRINCESS ELIZABETH AND PRINCESS MARGARET

THE GREAT DICTATOR

1941

General Erwin Rommel

Balkans surrender

27 APRIL

The Nazi swastika flag is flying on the Parthenon, the famous ancient temple that overlooks the Greek capital, Athens. Greece was forced to surrender to the German army on 21 April. The British soldiers who were garrisoned around Athens fought a slow retreat, covered by Greek infantry, to a point on the coast south of Athens where they were able to evacuate their army by sea. Yugoslavia has also surrendered to the German Blitzkrieg. The German invasion of Yugoslavia followed the overthrow of the pro-Nazi government of Prince Paul of Yugoslavia on 27 March. The Yugoslav armed forces were poorly armed and bitterly divided, and were able to offer little resistance to the far superior force of the German army.

AIR RAID SAFETY

It is the job of British air raid wardens to make sure that people are safe during an air raid. They wear special uniforms with a blue helmet so that they can be easily recognized. The wardens help rescue teams and firefighters.

Rommel arrives in Tripoli

12 FEBRUARY

The British army in north Africa has a new force to reckon with. German troops have arrived in Tripoli, Libya, to reinforce their Italian allies, who have suffered a series of defeats at the hands of the British. In command of the German force, known as the Afrika Korps, is General Erwin Rommel, a formidable leader who made a name for himself last year at the head of a tank division during the occupation of France.

Artist's impression of German dive bombers flying over the city of Athens

JANUARY–APRIL

JAN The Italian-held port of Tobruk in Libya falls to triumphant UK and Australian troops.

JAN Irish writer James Joyce, author of *Ulysses* and *Finnegan's Wake*, dies in Switzerland aged 58.

JAN The first aeroplane ejection seat is tested in the German Heinkel *He 280* jet fighter.

JAMES JOYCE

MAR US president Franklin D Roosevelt signs the Lend Lease Act, a programme promising aid to the Allies.

JAN Tamara Lobora of the USSR becomes the first woman camera operator to shoot a feature film.

FEB In the UK the Royal Air Force (RAF) establishes the first air-sea rescue team.

MAR In the UK, war work becomes compulsory for all women without young children aged 16 to 49.

FEB *Mother Courage and her Children* by German playwright Bertolt Brecht opens in Switzerland.

FEB In the UK, a policeman suffering from septicemia is cured by the new drug penicillin.

MAR Bulgarian prime minister Bogdan Philoff signs the Tripartite Pact, allying Bulgaria with Germany and Italy.

MAR US film *The Thief of Baghdad*, an Arabian Nights story with amazing special effects, is released.

PRIME MINISTER BOGDAN PHILOFF

APR The first playgroup for pre-school children is opened in Wellington, New Zealand.

1941

London blitzed by German bombers

St Paul's Cathedral has survived the raid

10 MAY

Bombers of the German air force last night launched a massive raid on London, Britain. In just a few hours, 550 German planes dropped hundreds of high-explosive bombs, starting over 2,000 fires and killing 1,436 people.

Many streets are impassable in the centre of the city and much of historic London has been destroyed. Other British cities have been heavily bombed in recent months but none has suffered such extensive damage and loss of life as London did last night.

"Unsinkable" ship is sunk

27 MAY

Germany claimed that her newest and fastest battleship, the *Bismarck*, was unsinkable. But the ship now lies at the bottom of the Atlantic after a merciless pounding by the British Royal Navy. The attack was prompted by the *Bismarck's* sinking of British ship HMS *Hood*.

Germans invade

22 JUNE

Hitler has broken Germany's non-aggression pact with Stalin and invaded the Soviet Union. In an operation codenamed Barbarossa, a massive onslaught by the German army began at dawn this morning. It has caught the USSR unawares. Already, on this first day of fighting, over 1,800 Soviet aircraft have been destroyed. It seems that the Germans are trying to achieve another Blitzkrieg victory, but the sheer size of the Soviet Union may make this impossible.

MAY–AUGUST

World Events	**MAY** Hitler's deputy Rudolf Hess crashlands in Scotland with an "important message".	**MAY** Major fascist strongholds in Italian-controlled east Africa surrender to UK troops.	**AUG** Churchill and Roosevelt agree the Atlantic Charter, an alliance between the UK and the USA.	**AUG** Soviet leader Joseph Stalin orders the destruction of a giant dam in order to hinder the Nazi advance.
Entertainment	**MAY** US premiere of Orson Welles' cinematic masterpiece *Citizen Kane*.	**MAY** US boxer Joe Louis successfully defends his world title for the seventeenth time.	**JUL** The BBC launches the UK's "V for Victory" campaign throughout Europe.	**AUG** Rabindranath Tagore, Nobel prize-winning Indian writer, dies aged 80.
Innovations	**MAY** Scientists develop the synthetic polyester fabric Terylene in the UK.	**MAY** The UK's Gloster E28/39, a top secret aircraft powered by a jet engine, makes its first flight.	**JUL** The first commercial TV broadcasting begins in the USA, with NBC and CBS competing.	**AUG** A company in Germany manufactures portable writing boards called clipboards.

CITIZEN KANE

ROOSEVELT AND CHURCHILL

1941

Winter slows Nazi advance

21 NOVEMBER

The German advance in the Soviet Union is starting to slow down. After many easy victories the German army is now approaching the Soviet capital, Moscow. But the Germans have found a new enemy – the savage Russian winter. Most of their soldiers are without winter clothing, and the engines in their trucks and tanks are freezing up. Meanwhile, the Soviets are receiving reinforcements of fresh troops from Siberia, better equipped to fight in the Arctic conditions.

German soldiers

Japanese attack Pearl Harbor

7 DECEMBER

Japan has made a devastating and unprovoked attack on the United States. Just before 8 am this morning about 360 Japanese aircraft burst through low cloud over the US Pacific fleet base at Pearl Harbor in Hawaii. It was the deadly beginning of a surprise strike that has crippled the US Pacific fleet. The Japanese fighters, dive-bombers, and torpedo-bombers were launched from a task force of aircraft carriers that had sailed in great secrecy to within 483 km (300 miles) of Pearl Harbor. The base was defenceless, its battleships riding at anchor, its aircraft parked wingtip to wingtip on the runways, and ammunition locked away. In less than two hours, eight of the US Pacific fleet's battleships had been either sunk or disabled and more than 2,400 people had been killed. Luckily for the United States, however, two aircraft carriers were not in the harbour at the time of the attack, and escaped damage.

SEPTEMBER–DECEMBER

SEP Mohammed Reza Pavlevi is the new 21-year-old shah of Iran. He promises to be a "completely constitutional monarch".

SEP US director John Huston makes an impressive debut with *The Maltese Falcon*, starring Humphrey Bogart.

OCT The first UK commercial flying-boat service begins operating from the UK to Cairo, Egypt.

AEROSOL CAN

SEP All Jews in Germany over the age of six are required to wear the Star of David in public as a "mark of shame".

OCT *Dumbo*, Walt Disney's lively animated film about a flying elephant, premieres in New York, USA.

OCT The world's first aerosol can, containing insect spray, is patented in the USA by Goodhue and Sullivan.

DEC Following the Japanese attack on Pearl Harbor, the USA and the UK both declare war on Japan.

NOV Repairs to the USA's famous presidents at Mount Rushmore are completed.

DEC The first Japanese merchant ship of the war is sunk by an US navy submarine.

RUSHMORE FACELIFT

DEC Italy and Germany declare war on the USA; President Roosevelt responds by declaring war on Italy and Germany.

NOV UK director Alfred Hitchcock's film *Suspicion* premieres in the USA.

DEC A Japanese fighter plane with a liquid-cooled engine makes its first flight.

HOME FRONTS

WORLD WAR II was fought not only on the battlefields but also on the home front. By 1943 a walk down any European city street was full of the reminders of war: men and women in their uniforms, bomb damage from air raids, gas masks, food shortages, and long queues. Posters urged the young and old to help in the war effort. Everything from scraps of iron for planes to leftover bones for glue was saved and recycled. Thousands of children were evacuated from cities to the countryside. Their teachers went with them, so that the children's education would not be interrupted.

FIRE SERVICE BADGE

Inflatable shelter

This cigarette card depicts a French-designed inflatable balloon shelter for protection in poison gas raids. This was one of many ingenious precautions that never actually went into mass production.

FAMILY LISTENING TO RADIO

Fire from the sky

The incendiary bomb was designed to set buildings ablaze during an air raid by generating intense heat. During a big attack, thousands of these bombs were dropped on cities, causing furious fires. It was vital that such incendiary bombs were dealt with as quickly as possible. This was the job of firefighters and wardens.

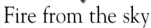
KILO MAGNESIUM (ELECTRON) INCENDIARY BOMB

Wartime radio

Radio audiences reached a peak in the war years. Families kept in touch with the daily progress of the war by listening to the news, but they also relied on the radio for entertainment. Comedy, drama, and children's programmes all helped to keep up people's spirits.

HARVESTING VEGETABLES IN A CATHEDRAL SQUARE, LENINGRAD (PETROGRAD), USSR

Harvesting food

During the war, blockades all over Europe and the rest of the world resulted in major food shortages. Everyone with a garden or an allotment was encouraged to grow vegetables and other crops. Fields and parks were dug up and turned into vegetable gardens to help supplement daily diets.

Eggs in tins

Eggs, like most other foodstuffs, were rationed. Some people kept a chicken coop in their garden, but most had to make do with dried eggs, which had the same nutritional value as fresh eggs but certainly did not taste as good.

Business as usual

Between 1940 and 1941, Hitler carried out a sustained bombing campaign against Britain known as the Blitz. Despite severe bomb damage, most people continued their normal daily routine.

DELIVERING MILK DURING THE BLITZ

Gas mask made of rubber

Head strap

War games

There were many war-related toys manufactured during the war to pass long evenings in the blackout, when windows were covered to stop enemy aircraft spotting a light. The aim of this particular game is to be the first to reach Berlin to assassinate Adolf Hitler.

RAFIE'S ROLLICKING TRIP To BERLIN

GET THE RAFIE TO BERLIN

Eye piece

"MICKEY MOUSE" GAS MASK

Masked

Over 38 million gas masks, some of them Mickey Mouse ones for children, were issued to the British public before war broke out. But the expected gas attacks never happened.

SCHOOL GAS MASK DRILL

Label states evacuee's destination

Air filter

Living in fear

All over Europe, families were broken up by the war. In Britain, two million children were sent to the countryside, and some were even sent overseas to Canada and Australia. In Germany, many children were evacuated in 1942 when Allied bombing increased. Some evacuees enjoyed being in the countryside, but most wanted to return home, preferring the bombs to being separated from their families.

133

1942

Yanks in UK

26 JANUARY
The first US GIs (so-called because their equipment is labelled Government Issue) have arrived in Britain. They came ashore at Belfast in Northern Ireland, where they received a warm welcome from the local residents.

Japanese tanks advance through Singapore

Singapore falls swiftly to Japan

15 FEBRUARY
The great naval base of Singapore has fallen to Japan. The island, which lies off the southern tip of the British colony of Malaya, was heavily fortified against a naval attack, but the Japanese bombarded the island from the land. Around 138,000 Allied troops have been captured by the Japanese. The fall of Singapore has deprived the Allies of their only major dry dock between Durban in South Africa and Pearl Harbor in Hawaii. In a radio broadcast to the British nation last night, Prime Minister Winston Churchill described the loss as "a heavy and far-reaching military defeat".

Yanks round up Japanese

31 MAY
Following the Japanese attack on Pearl Harbor, the US government has rounded up all citizens of Japanese descent living in the United States and sent them to detention camps in the deserts of the west. There are no criminal charges against these people, but their guards have strict instructions to shoot anybody who tries to escape.

Battle of Midway

6 JUNE
The Japanese have suffered their first major defeat in a naval battle off Midway Island in the Pacific. The US fleet used a special code-breaking machine to break the Japanese naval code and so intercept a top-secret message. This gave them advance warning of a plan to bomb Midway Island. As the Japanese attacked the island with dive-bombers the US fleet in turn launched a surprise naval attack on the Japanese fleet sinking four of its aircraft carriers.

JANUARY–JUNE

World Events	**APR** The people of Malta are awarded the UK George Cross for enduring German bombing.	**JUN** SS deputy chief Reinhard Heydrich, "the butcher of Moravia", is assassinated in Czechoslovakia by Resistance agents.	**JUN** Major General Dwight Eisenhower is given command of all US forces in Europe from headquarters in the UK.	**JUN** In France, all Jews over the age of six are ordered to wear the Star of David on their clothes at all times.
Entertainment	**JAN** US film star Carole Lombard is killed in a TWA airliner crash near Las Vegas, USA.	**FEB** US bandleader Glenn Miller's song *Chatanooga Choo Choo* sells one million copies and wins a gold disc.	**APR** Spencer Tracy and Katharine Hepburn star in the US film comedy *Woman of the Year*.	**MAY** US athlete Cornelius Warmerdam sets a record for the pole vault of 4.78 m (15.7 ft).
Innovations	**MAR** The BBC broadcasts a daily Morse code news bulletin to the French Resistance. **GEORGE CROSS**	**APR** The first T-shirts are manufactured for sailors serving in the US navy.	**JUN** Nylon parachutes are used for the first time in Hertford, in the UK. **DWIGHT EISENHOWER**	**JUN** The Co-operative Society of Romford launches the first UK self-service grocery store.

1942

Dieppe disaster

19 AUGUST

A reconnaissance raid on the German-held seaport of Dieppe in northern France has ended in disaster for the Allies. Several thousand UK, US, Canadian, and Free French troops landed on the beaches, but the Germans were waiting for them. Over 3,000 soldiers, mostly Canadians, lost their lives.

Victory for Monty at El Alamein

4 NOVEMBER

The British Eighth Army, led by flamboyant commander General Montgomery, today succeeded in halting the German Afrika Corps at El Alamein outside Cairo in Egypt. Throughout the summer Montgomery has assembled 230,000 soldiers and equipped them with the latest US tanks. On 23 October the British artillery opened fire with the heaviest barrage the African continent has ever known, bringing Italian and German troops to a standstill. Erwin Rommel, commander of the Afrika Corps, was on sick leave when the battle broke out. He rushed back to find the Eighth Army smashing defences, destroying tanks, and taking prisoners.

Sinatra's debut

30 DECEMBER

New York's Paramount Theatre has witnessed the birth of a new singing sensation – the young star Frank Sinatra. The 27-year-old has the potential to become one of the United States' most popular crooners.

WAR DOLL
Vogue Dolls have issued this figure in the USA to mark the formation of Women Accepted for Volunteer Emergency Services. The new recruits will perform non-combat duties!

JULY–DECEMBER

JUL The German Sixth Army launches an assault on the city of Stalingrad in the USSR.

JUL US actor James Cagney stars in the patriotic musical film comedy *Yankee Doodle Dandy*.

JUL The first jet fighter, the German Messerschmitt *Me 262*, makes its maiden flight.

IRVING BERLIN

JUL A death camp at Treblinka, to be used for the mass murder of the Jewish people, is opened by the Germans in Poland.

JUL Irving Berlin's musical *This is the Army* opens at the Broadway Theatre in New York, USA.

JUL The Oxford Committee for Famine Relief (OXFAM) is founded by Gilbert Murray in the UK.

NOV Operation Torch gets underway as General Eisenhower leads the Allied landings in Morocco and Algeria.

NOV *Stars and Stripes*, a daily paper for US GIs in Europe, is first published in the UK.

OCT The *XP-59* turbojet aircraft is successfully tested in the air for the first time in the USA.

WILLIAM BEVERIDGE

DEC The Beveridge Report, a blueprint for UK postwar social security by Sir William Beveridge, is made public.

DEC US singer Bing Crosby has a big hit with the timely song *White Christmas*.

DEC Physicist Enrico Fermi conducts a sustained nuclear chain reaction test in the USA.

1943

Play it, Sam

14 JANUARY

As Allied leaders meet for a conference in the north African city of Casablanca, movie-goers are flocking to see *Casablanca*, Warner studio's romantic war drama starring Humphrey Bogart as Rick and Ingrid Bergman as the unforgettable Ilsa.

A LITTLE PRINCE

French pilot and author Antoine de Saint-Exupéry has written a delightful story called *The Little Prince*. It tells the tale of a pilot who accidentally lands in a desert, where he meets a charming little boy from outer space. The inspiration for the book grew out of the author's own experience when he crashed in the Libyan desert while attempting to set a new flying record.

German army surrenders at Stalingrad

31 JANUARY

Amid the savage snows of the Soviet winter, the German Sixth Army has suffered a shattering defeat at the hands of the Soviet Red Army in Stalingrad. Commanded by Field Marshal Paulus, the German army has been suffering heavy losses since fighting first broke out last August. The German army reached Stalingrad last September, but by November the Soviets had closed in on them. Field Marshal Paulus twice rejected a surrender ultimatum from the Soviets although his position was hopeless. Finally, when he was on the point of giving way, Hitler himself refused to grant the order for evacuation and instead instructed his army to "hold their positions to the last man". This they tried to do, and it cost in total the lives of 300,000 German troops as well as 450,000 of their Italian and Romanian allies. A further 108,000 Germans have been captured and marched off to prison camps.

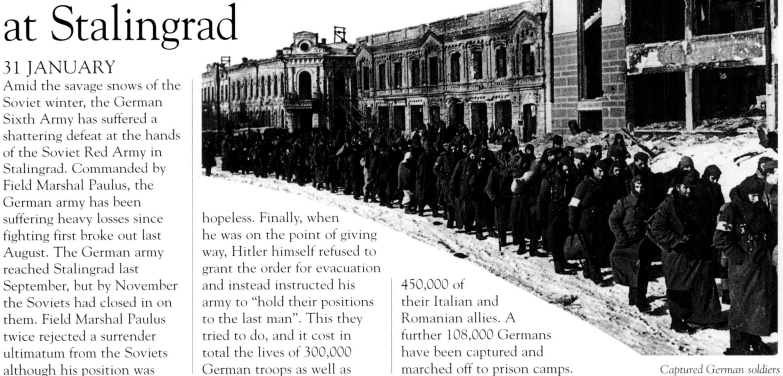

Captured German soldiers

	JANUARY–MARCH		
World Events	**JAN** Allied troops take Tripoli, the last remaining Italian-held city in Libya.	**JAN** UK RAF Mosquito bombers launch the first two daylight raids on Germany's capital Berlin.	**FEB** Indian social reformer Mahatma Gandhi begins a 21-day hunger strike in protest over his imprisonment in Poona.	**MAR** In Frankfurt, Germany, several key bridges along the River Oder are destroyed by saboteurs.
Entertainment	**MAR** *Mrs Miniver* wins an Academy Award for best film in Hollywood, USA.	**MAR** The musical *Oklahoma!*, set in the US midwest, opens at the St James' Theatre in New York, USA.	**MAR** The fantasy adventure film *Baron Münchhausen* opens in Berlin, Germany, after three years in production.	**MAR** Soviet composer Sergei Rachmaninov dies at his Beverly Hills home in the USA, aged 69.
Innovations	**JAN** Thornycroft *Terrapin I*, an amphibian tank for military use, is tested in the UK.	**JAN** French naval engineer Jacques-Yves Cousteau successfully tests his "Aqua-Lung" breathing apparatus.	**FEB** The first telephone answering-machine able to give and receive messages is developed in Switzerland.	**MAR** The first kidney machine is developed in secret for the Dutch resistance by Willem Kolff.

OKLAHOMA! PREMIERES

BARON MÜNCHHAUSEN

1943

Massacre of the Warsaw ghetto

19 APRIL

News is reaching the rest of the world of a bloodbath in Poland's Warsaw ghetto, with 40,000 Jews murdered by German troops. After the Nazis invaded Poland in 1939 they forced 450,000 Jews into the ghetto, cutting them off from the rest of the city.

Since then, many have been sent to unknown destinations, while others have perished. Today German troops were ordered in to clear out the remaining 60,000 inhabitants, and were met with fierce resistance by armed Jews. However, the Jews' defiant gesture has proved futile.

Allies capture North Africa

12 MAY

The Italian and German armies in North Africa have surrendered. After a long, hard battle following the British victory at El Alamein in November 1942, the German Afrika Corps and its Italian allies have been pushed into a pocket of land inside Tunisia from which there is no escape. This afternoon, the British commander in Tunisia radioed the British prime minister Winston Churchill, telling him, "All enemy resistance has ceased. We are the masters of the North African shores."

"Bouncing" bombs dropped

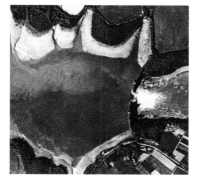

Aerial view of Ruhr floods

16 MAY

In one of the most daring air raids of the war, a small number of British Lancaster heavy bombers, led by Wing Commander Guy Gibson, blasted three dams and caused floodwaters to destroy much of the Ruhr, Germany's industrial heartland. The Lancasters dropped new "bouncing" bombs – huge depth charges designed to bounce across the water, hit the dams' walls, and explode.

APRIL–JUNE

APR The German army discovers a mass grave of over 4,000 Polish officers in the Katyn Forest, Poland.

MAY RKO release the horror film *I Walked With a Zombie* in Hollywood, USA.

APR In Baltimore, USA, Judy Johnson is the first female jockey to win a professional horse race.

BLETCHLEY PARK HEADQUARTERS

MAY The Allies begin a major bombing campaign aimed at Italian cities and military bases.

MAY French director Jean Renoir releases the film *This Land is Mine* in the USA.

JUN Code-breaking "bombes" decipher German Enigma messages at Bletchley Park, UK.

MAY In the UK, part-time war work becomes compulsory for all UK women who are aged between 18 and 45.

JUN UK actor Charlie Chaplin marries Oona O'Neill, daughter of playwright Eugene O'Neill.

JUN In the UK, the General Post Office (GPO) introduces the first pre-stamped aerogrammes.

LESLIE HOWARD

JUN The new French Committee of Liberation led by General de Gaulle pledges to liberate French territory.

JUN UK actor Leslie Howard goes missing when his plane is shot down in the Bay of Biscay.

JUN SCUBA (self-contained underwater breathing apparatus) aqualung manufactured in France.

1943

Ladislao Biro on the ball

10 JUNE

The Hungarian hypnotist and journalist Ladislao Biro has patented a revolutionary writing pen. Four years ago, when working as an editor on a magazine in Budapest, Biro first thought about using printer's quick-drying ink in a pen. Now his remarkable pen has been perfected. It combines a rotating steel ball-point with a tiny tube containing quick-drying ink.

Soviet tanks firing a barrage against Waffen SS and Wehrmacht opposition

German army smashed at Kursk

13 JULY

Today Adolf Hitler ordered a German withdrawal in the greatest tank battle of the century. The German attack began seven days ago on the flat cornlands around Kursk in the Soviet Union. Hitler, who was desperate for a victory following his disaster at Stalingrad, had attached enormous importance to the offensive. The finest divisions of the Wehrmacht and Waffen SS, equipped with 3,000 armoured vehicles including new Tigers, the most powerful tanks yet built, tried to batter their way through the heavily fortified Soviet defences. The battle reached a climax yesterday when 1,500 German and Soviet tanks fought at close range. The Soviet tanks proved superior, with greater firing power. They pushed their way through minefields, anti-tank guns, and mud with great efficiency. After a week of ferocious fighting the Germans have now been driven back. The Soviet army is now preparing to launch its own attack on the dispirited enemy, using fresh troops.

JULY–SEPTEMBER

	World Events	Entertainment	Innovations

JUL A severe famine grips the province of Bengal in north-east India.

JUL Ingrid Bergman stars in the US film *For Whom the Bell Tolls*.

JUL DUKW 2.5 tonne US amphibian supply craft used for Sicilian landings.

FAMINE IN BENGAL

JUL In Italy, Mussolini is overthrown and Marshal Pietro Badoglio forms a new government.

JUL US Hollywood stars Rita Hayworth and Orson Welles are married in Santa Monica, USA.

AUG Allied intelligence reports that Germany is testing a new flying bomb in Blizna, Poland.

JUL Jean Moulin, president of the French National Resistance Council, is captured and executed by the German Gestapo.

JUL An Allied bombing raid on Rome in Italy manages to avoid hitting major historic sites and buildings.

AUG The German Luftwaffe launches the Hs 293, the first guided missile, in an attack over the Bay of Biscay.

JEAN MOULIN

AUG UK RAF bombers attack a top-secret Nazi rocket base at Peenemünde in northern Germany.

SEP US actor Paul Robeson is the first black American to star in the Broadway production of *Othello*.

SEP A new tax scheme called PAYE, Pay As You Earn, is announced in the UK to reduce income tax evasion.

1943

Allies take Palermo

22 JULY

The race to capture the Sicilian capital of Palermo has been won by the United States. It began on 9 July when United States airborne troops touched down on the southern tip of the island of Sicily. In a rapid thrust to the north, US troops reached Palermo yesterday, trapping an estimated 45,000 German and Italian troops. The US army, commanded by the flamboyant General George Patton, received a raptuous welcome from the local Sicilians, who frantically scrambled to acquire any US cigarettes and chocolate. The remaining German defenders of Sicily are now retreating towards the town of Messina, from where they plan to evacuate their forces to mainland Italy. The victory has given the Allies access to a new airfield, from which their planes can strike at the German and Italian positions.

US soldiers drive through the streets of Palermo

Smoking ruins in the city of Hamburg

Fierce bombing in Hamburg

2 AUGUST

The centre of the German port of Hamburg has been devastated by a series of Allied air raids. Bombing day and night, the British RAF bombers and US air force have created huge firestorms that have killed at least 50,000 people and destroyed over 250,000 homes. The city's shipyards and factories have been reduced to rubble, with the Nazi propaganda chief Josef Goebbels declaring the air raids "a catastrophe".

Italy joins forces with the Allies

13 OCTOBER

Italy has declared war on Germany. Marshal Pietro Badoglio, the successor of Benito Mussolini, opened talks with Allied troops after they landed on the Italian mainland three weeks ago. German troops have moved in quickly to fill the vacuum left by their Italian allies.

Marshal Badoglio

OCTOBER–DECEMBER

OCT In Sweden, 4,200 UK prisoners of war are exchanged for Germans in the first major exchange of the war.

OCT Austrian theatre producer and director Max Reinhardt dies in the USA aged 50.

OCT Penicillin is first used to treat wounds of Allied soldiers fighting in the Mediterranean.

PENICILLIN CULTURE

OCT Allied leaders meet Chinese leader Chiang Kai-shek in Cairo, Egypt, to discuss measures to defeat Japan.

NOV Leonard Bernstein makes his debut conducting the New York Philharmonic Orchestra in the USA.

OCT The first children's adventure playground opens in Copenhagen in Denmark.

NOV Allied leaders Churchill, Roosevelt, and Stalin attend a summit in Teheran, Iran, to co-ordinate war strategies.

DEC The musical production of *Carmen Jones* opens on Broadway, New York, USA.

OCT Irish coffee is invented by an Irish chef to warm trans-atlantic flying-boat passengers.

TEHERAN CONFERENCE

DEC The Soviet army launches an offensive in the Ukraine after regaining two-thirds of Soviet territory from Germany.

DEC Beatrix Potter, creator of Peter Rabbit, dies in the UK aged 77.

DEC The first electronic computer *Colossus I* is built in the UK.

WOMEN AT WAR

CIVILIANS HAD A VITAL PART to play in World War II. Women were thrust into the front line of the war effort, taking the place of men who had joined the armed services. They worked in shipyards and factories, drove ambulances in air raids, and were called up to join the army, navy, and airforce. In the Soviet Union some women flew fighter aircraft. By 1943 most unmarried women in Britain between the ages of 20 and 40 were working for the war effort. In Australia, Canada, and Britain, women joined the Women's Land Army, and in factories in the United States they often made up the majority of the workforce.

Mothers of invention

This 1942 German poster urges women to give their old clothes for the war effort. From 1941 all new clothing and footwear in Germany went to the armed forces. When cotton thread ran out, women darned and repaired their clothes using string dyed with shoe polish.

Modest protection

At the beginning of the war the fear of attack by poison gas was very real. Civilians had to carry gas masks with them at all times. Some women used elegant bags like this one to conceal them.

UTILITY SILK STOCKINGS

SHOPPING WITH A RATION BOOK

Professional shoppers

In all the warring countries, the ration book was a vital item in every household. The food coupons ensured a dull but healthy diet. Although rationing promised fair shares for everyone, it also created a thriving black market. Women became expert at finding bargains, haggling, and swapping coupons for less available food.

Inventive wartime fashion

With strict rationing everywhere, the "utility look" became the wartime fashion for women. It cut out all unnecessary frills, with the materials used and prices charged closely controlled by governments. Silk stockings were a particularly rare item, but women were inventive and painted their legs with make-up instead. In France, women used flowers, feathers, and even woodshavings to decorate hats.

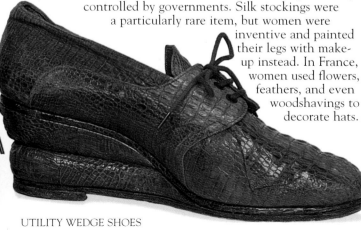

UTILITY WEDGE SHOES

A WOMAN OPERATING A SEARCHLIGHT

Anti-aircraft command

During the war, thousands of women served alongside men in anti-aircraft batteries. They handled searchlights, drove army trucks, and plotted the paths of enemy aircraft on radar. In some countries women were allowed to operate anti-aircraft guns.

Headscarfs became wartime fashion for working women

Women workers wore mens' uniforms including heavy helmets

Women rarely wore trousers in public before the war

WOMEN WELDERS FOR AN ARMAMENTS FACTORY

Role model "Rosie"

The fictional "Rosie the Riveter" posed on the cover of the US *Post* magazine in 1943. She was the symbol of thousands of real "Rosies" working in the US war industry. The money they made and the skills they acquired gave women workers a new confidence, as well as independence from their traditional responsibilities.

The land girls

Over 80,000 women served in the Women's Land Army in Britain. Many Australians and Canadians also chose to work in the fields to provide food for the war effort. Some worked in the timber industry felling trees and working in sawmills. Others were milkmaids, harvesters, or even rat-catchers.

"Doing your bit"

Many women became factory workers during the war, taking jobs in industry that had previously been carried out exclusively by men. There was a vital need for workers in munitions factories, but women also proved to be expert welders, crane operators, and lorry drivers. They were paid less than the men, however, and when the war ended most women were made to leave their jobs for the men returning home from the forces.

1944

A Russian soldier surveys the city

Soviet Union smashes siege line

27 JANUARY

The long siege of Leningrad is finally over. For 900 days, the Nazis have been trying to starve the people of this Soviet city into submission. However, the advancing Red Army has succeeded in driving the Germans back beyond artillery range. The Nazi strategy had nearly succeeded. During the long, harsh winters, as many as 300 people a day died of hunger, illness, or the cold. In all, about one million people perished in the city. Despite this, the citizens of Leningrad fought back, managing to hold out until the Soviet armoured forces attacked, driving the Nazis away.

Mondrian dies

1 FEBRUARY

The famous Dutch artist Piet Mondrian has died. Mondrian has been described as the painter of geometry, as his canvases are based entirely on straight-sided forms, like *Composition No. III with red, yellow, blue* c. 1935 (left).

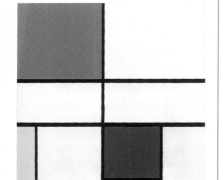

Freedom for Rome

4 JUNE

Troops of the US Fifth Army have entered Rome. Their commander, the flamboyant general Mark Clark, had made the Italian capital his principal objective and was determined to beat all the other Allied armies to the prize, even if it meant ignoring the orders of the overall commander in Italy, the British general Sir Harold Alexander. Only three days ago, Hitler ordered the German commander, Field Marshal Albert Kesselring, to withdraw and declared Rome an "open city", sparing it from the destruction likely to be caused by street battles. Happily, the city's historic sites have been untouched by the ravages of war. Now the Germans are gone and the streets are flooded with excited Italian civilians who crowd around the US soldiers, welcoming them with open arms. Many of the US troops are utterly exhausted from the hard fighting in Italy and, after accepting gifts of wine, they slump down to sleep wherever they are in the streets. General Clark is the hero of the hour, but critics are suggesting that his well-known hunger for publicity has upset Allied plans.

JANUARY–MARCH

World Events	**JAN** Allied troops land on the beaches of Anzio in southern Italy to outflank German defence lines.	**FEB** US forces launch "Operation Brewer", an assault on the Japanese-occupied Admiralty Islands in the Pacific.	**FEB** UK RAF Mosquitoes stage a precision raid on Amiens, France, to free French Resistance leaders.		**MAR** A large Allied force is dropped into Burma by glider and strategically positioned ready to attack the Japanese.
Entertainment	**JAN** French dramatist and war hero Jean Giraudoux dies aged 61.	ANZIO LANDINGS	**JAN** Eleven-year-old Elizabeth Taylor stars in *National Velvet*, made by the US MGM studio.	**JAN** Norwegian artist Edvard Munch, a founder of Expressionism, dies aged 80.	**FEB** The BBC plans to develop schools radio to accompany a new education system in the UK.
Innovations	**JAN** Helicopters are used in warfare for the first time by the USA army.		**JAN** The first printed circuit boards are used in electronic equipment for warfare.	**FEB** The first night reconnaissance photographs are taken by the US airforce over Italy. ARTIST EDVARD MUNCH	**MAR** The first ballpoint pens are manufactured for use by the RAF in the UK.

1944

Allied troops storm Normandy beaches

6 JUNE

In an operation codenamed "Overlord", two Allied armies, with over 100,000 US, British, and Canadian troops, landed at dawn today on the Normandy coast in northern France. The order to invade came from General Eisenhower, the supreme commander in Europe. First, airborne troops landed behind the German coastal defences to provide cover for troops, who stormed the beaches in amphibious tanks, fighting through Nazi defences to liberate the first pieces of French soil. The most serious resistance from the Germans took place on a beach that was codenamed "Omaha", where heavy fighting caused 3,000 Allied casualties. The preparations for the landings in Normandy had been intense. An air offensive on German communication lines in northern France lasted several weeks and the Allies used an elaborate deception to convince the Nazis that the main attack would begin in the Pas de Calais rather than Normandy. Further troops go ashore tomorrow.

APRIL–JUNE

APR Japanese forces are defeated by the UK Fourteenth Army at Kohima, in Assam, a state in north-east India.

APR US actress Marlene Dietrich entertains the Allied troops in Italy and north Africa.

APR Quinine, used as a treatment for malaria, is synthesized by scientists at Harvard University in the USA.

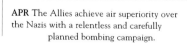

DR LEAKEY

APR The Allies achieve air superiority over the Nazis with a relentless and carefully planned bombing campaign.

MAY *Gaslight*, a thriller suspense starring Charles Boyer and Ingrid Bergman premieres in the USA.

MAY UK anthropologist Dr Leakey discovers fossils and tools used by people in the Old Stone Age.

APR The first of 500,000 prefabricated homes designed for bombed-out families go on show in London in the UK.

MAY French existentialist writer Jean-Paul Sartre's new one-act play *No Exit* opens in Paris, France.

MAY The first eye bank is opened by Manhattan and New York hospitals in New York, USA.

JUN Iceland, which has shared a royal family with Denmark since 1381, becomes the Republic of Iceland.

JUN US actor Gregory Peck makes his screen debut playing a resistance fighter in *Days of Glory*.

ICELAND'S FLAG

JUN For the first time, napalm, a highly inflammable substance, is used in warfare by the UK army.

1944

V-1 launched

13 JUNE

Adolf Hitler has unleashed Germany's flying bomb on the south of England. This deadly pilotless sub-winged

weapon flies at a speed of 563 km/h (352 mph) over a range of 257 km (161 miles). Launched from catapult ramps in the Pas de Calais in northern France, the V-1 is guided by a gyroscopic compass and driven by a pulse jet engine. Its warhead carries an incredible one tonne of high explosives. When the V-1 reaches a measured distance, the engine stalls and the bomb falls to earth, exploding within 15 seconds of impact. The bombs have already scored direct hits on vulnerable places, including a convent, a church, and a hospital. The British public have been warned to take cover if they hear the curious engine-noise stop. The popular belief is that as long as you can still hear the engine you are safe.

WAR GAMES

Toys are scarce in wartime, but British children are having plenty of fun collecting these miniature flags issued free with national newspapers. Children can use them to chart the strategic positions of the Allied and opposing forces on a map of the world.

Hermann Goering and leading Nazis examine Hitler's wrecked headquarters

Hitler death attempt

20 JULY

Adolf Hitler has survived an assassination attempt at his "Wolf's Lair" headquarters in East Prussia. A suitcase bomb was planted under a table in Hitler's conference room. It caused a huge explosion, shattering the entire room and killing three senior Nazi officers, although Hitler escaped with only minor cuts and burns. The assassination attempt was led by Claus von Stauffenberg, a crippled war hero who fought in the USSR in 1943. The band of plotters face certain execution. The Führer has taken his near escape as a sign that fate is preserving him to continue his important life's work.

JULY–SEPTEMBER

World Events	**AUG** The UK parliament passes an education act to provide all children with free education.	**SEP** V-2 rockets, the deadly successors of the V-1s, are launched on London, UK, from bases in Holland and Germany.	**SEP** In Germany, all males aged 16 to 60 are called up for compulsory service in the Volkssturm ("home guard").	**SEP** The Allies liberate Antwerp in Belgium and destroy the V-1 flying bombsite in the Pas de Calais in northern France.
Entertainment	**JUL** US comedian Bob Hope entertains Allied forces with his comedy show in the Solomon Islands.	**SEP** Warner Brothers release the hilarious comedy *Arsenic and Old Lace*, starring US actor Cary Grant.	**SEP** US dancer and actor Fred Astaire puts on a private show for Allied forces stationed in France.	**SEP** Laurence Olivier and Ralph Richardson star in *Richard III* at the New Theatre in London, UK.
Innovations	**JUL** John Logie Baird attempts an "all-electronic" colour television system in the UK. **BOB HOPE**	**AUG** Germany introduces postcodes, a form of address coding to make the delivery of mail more efficient.	**AUG** The German Messerschmitt *Me 262A-2 Sturmvogel*, ("Stormbird") is used in battle for the first time. **VOLKSSTURM**	**SEP** The Swedish Volvo PV44 is the first car to be fitted with a laminated glass windscreen.

1944

Paris liberated by the Allies

25 AUGUST

After four years of Nazi occupation, Paris has at last been liberated. Adolf Hitler planned to have the French capital demolished rather than allow it to fall into Allied hands, but General von Choltitz, the German commander in Paris, defied Hitler and surrendered the beautiful city intact. The first Allied forces to enter Paris, to the ecstatic jubilation of the Parisians, were the French Fourth Armoured Division led by General Jacques Leclerc. In the evening, the popular General de Gaulle marched through the crowds lining the Champs Elysées.

Japanese navy crushed at Leyte

26 OCTOBER

This evening United States warships are in pursuit of the battered survivors of the Japanese navy after a three-day battle off the coast of the Philippines. General Douglas MacArthur, overall land commander in the Pacific, has landed on the central Philippine island of Leyte to congratulate his troops on their successful invasion of the island. Commenting on the sea battle, he declared that "the Japanese navy has suffered its most crushing defeat of the war".

MacArthur addresses US troops

OCTOBER–DECEMBER

OCT Field Marshal Rommel commits suicide rather than face the consequences of his participation in the plot to kill Hitler.

OCT The Martha Graham Dance Company perform Aaron Copland's ballet *Appalachian Spring* in the USA.

OCT Two Messerschmitt *Me 262A* fighters become the first jet aircraft to be shot down in aerial combat.

FIELD-MARSHAL ERWIN ROMMEL

NOV Franklin D Roosevelt wins a record fourth term as US president with 432 votes over Republican Thomas Dewey.

DEC The Green Bay Packers defeat the New York Giants in the US national football league championship.

NOV US surgeon Alfred Blalock performs the first successful heart operation on a newborn baby.

NOV Three UK RAF Lancaster bombers sink the German *Tirpitz* warship in the Tromso Fjord in northern Norway.

DEC US film *National Velvet* is released in Hollywood, starring 11-year-old UK actress Elizabeth Taylor.

DEC Chemists in the UK develop chromatography, a technique used to separate mixtures of liquids or gases.

NATIONAL VELVET

DEC Civil war erupts in Greece when the National People's Liberation Army (NPLA) seizes part of Athens.

DEC US singer Glenn Miller's plane is reported missing on a routine flight over the Channel.

DEC In the UK, Decca Records release the first high-fidelity (hi-fi) recordings.

1940 SOE SET UP TO CO-ORDINATE
RESISTANCE GROUPS IN EUROPE

1940 CHARLES DE GAULLE ESTABLISHES
FREE FRENCH NATIONAL COMMITTEE

1942 TITO ORGANIZES
YUGOSLAV UNDERGROUND

OCCUPATION AND RESISTANCE

BY THE SUMMER OF 1942 German conquests in Europe stretched from the Atlantic coast of France to the Caucasus mountains in the Soviet Union. The industry, agriculture, and workforces of these vast occupied territories became the property of Germany. The German treatment of the nations they occupied varied. In Poland, the population was used as a source of slave labour, and in Greece thousands of people starved to death when most of the country's food stocks were seized by the German army. Underground resistance groups were established in many places, but their success was often influenced by the geography of the region. In mountainous areas like Yugoslavia, resistance groups found it easier to operate undetected. In flat countries such as the Netherlands and Denmark, passive resistance in the form of strikes, posters, and patriotic graffiti was more common.

Hidden map

Secret maps could be hidden beneath the surface of some seemingly ordinary playing cards for use by British agents working in Europe.

ODETTE SANSOM

Secret agent

Odette Sansom was recruited as a radio operator by the British Special Operations Executive (SOE). She worked in France with agent Peter Churchill until they were captured by the Germans. Released at the end of the war, Sansom was awarded the George Cross for her bravery.

German soldier choosing a postcard to send home

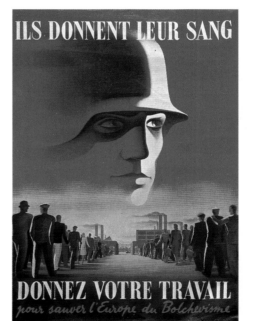

ILS DONNENT LEUR SANG

DONNEZ VOTRE TRAVAIL
pour sauver l'Europe du Bolchevisme

Nazi propaganda

This German propaganda poster urges French workers to join the fight against communism. Germany's war industry relied on "volunteers" from the occupied countries as well as slave labour from Eastern Europe, and French prisoners-of-war. Enforced recruitment drove many young men into resistance groups.

Life in occupied Paris

Under occupation, Paris remained the playground city of Europe as German soldiers packed its cafes, theatres, and clubs. For most of the French, life went on as usual. Posters reminded them that, if they offered no resistance, their families and property would be safe. However, many bars and restaurants were reserved exclusively for German soldiers, and the Nazi swastika hung from the Eiffel Tower.

Puppet prime minister

Vidkun Quisling led the Norwegian Nazi Party before the war, and when the Germans invaded in 1940 they installed him as head of the Norwegian government. Disliked by most Norwegians, he acted as a puppet for the Germans. After the war Quisling was tried for treason and executed in 1945. His name has been adopted as an international byword for traitor.

1942 CZECH RESISTANCE ASSASSINATES
GENERAL REINHARD HEYDRICH

1944 GERMAN RESISTANCE PLANTS
BOMB IN HITLER'S HEADQUARTERS

1945 VIOLETTE SZABO AWARDED FRENCH
CROIX DE GUERRE FOR COURAGE

Secret radios

SOE agents in occupied Europe used radios concealed
in suitcases to send coded messages. Agents also carried
a range of weapons, such as explosive pens, bicycle pumps
that concealed a single-action shotgun, and silent pistols
that could be hidden in clothing.

*Headphones allowed
agents to listen to
broadcasts silently*

*Transmitter works
from mains or
battery power*

Ever vigilant

"Keep quiet! The Germans
have fled, but their spies
remain!" Posters like this
were produced by the Allies
after the liberation of France
in 1944 to remind the
French that Germany
still posed a threat.

*Apparatus packs into
a suitcase and weighs
14.5 kg (32 lbs)*

In disguise

There were over
11,000 agents in
the British Special
Operations Executive
(SOE). The SOE was
set up in July 1940 to
gather information in
German-occupied
Europe, carry out sabotage,
and support resistance groups. In
the words of Winston Churchill, the British
prime minister, their aim was to "set Europe ablaze".

*Voltage
adjuster*

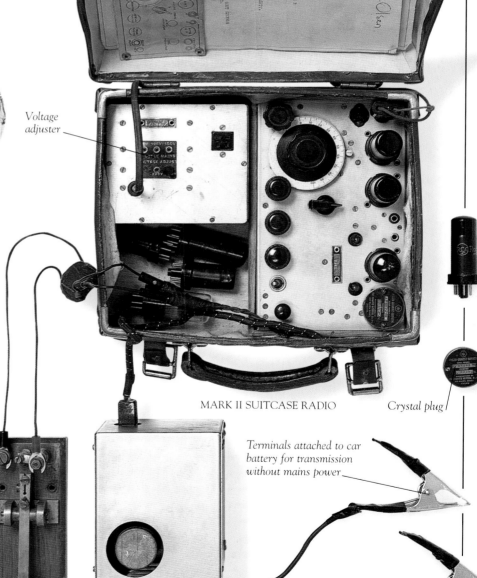

FRENCH RESISTANCE FIGHTERS BEING BRIEFED

MARK II SUITCASE RADIO

Crystal plug

Secret force

The French Maquis was set up in 1943, after
the Germans demanded 400,000 men to work in
German industry. To avoid forced labour, thousands
formed resistance groups in remote countryside
regions. By May 1944, the Maquis numbered 35,000
although only about 8,000 had enough ammunition
for more than one day's serious fighting. After
D-Day in 1944, thousands of tonnes of equipment
was parachuted to the Maquis, who attacked
the Germans in central and southern France.

*Terminals attached to car
battery for transmission
without mains power*

Tapping key

1945

Allies flatten Dresden in single night of bombing

US capture Iwo Jima

15 FEBRUARY

The beautiful and historic city of Dresden in Germany has been devastated by an Allied bombing raid. For three nights nearly 800 British Lancaster planes and 300 US Flying Fortresses have ruthlessly obliterated many of the grandest architectural monuments of this showpiece city. Dresden has suffered so few bombing raids that all its anti-aircraft guns have been removed. The death toll is thought to be as high as 100,000, many of them refugees, with total casualties estimated at around 400,000. The bombing has aroused widespread criticism. In Britain, some observers have accused the chief of the RAF Bomber Command, Air Marshal Sir Arthur Harris, of clinging, despite everything, to his controversial theory that terror-bombing can by itself destroy the enemy's will to fight. Senior Allied military officers are in uproar about the need to attack such a strategically unimportant target. They would have preferred to see the bombers step up attacks on German communications and oil installations.

US marines hoist the Stars and Stripes on Mount Suribachi

23 FEBRUARY

The United States' flag has been raised on the peak of Mount Suribachi, the highest point on the tiny Pacific island of Iwo Jima, where Japanese troops were firmly entrenched. A savage attack on the heavily fortified island began four days ago when US battleships, cruisers, and aircraft carriers began relentlessly pounding the whole island. Taking control from the Japanese has cost the lives of 6,800 US servicemen and wounded 18,000 others. Many days of fighting still lie ahead before this speck in the ocean can be turned into an airbase from which to bomb the neighbouring islands of Japan.

Dresden devastated after a night of bombing

JANUARY–FEBRUARY

World Events	**JAN** US president Franklin D Roosevelt is inaugurated for a record fourth term in office.	**JAN** Seven thousand people are killed when the German *Wilhelm Gustloff* is sunk by a Soviet submarine in the Baltic sea.	**JAN** The Soviet Red Army discover the horrors of the Auschwitz concentration camp in Poland, where millions of Jews died.	**FEB** Winston Churchill, Joseph Stalin, and Franklin D Roosevelt carve up the postwar world at Yalta, in the Ukraine.
Entertainment	**JAN** US singer Perry Como has a hit with *Till the End of Time*.	**JAN** Sergei Eisenstein's film *Ivan the Terrible* is released in the USSR's capital Moscow.	**JAN** Brazilian musician Villa Lobos composes the musical score for the film *The Green Mansions*.	**FEB** Walt Disney premieres his latest cartoon feature *The Three Caballeros* starring Donald Duck.
Innovations	**JAN** The world's first fluoridated water supply is available in Michigan, USA.	**JAN** Soviet scientists start to develop high-thrust liquid-propellant rocket engines.	**FEB** A vertically launched rocket interceptor crashes on its first manned test flight in the USSR.	**FEB** The USSR begins flight trials of the *RD-100* rocket engine, a version of the German V-2.

WILHELM GUSTLOFF

THE YALTA CONFERENCE

1945

Les Enfants du Paradis

9 MARCH

A remarkable new film *Les Enfants du Paradis* ("The Children of Paradise"), has premiered in Paris, France.

This epic story, set in the theatre world of Paris, has become a symbol of the hopes for the rebirth of France after German occupation.

Hitler kills himself

30 APRIL

Adolf Hitler has committed suicide in his bunker beneath the Reich Chancellory garden in Berlin. Hitler had refused pleas from his generals to escape from the German capital. Yesterday, as Soviet shells and rockets were raging above in the battle for Berlin, Hitler married Eva Braun, the woman who has been his mistress since 1932. Hitler and Braun withdrew to their private quarters where they both bit into lethal cyanide capsules. Simultaneously, Hitler shot himself with a pistol. Their bodies were then carried upstairs and into the gardens by their aides where they were doused with petrol and burned, along with great piles of Nazi documents. Only ten days ago, Hitler celebrated his 56th birthday.

Hitler and Eva Braun

F D R dies on eve of victory

12 APRIL

Franklin D Roosevelt has died of a brain haemorrhage. While resting at the resort of Warm Springs in Georgia, the US president complained of a headache. A few hours later he was dead. When informed of her husband's death, Mrs Roosevelt said, "I am more sorry for the people of this country and of the world than I am for ourselves."

MARCH–APRIL

MAR Japanese schools and universities are shut down and everyone over the age of six is ordered to do war work.

MAR The US film *The Picture of Dorian Gray*, based on Oscar Wilde's novel, is released.

APR Hungarian scientists succeed in reflecting radar signals from the Moon.

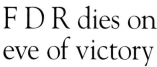

CAROUSEL OPENS ON BROADWAY

APR In Germany, the Soviet army launches an offensive aimed at capturing Berlin from its bridgehead on the River Oder.

APR Oscar Hammerstein's US musical *Carousel* opens at New York's Majestic Theatre, USA.

APR The Heinkel *He 162* is the first aircraft to go into service with a operational ejector seat.

APR Mussolini and his mistress Clara Petacci are shot by Italian partisans in the Piazza Loretto in Milan, Italy.

APR Sylvester the cat makes his first appearance in *Life with Feathers*, a new cartoon released by Warner Brothers.

APR Hungarian scientist Lajos Jánossy investigates the effects of cosmic rays upon the Earth's atmosphere.

APR The Soviet army takes Vienna in Austria, and installs Karl Renner as prime minister of the provisional government.

APR US jazz-band leader Lionel Hampton releases his *All American Award Concert* album to great acclaim.

BENITO MUSSOLINI

APR Dr Claus Maertens invents the comfortable Doc Marten shoe after he suffers a ski injury while on holiday.

1945

Truth revealed as death camps discovered

Survivors tell their stories to the GI liberators

Slave labourers found by US troops at Buchenwald camp

30 APRIL

Allied troops have uncovered the horrifying truth of the Nazi concentration camps. Hundreds of thousands of Jews had been rounded up by the Nazis and shipped to concentration camps across occupied Europe as part of Hitler's "final solution" to eliminate the Jewish race. Political, religious, and sexual "undesirables" faced a similar persecution. Soviet, British, and American soldiers liberating death camps such as Belsen, Treblinka, and Auschwitz were greeted by

pits piled high with rotting corpses and survivors who were little more than walking skeletons. The survivors have described how the inmates were separated on arrival, most of them herded into the "shower rooms" where they were gassed to death. The rest were forced to work as slave labour until starvation and appalling living conditions weakened them and they too were gassed. Women and children were often forced into prostitution and, at some

camps, the inmates were experimented on by Nazi scientists. Despite every effort being made to save the emaciated prisoners, hundreds are dying every day.

The Allies have known about the camps for years, but were so preoccupied by strategic campaigns that they did not select them for bombing.

MAY–JUNE

World Events	**MAY** UK broadcaster William Joyce, "Lord Haw-Haw", is arrested on a charge of treason.	**MAY** Heinrich Himmler, chief of Nazi Germany's SS and Gestapo, commits suicide while he is in UK custody.	**JUN** In the Battle of Okinawa, Japanese Kamikaze pilots crash their aircraft into enemy targets, killing 5,000 US seamen.	**JUN** In Ottawa, the capital of Canada, MacKenzie King's Liberal Party is returned to power in a general election.
Entertainment	**MAY** The US actress Judy Garland stars in romantic war film *The Clock*.	**MAY** US singer Doris Day and the Les Brown Orchestra have a hit with the song *Sentimental Journey*.	**MAY** German director Max Ophüls releases his latest film *From Mayerling to Sarajevo* in Paris, France.	**JUN** Benjamin Britten's opera *Peter Grimes* premieres at London's recently opened Sadler's Wells Theatre, in the UK.
Innovations	**MAY** Tridione is developed to treat postwar convulsive disorders such as epilepsy.	**MAY** UK scientist Arthur C Clarke advocates geostationary orbit for global communications.	**MAY** Wernher von Braun and other German rocket scientists surrender to US Seventh Army.	**JUN** The UK government introduces the family allowance, a weekly payment to help all families.

THE CLOCK

KAMIKAZE PILOT

1945

Montgomery accepts German surrender terms

4 MAY

In a tent on the desolate Luneburg Heath, south of Hamburg, Germany, Field Marshal Montgomery today received the first surrender of the German forces – all those in northwest Germany, Holland, and Denmark. The Allies expect the final surrender of the German high command to take place within the next few days.

General Friedenburg signs the surrender terms

Allied victory

7 MAY

Germany surrendered unconditionally to the Allies at 2.41 this morning. The German High Command made their final surrender in a little red schoolhouse in Reims in France. General Bedell Smith signed for the Western Allies and General Ivan Suslapatov was chief witness for the Soviet Union. Since then, German troops have been giving themselves up to the Allies in droves.

German troops surrender to the Allies

Victory in Europe

8 MAY

Dull skies and drizzle have not dampened the British celebrations of Victory in Europe (VE) Day. In London, delirious crowds headed for Buckingham Palace to cheer the royal family. As darkness fell, the British capital was ablaze with floodlights and fireworks for the first time since war broke out in 1939. At street parties across the nation, bonfires topped with effigies of Adolf Hitler and his henchmen were lit to mark the end of Nazi Germany. There

have been similar scenes of celebration in Paris and Rome. In Moscow, in the Soviet Union, captured German flags were piled at the feet of the Soviet leaders in Red Square.

Children celebrating the end of the war at a street party

JULY–AUGUST

JUL At the Potsdam Conference in Germany Allied leaders disagree over where Germany's postwar boundaries should be drawn.

AUG The USA unleash a second atomic bomb on the city of Nagasaki in Japan, killing over 65,000 innocent men, women, and children.

AUG Marshal Pétain, former premier of France, is sentenced to death but reprieved by General De Gaulle because he is 89 years old.

AUG Following the defeat of Japan, conflict breaks out in that country between the nationalist government and the communists.

JUL The BBC broadcasts *The Robinson Family*, the first daily drama serial in the UK.

NAGASAKI OBLITERATED

AUG US jazz musician Charlie Parker has a hit with the popular tune *Now's the Time*.

AUG The Czechoslovakian government nationalizes all the country's film companies.

THE LOUVRE

AUG The Louvre art museum in Paris, France, is re-opened to the general public.

JUL The first atomic explosion takes place in Almogordo in the New Mexico desert, USA.

JUL A vaccine against virus A and B influenza is used on the US army for the first time.

AUG Benadryl is developed in the USA to treat common allergies such as hayfever and asthma.

AUG Finnish scientist Arturri Virtanen develops a method for preserving cattle fodder.

1945

Devastating bomb dropped on Japan

6 AUGUST

At 8.15 am this morning an American bomber plane called *Enola Gay* released its solitary bomb over the city of Hiroshima in Japan, and a new era in warfare began. As a result of a single atomic explosion, an estimated 80,000 people were killed instantly, and much of Hiroshima has simply ceased to exist. The people at the centre of the blast have been completely vaporized, with charred shadows their only remains. Radiation levels in the area are dangerously high. A mushroom-shaped cloud of smoke and dust rising 8 km (5 miles) in the air above the city is all that can be seen. Relying on the explosive power of an atomic reaction, the atom bomb has been developed by an international team of scientists in the United States in a top-secret project codenamed "Manhattan". The US launched the attack after Japan failed to surrender unconditionally, although rumours persist that this unprecedented use of nuclear weapons was unnecessary. What is clear now is that Japan will now either have to surrender or face further nuclear attacks. The Allies believe the attack will lead to an end to the war.

CHILD VICTIMS

The young survivors of the Hiroshima bomb wear masks over their noses and mouths. The masks help to combat the odour of death clinging to the city's ruins. People are living in makeshift shelters in the blasted wastelands of both Hiroshima and Nagasaki.

SEPTEMBER–OCTOBER

World Events

SEP UK troops take control of the colony of Hong Kong as Japanese troops return to Japan.

OCT French traitor Pierre Laval is denied the right of appeal after being sentenced to death for collaborating with the Germans.

OCT Egypt, Iraq, Syria, and Lebanon form the Arab League and warn that the creation of a Jewish state will cause trouble.

OCT Colonel Juan Perón takes over the government of Argentina again, only eight days after he had been ousted by the army.

Entertainment

SEP The Italian film *Rome, Open City* is unpopular as it reminds people of the war.

SEP Former child actress Shirley Temple marries John Agar in Hollywood, California, USA.

OCT US star Joan Crawford returns to the screen in *Mildred Pierce*, the story of an over-achieving woman.

OCT The Moscow Dynamo football team leaves the USSR for a tour of the UK and wins every match.

PIERRE LAVAL

JOAN CRAWFORD

Innovations

SEP The Universal Jeep, the first Jeep for civilian use, is produced in the USA.

SEP A helicopter crosses the Channel between France and the UK for the first time.

OCT Fluorescent lighting is first used in Europe in an underground station in London, UK.

OCT The first microwave oven is patented by the Raytheon Company in the USA.

1945

Victory celebrations

Crowds celebrate in the streets of New York

Official surrender

2 SEPTEMBER

This morning grey skies hung over Tokyo Bay as a formal Japanese delegation arrived on the deck of the US battleship *Missouri* to sign an unconditional surrender. The Japanese conceded defeat after a second atomic bomb killed over 65,000 people in the city of Nagasaki. Although the Allies celebrated victory last month, today's ceremony means that World War II is officially over.

Japanese delegation arrives to sign surrender

15 AUGUST

Last night's news that Japan has decided to surrender has sparked off celebrations in the United States and Australia. In San Francisco, on America's west coast, the news was greeted with a wild wailing of air raid sirens, the honking of car horns, and the hooting of ship's sirens. Traffic has been brought to a halt in cities right across the United States as singing, cheering, and dancing crowds fill the streets. In Washington DC the military police were called in to keep a huge and excited mob from invading the White House, and in New York an estimated two million people jammed Times Square. In Sydney, Australia, a million people let their hair down, mobbing army trucks and Jeeps, snatching off servicemen's hats, and swapping kisses. In stark contrast, the citizens of Tokyo, Japan, shuffled through their ruined city to the gates of the emperor's palace, where they stood and wept.

Ho Chi Minh's new republic

2 SEPTEMBER

After hearing news of the Japanese surrender, Ho Chi Minh, leader of Vietnam's communist-dominated Viet Minh Party, has declared the country a republic. The former French colony in southeast Asia had been occupied by the Japanese since 1941. Armed by the Americans, the Viet Minh have today taken control.

NOVEMBER–DECEMBER

NOV Marshal Tito's National Front Party wins an overwhelming majority in a general election in Yugoslavia.

NOV Popular jazz artist Woody Herman releases a hit album called *The Thundering Herd*.

NOV The first air-sea rescue by helicopter is carried out by the US army off Long Island Sound.

NUREMBERG TRIALS

NOV The trial of 21 leading Nazis is opened in Nuremberg, Germany, before an Allied International Military Tribunal.

NOV "Bebop" is the new sound sweeping across the USA. Small "combos" play loud, fast music.

NOV US chemist Earl W Tupper develops airtight plastic boxes called "Tupperware".

NOV General Charles de Gaulle is elected the president of the provisional government in France.

NOV Jerome Kern, US composer of many well-loved hits including *Show Boat*, dies aged 60.

DEC The first car-stickers are manufactured by Forest Gill at the Gill Studios, Kansas, USA.

JEROME KERN

DEC Mussolini's daughter Edda Mussolini Ciano is jailed for two years in Italy for aiding fascism.

NOV Film critics warmly receive UK director Alfred Hitchcock's latest thriller *Spellbound*.

DEC A new fabric called Lurex is manufactured by Dobecknum Co, Cleveland, Ohio, USA.

1939 IGOR SIKORSKY
DESIGNS THE HELICOPTER

1939 THE GERMAN HEINKEL *178*
IS THE FIRST JET AIRCRAFT

1940 US ARMY INTRODUCES
THE ALL-PURPOSE JEEP

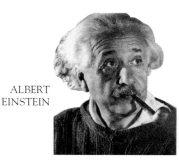

TECHNOLOGY OF WAR

SCIENTISTS AND TECHNICIANS played a vital role in World War II. Many of the most important battles were fought not on the front line but in laboratories and factories. Science was applied to every aspect of each country's war effort, from developing weapons to devising a healthy and tasty diet from the increasingly rationed food supplies. The demands of war also speeded up research on technologies which had been started in the 1930s, including radar, computer sciences, atomic fission, and the jet aircraft. War brought together the forces of science and industry as no peacetime event could have done. However, other scientific advances, such as the invention of the atom bomb, cast a shadow over the world that remained for years to come.

ALBERT
EINSTEIN

Intelligent advice

The brilliant physicist Albert Einstein fled Nazi Germany for the US in 1933. He warned President Roosevelt of the dangers if Germany became the first to develop an atom bomb.

Enigma variations

The signals from the German "Enigma" machine, which was used for secret military communications, baffled the enemy cipher experts for many years. When the operator pressed a letter key, rotors working under the keyboard made a different letter appear on the display board. The receiving Enigma machine reversed this process. The British breaking of the Enigma code was one of the great technical feats of the war.

MASS PRODUCTION OF MESSERSCHMITT AIRCRAFT

Air attack

Willy Messerschmitt began work on the German *Me109* in 1934, and by the outbreak of war it had became one of the most outstanding fighter planes in the world. It was built in greater numbers than any other German combat aircraft. The most numerous aircraft of the war was the Soviet *Il-2 Stormovik*. Over 35,000 were built between 1941 and 1945 in three huge factories.

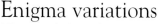
Rotor cylinder

Code letters

Letter key

GERMAN ENIGMA
CIPHER MACHINE

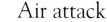
Front panel

Exploding pigs

Nicknamed "Pigs", these Italian underwater torpedo craft had a detachable warhead in the nose. The two-man crew would fix the warhead to the hull of an enemy ship. A time fuse in the bomb allowed them to escape before it exploded. In December 1941, Italian human torpedoes badly damaged two British battleships in Alexandria Harbour in Egypt.

Warhead

A RADAR DISPLAY

Rocket man

Wernher von Braun was the technical director of the secret German rocket establishment at Peenemünde from 1934 where he created deadly missiles such as the V-1 and V-2 rockets. At the end of the war, von Braun, together with other German rocket scientists were captured and taken to the United States where they played an important role in the creation of the US space programme.

OPPENHEIMER INSPECTS THE REMAINS OF THE SITE

Bombsite

The men who designed the atom bomb, scientist Robert Oppenheimer and US general Leslie R Groves, tested the bomb in New Mexico before it was dropped over Japan.

Early warning

This radar display is tracking enemy aircraft from an American aircraft carrier in the Pacific. The word "radar" stands for RAdio Direction And Ranging, a phrase coined in 1942. Developed in the 1930s, it was one of the key technologies of the war. In the Battle of Britain, the British used ground radar to detect enemy bomber formations. Later, radar was carried in German bombers to help find targets, and by the Allies in the vast spaces of the Pacific to find the enemy and to range the guns on their warships.

ENIAC COMPUTER

Mechanical mind

The first successful general purpose computer was called ENIAC (short for Electronic Numerical Integrator And Calculator). It was designed by American scientists John Mauchley and John Eckbert and weighed 30 tonnes. The computer increased processing speeds a thousand times but had to be partially rewired each time it was programmed.

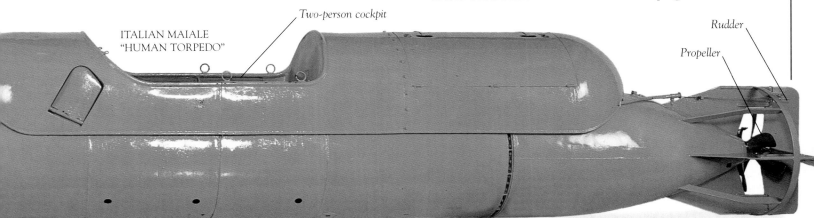

Two-person cockpit

ITALIAN MAIALE "HUMAN TORPEDO"

Rudder

Propeller

1946

Nations united

11 JANUARY

The general assembly of the United Nations has held its first session in London. British prime minister Clement Attlee told the gathered representatives of 51 nations, "Our aim is the creation of justice and security."

"Iron Curtain" division in Europe

5 MARCH

Britain's wartime leader Sir Winston Churchill has found a new enemy to fight – the threat of communism. In a speech he gave while touring the United States he warned that "an Iron Curtain has descended across Europe". He believes that the differences between the capitalist and communist countries are irreconcilable, and the USSR is commited to expansionism. He urged an alliance between the United States and Britain to counter Soviet aggression.

WESTERN EUROPE   EASTERN EUROPE   IRON CURTAIN

Palestine splits

1 MAY

A new plan for Palestine, drawn up by Britain and the United States, threatens to lead to bloodshed. The plan proposes that Palestine be divided into separate Jewish and Arab states. However, it seems certain that both Jews and Arabs will reject the plan. Jews all over the world consider Palestine to be their homeland, and many thousands have made their way there to settle.

Jews climb aboard refugee ship

JANUARY–JUNE

World Events	**JAN** Emperor Hirohito of Japan declares his divinity a "false conception" founded in fiction.	**FEB** Colonel Juan D Perón is elected as the president of Argentina for a six-year term, despite heavy opposition from the US.	**FEB** Anti-UK protestors and riot police clash in Bombay, India, and over 60 Indians are killed and 500 injured.	**JUN** Italian women are able to vote in national elections for the first time. Enrico de Nicola is elected president.
Entertainment	**JAN** UK director David Lean's film of *Great Expectations* premieres.	**MAY** US film star Lana Turner heads the cast of the menacing film *The Postman Always Rings Twice*.	**JUN** Television licences, to raise revenue to support the BBC, are introduced in the UK.	**JUN** The BBC revives TV broadcasts in the UK interrupted by the war.
Innovations	**FEB** US company IBM introduces a new electronic calculator using vacuum tubes.	**MAY** Dr Spock's *Common Sense Book of Baby and Child Care* is published in the USA.	**MAY** A huge 14-tonne German V-2 rocket climbs 120 km (75 miles) in a US missile test.	**JUN** Scot John Logie Baird, the first to demonstrate TV pictures, dies aged 58.

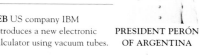

PRESIDENT PERÓN OF ARGENTINA

ITALIAN WOMEN GET THE VOTE

1946

Two-piece shock

5 JULY

A sensation was caused in Paris today by the "bikini" bathing dress – or rather – undress! This new costume, named after Bikini Atoll in the Pacific is a two-piece affair and can be packed into a matchbox or pulled through a wedding ring. The world's tiniest costume was worn by 19-year-old Micheline Bernardini, a nude dancer from the Casino de Paris, at a contest at the Molitor swimming-pool to find the most beautiful bather of 1946.

Micheline Bernardini models the new bikini

The longest screen kiss

22 JULY

UK director Alfred Hitchcock has defied the censors with his new film *Notorious*. Cary Grant keeps Ingrid Bergman in his arms for the longest embrace in screen history, his kiss only interrupted by a telephone call.

Top Nazis sentenced

16 OCTOBER

The war crimes trial being held at Nuremberg, Germany, is over and sentence has been passed by the panel of judges representing the Allies. Of the 21 Nazi leaders on trial, 11 have been sentenced to death and the rest received heavy prison sentences.

However, the biggest war criminals of all are absent from the trial. Adolf Hitler and SS Chief Heinrich Himmler both committed suicide at the end of the war and Hitler's secretary Martin Bormann is missing.

JITTERBUGGING

US armed forces stationed in Europe have started a Jitterbug dance craze. The dance was first seen in the United States in the 1930s and has now spread to many parts of the world. Dancers Jitterbug to swing and boogie-woogie. Both partners need to be athletic in order to complete the Jitterbug's "under-arm swing".

JULY–DECEMBER

JUL In the worst anti-Jewish pogrom since war ended, 39 Jews and four Poles are killed in Poland.

AUG H G Wells, UK author of *The Time Machine* and *The War of the Worlds*, dies aged 79.

JUL The US military conduct the first underwater atomic explosion off the Bikini Atoll in the Pacific.

BEAUTY AND THE BEAST

AUG Chinese communist leader Mao Zedong orders an all-out civil war against the nationalists.

DEC French film director Jean Cocteau's *Beauty and the Beast* wins the Louis Delloc Prize.

SEP The first car with electrically operated windows, the Daimler DE36, is manufactured in the UK.

OCT Nazi Hermann Goering commits suicide by swallowing cyanide hours before he is due to be executed.

DEC US boxer Sugar Ray Robinson wins the welterweight championship in New York City.

NOV A non-smudging ballpoint pen called the Biro after its Hungarian inventor goes on sale in the UK.

SUGAR RAY ROBINSON

NOV The National Health Service (NHS) is created in the UK by the Labour government.

DEC Swiss mystic author Herman Hesse wins the Nobel Prize for Literature.

DEC UK scientists Donald Hay and Edward Appleton discover that sunspots emit radio waves.

1947

Dior unveils "New Look"

12 FEBRUARY

French designer Christian Dior has created a fashion sensation with his "New Look". The elegant, feminine designs are certain to be a big hit with women hungry for something new. The dresses feature a narrow waist, tight bodice, and padded hips.

"New-Look" style suit

Anne Frank's diary published

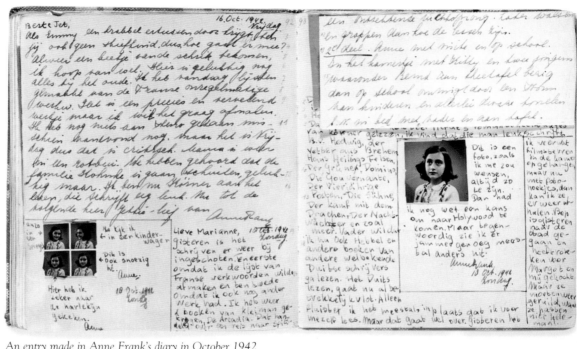

An entry made in Anne Frank's diary in October 1942

15 JUNE

"In spite of everything I still believe people are really good at heart." These moving words come from one of the pages of a diary kept by a young Jewish girl called Anne Frank during the war. When the Nazis overran Holland in 1940 the Frank family went into hiding. Day after day, in constant fear of being discovered, Anne took comfort from the pouring out of her thoughts in her diary. After two years the family was betrayed by Dutch informers, arrested by the Gestapo (secret police), and sent to concentration camps. Anne died of typhus in March 1945. Her father has had his daughter's remarkable writings published and now millions of readers can gain some insight into the nightmare of living through the Holocaust.

DEAD SEA SCROLLS

A great archaeological find has been made in Palestine. A young herdsman stumbled upon some jars filled with ancient manuscripts in a cave by the Dead Sea. Some of them have been dated to 200 BC.

JANUARY–JUNE

World Events	**FEB** In Germany, UK and US agents round up hundreds of Nazis who have been in hiding.	**MAR** In the UK, Lord Mountbatten is appointed viceroy of India in order to oversee the transfer of government to India.	**MAR** Henry Ford, who changed the car industry with his mass-produced Model T, dies in the USA aged 83.	**JUN** US secretary of state George Marshall reveals his plan for the reconstruction of postwar Europe.
Entertainment	**FEB** The lively musical *Brigadoon* opens at the Ziegfeld Theatre, in New York, USA.	**APR** In the USA, Jackie Robinson is the first black American to play in major league baseball since 1884.	**JUN** The musical *Annie Get Your Gun* opens to rave reviews in the West End of London, UK.	**JUN** UK actor Laurence Olivier is awarded a knighthood for his contribution to the theatre.
Innovations	**JAN** UK scientist J A Sargrove is the first to develop a printed circuit board.	**MAR** In the UK, prime minister Clement Attlee makes the first party political broadcast on BBC radio.	**APR** The first duty-free shop selling wines and spirits opens at Shannon Airport in Ireland.	**APR** The first microwave ovens go on sale in the USA, but they fail to make an impact on the public.

JACKIE ROBINSON

THE MARSHALL PLAN

1947

Independent India

15 AUGUST

After 163 monumental years the sun has set on the British Raj. The British colony of India was today replaced by the independent countries of India and Pakistan. Lord Mountbatten has relinquished his title as viceroy and become governor-general of the new dominion of India. Fearing the outbreak of civil war between the conflicting communities of Hindus and Muslims, Mountbatten had been negiotating partition plans since 1946. Last June, he held talks with Jawaharlal Nehru, leader of the

Congress Party, and Mohammed Jinnah, leader of the Muslim League. Broad agreement was reached on plans for the partition, but Mahatma Gandhi, who worked closely with Nehru to achieve independence, adamantly opposed the division of India. He had hoped the country would remain united and urged that Hindus and Muslims live in peace.

Jawaharlal Nehru with Mahatma Gandhi

Yeager shatters sound barrier

14 OCTOBER

Daredevil US pilot Chuck Yeager has become the first person to fly faster than the speed of sound. At Muroc Dry

Lake in California, Yeager piloted his bullet-shaped aerodynamic Bell *X-I* rocket plane smoothly through the sound barrier at a fantastic speed of 1,120 km/h (700 mph).

Witchhunt in Hollywood

26 NOVEMBER

In Hollywood, film capital of the world, a hunt for undercover communists has wrecked the career of ten leading US writers and film directors. The

so-called "Hollywood Ten" refused to appear before a congressional committee to answer questions about their political activities. Because of this, they have been cited for contempt of Congress, blacklisted, and given prison sentences. Edward Dmytryk (above), the director of the highly successful film *Crossfire*, has been dismissed by RKO. Several actors, including Humphrey Bogart, Gene Kelly, and Jane Wyatt, plan to protest against the running of the committee.

JULY–DECEMBER

SEP In the newly partitioned India, thousands are killed as riots break out between Hindus and Muslims.

AUG US actor Danny Kaye stars in the film comedy *The Secret Life of Walter Mitty*.

SEP The first frozen orange juice concentrate is manufactured by a citrus co-operative in the USA.

THE ROYAL UK NEWLY WEDS

NOV Princess Elizabeth, daughter of King George VI, marries Lieutenant Philip Mountbatten in London, UK.

OCT Twelve-year-old Julie Andrews stars in the musical show *Starlight Roof* in the UK.

OCT President Truman makes the first presidential address to the US nation on the television.

NOV The UN general assembly votes in favour of the partition of Palestine and the emergence of a new Jewish state.

NOV The Edinburgh Festival of Music and Drama is founded in Scotland.

NOV In Romania, Anna Pauker becomes the first female foreign minister.

MIRACLE ON 34TH STREET

DEC The Greek government dissolves the communist-controlled National Liberation Front.

DEC The children's film *Miracle on 34th Street* opens to crowds in the USA.

DEC The first transistor is patented by US physicist William Shockley.

1945 CIGARETTES ARE USED TO BARTER
FOR FOOD AND OTHER ESSENTIAL ITEMS

1946 UK GI BRIDES LEAVE THEIR
HOMES FOR A NEW LIFE IN THE USA

1946 THE UNITED NATIONS
HOLD THEIR FIRST SESSION

AFTER THE WAR

WORLD WAR II was responsible for an estimated fifty-five million deaths, and many were innocent civilian victims. Huge areas of Europe and southwest Asia had been bombed and devastated. Not only were military targets hit, but houses, schools, and road and rail networks lay in ruins. Famine loomed and the roads of Europe and southwest Asia were clogged with thousands of refugees. Soldiers returning to their native countries found their homes destroyed and their families scattered. Yet amid the gloom there was a growing hope for a new world that would be free of tyranny.

Welcome home

As the guns of war fell silent in Europe and the Far East, millions of servicemen returned home and tried to settle back into family life. But many returned to find changed circumstances. They found the task of re-adjusting difficult, and this led to a soaring divorce rate in the first few years after the war.

Demobilization

After World War I soldiers had been promised "a land fit for heroes", but all they found was unemployment. At the end of World War II governments were determined not to make the same mistake again. But it was an expensive task to return millions of men and women to civilian life. Some countries were bankrupt, while others were deeply in debt. In Britain, each demobilized soldier received a government gift of £199 and a complete set of new clothing.

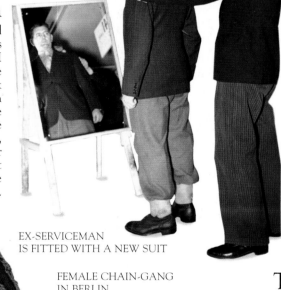

EX-SERVICEMAN
IS FITTED WITH A NEW SUIT

FEMALE CHAIN-GANG
IN BERLIN

Pre-fabrication

Britain had the worst housing shortage of any Allied country. The new Labour government set out to build 400,000 new houses a year, but fell short of the target. A stop-gap solution was the temporary, quick-to-assemble pre-fabricated house. The "pre-fab" was intended to last ten years, but continuing shortage of accommodation meant that many of them had to be used for much longer.

The re-building of Europe

Bombing raids had frequently targeted civilian centres and there were many European cities in ruins. Public buildings, factories, and transport systems were severely damaged, and food, fuel, and water in desperately short supply. People were half-starved and forced to take refuge anywhere that they could. In postwar cities in Germany, women outnumbered men, and in Berlin it was a common sight to see "chain gangs" of women who were paid a small sum of money to help in the painstaking task of clearing away the rubble from the streets and bombsites of their city.

Miraculous recovery

Immediately after the war, most German citizens simply concentrated on survival. But, after ten years of foreign investment and efficient town-planning, Germany became one of the first European nations to recover from the trauma of war. Unlike the Allies, Germany had no huge military loans to pay back. So the Germans were able to re-build their factories and new businesses once again flourished.

A land of prosperity

By 1945 the USA was the richest and most powerful nation in the world. It remained physically untouched by war; factories continued to make new goods and there was no food rationing. The postwar economy leapt ahead of the rest of the world bringing new prosperity to millions of people. Farmers' incomes quadrupled and the wages of industrial workers rose by 70 per cent. To Europeans recovering from the harshness of war, the USA seemed like the land of plenty.

JAPANESE ORPHAN

Label states destination of orphan

Sweet rations

In Britain, food rationing increased after the war. In July 1946 even bread was rationed, a measure introduced to help feed people in the British-occupied zone of Germany. It was not until the 1950s that people could enjoy unlimited quantities of luxury items such as sweets and chocolates.

The aftermath of the atomic bomb

The atomic bombing of the Japanese cities of Hiroshima and Nagasaki shocked the world. Both cities were devastated and most of the population died. For months after, those who had survived the blasts suffered from radiation sickness and developed cancers linked to radiation. In later years there were other consequences, such as birth defects. The final death toll in Hiroshima alone has been estimated at nearly 300,000. Countless refugees, many of them small children, were left homeless and without their families to care for them.

THE WASTELAND OF HIROSHIMA

1948

Gandhi mourned across India

31 JANUARY

In India, thousands of people have gathered on the banks of the River Jumna to mourn the death of their spiritual leader Mahatma Gandhi. The spiritual father of Indian independence was shot three times yesterday by one of his countrymen at a prayer meeting in New Delhi. The assassin, who was identified as Nathuram Godse, a fanatical Hindu, was immediately seized by police and led away from the hysterical crowd. Mahatma Gandhi's body has been cremated and his ashes cast into the river.

Czech communists stage coup

Clement Gottwald

25 FEBRUARY

A communist coup has toppled the fragile coalition government of President Eduard Benes in Prague, Czechoslovakia. The Communist premier Clement Gottwald has seized power and President Benes has announced the resignation of all of the centre and right-wing ministers of the previous government.

Israel proclaimed

14 MAY

The Jewish leaders Chaim Weizmann and David Ben-Gurion have declared the independence of the new Jewish state of Israel. The announcement, which was timed to coincide with the departure of British troops, seems certain to commit the new nation to a war with its neighbouring Arab states. Egyptian troops are already massing on Israel's southern border. The Jews are greatly outnumbered but are still braced to defend themselves. However, their 30,000-strong defence force has no aircraft, tanks, or heavy artillery. The troubles began when the UN general assembly would not affirm the boundaries for the new state's borders. The only hope for true peace lies in persuading Jews and Arabs to find common ground in some of the partition proposals that were put to the United Nations last November.

Prime Minister David Ben-Gurion

President Chaim Weizmann

JANUARY–JUNE

World Events	**JAN** The Union of Burma is proclaimed an independent republic in jubilant celebrations.	**MAY** In South Africa, David F Malan of the segregationalist Nationalist Party becomes the new prime minister.	**MAY** In Hungary, the Social Democrats and the Communists merge to form the Hungarian Workers' Party.	**JUN** In the USA, the Selective Service Act requires all men aged 18 to 25 to register for military duty.
Entertainment	**JAN** UK actress Vivien Leigh stars in the romantic film drama *Anna Karenina*.	**FEB** The celebrated Soviet film director Sergei Eisenstein dies of a heart attack at the age of 50.	**JUN** World heavyweight champ Joe Louis knocks out Joe Walcott to retain his title in the USA.	**JUN** US poet T S Eliot, who wrote *The Wasteland*, is awarded the Nobel Prize for Literature.
Innovations	**FEB** The UK General Certificate of Education (GCE) comes into use.	**JUN** US scientist A E Mirsky discovers ribonucleic acid (RNA) in human chromosomes.	**JUN** Record producers Columbia introduce the first US long-playing commercial vinyl records.	**JUN** Scrabble, the word game devised by architect Alfred Mosher Butts, is launched in the USA.

DAVID F MALAN

LONG-PLAYING RECORD

1948

Blockade beaten

30 JUNE

An armada of transport is being assembled to feed the starving citizens of the Western-occupied zones of Berlin, the German capital. Since the end of the war Germany has been divided into four zones, each run by one of the victorious Allies. Berlin, which lies deep in the heart of the Soviet zone of Germany, is also divided into four zones. Since 1945, relations between the Soviet Union and the West have grown worse. On 23 June the Soviet army blocked all road and rail links. The first supply plane flew into the besieged city four days ago, and now 200 aircraft are flying in daily delivering 2,500 tonnes of much-needed food.

A US plane carrying supplies lands in the German capital, Berlin

ACTION PAINTING

US artist Jackson Pollock has shot to fame with "action" paintings such as *Alchemy*. This unique artist does not use a brush and palette. Instead, he fixes his canvas to the floor and drips paint over the surface in huge sweeping rhythmic patterns.

Tito breaks with Stalin

1 JULY

Marshal Tito is determined to prevent the Soviet Union from gaining control over Yugoslavia. Outraged, Soviet leader Josef Stalin expelled Yugoslavia from the Soviet-controlled Cominform (the international organization of communist parties) three days ago. The Yugoslavs have rallied around Tito to face the threat of an economic blockade and invasion.

Marshal Tito

JULY–DECEMBER

AUG The Republic of South Korea is proclaimed in Seoul with Syngham Rhee as president.

JUL King George VI of the UK opens the first post-war Olympic Games in London, UK.

JUL The world's first turbine-propeller aircraft, the UK Vickers *Viscount*, makes its maiden flight.

THE BICYCLE THIEF

SEP Communist leader Kim Il Sung proclaims the People's Republic of North Korea in Pyongyang.

NOV Vittorio de Sica's latest film *The Bicycle Thief* is praised by the film critics in Rome, Italy.

NOV Edward Herbert Land's Polaroid camera proves very popular with the US public.

SEP Count Folke Bernadotte, the UN mediator in Israel, is assassinated there by Jewish terrorists.

NOV US actor Gene Kelly stars as D'Artagnan in the film *The Three Musketeers*.

DEC In the USA, Richard and Maurice McDonald open a drive-in hamburger cafe.

McDONALD'S DRIVE-IN

DEC Seven Japanese officials are hanged in Tokyo following conviction as war criminals.

NOV Norman Mailer's war novel *The Naked and the Dead* is published.

DEC In Switzerland, Georges de Mestral invents Velcro, a new clothes fastener.

1949

Nato alliance forged

18 MARCH

Agreement has today been reached among western European countries and the United States to form a new military alliance to deter the threat of a Soviet attack. The alliance is to be called the North Atlantic Treaty Organization (NATO) and is being described by US officials as an "antidote to fear". The final agreement will be signed by leaders of the 12 countries next month. However, some commentators fear that it will polarize the world into two armed camps.

Hamlet takes five Oscars

24 MARCH

It was *Hamlet*'s night at America's famous Academy Awards ceremony where the film scooped five Oscars. The British actor Laurence Olivier won the best actor award for his role of Hamlet in a film he also directed.

Italian champs perish in air crash

4 MAY

Italian football fans are in a state of shock tonight after hearing the tragic news that the whole Torino football team has been wiped out by a horrific plane crash. The team was on its way back from a tour of Portugal when the plane they were flying in crashed into the 802-m (2,200-ft) high Mount Superga on the outskirts of Turin in Italy. Thirty people are believed to have lost their lives in the disaster. The all-conquering Torino football team was on the verge of winning an amazing fifth successive league championship.

Remains of the plane carrying the Italian team

AUTOMATIC ROBOT

This amazing new Japanese robot is sure to appeal to children of all ages. It has a clockwork motor that allows it to walk all by itself. It is made of tin plate and has a humanoid appearance. Toy manufacturers are predicting that robots will be one of the most popular toys this Christmas.

JANUARY–JUNE

World Events	**JAN** Race riots between Indians and Africans in South Africa result in 106 deaths.	**FEB** Army leaders in Argentina try to force Eva Perón out of public life but Juan Perón threatens to resign as president.	**APR** The newly proclaimed independent Republic of Ireland leaves the UK Commonwealth.	**JUN** President Truman tries to calm anti-communist hysteria in the USA which was fuelled by "loyalty" investigations.
Entertainment	**JAN** The first Emmy TV Awards are presented in Hollywood, USA.	**FEB** German Jews protest at the Berlin premiere of hit film *Oliver*, accusing it of being anti-semitic.	**FEB** Arthur Miller's provocative new play *Death of a Salesman* premieres in New York, USA.	**MAR** US boxer Joe Louis, nicknamed the "Brown Bomber", retires as the world heavyweight champion.
Innovations	**JAN** New "micro-groove" 45-rpm records are invented in the USA.	**MAR** US air force pilots complete the first nonstop, round-the-world flight in *Lucky Lady II*.	**APR** The first Telethon is held in the USA with Milton Berle staying on air for 14 hours to raise money for charity.	**MAY** The first heliport, a landing pad specially made for helicopters, is installed in New York, USA.

SCENE FROM OLIVER

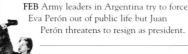

DEATH OF A SALESMAN

1949

Adenauer is new German chancellor

23 MAY

First results of the German election indicate that Dr Konrad Adenauer has won the race to be first chancellor of the Federal Republic of Germany. The new state, made up of the American, French, and British zones of occupation, but not the Soviet zone, will come into being tomorrow. In recent months a constitution has been agreed that provides for a federal form of government and, remembering the recent Nazi atrocities, has built-in safeguards against the abuse of human rights.

Mao proclaims new republic

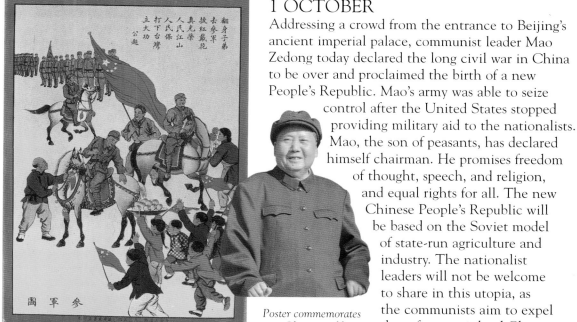

Poster commemorates new China republic

1 OCTOBER

Addressing a crowd from the entrance to Beijing's ancient imperial palace, communist leader Mao Zedong today declared the long civil war in China to be over and proclaimed the birth of a new People's Republic. Mao's army was able to seize control after the United States stopped providing military aid to the nationalists. Mao, the son of peasants, has declared himself chairman. He promises freedom of thought, speech, and religion, and equal rights for all. The new Chinese People's Republic will be based on the Soviet model of state-run agriculture and industry. The nationalist leaders will not be welcome to share in this utopia, as the communists aim to expel them from mainland China.

Peace in Greece

16 OCTOBER

For Greeks the horrors of war are finally over. The civil war, which broke out when the Germans pulled out in 1944, has today ended. With aid from the United States, the Greek government has now defeated the communist-controlled guerrillas in their mountain strongholds. However, the many atrocities committed by both sides has left Greeks bitterly divided.

JULY–DECEMBER

JUL The Pope declares that any supporters of communism will be excommunicated from the faith.	**SEP** The USSR tests its first atomic bomb to the alarm of the USA as well as that of western Europe.	**OCT** Soviet premier Joseph Stalin sets up a communist German state in the Soviet-controlled zone of that country.	**DEC** A total of 124,245 Germans are reported to have crossed over the border from East to West Germany this year.
JUL George Orwell's novel about the dangers of totalitarianism, *Nineteen Eighty-Four*, sells out in UK bookshops.	**SEP** Spy thriller *The Third Man* starring Orson Welles wins the Grand Prix at the Cannes Film Festival.	**NOV** A report in the UK shows that television is taking over from cinema.	**DEC** US film *On the Town's* song *New York, New York* is a big hit.
JUL Silly Putty is accidentally discovered by a US chemist while working on silicon compounds.	**JUL** "Three-stripe" running shoes (trainers) with moulded rubber soles are launched in Germany by Adidas.	**JUL** UK engineers develop the De Havilland *Comet* jet airliner, the world's first jet airliner.	**NOV** The first disposable nappies, called Paddipads, go on sale in the UK.

NINETEEN EIGHTY-FOUR

MAIDEN FLIGHT OF COMET JET

1950

Atom spy jailed

6 MARCH
Scientist Klaus Fuchs, sentenced to 14 years' imprisonment this month for passing vital atomic secrets to the USSR, has made further confessions about his Soviet contacts. Western intelligence services are now broadening their operation to uncover the spy network through which the secrets were betrayed.

Atomic secrets spy Klaus Fuchs

War breaks out in Korea

25 JUNE
At dawn today the communist People's Republic of North Korea launched a surprise invasion of the Republic of South Korea with the intention of unifying the Korean peninsula. It is expected that the United Nations security council will condemn the North Koreans and call for them to withdraw. Prior to the invasion, huge numbers of refugees had fled from the communist regime in the North across the 38th Parallel of Latitude. This marks the border between the two states and follows the line that divided the occupying forces of the Soviet Union and the United States at the end of World War II. The Soviet troops withdrew from the North only last year, and a US military government was in control of the South until 1948. It seems highly likely that both the Soviet Union and the USA will become involved in this new conflict.

Korean refugees

England lose 0–1 to the USA

Soccer shocker

28 JUNE
The English football team has suffered a shock defeat at their national sport in the first round of the World Cup. Despite constant attacks, they lost 0–1 to rank outsiders the United States at Belo Horizonte, Brazil.

JANUARY–DECEMBER

World Events	**JAN** Under Jawaharlal Nehru's leadership, India becomes the world's largest democratic republic.	**JUN** In Canberra, Australia, Prime Minister Menzies promises a 3,000-strong force to support US troops in Korea.	**SEP** Jan Smuts, the former Boer guerrilla leader and renowned South African statesman, dies aged 80.	**SEP** A United Nations force led by General MacArthur lands at Inchon in South Korea in an attempt to recapture Seoul.
Entertainment	**JAN** Carol Reed's film *The Third Man* premieres in the UK.	**APR** Soviet ballet dancer and choreographer Vaslav Nijinsky dies in London, UK, aged 60.	**AUG** US swimmer Florence Chadwick swims the Channel in 13 hours 23 mins, beating the women's record.	**NOV** Irish dramatist and critic George Bernard Shaw, author of the play *Pygmalion*, dies aged 94.
Innovations	**FEB** Diners' Club credit cards are launched in the USA by Ralph Schneider.	**JUN** The first human kidney transplant is performed by US surgeon R H Lawler.	**JUL** The production of television sets in the UK has increased by 250% in a single year.	**OCT** In London, UK, the Bowler family celebrates the centenary of that UK institution, the bowler hat.

FIRST CREDIT CARD

the Diners' Club
CREDIT IDENTIFICATION CARD
SIGNATURE
EXPIRES JUNE 30, 1951
SUBJECT TO TERMS OF REVERSE SIDE

JAN SMUTS DIES

1951

Genius machine

14 JUNE

Two brilliant US engineers, John Eckert and John Mauchly, have invented the most advanced form of digital computer to date. It is called UNIVAC (Universal Automatic Computer) and can read 7,200 digits per second. UNIVAC uses in the US Census Bureau in Philadelphia where it will be used for processing vast amounts of data. It will completely change the business-machine industry.

magnetic tape to put in information (input) and take out information (output). Unlike its forerunners, this computer can handle both numbers and alphabetical characters equally well. UNIVAC has been installed

UNIVAC, the world's first commercial computer

UNITED NATIONS MOVES HOUSE

The new United Nations headquarters in New York, USA, are being made ready for the first session next year. Building work began in 1947 and was completed in 1950. The modern skyscraper was designed by an expert international committee of architects led by Wallace Kirkman Harrison.

Hero for a new generation

16 JULY

One of this season's most original books is *The Catcher in the Rye* by US writer J D Salinger. The novel's hero is a troubled but funny prep-school drop-out who is called Holden Caulfield. He gives his own account of a series of events which led to him "cracking up". The story follows Holden on a two-day trip to New York where he observes the adult world around him with a mixture of innocence and irony. Holden's opinion of grown-ups – a bunch of "phonies" – and his delinquent behaviour may prove controversial. But this is a book that speaks of teenage alienation with insight and understanding, and it seems certain to become a favourite with the younger generation.

J D Salinger

JANUARY–DECEMBER

JAN United Nations forces repel a joint Chinese and North Korean offensive near the 38th Parallel.

MAY Soviet Mikhail Botvinnik retains his world chess crown at the chess championships in Moscow.

JAN The celebrated German motor car engineer Ferdinand Porsche dies at the age of 76.

USA TESTS A-BOMB

APR US President Truman fires commander of the UN forces General MacArthur after he threatened to invade China last month.

JUL Ace Argentine racing driver Juan Fangio wins the victor's laurels at the European grand prix in France.

APR The US Atomic Energy Commission begins A-bomb tests in the Nevada desert.

MAY Blacks and people of mixed race are removed from the electoral register in South Africa, and therefore cannot vote.

AUG In the USA, New York's WCBS TV broadcasts the first baseball game in colour.

AUG Deutsche Grammophon launches the first 33 rpm long-playing record.

PORSCHE AT UK MOTOR SHOW

NOV One million South Koreans are reported to have died since the onset of the Korean War in 1950.

DEC East Germany turns down an invitation to take part in the 1952 Olympics.

OCT In the UK a Porsche, the first German car exhibited since the end of WWII, is a success.

1952

Teenage tennis champion wows Wimbledon

5 JULY

A determined young Californian, Maureen Connolly, has won the prestigious Wimbledon women's singles tennis title at her first attempt, at the age of only 17. In the final, Connolly gradually wore down her opponent, fellow American Louise Brough, with her steady backhand and sure groundstrokes. She won in straight sets – 7–5, 6–3. With this victory "Little Mo", as she is known to her fans, becomes the youngest All-England champion since 15-year-old Lottie Dodd won in 1887. Having taken the US women's singles title at the age of 16, Little Mo seems certain to dominate the world of tennis for years to come.

"Little Mo" Connolly at Wimbledon

Evita is dead

26 JULY

Eva Perón, the charismatic wife of Argentine president Juan Perón, has died of cancer at the age of 33. As Argentina's first lady, she provided a unique and glamorous figurehead. She was adored by the poverty-stricken "descamisados", or "the "shirtless ones", whose rights she championed. To them, she was known simply as "Evita". Before she got married to labour minister Perón, Eva worked as an actress, and her dramatic talents proved a great asset. In 1945 when her husband was arrested for treason, she made an impassioned radio broadcast for the workers to rise up on his behalf. He was quickly released. When Juan Perón became president, Eva virtually ran the health and labour ministries and succeeded in winning the vote for women, legalizing divorce, and improving education. But Eva had her critics. Many held her at least partly to blame for the corruption and brutality of her husband's regime.

Eva Perón

Zátopek (left) during the marathon

Three Olympic golds for Czech

27 JULY

This week at the 15th Olympic Games in Helsinki, Finland, a 29-year-old Czechoslovakian runner has stunned everyone. Emil Zátopek has won the 5,000 metres, the 10,000 metres, and the marathon in record times, earning the nickname the "Czech Express"!

JANUARY–JUNE

World Events

FEB King George VI of the UK dies aged 56 and Princess Elizabeth accedes to the throne.

MAR Dr Kwame Nkrumah is elected as prime minister of the Gold Coast, the first African prime minister south of the Sahara.

APR US President Truman signs a peace treaty with Japan to mark the official end of World War II in the Pacific.

JUN In South Africa, blacks, Indians and mixed race begin a non-violent campaign against the imposition of apartheid.

Entertainment

JAN The Indian International Film Festival, the first festival of its kind in India, opens.

MAR A dazzling new musical, *Singin' in the Rain* starring singer and dancer Gene Kelly, opens in the USA.

MAR UK actress Vivien Leigh wins an Oscar for her role in the hit film *A Streetcar Named Desire*.

MAY René Clément's moving film about the effects of war on two children, *Jeux Interdits*, opens in Paris, France.

Innovations

MAR An artificial heart is first used in an operation at Pennsylvania Hospital, USA.

PRIME MINISTER NKRUMAH

MAR Two USAF *F-84 Thunderjets* make the longest sustained jet flights from the USA to Germany.

MAY UK airline BOAC begins the first jet passenger service from the UK to South Africa.

OSCAR WINNER VIVIEN LEIGH

JUN The USS *Nautilus*, the world's first nuclear-powered submarine is launched in the USA.

1952

USA tests H-bomb

A vast mushroom cloud rises over Eniwetok Atoll in the South Pacific

1 NOVEMBER

According to eyewitness accounts, a small island off Eniwetok Atoll in the South Pacific Ocean has been completely obliterated in a US nuclear test explosion. Radioactive dust rose in a huge cloud 40 km (25 miles) high and 160 km (100 miles) wide over the test site. The blast is believed to have been caused by a new kind of weapon called a hydrogen bomb or H-bomb. It is a thermo-nuclear device powered by a fusion reaction, rather than the fission reaction of the atom bomb.

This devastating superbomb explodes with a force that is an incredible 500 times greater than the atom bomb that destroyed the Japanese city of Hiroshima at the end of World War II. Many atomic scientists, such as Robert Oppenheimer and Enrico Fermi, are opposed to the idea of the H-bomb. It is believed that Soviet scientists will soon produce their own H-bomb. When both the superpowers, the United States and the Soviet Union, are equipped with such weapons, a war in the future will be a terrifying prospect.

Nobel Peace Prize for noble doctor

10 DECEMBER

German-born Albert Schweitzer has been awarded the Nobel Peace Prize for his efforts on behalf of "the brotherhood of nations". A brilliant scholar and musician, he became a doctor of medicine in 1913 in French Equitorial Africa using a chicken coop as his first consulting room. With his wife Hélène Bresslau, he set up a large mission hospital at Lambaréné. He intends to use the Nobel prize money to establish a leper colony.

Albert Schweitzer in Africa

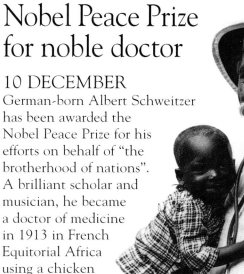

MONTESSORI EXPERIENCE

The pioneering educator Dr Maria Montessori died this year at the age of 82. She opened her first school in 1907, and designed an educational system aimed at helping children develop their intelligence and independence. She wrote several books, including *The Montessori Method*, and her schools are now established all over Europe.

JULY–DECEMBER

JUL After his abdication, King Farouk of Egypt, the "playboy king", sails out of Alexandria in his luxury yacht.

JUL US film actor Gary Cooper stars in the popular moralistic Western *High Noon*.

SEP *This is Cinerama*, the first film in wide-angle Cinerama is shown in New York, USA.

KING HUSSEIN OF JORDAN

AUG Still a schoolboy, Crown Prince Hussein becomes king of Jordan when his father is pronounced too ill to rule.

SEP In the USA, actor Charlie Chaplin is investigated as a communist sympathizer.

NOV A Swedish Airways plane is the first passenger airliner to fly over the North Pole.

OCT The UK declares a state of emergency in Kenya as Mau Mau terrorist attacks increase in the fight for independence.

NOV New Greek opera singer Maria Callas wins warm ovations in the UK for Bellini's *Norma*.

NOV In Cyprus, archaeologists discover a 2,000-year-old mosaic depicting Homer's tale *The Iliad*.

DEC In Brazil, the government forms a Coffee Institute to increase the national output of coffee.

NOV The *New Musical Express* publishes the first singles record chart in the UK.

BRAZILIAN COFFEE BEANS

NOV *Bwana Devil*, a 3-D film where lions "leap" from the screen, opens.

CINEMA OF THE FIFTIES

BEFORE THE 1950S cinemas were the only places where people could watch moving pictures. Then television arrived. As more families bought television sets, cinema companies had to find bigger and better attractions to tempt viewers to leave their living rooms. TV programmes were broadcast in black and white on small screens, so movie companies developed spectacular new "wide-screen" techniques like Cinerama and CinemaScope. In brilliant colour, with stereophonic soundtracks, wide-screen movies promised "real-life" action. Perhaps the strangest movie device of all was Smell-o-vision, where scents were pumped into the cinema.

Drive-in movies

By the end of the 1950s there were 4,000 drive-in cinemas in the open air throughout the United States. As many as 2,000 cars in curved rows could face the large screen, and small speakers were placed inside each car for sound.

Rockin' soundtrack

In 1955 *The Blackboard Jungle*, a film about rebellious teenagers, opened and closed with the song *Rock Around the Clock* by Bill Haley and the Comets. Young audiences went wild when it was played and soon many of the new "teen" genre movies were featuring rock 'n' roll soundtracks.

3-D cinema

One of the craziest gimmicks was 3-D cinema. Audiences had to wear special glasses to get the 3-D effect which made the action appear to burst from the screen. In 1952, the action film *Bwana Devil* promised "a lion in your lap".

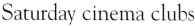

3-D VISION GLASSES

Childhood fantasy

The Red Balloon was a French fantasy film about a little boy who is followed through Paris by a friendly red balloon. When jealous schoolfriends burst the balloon, all the balloons of Paris converge upon the boy and lift him up into the sky. This charming little tale won an Oscar for best original screenplay in 1956.

THE RED BALLOON

ROY ROGERS

Saturday cinema clubs

Cinemas put on special Saturday morning shows for children which were hugely popular in the days before most people had television. The programmes featured animal characters such as Lassie the dog and Champion the Wonder Horse, and cowboy heroes like Roy Rogers and his horse Trigger. Many cinemas also held talent contests for the children in the ice-cream intervals.

Science-fiction

Although films about invaders from outer space and robots were popular, they were made with small budgets and without big-name actors. Some sci-fi films of the Fifties carried a serious message. The alien invaders in *The Day the Earth Stood Still* (1951) came to warn the Earth about the dangers of modern warfare.

ALIENS IN *THE DAY THE EARTH STOOD STILL*

GODZILLA

Glassy eyes

Special effects

Fantasy films like the Japanese feature *Godzilla* used special effects to create amazing screen monsters. They thrilled cinema audiences in the Fifties, but today they look clumsy and almost comical alongside the modern computer-generated images.

Big-budget epics

Wide-screen blockbusters were a feature of the 1950s, with their lavish sets, expensive all-star casts, as well as thousands of extras. *Ben Hur* (1959), a big-budget epic about a Roman gladiator, showed how successful they were when it won 11 Oscars.

CHARLTON HESTON STARS IN *BEN HUR*

Fish-like mouth

Moulded rubber mask

Webbed hands with sharp claws

Fins

Scaly suit made up of different sections

THE CREATURE FROM THE BLACK LAGOON

Marine monster

The Creature from the Black Lagoon (1954) featured a weird amphibious monster. The script was tacky, but the stunning underwater photography and convincing half-man, half-fish creature drew in large audiences.

171

1953

Death of a dictator

5 MARCH

Joseph Stalin, the leader of the Soviet Union for almost 30 years, has died from a brain haemorrhage at the age of 73. In 1917, Stalin was involved in the communist takeover of tsarist Russia, led by Lenin and resulting in the creation of the Soviet Union. Although Lenin later found him "rude and uncomradely", Stalin swiftly rose to power when Lenin died in 1924.

Stalin's series of "five-year plans" helped to modernize the vast country and, during World War II, he established the Soviet Union as a world power. He also created a totalitarian state, crushing all opposition. Stalin ("man of steel") was also nicknamed "Uncle Joe", showing that his people regarded him as both dictator and protector.

The body of Stalin lying in state in the Hall of Columns, Moscow

STEPPING OUT

Spike heels, or stilettoes, are all the rage with fashionable women. However, these elegant, ultra-high heels have their drawbacks – the wearer looks delightfully sophisticated unless she gets them caught in a pavement or grating!

Charlie's life in exile

17 APRIL

Charlie Chaplin, the brilliant movie star and director, will never return to the United States, his home for over 40 years. Last autumn, when he left his adopted country to promote the film *Limelight*, British-born Chaplin was banned from returning because he was suspected of supporting communism. Chaplin has surrendered his re-entry permit, protesting that he has been the object of "vicious propaganda".

Scientists discover the key to life

The scientists with their DNA helix

25 APRIL

Francis Crick and James Watson, two scientists at Cambridge University in the UK, have unlocked one of the mysteries of life. They have discovered the structure of DNA, the chemical which makes the genes that pass on hereditary characteristics. The DNA molecule is made up of two intertwined strands – a double helix. Scientists can now work out how living things reproduce themselves.

JANUARY–JUNE

World Events	JAN Yugoslav communist leader Josip Broz, known as Tito, is elected president of Yugoslavia.	FEB Flooding in Holland leaves over 1,000 dead after dykes burst, and nearly 300 drown in the UK's east coast flood.	APR UN and communist prisoners-of-war are swapped at Panmunjon, Korea, but the war continues.	JUN Egypt is proclaimed a republic after army leaders depose King Fuad, infant son of ex-king Farouk.
Entertainment	JAN US country singer Hank Williams dies of a heart ailment aged only 29.	FEB French actor Jacques Tati stars in *Monsieur Hulot's Holiday*, a film about an accident-prone bachelor.	MAR Soviet composer Sergei Prokofiev, whose works included *Peter and the Wolf*, dies aged 61.	MAY US writer Ernest Hemingway wins a Pulitzer Prize for his book *The Old Man and the Sea*.
Innovations	JAN The UK grounds all *Stratocruiser* aircraft after finding an engine defect.	FEB US film company Twentieth Century Fox announces the advent of wide-screen CinemaScope.	MAR US virologist Dr Jonas Salk successfully tests a vaccine against the disease polio.	MAY US architect Frank Lloyd Wright receives a National Institute of Arts and Letters medal.

YUGOSLAV PRESIDENT TITO

COMPOSER SERGEI PROKOFIEV

1953

Peak pioneers

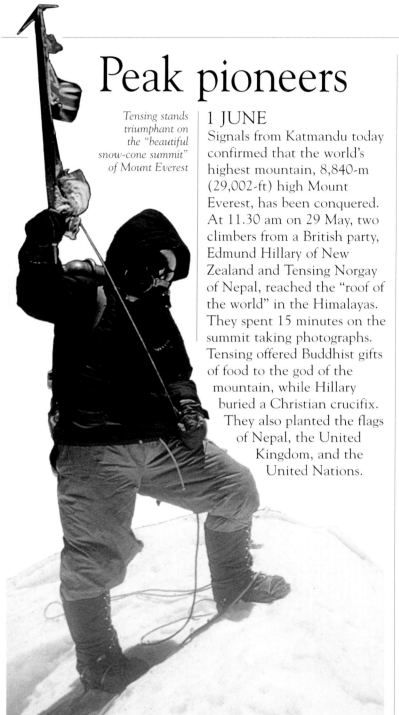

Tensing stands triumphant on the "beautiful snow-cone summit" of Mount Everest

1 JUNE

Signals from Katmandu today confirmed that the world's highest mountain, 8,840-m (29,002-ft) high Mount Everest, has been conquered. At 11.30 am on 29 May, two climbers from a British party, Edmund Hillary of New Zealand and Tensing Norgay of Nepal, reached the "roof of the world" in the Himalayas. They spent 15 minutes on the summit taking photographs. Tensing offered Buddhist gifts of food to the god of the mountain, while Hillary buried a Christian crucifix. They also planted the flags of Nepal, the United Kingdom, and the United Nations.

A new Elizabethan era begins

2 JUNE

A new Elizabethan age began when Queen Elizabeth II of Great Britain was crowned today in Westminster Abbey, London. She succeeded to the throne last year on the death of her father King George VI. Millions of television viewers all over the world watched the coronation service as the new 27-year-old queen pledged herself to the service of her people in Great Britain and the Commonwealth.

Rebel leader

Marlon Brando in Laslo Benedek's The Wild One

30 DECEMBER

Rebel teenagers have a new hero – the leather-clad biker played by Marlon Brando in a new film *The Wild One*. The film follows the story of a motorcycle gang that descends on a small Californian town and wreaks havoc. Brando is the tough but sensitive gangleader Johnny who, when asked what he is rebelling against, replies "What've you got?"

JULY–DECEMBER

JUL The Korean armistice is signed at Panmunjom after three years of fighting and the loss of over two million lives.

JUL *Gentlemen Prefer Blondes*, a US film musical starring Jane Russell and Marilyn Monroe, opens.

SEP The first film in widescreen CinemaScope, *The Robe*, premieres in Hollywood, USA.

KOREAN ARMISTICE

AUG Over 1,000 are reported dead in Greece's Ionian islands after they are hit by earthquakes and huge tidal waves.

JUL US golfer Ben Hogan wins his third golf masters tournament in one year.

AUG Soviet prime minister Georgi Malenkov claims the USSR has the H-bomb.

AUG The shah flees Iran after a failed attempt to topple the nationalist leader Mohammad Mossadegh.

NOV Fiery Welsh poet Dylan Thomas dies at the Chelsea Hotel, New York, USA, aged only 39.

NOV The US Bell X-1A rocket-powered plane flies at over 2,560 km/h (1,600 mph).

YETI FOOTPRINT

NOV French soldiers capture Dien Bien Phu in Vietnam from the communist Viet Minh forces.

DEC UK PM Winston Churchill wins Nobel Prize for Literature for his historical works.

DEC A UK-led expedition sets out to find the legendary yeti in the mountains of Nepal.

1954

New vaccine

12 APRIL
The first vaccine against polio, a disease that affects thousands of children, is being tested on nearly one million children in the United States. Dr Jonas Salk made the breakthrough after discovering that polio is caused by a virus. He hopes that the disease will now be wiped out.

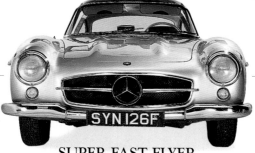

SUPER-FAST FLYER
Mercedes has used race-track technology to make a new high-speed supercar, the 300SL *Gullwing*. With its roof-hinged "gullwing" doors open, it looks like a bird, and can fly along at a top speed of 225 km/h (140 mph).

Roger Bannister wins the battle to smash the four-minute mile barrier

Bannister breaks four-minute barrier

6 MAY
Just under one hundred years ago, the world record for running the mile stood at four minutes 55 seconds. No one thought it could be run in under four minutes. But today in Britain an athlete finally achieved the impossible. Roger Bannister, a 25-year-old medical student, ran a mile in three minutes 59.4 seconds at Oxford. Some experts had feared that the enormous exertion might kill him. Bannister survived, but said afterwards that he was actually "prepared to die".

Beleaguered French troops at Dien Bien Phu

French defeated in Vietnam

7 MAY
The Vietnamese came closer to throwing off French rule today. Vietnam is a part of France's empire in Indo-China but, since 1945, communist rebels known as the Viet Minh have been fighting to win back control of their own land. After a 55-day siege, they have now captured the strategically placed French fortress of Dien Bien Phu. This defeat may end French efforts to hold on to Indo-China.

JANUARY–JUNE

World Events	**JAN** President Eisenhower of the USA proposes that the vote be given to all 18-year-olds in the country.	**APR** UK security forces in Kenya mount the biggest round-up of Mau Mau terrorist suspects in the 18-month-old state of emergency.	**MAY** The government of Thailand offers bases to Western countries from which to fight communism in southeast Asia.	**JUN** US President Eisenhower says he will prevent Senator McCarthy from investigating the CIA for communist infiltrators.
Entertainment	**JAN** Marilyn Monroe marries US ex-baseball player Joe DiMaggio.	**APR** Frank Sinatra, star of the US film *From Here to Eternity*, wins an Oscar for best actor.	**APR** One of two famous brothers who pioneered the cinema, Auguste Lumière dies in Lyon, France, aged 91.	**JUN** Mississippi-born singer Elvis Presley records his first single in the USA, *That's All Right Mama*.
Innovations	**JAN** The USA launches the first nuclear-powered submarine, *Nautilus*. **FIRST NUCLEAR SUBMARINE**	**JAN** The first electronic computer is put into regular operation by a UK business.	**MAR** The Japanese crew of the *Lucky Dragon* suffer radiation sickness after US H-bomb tests at Bikini Atoll. **CINEMA PIONEER LUMIERE**	**JUN** The tomb of Pharaoh Sankhet which dates from 2750 BC, is uncovered at Sakkara in Egypt.

1954

Segregation in the southern states – separate water fountains for blacks and whites

On the road to racial equality

17 MAY
A major blow for racial equality was struck today in the United States. The Supreme Court overturned an 1846 law which states that education can be "separate but equal". The new ruling means it is now illegal for black children to be barred from white schools. At present, 2.5 million black pupils in the southern United States are educated in poorly equipped schools, separated from white children.

First atomic power station

27 JUNE
The world's first atomic power station opened today at Obninsk in the Soviet Union. The nuclear reactor can generate 5 megawatts of electricity, enough for a town of 5,000 people. It proves that nuclear energy can be used for beneficial purposes.

Inside the Obninsk atomic power station

McCarthy's witchhunts over

2 DECEMBER
US senator Joseph McCarthy was today condemned by the Senate for misconduct. For four years his opponents have been awaiting such a verdict, and they hope it will mean that McCarthy's spell over the American people has finally been broken. Since 1950 McCarthy has been waging a campaign to root out communist "spies and infiltrators" in the state department and, more recently, the army. Lacking hard evidence, McCarthy's committees have relied upon whispers and rumours to back up their accusations. This has led to an uncontrolled wave of anti-communist hysteria – "reds under the bed" have been suspected everywhere from Hollywood to the White House. Now it is possible that McCarthy's rule of terror may at last be over.

Senator McCarthy, left, challenges US army chiefs

JULY–DECEMBER

JUL In Geneva, it is agreed that Vietnam will be divided along the 17th Parallel, with the communists controlling the north.

SEP World heavyweight boxer Rocky Marciano beats Ezzard Charles for his 47th consecutive victory in the USA.

AUG UK firm Rolls-Royce announces it has developed a vertical take-off jet, nicknamed the "Flying Bedstead".

AUG The UN officially withdraws from Korea, one year after the ceasefire was signed at Panmunjon.

NOV French painter Henri Matisse, one of the leaders of the colourful Fauvist art movement, dies aged 84.

NOV A Scandinavian airline begins the first passenger flights to the USA over the North Pole.

HENRI MATISSE

SEP Over 1,000 people are feared dead, and an estimated 36,000 are homeless, as a huge earthquake hits Algeria.

DEC US writer Ernest Hemingway, author of *A Farewell to Arms*, wins the Nobel Prize for Literature.

NOV The US National Cancer Institute claims a link between cancer and cigarette smoking.

AUTHOR ERNEST HEMINGWAY

DEC In South Africa, the prime minister Johannes Strijdom calls for the imposition of stricter apartheid laws.

DEC UK runner Roger Bannister retires from athletics to devote himself to his medical practice.

DEC The USS *Forrestal* is the first aircraft carrier to be built that has an angled flight deck.

FIFTIES TOYS AND GAMES

IN THE 1950S mass production and the introduction of plastic meant that children were able to choose from a wider range of toys than ever before. As well as more traditional toys such as tinplate cars and board games, cheap plastic novelty toys such as the hula hoop, the day-glo yo-yo, and the frisbee became runaway successes and developed into the latest fads. One of the most popular mass-produced toys was the US Barbie® doll, the first ever "fashion model" doll with a wardrobe of different outfits. At only $3, these fashion dolls were not expensive, and over 350,000 of them were sold in the first year alone. Once toy manufacturers realized the potential of this fast-growing market, the race was on to find the next worldwide craze.

To keep the hoop spinning, you had to swivel your hips

Hoop mania

Wooden hoops originated in Australia, but when a plastic version of them was launched in the United States in 1958, 25 million were sold in four months. Everyone wanted a plastic hoop and the craze soon spread worldwide.

TIN-PLATE MOTORCYCLIST

FRICTION-DRIVEN TOY CAR

Mechanical tin toys

In the 20 years after World War II, Japanese toy manufacturers mass-produced imaginative and inexpensive toys for children which sold all over the world. They pioneered the use of plastic, but also made a wide range of tin-plate cars, trains, motor-cycles, and space vehicles. Some of them had built-in battery-operated mechanisms that enabled them to perform noisy special effects.

The changing face of the Barbie® doll

FIRST EVER BARBIE, 1959

ENCHANTED EVENING BARBIE, 1961

LIVE ACTION BARBIE, 1971

DAY TO NIGHT BARBIE, 1985

ULTRA HAIR BARBIE, 1993

Tiny trucks

Miniature motor vehicles that were inexpensive to make and buy became very popular in the 1950s. Japanese firms pioneered the use of plastic, but also manufactured a wide range of tinplate replicas of cars, lorries, pick-up trucks, and diggers that were so desirable that even adults began collecting them!

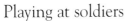

Playing at soldiers

Combat dolls for boys to play with became popular from the early 1950s onwards. In Britain, Action Man came with a range of outfits and military accessories. He was closely related to GI Joe of the United States, Combat Joe of Japan, and Falcon of Brazil. These new toy soldiers soon became household names and millions were sold each year throughout the world.

Disc made of moulded plastic

Stick-on insignia

TOY
ROCKET
SHIP

Inspired science-fiction

The real-life space race between the United States and the Soviet Union began in 1957, but even before that people were fascinated with outer space and UFOs. Fantasy toys like ray guns, rocket ships, and flying saucers were much in demand. Toys and other merchandise were often specially produced to tie in with popular cartoon characters and futuristic films and TV shows.

Perspex bubble

Flying objects

Flying discs became one of the biggest fads of the 1950s. These plastic toys were controlled with a flick of the wrist and became an instant success on beaches and in city parks. The first world champion was crowned in 1968.

Flashing light adds a new dimension

FLYING
SAUCER WITH
FLASHING LIGHTS

1955

Charlie Parker

Einstein's time is up

18 APRIL
One of the world's greatest scientists, Albert Einstein, died today at Princeton, USA, his home since 1933. He was 76 years old. Einstein, born in Germany, was the founding father of modern physics. His revolutionary theory of relativity changed the way scientists thought about time and space, and his equation, $E = mc^2$, was the key to the development of nuclear energy. Einstein was a modest, philosophical man who loved classical music. Although his discoveries led to the creation of the atomic bomb, he was a leading campaigner for world peace.

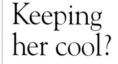

Albert Einstein

Marilyn cools off in steamy New York City

Goodbye to all that jazz

12 MARCH
One of the leading talents of modern jazz, Charlie "Yardbird" Parker, has died in the USA at the age of only 34. The self-taught alto saxophonist from Kansas City changed the way jazz is played. In the early 1940s he helped to create a new music style called "bebop" with other young jazz musicians such as Dizzy Gillespie. Parker will be remembered for his inspired improvisations.

Keeping her cool?

13 JUNE
Publicity posters for Marilyn Monroe's new movie *The Seven-Year Itch*, which opened last week, have been creating quite a stir. The 29-year-old screen goddess is shown standing over a grating, her skirt billowing in an uprush of air from the subway. Pressure from the League of Decency forced Loew's State Theatre in New York, USA, to remove their giant poster.

JANUARY–JUNE

World Events	**FEB** Nikita Khrushchev emerges as the new leader of the USSR, replacing Georgi Malenkov.	**MAR** Floods in New South Wales, Australia, kill 200 people and 300,000 sheep, and leave 44,000 people homeless.	**MAY** The Warsaw Pact is signed by all the communist countries of eastern Europe to form a new military alliance.	**MAY** The Allied high commission, which has held sovereignty since the war, abolishes itself and gives sovereignty to West Germany.
Entertainment	**MAR** French fashion designer Christian Dior's spring collection introduces the A-line skirt.	**MAR** US actor Marlon Brando wins an Oscar for his performance as Terry Molloy in the film *On the Waterfront*.	**JUN** In France, three cars plough into the crowd at the Le Mans race track, killing 80.	**JUN** US high jumper Charles Dumas is the first person ever to clear 2 m (7 ft).
Innovations	**JAN** RCA demonstrates a new music "synthesizer" in New York, USA.	**JAN** The WHO (World Health Organization) says that atomic waste poses a serious health risk.	**JAN** In the UK, archaeologists confirm that fossilized "Piltdown Man" was a complete hoax.	**JUN** Kanchenjunga in the Himalayas, the highest unclimbed peak, is conquered by a UK team.

DIOR'S NEW A-LINE

HIGH-JUMPER CHARLES DUMAS

1955

Disney's wonderland

18 JULY

The world has never seen anything like it. Famous US film-maker Walt Disney has fulfilled his dream of creating a "Never-Never Land" for children. His trail-blazing amusement park, called Disneyland, opened today at Anaheim near Los Angeles. It is divided into three different realms known as Fantasyland, Adventureland, and Frontierland. Visitors can take a ride on a Mississippi riverboat, experience the Wild West, sail in a pirate galleon, or fly through a moonscape. Over five million people from around the world are expected to visit this magical kingdom every year.

THE SHARK

Citroën have launched their futuristic new car, the Citroën DS Décapotable. Nicknamed "the Shark" because of its sleek nose, the DS is stylish and practical, with semi-automatic gears.

Talented actor dies young

30 SEPTEMBER

James Dean, the US actor whose good looks and cool style quickly made him one of Hollywood's hottest stars, has died in a car crash outside Los Angeles. He was only 24. Dean's performance as a teenage rebel in his first film, *East of Eden*, was highly acclaimed. Two more movies, *Rebel Without a Cause* and *Giant*, have yet to be released.

James Dean, who lived too fast and died young

Flying saucers – no evidence

Photograph of an Unidentified Flying Object, or UFO, in Nevada, USA

25 OCTOBER

Whatever science-fiction writers and film-makers might say, there are no such things as flying saucers – and that's official. The US air force has just concluded an eight-year-long investigation into the UFO phenomenon and has found no evidence to suggest the existence of any alien spacecraft in our skies.

JULY–DECEMBER

JUL The first East-West heads of government meeting since 1945 takes place in Geneva, Switzerland.

JUL French cyclist Louison Bobet becomes the first man to win the Tour de France three times.

JUL The world's most eminent scientists sign a declaration condemning nuclear warfare.

CYCLIST LOUISON BOBET

SEP In Buenos Aires Juan Perón is overthrown and General Eduardo Lonardi becomes provisional president of Argentina.

JUL Turkish-born UK oil magnate Calouste Gulbenkian dies, leaving millions for art and charity.

JUL UK's Donald Campbell is the first to exceed 320 km/h (200 mph) in his turbo-jet hydroplane *Bluebird*.

NOV After terrorist attacks and the breakdown of talks between the UK, Greece, and Turkey, a state of emergency is declared in Cyprus.

JUL Canadian swimmer Marilyn Bell, aged 17, is the youngest person to swim the Channel.

SEP In the UK, MG Cars unveils a popular new sports model, the MG-A.

CHANNEL SWIMMER MARILYN BELL

DEC The United Nations admits 16 new countries as members, but refuses membership to Mongolia and Japan.

AUG Nobel prize-winning German novelist Thomas Mann dies in Switzerland.

OCT In the UK the BBC demonstrates colour TV at Alexandra Palace, London.

1956

US bus boycott

Mrs Rosa Parks sits in the whites-only section of a bus in Montgomery, Alabama

29 FEBRUARY

In the southern American state of Alabama, the fight for full civil rights for black people continues. Late last year the Interstate Commerce Commission ordered that black citizens should be able to sit wherever they choose on public transport. However, Rosa Parks, a black woman living in Montgomery, Alabama, has been arrested for sitting at the front of a bus in a section still set aside for whites. After her arrest, black protesters in Montgomery organized a bus boycott and 115 of them were also jailed. Now huge crowds, supported by civil rights leader Dr Martin Luther King, are demanding an end to any kind of "segregation".

Prince Rainier of Monaco marries beautiful American movie queen

19 APRIL

Today on the French Riviera, a fairytale marriage was celebrated in front of more than 1,000 guests. The groom was Prince Rainier III, ruler of the tiny principality of Monaco. His bride was Grace Kelly, the US movie queen famous across the world for her "iceberg beauty". Guests at the Catholic ceremony included dignitaries from 25 nations, and countless others watched the event on television. Grace Kelly, the young star from Philadelphia, has appeared in 11 films, and won an Academy Award for best actress in 1954 for her role in *The Country Girl*. As a real-life princess she intends to retire from an acting career. From now on her face will be appearing on postage stamps, not in publicity photographs.

Prince Rainier and Princess Grace marry

FROM THE HEART
Emil Nolde, the great German Expressionist painter, has died. Nolde was fascinated by primitive art, and the use of rich colours to show emotion. His dramatic works include *Night of Sunflowers*.

JANUARY–JUNE

World Events

JAN The Sudan, Africa, is declared an independent republic, ending the joint Anglo-Egyptian administration.

FEB The US and UK governments sign a declaration warning developing countries against Soviet aid.

MAR Pakistan is proclaimed an Islamic republic, with Major-General Iskander Mirza its first president.

MAR Soviet leader Khrushchev denounces Stalin as a brutal and criminal murderer in a speech to the Communist Party élite.

Entertainment

JAN UK author A A Milne, famous for his stories about Winnie-the-Pooh, dies aged 74.

JAN The seventh winter Olympic Games open with a flourish in Cortina d'Ampezzo in Italy.

APR US world heavyweight boxing champion Rocky Marciano retires after 49 fights and 49 wins.

JUN Austrian conductor Herbert von Karajan becomes the artistic director of the Vienna State Opera.

Innovations

JAN In the UK, the Astronomer Royal dismisses the idea of space travel as "bilge".

A A MILNE'S CHARACTER EEYORE

APR In Chicago, USA, a device that records TV programmes onto tape is first demonstrated.

MAY The USA drops an H-bomb from a plane for the first time, over Bikini Atoll in the Pacific.

ROCKY MARCIANO RETIRES

MAY In France, Teflon Co markets a Teflon-coated frying-pan as the first non-stick kitchenware.

1956

Suez Canal seized

26 JULY

Serious trouble is brewing in Egypt. The president, Colonel Gamal Abdel Nasser, has seized control of the Suez Canal, which runs through his country. Opened in 1869 and controlled by an Anglo-French company, the 165-km (103-mile) long waterway is vital for carrying Middle Eastern oil supplies through Egypt to Europe. Colonel Nasser aims to build a high dam at Aswan with the money the canal generates. His seizure of the canal comes after the United States and Britain refused to fund the project. The Egyptian people seem to have approved their president's actions. As for the outraged British and French, he says that they can "choke to death on their fury". The two countries will now have to decide what action to take.

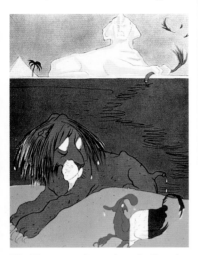

The Egyptian sphinx whips the British lion and the French hen at Suez

Perfect pitching

8 OCTOBER

Sporting history was made in the United States today, during the fifth game in the baseball World Series. Don Larsen, pitching for the New York Yankees against the Brooklyn Dodgers, tossed the first-ever perfect game, stopping every Dodger batter from reaching first base.

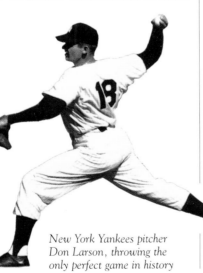

New York Yankees pitcher Don Larson, throwing the only perfect game in history

Uprising in Hungary

A captured Soviet tank flies the Hungarian flag in Budapest

26 OCTOBER

Since 1946 Hungary has been part of the Soviet Union's communist empire. Now, in the capital Budapest, rebels have destroyed the huge bronze statue of Stalin, and many thousands have died fighting with Soviet forces stationed in Hungary. Prime Minister Imre Nagy has sympathy for the rebels, but Soviet troops are said to be massing on the Hungarian border with East Germany.

Screen goddess

28 NOVEMBER

French actress Brigitte Bardot is the beautiful star of the new film *And God Created Woman*, directed by her husband Roger Vadim. Her sensual character has shocked Hollywood, but Vadim says she is simply a liberated and beautiful young woman.

Bardot in And God Created Woman

JULY–DECEMBER

SEP The USSR and Japan agree to end their state of war, in place since World War II, and to restore full diplomatic relations.

AUG German dramatist Bertolt Brecht, whose work included *The Threepenny Opera*, dies in Berlin aged 58.

AUG Generating begins at Calder Hall in the UK, the world's first large-scale atomic power station.

ELVIS PERFORMS LIVE ON TV

OCT In Egypt, Anglo-French forces bomb the Suez Canal area after the UN calls for a ban on the use of force by its members.

SEP In the US, Elvis Presley performs live on the Ed Sullivan Show, viewed by 82% of the potential audience.

SEP US air force pilot Kincheloe flies a Bell *X-2* rocket aeroplane to an altitude of 38,376 m (125,907 ft).

NOV Anglo-French forces move into Egypt and seize control of the Suez Canal zone from the Egyptians.

SEP The Bill Haley film *Rock Around the Clock* causes "Teddy Boys" to riot in UK cinemas.

OCT Clarence Birdseye, inventor of a process for deep-freezing food, dies in the USA.

UN TROOPS MOVE INTO EGYPT

NOV The UN imposes a ceasefire on the Anglo-French allies, and sends troops into Egypt to control the canal.

NOV Italy now has the greatest number of cinemas in Europe – more than 17,000.

NOV Work begins on an engineering marvel – the Kariba High Dam in Rhodesia.

ROCK 'N' ROLL

BILL HALEY

IN THE MID-1950s a new kind of music sprang into being in the United States. Fast, loud, and upbeat, it became known as rock 'n' roll. Rock had its roots in the musical styles of black Americans such as rhythm-and-blues and boogie-woogie, but it suddenly took off when white singers began adapting these styles for their own music. No one had ever heard anything like it before. All over the world, the loud, exciting dance tunes with outrageous-sounding lyrics appealed to teenagers who worshipped screen rebels like James Dean and Marlon Brando. Rock 'n' roll offered a whole new approach to life with its own cool style, crazy dances, hip language, and above all its sense of being young and modern.

Rock pioneer

With the Comets, Bill Haley hit the big time in the USA with *Rock the Joint*, and became an international rock icon.

New grooves

A decade after World War II, the United States was enjoying an economic boom and young people had money to spend. Manufacturers began to target the growing teenage market – selling goods like portable record players that could be played in bedrooms away from the family living-room!

ELVIS PRESLEY

Star singles

During the 1950s, singles were released on cheaper, smaller vinyl discs that played at 45 rpm (revolutions per minute). They were much better value than the heavier 25-cm (10-in) 78 rpm records, and teenagers bought them in their thousands.

ORIGINAL 45 OF *JAILHOUSE ROCK* BY ELVIS

CHUCK BERRY

The rock 'n' roll poet

Chuck Berry developed a distinctive rock 'n' roll style from his rhythm-and-blues roots. He merged hard-driving, chiming guitar sounds with lyrics that spoke about the joys and trials of being young in the 1950s. Songs like *Sweet Little Sixteen* and *Johnny B Goode* influenced many later musicians.

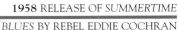
The King

The sheer excitement of Elvis Presley's mid-1950s hits – *Heartbreak Hotel, Jailhouse Rock, Teddy Bear,* and *All Shook Up* – was matched only by the sensational way he performed them live. He was unlike any other white American singer because he "sang black" with emotion and verve. Elvis swung his hips and curled his lip in a way that captured the hearts of millions of teenage girls, but outraged their parents.

Rock 'n' roll style

Rock 'n' roll was about style as well as music. You had to look good if you played, or even if you were simply listening. The coolest men wore their hair brushed up away from their foreheads and held it in place with greasy haircream.

Jumping jukeboxes

During the 1930s in the United States live music in roadhouses known as "juke joints" gave way to coin-operated machines offering a wide choice of records to play. By the 1950s these "jukeboxes" were hugely popular, particularly with teenagers. *Billboard* magazine's Hot 100 singles chart, launched in 1958, was based on both record sales and the number of jukebox plays.

WURLITZER JUKEBOX

LITTLE RICHARD

The wild man

"Awopbopaloobopawopbamboom!" shrieked Little Richard in his first big hit *Tutti Frutti*, in 1956. His acrobatic antics at the piano thrilled his audiences, and more frenzied hits followed such as *Long Tall Sally* and *Good Golly Miss Molly*. But in 1957 Little Richard suddenly gave up rock 'n' roll music to become a church minister. He later returned to the stage to sing gospel.

ELECTRIC GRETSCH GUITAR 1959

"Pickups"amplify vibrations from the strings

Tremolo arm to vary pitch

Volume control

Electric guitar

Rock 'n' roll music depended heavily on the electric guitar. With its unlimited volume and its power to produce a whole range of new sounds, it revolutionized popular music.

BUDDY HOLLY

Hit writer

Buddy Holly was one of the greatest rock 'n' roll songwriters. Between 1957 and 1959, he had seven hit singles, some with his group the Crickets and some as a solo performer. Songs such as *Peggy Sue* became instant classics. The world was stunned when he died in a plane crash in 1959, aged only 22.

183

1957

An ace for Althea

6 JULY

US tennis player Althea Gibson wrote herself into the record books this week by becoming the first black woman to win the most coveted prize in tennis – the singles title at Wimbledon, England. In the final she beat Darlene Hard 6–3, 6–2 and has played the whole tournament without dropping a single set. Thirty-year-old Gibson began her tennis career playing paddle tennis on the streets of Harlem, New York, in the United States. She is the first black player to win a major tennis tournament.

*Wimbledon winner
Althea Gibson*

Composer Leonard Bernstein

West Side hit

26 SEPTEMBER

West Side Story, an exciting new musical by US composer Leonard Bernstein and the lyricist Stephen Sondheim, opened today on Broadway in New York. An updated version of the very popular Shakespeare play *Romeo and Juliet*, it is a moving love story set in New York's rough gangland.

A WAY WITH WORDS

US writer Dr Seuss has found a brilliant way to interest children in reading. His new book, *The Cat in The Hat*, uses only 175 simple words, but is written in comic verse. It tells of an anarchic cat who tries to persuade two children that they want to have "lots of good fun that is funny".

Formula One champion

4 AUGUST

Argentine racing driver Juan Manuel Fangio has done it again. In West Germany the 46-year-old driver, who is nicknamed "Cheuco" ("bandy legs"), has won his 24th grand prix race, picking up his fifth world championship in seven years. Driving for Maserati, he broke the lap record by a staggering 11 seconds at the Nurburgring racing track. Fangio thrilled the 200,000 spectators by coming from behind to win. He is the most successful Formula One driver there has ever been.

JANUARY–DECEMBER

World Events	**JAN** In the UK, Harold Macmillan becomes prime minister when Anthony Eden resigns.	**MAR** Six nations – France, West Germany, Italy, Belgium, Holland, and Luxembourg – set up the European Common Market.	**AUG** After 170 years of UK rule, Malaya achieves its independence and elects its first president, Abdul Rahman.	**SEP** Dr François Duvalier, popularly called "Papa Doc" by the people of Haiti, is elected president of that country.
Entertainment	**JAN** US film star Humphrey Bogart, tough, cool hero of over 50 movies, dies aged 57.	**MAY** US star Burt Lancaster is legendary lawman Wyatt Earp in the film *Gunfight at the OK Corral.*	**AUG** US comedian Oliver Hardy, the plump half of the comedy duo Laurel and Hardy, dies aged 65.	**SEP** Finnish composer Jean Sibelius, probably most famous for his Seventh Symphony, dies aged 91.
Innovations	**JAN** Danish architect Joern Utzon is to be the designer of the Sydney Opera House, Australia.	**FEB** The first portable electric typewriter is marketed by Smith Corona of Syracuse in the US.	**OCT** The USSR launches *Sputnik I*, the first artificial satellite to go into space.	**NOV** A dog called Laika is the first animal to be sent into space aboard the Soviet spacecraft *Lunik II*.

HAROLD MACMILLAN

"PAPA DOC" DUVALIER

1958

Elvis signs up for the army

Elvis loses his quiff to the army barber

24 MARCH

Elvis Presley was today drafted into the US army for his national service. His call-up was postponed so that he could finish filming *King Creole*. The 23-year-old singer will serve for two years, and see his monthly earnings of $100,000 drop to just $83.20!

President de Gaulle

21 DECEMBER

The former wartime leader General Charles de Gaulle was today elected president of France by an overwhelming majority. The French hope that de Gaulle's talents as a politician will again steer France through a difficult period – this time the country seems to be on the brink of civil war over the fraught question of Algerian independence. French settlers in Algeria are determined to keep the colony under their control, but de Gaulle is hoping for a compromise with the Algerian nationalists. He will be president of France for the next seven years.

Brazilian magic

29 JUNE

The Brazilian football team has won the sixth World Cup, beating the host nation Sweden 5–2 in the final. The Brazilians played dazzling football throughout the whole competition, particularly 17-year-old prodigy Pelé, whose sensational goal-scoring seemed unstoppable.

17-year-old soccer star Pelé

JANUARY–DECEMBER

MAY In Algeria, 40,000 French settlers riot against the deal the French government have made with the Algerian nationalists.

JUN Greek-Cypriot leader Makarios rejects the UK peace plan for Cyprus; clashes with the Turkish-Cypriots on the island continue.

JUN Two years after the Hungarian uprising, former prime minister Imre Nagy is executed, causing much anger.

JUL King Faisal II, the crown prince, and Iraq's prime minister are murdered in an army coup and a republic is formed.

JAN In France the first collection of 23-year-old couturier Yves St Laurent is a great success.

FEB In Germany, eight of the UK's Manchester United football team are killed in a plane crash.

MAR West Indian cricketer Gary Sobers scores a record 365 runs playing against Pakistan.

AUG Australian runner Herb Elliot breaks two world records for the mile and 1,500 metres.

JAN The USA launches its first satellite, *Explorer I*, from the launch pad at Cape Canaveral in Florida.

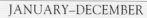

THE GERMAN PLANE CRASH

AUG US nuclear submarine *Nautilus* makes the first undersea voyage beneath the North Pole.

OCT The USSR agrees to lend money to President Nasser of Egypt to build the Aswan Dam.

CRICKETER GARY SOBERS

DEC The world's largest oil tanker, able to carry 1,021,000 barrels, is launched in Japan.

185

1959

New leader for Cuba

2 JANUARY

Following a coup on the Caribbean island of Cuba, President Fulgencio Batista has fled to the Dominican Republic. Since 1952 Batista has run Cuba as a police state, favouring the interests of the wealthy élite at the expense of ordinary citizens. In 1956 his opponents began to make guerrilla attacks from the mountains. Known as "los barbudos" ("the bearded ones"), they were led by a young lawyer called Fidel Castro and his second-in-command, Ernesto "Ché" Guevara. Now the small band of guerrillas has become a national movement. In yesterday's coup, Castro rode triumphantly into the capital Havana. The new regime is to have a president, Dr Manuel Urrutia, but it seems that Castro will be Cuba's premier. Hopes are high that this revolution will transform life for ordinary Cubans.

Fidel Castro, the new revolutionary leader of Cuba

CUDDLY TEDDIES?
Many teenagers have a new and distinctive style. The notorious "Teddy Boys", who have a reputation for gang fights, are named for their long, Edwardian-style drape jackets, drainpipe trousers, crêpe-soled shoes, and slicked-back hair.

The Dalai Lama flees Tibet

The Dalai Lama, a fugitive in India

19 APRIL

The Dalai Lama, Tibet's Buddhist spiritual leader, is safe at last. Since 1950 Tibet has been ruled by the Chinese, who have dealt brutally with recent Tibetan attempts to regain independence. The Dalai Lama was smuggled out of Lhasa, Tibet's capital, at the end of March. He travelled over the mountains by yak, avoiding Chinese patrols, and has found sanctuary in India. Today 7,000 Tibetans gave him a rousing welcome at the West Bengali town of Siliguri before he set off to meet the Indian prime minister, Mr Nehru.

JANUARY–JUNE

World Events	**JAN** In North America, Alaska becomes the 49th, and the largest, state in the USA.	**MAR** Over 3,000 people are reported dead after a hurricane hits the island of Madagascar off the east coast of Africa.	**APR** Cuban revolutionary leader Fidel Castro says the USA can keep its naval base at Guantanamo Bay in Cuba.	**JUN** In Dublin, 76-year-old Éamon de Valera, three times prime minister of the Republic of Ireland, becomes president.
Entertainment	**JAN** US movie mogul Cecil B de Mille, famous for his epic films, dies aged 77.	**FEB** Rock singing legend Buddy Holly dies in a plane crash in Iowa, USA, aged 22.	**MAR** Marilyn Monroe, Jack Lemmon and Tony Curtis star in the US film *Some Like It Hot*.	**MAR** US thriller writer Raymond Chandler, creator of detective Philip Marlowe, dies aged 70.
Innovations	**JAN** The Soviet *Lunik I* spacecraft flies past the Moon into orbit around the Sun.	**APR** The St Lawrence Seaway linking the Great Lakes to the Atlantic Ocean opens in the USA.	**APR** US architect Frank Lloyd Wright, master of innovative building design, dies aged 89.	**MAY** The UK's Jodrell Bank radio telescope transmits radio messages to the USA via the Moon.

CECIL B DE MILLE

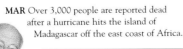

SOME LIKE IT HOT

1959

New miniature car is launched

18 AUGUST

In the United Kingdom, the British Motor Corporation is launching a very innovative small car. The new Morris Mini looks just like a box on wheels, but in fact it has been carefully designed by Alec Issigonis to be both practical and cost-effective. By placing the four small wheels at the corners and mounting the engine sideways, Issigonis has created a surprising amount of space inside. The car also sits very low on the road.

The great quiz show scandal

Van Doren apparently pondering on air

2 NOVEMBER

The hugely popular US TV quiz show *Twenty-One* is today at the centre of a national scandal. The current champion of the quiz show, Professor Charles Van Doren, has admitted that he had won $129,000 dishonestly – he had been shown the answers in advance. The former champion Herbert Stempel was so upset at being ousted in favour of Van Doren that he spilled the beans.

Antarctica is saved

1 DECEMBER

Only last year "the last great journey in the world" was completed when a small expedition led by English explorer Vivian Fuchs travelled across the frozen continent of Antarctica. Now the South Polar region is in the news again as 12 countries, including the United States, Britain, and the Soviet Union, sign a historic international agreement not to claim any part of it for themselves. Military bases there are to be banned, as are nuclear experiments and the dumping of nuclear waste. But the scientists of all nations will be allowed free access to the frozen continent to carry out research into the climate and geology, as well as the wildlife of one of the world's last wildernesses.

An Antarctic king penguin

JULY–DECEMBER

AUG The volcanic islands of Hawaii in the central Pacific Ocean become the 50th state of the USA.

JUL US singer Billie Holiday, one of the greatest voices of jazz, dies at the age of 44.

JUL Australian airline Quantas makes its first flight across the Pacific from Sydney to the USA.

HAWAII, THE 50TH US STATE

SEP Ceylon's prime minister Solomon Bandaranaike dies from wounds after being shot by a Buddhist monk.

AUG US sculptor Sir Jacob Epstein, who lived most of his life in London, UK, dies aged 79.

JUL In the UK, a hovercraft makes a first sea crossing between England and France.

NOV In Havana, Cuba, Major Ernesto "Ché" Guevara, Castro's right-hand man, becomes head of the Cuban national bank.

SEP Soviet leader Khrushchev is angry when, for security reasons, he cannot visit Disneyland on his USA tour.

SEP The USSR's space probe, *Lunik II*, scores the first direct hit on the surface of the Moon.

PRESIDENT MAKARIOS

DEC Archbishop Makarios, leader of the Greek Orthodox church, becomes first president of the new republic of Cyprus.

OCT UK actor Errol Flynn, famous for his swashbuckling roles in adventure movies, dies aged 50.

OCT The Soviet *Lunik III* sends back the first-ever photographs of the dark side of the Moon.

THE LEISURE BOOM

BY THE MID-1950S many countries were finally recovering from the effects of World War II. Improved methods of mass production meant that luxury goods could be cheaply produced and more people than ever before could afford labour-saving devices such as vacuum cleaners and washing machines. This left extra time for recreational activities and the leisure industry boomed. As economies prospered, people also found that they had more money to spend. A wide range of goods and services, from glossy magazines and portable record players to plastic toys and package holidays, flooded the growing market of prosperous consumers.

Watersports

As more people spent time at the seaside, watersports took off. It was possible for many to take up exciting hobbies such as water-skiing.

Family holidays

Holiday camps were not new in the 1950s, but they became increasingly popular worldwide as more and more people earned enough money to take an annual holiday. Families stayed in chalets and took part in communal games, sports, and competitions.

Hairdryer hood

Home magazine

TWO WOMEN RELAX AT THE HAIRDRESSER'S

Taking five

By using labour-saving household appliances, 1950s housewives were able to take a breather more often. Shopping in the new supermarkets also helped them to save time because they could make all their purchases under one roof. As a result, consumer goods such as magazines aimed specifically at women grew in number.

Leisurewear

Before the 1950s, there was no such thing as leisurewear. People wore the same sorts of clothes for both work and recreation. But, in the 1950s, people began to adopt more casual clothes for leisure pursuits. Blue denim jeans in particular became hugely popular throughout the world.

1955 DISNEYLAND THEME PARK
OPENS IN CALIFORNIA, USA

1958 FIRST PASSENGER JETS SPEED
UP INTERNATIONAL TRAVEL

1958 WOMEN'S MAGAZINES
MULTIPLY AS READERSHIP GROWS

Sunshine holidays

In the 1950s, tourism became big business. Air travel was still expensive, but holiday companies began to offer cheaper charter flights to overseas destinations. The Mediterranean coasts of France, Italy, and Spain attracted thousands of holiday-makers looking for cut-price vacations in the sun, and new resorts sprang up to cater for the growing numbers of tourists.

Sunglasses were a vital fashion accessory

Carefully groomed hair

On the beach

In glamorous resorts along the French Riviera, looking good on the beach was very important. A beach holiday often meant buying a whole new wardrobe of leisure clothes. Boned bathing costumes like this one were stylish without being too revealing.

Casual jacket

It's a strike!

Like cinemas, dance halls, and bingo clubs, bowling alleys drew large numbers of people with time and money to spend. Bowling alleys encouraged families to visit by providing soft drinks and fast food, and from 1952 many alleys became mechanized, with machines replacing the "pin-boys" to re-set the "skittled" (knocked over) pins.

Soft-soled bowling shoes

BOWLING BALL

Short skirt with rows of frills

Chiffon scarf

Painted toenails

PINS

1960

Sharpeville massacre

The terrible scene at Sharpeville

21 MARCH

Today in South Africa, 69 people were killed and 186 left wounded in a deadly confrontation that will surely deepen the existing crisis there. The country's troubles stem from the South African government's racial policy, know as apartheid. This policy is intended to separate the black and white races, and ensure the domination of the black majority by their white rulers. South Africa's white minority government has introduced laws that deny the black population many of their basic rights, and since 1956 only whites have been allowed to vote. Today's tragedy occurred in the black township of Sharpeville, in the Transvaal, when 15,000 blacks staged a demonstration against the "Pass Laws". These laws demand that blacks stay in their own areas, not travelling out of them without permission. When they saw the crowd of blacks approaching, local white police officers opened fire. Within minutes the scene looked like a battlefield, with bodies sprawled everywhere. Police commander Colonel D H Pienaar commented afterwards, "If the natives do these things, they must learn their lesson the hard way."

CAPITAL OF HOPE

In April, the futuristic city of Brasilia became Brazil's new capital. Brasilia's apartment blocks have all been built in the same modern style to avoid any class distinction, and the congress is housed in impressive twin towers.

Champions of Europe – again!

18 MAY

It seems that wonder-team Real Madrid are unbeatable. The Spanish football stars have won the European Cup for the fifth year running. This time they beat West Germany's team Eintracht Frankfurt 7–3 in front of a spellbound crowd at Hampden Park in Glasgow, Scotland. Three of their goals were scored by Argentine star Alfredo Di Stefano. All the others were scored by the Hungarian Ferenc Puskas, nicknamed the "Galloping Major" by his teammates. They claim that Puskas uses his left foot to juggle the soap in the shower.

European Cup winners Real Madrid

Historic votes cast in Ceylon

21 JULY

The world has its first woman prime minister today. She is Mrs Sirimavo Bandaranaike, leader of the Sri Lanka Freedom Party, who won the country's general election yesterday with 75 seats out of a possible 150. Her rise to power has been swift. She entered politics last year, after her husband Solomon, the prime minister, was assassinated.

JANUARY–JUNE

World Events	**JAN** In Egypt, President Nasser lays the foundation stone of the Aswan High Dam as work begins.	**MAR** An earthquake, followed by a tidal wave and widespread fire, kills over 12,000 in the Moroccan resort of Agadir.	**MAY** Adolph Eichmann, the German SS officer who masterminded Hitler's "Final Solution" is captured by the Israelis.	**JUN** The UK- and Italian-ruled Somaliland territories gain their independence, uniting to form Somalia on 1 July.
Entertainment	**JAN** Algerian-born French writer Albert Camus, author of *The Outsider*, dies aged 46.	**FEB** The eighth Winter Olympics opens in Squaw Valley, USA, with a ceremony staged by Walt Disney.	**MAR** Joy Adamson's *Born Free*, the true story of Elsa, an African lioness, is published.	**APR** In the USA, William Wyler's film *Ben Hur* wins a record 11 Oscars.
Innovations	**FEB** Israeli archaeologists unearth 1,700-year-old Biblical parchment scrolls. **ALBERT CAMUS**	**MAR** The Jodrell Bank Telescope in the UK contacts a US satellite 655,000 km (409,375 miles) away.	**APR** The first weather satellite, *Tiros 1*, sends pictures of the USA from a height of 724 km (453 miles). **ELSA THE LIONESS**	**MAY** The world's longest liner, the SS *France*, is launched in France by Mme de Gaulle.

1960

The master of suspense

10 AUGUST

British film director Alfred Hitchcock certainly knows how to keep an audience on the edge of its seat. He believes that the greatest feeling of suspense comes when people know exactly what to expect – because then waiting for it to happen can drive them almost crazy. In his latest film *Psycho* trouble is plainly in store when Janet Leigh, playing a young secretary on the run with stolen money, checks into a strange, deserted motel. She eats dinner with the owner's son, twitchy Norman Bates (played by Anthony Perkins), then decides to take a shower before bed.... But to find out what happens you must wait in suspense until you see this chilling film yourself.

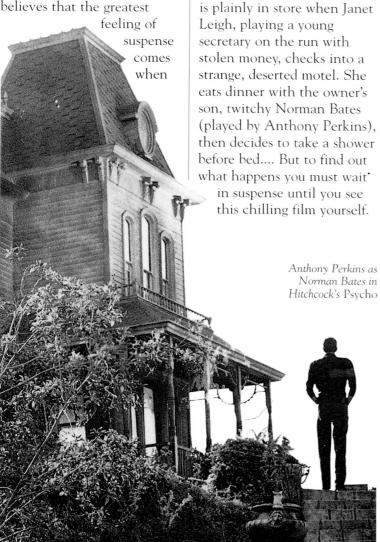

Anthony Perkins as Norman Bates in Hitchcock's Psycho

African man's marathon feat!

Abebe Bikila of Ethiopia

10 SEPTEMBER

Until now, no African athlete has ever won an Olympic gold medal in a track or field event. Today in Rome, the barefoot Ethiopian runner Abebe Bikila won the marathon in 2 hours 15 mins 16.2 secs.

Presidential debate live on TV

26 SEPTEMBER

In November this year the people of the United States will go to the polls to elect a new president. Tonight they were given an early chance to decide which way to vote – they were able to tune in to a special live debate between the Republican candidate Richard Nixon and his Democrat rival, John F Kennedy. The clash was fairly gentle but, while TV viewers were impressed by Kennedy's good looks and relaxed manner, listeners who heard the debate on the radio felt Nixon came out on top.

Kennedy and Nixon prepare to do battle

JULY–DECEMBER

JUL In the Congo, Africa, Colonel Mobutu leads the Congolese army into mutiny against incumbent President Lumumba.

JUL In the UK, Donald Campbell successfully takes his new £1 million *Bluebird* car for its first test run.

JUL US submarine *George Washington* launches Polaris nuclear missiles for the first time.

PATRICE LUMUMBA

AUG Fidel Castro nationalizes all US-owned property in Cuba in retaliation for what he considers "US economic aggression".

AUG Australian Jack Brabham becomes the new Formula One champion after winning the Portuguese grand prix.

AUG The USA puts the world's first communications satellite *Echo 1* into orbit round the Earth.

OCT The UK's largest colony Nigeria gains its independence under Prime Minister Balewa, and joins the Commonwealth.

SEP US sprinter Wilma Rudolph, once a polio victim, wins an amazing three Olympic golds.

SEP Ten skeletons are discovered by archaeologists in 3,800-year-old graves at Stonehenge in the UK.

US ATHLETE WILMA RUDOLPH

OCT Thousands of people die in east Pakistan as the country is battered by a tidal wave and hurricane.

NOV UK jury rules that D H Lawrence's *Lady Chatterley's Lover* is not an obscene book.

OCT In the UK, Hawker Siddeley's *P.1227* vertical take-off aircraft is tested.

1961

Youngest US president sworn in

20 JANUARY
In Washington today John Fitzgerald Kennedy was sworn in as the new president of the United States. At 43, he is the youngest man to hold the office, and he is also the first Roman Catholic. In his rousing ten-minute inaugural speech

President Kennedy

he said, "The torch has been passed to a new generation of Americans," one that was still "proud of our ancient heritage". He also encouraged his fellow citizens to "ask not what your country can do for you – ask what you can do for your country."

Ham is the first chimp in space

31 JANUARY
In 1957 the Soviet Union put a dog into space and today the United States has sent up a monkey called Ham.

Ham receives a well-earned apple

The chimpanzee was blasted 240 km (150 miles) into space in a *Mercury* capsule for an 18-minute flight. After he had safely splashed down and was on board the recovery ship, Ham was given an apple as a reward for his successful performance in the operation. He is now heading back to Cape Canaveral in Florida, where experts from the space programme are waiting to "debrief" him on his mission.

Bay of Pigs invasion

19 APRIL
The United States is suffering a serious blow to its pride over the prickly issue of Cuba. Relations between the small Caribbean island and her mighty neighbour have steadily worsened since Fidel Castro's revolutionaries seized power in 1959. Castro soon began moving smoothly towards a communist system of government, backed by the Soviet Union. Only two days ago, 1,500 Cuban exiles returned to the island to mount an invasion, which

they hoped would start an uprising against Castro. No US forces were involved, but they clearly supported the landing at the Bay of Pigs, an inlet on Cuba's coast 145 km (91 miles) southwest of the port of Havana. However, now the invasion has failed, and US President Kennedy and Soviet premier Khrushchev have given each other blunt warnings not to interfere in Cuba's internal affairs. It seems almost inevitable that this island will cause trouble between the two powers.

Cuban anti-communist troops plan their attack

JANUARY–JUNE

World Events	**JAN** In New Delhi, India, the Russian Orthodox Church is elected to the World Council of Churches.	**MAR** The US government announces it is increasing aid to the Laos government in its fight against the Pathet Lao communists.	**APR** In New York in the USA, the UN votes 83–0 in favour of censuring South Africa for its racial policy of apartheid.	**JUN** Iraq lays claim to Kuwait, after the UK officially ends its protectorate over the small oil-rich sheikdom in the Middle East.
Entertainment	**JAN** US novelist Dashiell Hammett, author of *The Maltese Falcon*, dies aged 66.	**MAR** UK conductor Sir Thomas Beecham, founder of the Royal Philharmonic Orchestra, dies.	**APR** South African golfer Gary Player wins the US masters championship by a single stroke.	**JUN** The leading male dancer with the Soviet Kirov Ballet, Rudolf Nureyev, defects in Paris, France.
Innovations	**JAN** In the UK, the one-millionth Morris Minor rolls off the production line. *DR LEAKEY AND HIS DISCOVERIES*	**FEB** UK anthropologist Dr Louis Leakey finds human fossils possibly one million years old in the USA.	**APR** The USSR's Yuri Gagarin orbits the Earth, and becomes the first man in space. *YURI GAGARIN, COSMONAUT*	**MAY** The USA puts a man in space, and Kennedy claims that they will be first to the Moon.

1961

A new wall divides Berlin

East Germans at work on the Berlin Wall

31 AUGUST

Today, the "Iron Curtain" dividing Europe that Britain's prime minister Winston Churchill warned about at the end of World War II became a reality. A network of concrete blocks and electric fences divides the city of Berlin. On 13 August, the East German authorities began building a huge wall to separate East and West Berlin, to the anger of people living on both sides. Since Germany was partitioned after the war, two million Germans have fled from the hardships and repression of communist East Germany into the West, mainly through Berlin. Now this route has been closed. But, even as the wall-builders block all the possible exit points that they can find, some refugees are still finding secret ways out. Two families have even swum across Berlin's canals to reach the West.

An East German soldier leaps through one of the last gaps in the Berlin Wall in a desperate bid for freedom

ELEGANT E-TYPE

Jaguar have unveiled their elegant and relatively inexpensive new E-type sports car. The rapturous world's press reported that "E stands for exhilaration, excitement, [and] ecstasy".

WWF founded

The giant panda is the new emblem of the World Wildlife Fund

11 SEPTEMBER

The World Wildlife Fund was officially formed and registered as a charity today, with its headquarters on the northern shores of Lake Geneva in Switzerland. Its aims will be to reverse and halt the destruction of the Earth's natural environment, and to help its human inhabitants live in greater harmony with nature. British ornithologist Max Nicholson and biologist Sir Julian Huxley have played major roles in bringing the fund into being. Its logo is a panda, a choice inspired by the recent arrival of Chi-Chi the panda at a British zoo.

JULY–DECEMBER

JUL Jomo Kenyatta is released after nine years of detention for his involvement with the Kenyan Mau Mau organization.

JUL US author Ernest Hemingway dies at the age of 61 from a self-inflicted shotgun wound.

JUL France launches a bathyscape to explore the 10,363-m (34,000-ft) Kurile Pit, an ocean chasm off Japan.

DAG HAMMARSKJÖLD

SEP Swedes take to the streets to mourn Dag Hammarskjöld, secretary-general of the UN, who died in a plane crash.

SEP Twenty-year-old US folk singer Bob Dylan inspires audiences in New York's famous Greenwich Village.

AUG The earliest surviving Roman mosaics in the UK are found at Fishbourne in southern England.

NOV In the USSR's de-Stalinization campaign, Lenin's mausoleum is re-opened after Stalin's body is removed.

OCT Leonard Bernstein's 1957 Broadway musical *West Side Story* is made into a film in the USA.

SEP US and UK governments call for a ban on all nuclear testing inside the Earth's atmosphere.

WEST SIDE STORY ON SCREEN

DEC In South Vietnam, James Davies has the dubious honour of being the first US soldier to be killed by Vietcong.

NOV James Thurber, the well-known US comic writer and illustrator, dies at the age of 66.

DEC US Lt Col Robinson flies a *Phantom II* at a record speed of 2,568.81 km/h (1,605.51 mph).

1962

Algeria independent

3 JULY

Today in a brief declaration, French president Charles de Gaulle "solemnly recognized" the independence of Algeria, bringing to an end a complex and bitter struggle that has been raging since 1954. The north African country was taken under French control in 1830. Subsequently many French colonists settled there, and after World War II any attempts to integrate Algeria more closely with France were resisted by the Algerians and French settlers alike. Recent terrorist activity by

Algerians celebrate their independence

both groups has made a peaceful solution unlikely, if not impossible. Now, after 132 years of French rule, the new republic of Algeria must work out its own destiny.

POP ART

A startling new artistic style has emerged in New York, USA. "Pop art" borrows images from everyday life and aims to make the viewer see them with a fresh eye. Andy Warhol's paintings of soup cans and Roy Lichtenstein's giant comic-strip cartoon frames are the masterpieces of the new genre.

Swan's song for the world's birds

16 AUGUST

A new book by US marine biologist Rachel Carson could have a profound effect on the way we now live.

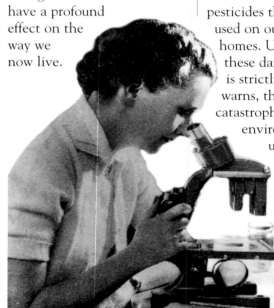

In *Silent Spring*, published today, she describes the side-effects of the artificial pesticides that are commonly used on our farms and in our homes. Unless the use of these dangerous chemicals is strictly controlled, she warns, they will have a catastrophic effect on our environment. She asks us to imagine a time when no birds sing and the trees bear no fruit, and to change the way we live to prevent this happening.

Scientist Rachel Carson

Marilyn Monroe found dead

Sad star Marilyn in her last film The Misfits

5 AUGUST

Marilyn Monroe was found dead today by her housekeeper. She lay in bed with an empty bottle of sleeping pills nearby. The 36-year-old actress had recently been fired from the film she was working on for Twentieth Century Fox. In an article in this week's *Life* magazine, she said, "Everybody is always tugging at you. They would all like a sort of chunk of you."

JANUARY–JUNE

World Events	JAN UK and US representatives walk out of talks about nuclear test ban treaties with the USSR.	FEB As US fears mount about the stockpiling of missiles, President Kennedy imposes an embargo on the import of all Cuban goods.	FEB The OAS secret army of French settlers steps up its terror campaign in Algeria to prevent independence.	MAY Nazi war criminal Adolf Eichmann, former SS colonel, is executed in Israel 24 months after his capture by Israeli agents.
Entertainment	JAN New Zealander Peter Snell breaks the world mile record in 3 mins 54.4 secs.	APR In Hollywood, USA, the film of the hit musical *West Side Story* wins ten Oscars.	JUN In Chile, Brazil retain the soccer World Cup, beating Czechoslovakia with a 3–1 victory in the final.	JUN US singer Stevie Wonder, who is only 12 years old, hits the top of the charts in the USA.
Innovations	FEB Astronaut John Glenn becomes the first American to orbit the Earth. **TELSTAR LAUNCHED** 	JUN The first communications satellite, the US *Telstar I*, relays television signals from space.	JUN In Paris, France, 130 men, women, and children die when an Air France Boeing 707 crashes. **12-YEAR-OLD STEVIE WONDER**	JUN The European Space Research Organization is established in Paris, France.

1962

Licensed to kill

Scotsman Sean Connery as Bond

1 OCTOBER

A suave screen hero makes his debut today in *Dr No*. Agent James Bond, code-named 007, is licensed to kill for the British secret service. Bond, played by Sean Connery, is based on the character created by Ian Fleming.

Khrushchev and Cuban leader Castro

Toy model of 007's Aston Martin with ejector seat

Back from the brink of a nuclear war

28 OCTOBER

The world breathed a huge sigh of relief today, as one of the most nerve-wracking weeks in history ended. Six days ago, US president John F Kennedy announced that a US spy plane had spotted Soviet nuclear missile bases on the Caribbean island of Cuba, 145 km (91 miles) from the east coast of the United States. Since World War II the two superpowers have been competing with each other for supremacy. When Castro's Cuba recently became a communist state, the Soviet Union took the opportunity to install nuclear weapons there – too close to the United States for comfort in President Kennedy's view.

Kennedy speaks to the press

He immediately ordered a naval blockade of the island and directed the US armed forces "to prepare for any eventuality". The possibility of the world's first nuclear war was looming unless the Soviets agreed to remove the weapons. As the tension mounted, messages flowed between Kennedy and the Soviet premier Nikita Khrushchev. A US pilot flying over Cuba was shot down and killed. In nearby Florida 200,000 US troops stood ready. Finally, today, Kennedy promised to lift the blockade and not invade Cuba, while Khrushchev agreed to remove the weapons.

JULY–DECEMBER

SEP After a brief civil war and elections, ruling council president Ahmed Ben Bella proclaims Algeria a socialist republic.

OCT Amnesty International, an organization set up to investigate the abuse of human rights all around the world, is formed.

DEC The first African-dominated government is formed in Northern Rhodesia under statesman Kenneth Kaunda.

DEC President Kennedy lifts the Cuban arms blockade and calls for an emergency phone link with the Soviet Kremlin.

AUG Nobel prize-winning Swiss author Hermann Hesse, who wrote *Steppenwolf*, dies aged 85.

NOV *How the West Was Won*, a US film featuring a buffalo stampede and Indian attack, is filmed in Cinerama.

DEC John Steinbeck, US author of *Of Mice and Men*, wins Nobel literature prize.

DEC Gregory Peck stars in *To Kill a Mockingbird*, a film about racism in the USA.

AUG The tunnel linking France and Italy under Mont Blanc in the Alps is completed.

SYMBOL OF AMNESTY INTERNATIONAL

AUG In the USA, the *Mariner II* space probe is launched towards Venus.

SEP In the UK, the world's first passenger hovercraft service completes a successful 3-month run.

HOVERCRAFT SERVICE

DEC US space probe *Mariner II* sends back the first close-up pictures of the planet Venus.

1963

Soviets put first woman in space

16 JUNE
Valentina Tereshkova from the Soviet Union became the first woman to go into space today. Twenty-six-year old lieutenant Tereshkova orbited the Earth in the spacecraft *Vostok 6* and, during the flight, spoke with the Soviet leader Nikita Khrushchev. He called her "Valya" and expressed his "fatherly pride" in her extraordinary achievement. The young cosmonaut who grew up on a farm, worked in a tyre factory and a textile mill before joining the Soviet space programme. She is also an amateur parachute jumper in her spare time. In 1962, she was picked for space training because of her dedication and obvious lack of fear.

Valentina Tereshkova ready for lift-off

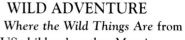

WILD ADVENTURE
Where the Wild Things Are from US children's author Maurice Sendak is a new classic in the making. The book's hero is plucky boy-rebel Max, whose brilliantly illustrated adventures with the "wild things" explore every child's anxieties and fantasies.

"I have a dream"

28 AUGUST
Over 200,000 demonstrators marched through the United States' capital, Washington DC, today to campaign for an end to discrimination against blacks. Civil rights leader Dr Martin Luther King inspired the huge crowd with a speech advocating justice and equality through non-violent means. He declared, "I have a dream that one day this nation will rise up and live out the true meaning of its creed: 'We hold these truths to be self-evident: that all men are created equal.' "

Black civil rights leader Dr Martin Luther King

JANUARY–JUNE

	World Events	Entertainment	Innovations
	FEB Willy Brandt is re-elected as mayor of West Berlin, Germany, with an overwhelming majority.	**FEB** A tennis racquet made of steel is patented by Lacoste in France.	**FEB** In the UK, surgeons at Leeds Infirmary announce a successful kidney transplant.

World Events

FEB Willy Brandt is re-elected as mayor of West Berlin, Germany, with an overwhelming majority.

MAR John Profumo, the UK's secretary of war, claims "no impropriety" in his relationship with 21-year-old Christine Keeler.

MAY Jomo Kenyatta is elected Kenya's premier in the country's first general election in the lead-up to independence.

JUN Giovanni Battista Montini is elected Pope Paul VI, succeeding Pope John XXIII who has died aged 81.

Entertainment

FEB A tennis racquet made of steel is patented by Lacoste in France.

BEATLES' HIT SINGLE PLEASE PLEASE ME

FEB UK group The Beatles release their first album, named after their hit single, *Please Please Me*.

APR David Lean's 1962 epic film *Lawrence of Arabia* wins seven Oscars, including best picture.

JUN After cast and director changes the most expensive film to date *Cleopatra* comes to the big screen.

ELIZABETH TAYLOR IN CLEOPATRA

Innovations

FEB In the UK, surgeons at Leeds Infirmary announce a successful kidney transplant.

MAR The first automatically controlled underground trains are introduced in London, UK.

MAY US astronaut Major Cooper lands in the Pacific after 22 orbits of the Earth in his *Mercury* capsule.

JUN A telephone hotline is set up for the first time between the White House and the Kremlin.

1963

Kennedy assassinated in Dallas

A nation mourns

President Kennedy in the motorcade, moments before his death

25 NOVEMBER

Twenty-four hours after John F Kennedy's suspected killer, Lee Harvey Oswald, was shot dead during a jail transfer, the United States president was buried at Arlington National Cemetery. Representatives of 93 nations came to pay their respects with the Kennedy family. After the service, John Junior, only three years old, saluted his father's coffin.

Jackie Kennedy with her children at the funeral

22 NOVEMBER

"President Kennedy is dead." Those four bleak words are now echoing across a shocked world. John F Kennedy, the 35th president of the United States, was shot in the head today as he was driven in an open-topped car through Dallas, Texas. In a flurry of shots, the president slumped down in the car as his wife Jackie tried to help, cradling his head. He died in the nearby Parkland Hospital, only 25 minutes after receiving the terrible head wound. He was 46 years old. John Connally, the governor of Texas, was also wounded in the shooting that turned a sunny day into the worst of nightmares. Connally's condition tonight is described as "serious". In the confusion following the shooting, police arrested Lee Harvey Oswald, a former US marine with recent Soviet contacts. Oswald strongly denies killing the president, but he is being treated as the prime suspect.

JULY–DECEMBER

AUG In the UK's greatest train robbery ever, £2.6 million in used banknotes is stolen from the Glasgow to London mail train.

SEP Scottish driver Jim Clark becomes the youngest Formula One champion.

JUL The first-ever Channel crossing by hydrofoil is made, between Belgium and the UK.

FRENCH SINGER EDITH PIAF

SEP Four girls are killed and 23 people injured when a bomb explodes in a church service in Alabama, USA.

OCT French singer Edith Piaf, whose anthem was *Je Ne Regrette Rien*, dies aged 74.

SEP In New Zealand, doctors give the world's first blood transfusion to an unborn child.

NOV A volcano erupts on the ocean floor, producing the new island of Surtsey, off the south coast of Iceland.

OCT Jean Cocteau, the French playwright, artist, poet, and novelist, dies aged 74.

OCT In the UK, a model of the Anglo-French *Concorde* supersonic plane is displayed.

SURTSEY, ICELAND'S NEW ISLAND

NOV Lyndon Baines Johnson is sworn in as the 36th president of the USA aboard the aircraft *Air Force 1*.

NOV UK author Aldous Huxley, who wrote *Brave New World*, dies aged 69.

NOV Viking remains found in Canada are dated at 500 years before Columbus.

1964

Boxing baby beats champ

25 FEBRUARY

In one of sport's great upsets, 22-year-old US boxer Cassius Clay has beaten the champion Sonny Liston to win the world heavyweight title. Before the fight, 43 of 46 US newspaper experts predicted that Liston could not lose because Clay had fought professionally only 20 times. But Clay's confidence was sky-high. Claiming that Liston was "too ugly to be a world champion", he proved too quick and skilful for the older man, beating him in six rounds at Miami Beach.

Cassius Clay, "the Louisville Lip"

Nelson Mandela

Life in prison for Mandela

14 JUNE

Three days ago, South African lawyer Nelson Mandela was sentenced to life imprisonment for sabotage and plotting to overthrow the government. Today he was taken from Cape Town to prison on Robben Island. Mandela is the leader of the banned ANC (African National Congress), which opposes the white South African government's racial policy of apartheid. His struggle to gain equality for the black population has won support the world over and many condemn the sentence.

Equal rights at last

3 JULY

President Lyndon B Johnson today signed the Civil Rights Act, the most far-reaching civil rights law in United States' history. Black campaigners for racial equality, led by Dr Martin Luther King, are at last achieving their aims. From now on, racial discrimination in workplaces, places of public accommodation, publicly owned facilities, and in union membership will be illegal. President Johnson, who comes from the south where racial tension is high, has asked his people to "close the springs of racial poison".

President Johnson shakes hands with King after signing the bill

ALL-GIRL MAGIC

In two months the hottest girl group in the United States, The Supremes, has had two number one hits there – *Where Did Our Love Go* and *Baby Love*. Diana Ross, Florence Ballard, and Mary Wilson used to sing together in church choirs in Detroit, but they are now recording with label Motown.

JANUARY–JUNE

World Events	**MAR** UN troops fly into Cyprus to attempt to keep the warring Greek and Turkish Cypriots apart.	**APR** Ian Smith becomes prime minister of Southern Rhodesia; he favours a unilateral declaration of independence against the UK.	**MAY** Jawaharlal Nehru, beloved prime minister of India since the country became independent in 1947, dies aged 74.	**JUN** Lal Bahadur Shastri, the former minister for home affairs, is sworn in as India's new prime minister in Delhi.
Entertainment	**FEB** The Beatles fly into Kennedy Airport, New York, USA, to an ecstatic reception.	**APR** Sidney Poitier is the first black US male to win an Oscar for his performance in the film *Lilies of the Field*.	**APR** UK rock group The Rolling Stones shock the Montreux Festival with their "dishevelled" appearance.	**JUN** Canadian-born tycoon and powerful newspaper magnate Lord Beaverbrook dies aged 85.
Innovations	**FEB** The UK and France agree to build a tunnel under the Channel to link them. **SIDNEY POITIER**	**APR** West German pilot Geraldine Mock is the first woman to complete a solo round-the-world flight.	**MAY** In Egypt, the course of the Nile is diverted so the next stage of the Aswan Dam can start. **INDIAN PM NEHRU**	**MAY** Soviet leader Khrushchev admits that the USSR uses its satellites to spy on other countries' activities.

1964

Japanese trains fly like a bullet

1 OCTOBER

Ten days before the Tokyo Olympic Games are due to begin, a new high-speed passenger rail service has opened today in Japan. The "bullet trains" will operate on a specially built trunk line along the busy 480-km (300-mile) route between the cities of Tokyo and Osaka. The new trains make the trip in just two-and-a-half hours, cutting the previous journey time by an amazing four hours.

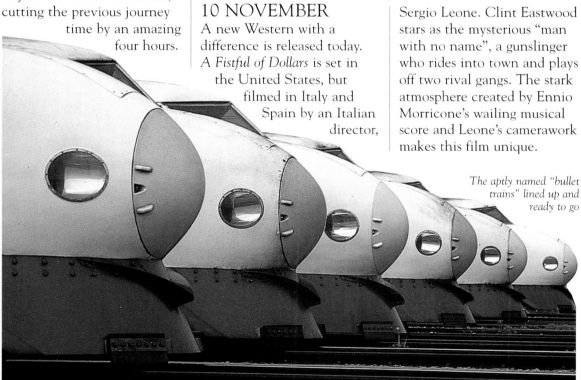

The aptly named "bullet trains" lined up and ready to go

Clint Eastwood in A Fistful of Dollars

Cool cowboy in spaghetti Western

10 NOVEMBER

A new Western with a difference is released today. *A Fistful of Dollars* is set in the United States, but filmed in Italy and Spain by an Italian director, Sergio Leone. Clint Eastwood stars as the mysterious "man with no name", a gunslinger who rides into town and plays off two rival gangs. The stark atmosphere created by Ennio Morricone's wailing musical score and Leone's camerawork makes this film unique.

Kenya becomes a republic

12 DECEMBER

The former British colony of Kenya in east Africa became a republic today. Its first president is Jomo Kenyatta, who has been prime minister since the country was granted self-government last year. At the independence ceremony in the capital Nairobi, the

Kenya's President Kenyatta (right)

British high commissioner described Kenyatta as "the wisest old bird in Africa". But he has a controversial past. In 1953 the British sentenced him to seven years in prison for his involvement with the violent Mau Mau terrorists.

JULY–DECEMBER

AUG President Johnson says the USA will take "all necessary action" against the communist regime in North Vietnam.

AUG South Africa is banned by the Olympic committee from the Tokyo Olympics for its apartheid policies.

JUL US satellite *Ranger VII* sends the first close-up pictures of the surface of the Moon back to Earth.

NIKITA KHRUSHCHEV

OCT At the age of 70, Soviet leader Nikita Khrushchev is deposed in favour of Leonid Brezhnev and Alexei Kosygin.

AUG UK writer Ian Fleming, creator of the hit series of books about fictional spy James Bond, dies aged 56.

SEP Europe's longest suspension bridge, the Forth Road Bridge, is opened in Scotland, UK.

OCT US campaigner for black civil rights, Dr Martin Luther King, who favours non-violent protest, is awarded the Nobel Peace Prize.

OCT In the Olympics, Australian swimmer Dawn Fraser, aged 27, retains her 100-m freestyle title.

NOV The world's longest suspension bridge, the Verrazano-Narrows Bridge, opens in New York, USA.

VERRAZANO-NARROWS BRIDGE

OCT China explodes its first A-bomb, becoming the fifth nuclear power along with the USA, USSR, UK, and France.

OCT US composer and lyricist of musical comedies, Cole Porter, dies aged 67.

DEC UK's Donald Campbell sets a world water speed record of 442.13 km/h (276.33 mph).

1957 *SPUTNIK 1*, FIRST ARTIFICIAL
SATELLITE IN SPACE, USSR

1961 *VOSTOK 1*, FIRST MANNED
SPACE EXPEDITION, USSR

1963 VALENTINA TERESHKOVA,
FIRST WOMAN IN SPACE, USSR

THE RACE TO THE MOON

IN 1961 PRESIDENT KENNEDY of the United States challenged the
Soviet Union to place a man on the Moon before the end of the
1960s. The idea of humans walking on the Moon had fired people's
imaginations for centuries, but it remained a dream until rockets
that were powerful enough had been invented. The Space Age
began in 1957 when the Soviets launched *Sputnik 1*, the
first satellite to orbit the Earth. It was closely
followed by the US satellite *Explorer 1*. The
Soviets led the race until 1965, putting the
first man into space and carried out
the first space walk. But in
1969 the United States
made the first manned
Moon landing.

Space dog

In 1957, the Soviets
sent a dog, Laika,
into space to see how
animals responded to
weightlessness. Her
condition was closely
monitored and the
information used
for later manned
expeditions.

Vostok 1

Soviet cosmonaut
Yuri Gagarin orbited
the Earth in the tiny
Vostok capsule, which
measured only 2.5 m (8.2 ft)
in diameter. Despite its minute
size, the capsule required a huge
disposable rocket to launch it into space.

*Radio
command
link aerial*

*Gagarin's
re-entry
module*

*Radio
aerial*

*Extendable
aerial*

*Television
camera*

*Petal-like
hinged panels*

LUNA 9

Lunar probe

In 1966, the Soviet lunar probe
Luna 9 was the first of its kind to
achieve a "soft landing" on the
Moon. The probe's innovative
design enabled it to bounce across
the Moon's surface before coming
to a gentle halt. Its "petals" and
antennae then opened, and a
TV camera sent back to Earth
the first-ever pictures of
the Moon's surface.

Radiator

*Gas pressure
bottles for life
support system*

YURI
GAGARIN

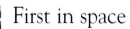

VOSTOK 1
SPACE
CAPSULE

*Final stage
engine*

*Engine to stabilize
rolling movement*

First in space

In 1961 Soviet leaders
were triumphant when
27-year-old Major Yuri Gagarin
became the first person ever to
fly in space. He orbited the Earth in
the *Vostok* spaceship, listening to music
by Tchaikovsky during the 108-minute
flight. Although Gagarin's space capsule was
controlled from the ground, the cosmonaut
carried a secret code that would unlock the
controls in the event that he became
unconscious and lost contact with Earth.

1965 ALEXEI LEONEV, FIRST
TO WALK IN SPACE, USSR

1965 GEMINIS 6 AND 7, FIRST TO
RENDEZVOUS IN SPACE, USA

1969 APOLLO 11, FIRST MANNED
MOON LANDING, USA

APOLLO 11
COMMAND MODULE

Apollo command module

On 21 July 1969, the United States won the race when the *Apollo 11* command module reached the Moon. Two astronauts, Neil Armstrong and "Buzz" Aldrin, landed on the surface, while the third member of the crew, Michael Collins, remained in lonely orbit in the 3-m (10-ft) high command module, in which all three crew members later returned to Earth.

Saturn V

In 1969 the giant US *Saturn V* rocket launched the *Apollo 11* manned mission to the Moon. The rocket stood 111 m (364 ft) high and, with fuel, weighed almost 3,000 tonnes. Each of the rocket's three stages was jettisoned after it had burned up its fuel. After the third-stage engine had fired, the combined command and service module section had enough momentum to coast across into the Moon's orbit.

SATURN V
ROCKET

BUZZ ALDRIN
STANDING ON THE
SURFACE OF THE MOON

One small step

As Neil Armstrong stepped from the lunar excursion module, he uttered the now historic words, "That's one small step for man, one giant leap for mankind." The astronauts spent just over a day on the Moon collecting samples of dust and rock, taking photographs, and making "kangaroo hops" in the Moon's low gravity. They planted an American flag before returning in the excursion module to dock with the command module and return home.

Space programme
Ten more US astronauts explored the Moon before the *Apollo* programme ended in 1972. Since then, both US and Soviet space probes have visited almost all of the planets in our solar system.

Docking radar

Tracking light

Small thruster engine to control flight

Crew hatch

Folding landing leg

Footpad stops leg sinking into Moon dust

MODEL OF *APOLLO 11*
LUNAR EXCURSION MODULE

1965

Flyaway eagle Goldie escapes into the park

21 FEBRUARY

London has a new tourist attraction. For ten days now, an escaped golden eagle from a zoo in Britain has been living in nearby Regent's Park, and attracting thousands of interested fans. Known as Goldie, the seven-year-old is enjoying stretching his wings properly for the first time in five years. So far he has resisted all efforts to recapture him and seems quite happy hopping from tree to tree.

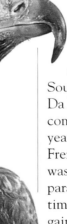

Goldie the golden eagle

USA enters conflict

Confidence is high as the first US troops arrive in Vietnam

31 MARCH

US President Johnson has sent 3,500 marines to give protection to the South Vietnamese air base at Da Nang from attacks by the communist Vietcong. Eleven years ago, in 1954, the former French territory of Vietnam was divided along the 17th parallel of latitude. Since that time, Vietcong guerrillas have gained ground in the South with the help of communist-controlled North Vietnam and China, while military advisers from the US have sought to strengthen the South's resistance. Last year, in the "Tonkin Gulf Incident", two US destroyers reported being fired upon by North Vietnamese torpedos, and US intervention has seemed inevitable. By sending in two battalions of front-line troops, they have shown that they are now prepared to become involved.

Oscar-winning magic musical

6 APRIL

The lady herself would have the perfect word for it: "Supercalifragilisticexpealidocious"! Walt Disney's film *Mary Poppins* has just won five Oscars in Hollywood. A musical comedy, it features a "practically perfect" nanny who amuses her young charges with all kinds of magical tricks. Disney combines live action with animation in amazing sequences.

Julie Andrews as Mary Poppins

JANUARY–JUNE

World Events	**JAN** UK statesman and inspirational wartime prime minister Sir Winston Churchill dies aged 90.	**FEB** Franco's blockade of Gibraltar, designed to force the UK to give "the Rock" back to Spain, begins to take effect.	**APR** The shah of Persia survives an assassination attempt in Teheran, but three of his entourage are killed.	**MAY** Queen Elizabeth II dedicates an acre of ground in the UK to the memory of assassinated US President Kennedy.
Entertainment	**FEB** Australian runner Ron Clarke breaks the 5,000-m world record.	**MAR** Zoo-keepers in London, UK, capture Goldie the eagle after his two weeks of freedom.	**MAR** Rodgers and Hammerstein's hit musical *The Sound of Music* is made into a captivating film.	**APR** The oldest footballer in Europe, the UK's Sir Stanley Matthews, retires aged 50.
Innovations	**FEB** In the UK, the one-millionth Mini comes off the production line.	**MAR** Soviet cosmonaut Colonel Alexei Leonov becomes the first man to walk in space.	**APR** Two new communications satellites are launched; the US *Early Bird* and Soviet *Molyna-1*.	**MAY** In Canada, the de Havilland *DHC-6 Twin Otter STOL* makes its maiden flight.

WINSTON CHURCHILL

STANLEY MATTHEWS IS TACKLED

1965

British Empire honours Beatles

26 OCTOBER

Today, British pop group The Beatles became the latest Members of the Order of the British Empire, or MBEs. They were presented with their medals by the Queen at Buckingham Palace, where a crowd of fans had gathered to catch a glimpse of their heroes. Some older MBEs have returned their medals in protest.

Paul, George, John, and Ringo show off their MBEs

UNICEF wins peace prize

UNICEF project helps children in Africa

10 DECEMBER

The United Nations Children's Fund was today awarded the Nobel Prize for Peace in Oslo, Norway. Founded in 1946 as UNICEF (which stands for the United Nations International Children's Emergency Fund) the society was set up to assist children in any country that was devastated by World War II. Since 1950, UNICEF has worked on long-term projects to improve the welfare of children, particularly in the developing countries. The organization helps to set up health services and nutrition programmes but still gives direct aid to children in crisis situations, wherever they are. UNICEF is financed by voluntary contributions from governments, organizations, and private individuals.

THE MODERNISTS

In Britain, Italian scooters like the Vespa are currently the height of chic with a youth cult called the Mods. Mods also favour snappy Italian-style clothes and music by The Who.

JULY–DECEMBER

JUL China signs various agreements with North Vietnam on economic and technical matters.

JUL In the Swiss Alps, Mme Vaucher is the first woman to climb the mighty Matterhorn.

JUL *Mariner IV*, launched from the USA last November, sends back pictures of Mars.

MATTERHORN, SWITZERLAND

AUG In the USA, race riots flare in an area of Los Angeles, with 28 people reported dead and 676 injured.

AUG UK photographer David Bailey marries French film star Catherine Deneuve.

AUG The Swiss-born architect Le Corbusier, known for his avant-garde style buildings, dies aged 77.

SEP The Argentine foreign minister restates his country's claim on the UK-ruled Falkland Islands to the United Nations.

NOV US film-maker Walt Disney announces plans for a second Disneyland in Florida, USA.

OCT A 1440 Viking map is found showing the Americas, 50 years before Columbus sailed there.

FERDINAND AND IMELDA MARCOS

DEC In Manila, with his wife by his side, Ferdinand Marcos is sworn in as sixth president of the Philippines.

DEC Mikhail Sholokhov, Soviet author of *Quiet Flows the Don*, wins the Nobel Prize for Literature.

DEC Two manned US *Gemini* spacecraft achieve the first rendezvous in space.

THE SWINGING SIXTIES

IN THE 1960s, skirts got shorter, hair got longer, and for the first time in the 20th century pop music became a driving force in society. This was especially true in Britain, home of The Beatles, whose songs provided a soundtrack to the era. "In this century", said US *Time* magazine in April 1966, "every decade has its city...and for the Sixties that city is London". England's capital teemed with artists, models, pop stars, photographers, fashion designers, and hairdressers, all dedicated to the creation of new styles for the young. The fashions they set caught on all over the world. So too did their message that life could be a party – "If you can remember the Swinging Sixties", someone joked later, "you weren't really there!"

French chic

In the 1960s London was swinging but France was the home of *chic*. Glamorous French singer Françoise Hardy helped to set a global trend by wearing her hair long and straight.

Let's Twist!
US singer Chubby Checker's 1960 hit *Let's Twist Again* launched the ultimate Sixties dance craze. "You move your hips like you're drying yourself with a towel," said Checker.

POLICE STRUGGLE TO HOLD BACK BEATLES' FANS

Beatlemania

By 1963 The Beatles had become so popular that their concerts were pandemonium. Their girl fans screamed so loudly that it was almost impossible to hear the band playing. "Beatlemania" soon spread across Europe and then the United States.

The Fab Four

The Beatles burst onto the popular music scene in 1962 with their first single *Love Me Do* and went on to become the most successful pop group of all time. Their music epitomized the 1960s. The songs they wrote had wit and intelligence and reflected the changing mood of the times. "If you want to know about the Sixties", said US composer Aaron Copland, "play the music of The Beatles".

GEORGE HARRISON

JOHN LENNON

RINGO STARR

Sensational long hair

PAUL McCARTNEY

"Drainpipe" trousers

Chelsea boots

THE BEATLES

MICK JAGGER

MARIANNE FAITHFUL

Pearly nail polish

Pale lipstick was vital for the Sixties look

Black eyeliner for outlining eyes

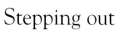

Less is more

In the 1960s there was a fashion revolution. The biggest sensation was caused by the outrageously short mini-skirt. Pioneered by English designer Mary Quant and French couturier André Courrèges, it was made popular by hip models such as Twiggy. Within a very short time, the mini was adopted by young women all over the world.

Vidal Sassoon hairstyle

False eyelashes

Stepping out

High-heeled, knee- or thigh-length boots looked just right with short mini-skirts. Made of leather or plastic, the boots rapidly became essential Sixties fashion accessories.

TWIGGY

Floral design woven in gold thread

Mick and Marianne

With their long hair and rebellious attitudes, Mick Jagger of The Rolling Stones and his girlfriend, solo singer Marianne Faithfull, embodied the renegade spirit of swinging London.

Some minis were as much as 15 cm (6 in) above the knee

PAISLEY-PATTERNED MORRIS MINI MINOR

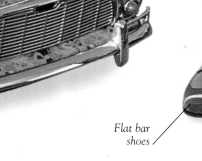

The Mini

Small was beautiful in the Swinging Sixties, whether you meant the mini-skirt or the BMC "Mini" car. In February 1965 the one-millionth vehicle rolled off the production line. Stylish and compact, it was perfect for London's trendies to use to dash around town.

Flat bar shoes

1966

India elects a new prime minister

19 JANUARY
Following the death eight days ago of Indian prime minister Lal Bahadur Shastri from a heart attack, his successor has now been elected. The new premier is Indira Gandhi, 48-year-old daughter of Jawaharlal Nehru, who was independent India's first prime minister in 1947. Mrs Gandhi, whose husband died in 1960, is the second widow to lead her country on the Indian sub continent – Mrs Bandaranaike of Ceylon was the first in 1960. Indira Gandhi's victory over her rival candidate Morarji Desai, the former finance minister, has pleased the Indian people, and tonight she pledged that she would "strive to create what my father used to call a climate of peace". She also intends to honour the peace agreement with Pakistan recently signed by Lal Shastri.

India's new prime minister, Mrs Indira Gandhi

Brezhnev emerges as new Soviet leader

8 APRIL
Since Nikita Khrushchev was ousted in 1964, the Soviet Union has lacked a clear leader. Today, however, following a typically secretive reshuffle at the Kremlin, Communist Party leader Leonid Brezhnev has taken the new title of general secretary. It appears that he now outranks Prime Minister Kosygin, President Podgory, and influential thinker Suslov. Brezhnev played a leading role in the coup of 1964, so there are fears that many of Khrushchev's reforms will now be reversed.

Leonid Brezhnev, the USSR's new general secretary

Musical wins best movie

Julie Andrews as another singing nanny

18 APRIL
The Sound of Music has won the Oscar for Best Film in Hollywood. This lively musical is set in pre-war Austria and follows the fortunes of the von Trapp family, whose father marries the governess of his seven children. The governess Maria is played by Julie Andrews, still fresh from her recent success in *Mary Poppins*. Many of the songs by Rodgers and Hammerstein are already well known from the Broadway stage version. Now, tunes like *Edelweiss*, *Do-re-mi*, and *My Favourite Things* will become the favourite songs of millions of film fans.

JANUARY–JULY

World Events	**JAN** In Accra, over 1,000 political prisoners are freed as an army coup topples Ghana's president Nkrumah.	**JUN** Éamon de Valera, known as "Dev", is elected president of Ireland for the second time, at the age of 83.	**JUN** James Meredith, the first black student admitted to the University of Mississippi, USA, in 1962, is shot on a civil rights march.	**JUN** US bombers hit fuel tanks in a raid over Hanoi, the first time that they have directly attacked the North Vietnamese capital.
Entertainment	**FEB** US actor Buster Keaton, the stone-faced comedy star of silent movies, dies aged 70.	**FEB** USSR novelists Andrey Sinyavsky and Yuri Daniel are imprisoned for "slandering the state".	**JUN** Legendary US folk singer Bob Dylan shocks audiences in London, UK, by playing the electric guitar.	**JUL** England beats West Germany 4–2 in the football World Cup final played in the UK.
Innovations	**FEB** Pictures from the Soviet spacecraft *Luna 9* show the Moon's surface to be solid.	**MAR** US astronauts Neil Armstrong and David Scott achieve the first successful space docking in *Gemini 8*.	**MAY** A missing US H-bomb, lost after a mid-air collision, is found in the Atlantic off the Spanish coast.	**JUN** The US unmanned *Surveyor* spacecraft is the first craft to land on the Moon.

IRISH PM DE VALERA

ENGLAND WIN WORLD CUP

1966

Cultural revolution in China

13 AUGUST

Mao Zedong, the leader of communist China, has started "a great proletarian cultural revolution". He claims it will create the ideal state in China which he dreamed of as a young man. Launched at a mass rally in Peking, the new movement is being led by huge numbers of students, organized into bands of "Red Guards". They are travelling around China with little red books quoting Mao's

thoughts, to remind people of the spirit of the great revolution of 1949. Party officials and "non-revolutionary" academics and artists are being targeted. Schools are being shut, and teachers and other intellectuals humiliated in the streets. A statement from Mao in 1927 is now appearing everywhere: "Revolution is not writing an essay, or painting a picture... revolution is an act of violence when one class overthrows another".

School buried

The slag heap engulfs the school

21 OCTOBER

A terrible tragedy has wiped out a whole generation of children today in Wales. The Aberfan coal mine's slag heap slipped suddenly, burying the village school. Local people are still working to find survivors, but 116 children and 28 adults have died.

First vertical take-off and landing aircraft

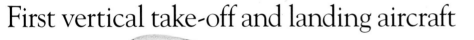

13 AUGUST

An astonishing new British plane has been unveiled at the Farnborough air show. Known as the Hawker Siddeley Harrier, it is the world's first vertical take-off and landing (VTOL) aircraft. A cross between a helicopter

and an aeroplane, it is a far cry from the wingless "flying bedstead" pioneered by Rolls-Royce in 1953. Its single engine has four nozzles, which are rotated downwards for take-off and landing, and backwards for flight.

STATUES MOVED

Since c.1200 BC, eight 20-m (66-ft) statues of Rameses II have guarded the temples of Abu Simbel in Egypt. Now the Aswan High Dam is very nearly completed, they are being moved to higher ground to avoid the rising waters.

AUGUST–DECEMBER

SEP Dr Hendrik Verwoerd, prime minister of South Africa, is assassinated by a parliamentary messenger in the House of Assembly.

NOV After the worst storms in Italy for over 1,000 years, the death toll is rising and there is "incalculable" loss to the nation's art heritage.

NOV In China, the Red Guard demand the dismissal of the Chinese heads of state Lui Shaopi and Deng Xiaoping.

DEC UK PM Harold Wilson and Ian Smith, leader of the rebel Rhodesian regime, meet for discussions.

AUG US runner Jim Ryun smashes the world mile record by 2.3 secs, running it in 3 mins 51.3 secs.

SEP Australian Jack Brabham is the first to win the world drivers' championship in his own car.

DEC Walt Disney, whose films and characters are loved by children around the world, dies aged 65.

DEC The Davis Cup for tennis remains with Australia for the third year after they beat India in the final.

AUG Soviet spacecraft *Luna 11* goes into orbit around the Moon and sends data back to Earth.

FLOODED FLORENCE, ITALY

AUG US *Lunar Orbiter 1* goes into orbit around the Moon and sends back pictures of the dark side.

NOV US *Gemini 12*, the last *Gemini* two-person mission, is crewed by Buzz Aldrin and James Lovell.

WALT DISNEY

DEC Soviet probe *Luna 13* lands on the Moon and sends back data about the soil.

1967

Bluebird takes final dive

The last moments of Donald Campbell and his Bluebird

4 JANUARY

Donald Campbell, the British world water-speed hero, has paid the ultimate price for attempting to smash his own world record. On Coniston Water in England's Lake District, he came within a fraction of a second of beating his record of 444.70 km/h (276.33 mph) when disaster struck. The jet-powered *Bluebird* leapt into the air, somersaulted, then plunged into the depths. His helmet, shoes, oxygen mask, and teddy bear mascot were found floating where the boat went down, but so far his body has not been recovered.

Ali refuses draft

30 APRIL

World heavyweight boxing champion Muhammad Ali, known as Cassius Clay before he changed his name and religion, has said that his Muslim faith will not allow him to fight as a soldier for the United States in Vietnam. Ali could face a minimum jail sentence of five years.

Football showdown

15 JANUARY

Today, in American football's first championship game between the two major leagues, the Green Bay Packers of the National Football League beat the Kansas City Chiefs of the American League 35–10 at the Los Angeles Coliseum. Green Bay coach Vince Lombardi, whose motto is "Winning isn't everything, it's the only thing", welcomed the victory.

DISNEY JUNGLE BEAT

Walt Disney's enchanting new cartoon film *The Jungle Book* is based on the novel of that name by English author and poet Rudyard Kipling. It tells the story of Mowgli, an Indian boy raised by wolves in the jungle. The soundtrack features some fine upbeat songs including *Bear Necessities*.

JANUARY–JUNE

World Events	**FEB** The USA launches Operation Junction City, its biggest assault against the Vietcong in Vietnam.	**MAR** Svetlana Alliluyeva, daughter of the late Soviet dictator Joseph Stalin, defects from the USSR to the West.	**APR** In a military coup in Greece, Colonel Papadopoulos seizes power from the democratic government.	**MAY** Colonel Ojukwu of the Ibo people proclaims the eastern region of Nigeria as the independent republic of Biafra.
Entertainment	**FEB** In the UK, fans run wild as US made-for-TV pop group The Monkees arrive on tour.	**MAR** US film star Judy Garland announces her return to the screen in *The Valley of the Dolls*.	**APR** Barefoot UK singer Sandie Shaw wins the Eurovision Song Contest with *Puppet on a String*.	**JUN** US film star Spencer Tracy, who has just completed *Guess Who's Coming to Dinner*, dies aged 67.
Innovations	**JAN** US astronauts Ed White, Gus Grissom, and Roger Chaffe die in a ground test fire.	**FEB** US nuclear scientist Robert Oppenheimer, head of the team that created the atom bomb, dies aged 62.	**MAR** In France, President de Gaulle launches the first French nuclear submarine.	**JUN** China detonates its first H-Bomb in Xiang Jang, a remote area of southwest China.

SVETLANA DEFECTS

COLONEL OJUKWU OF BIAFRA

1967

The Six-Day War

10 JUNE

For the third time in 21 years, the constant tension between the state of Israel and its Arab neighbours has erupted into full-scale warfare. It began six days ago, when the Israelis launched surprise strikes from land and air. As Israeli troops swept across Egyptian and Jordanian land, the UN security council called for an immediate ceasefire. Two days later, Jordan and Egypt had agreed to this, but Israel fought on, attacking Syria. Finally, on the sixth day, the Israelis have halted their advance and observed the UN ceasefire. They have taken over Arab territories that are many times larger than Israel itself, but the cost of the advance has been great – more than 100,000 people are feared dead.

Israeli soldiers at the Wailing Wall

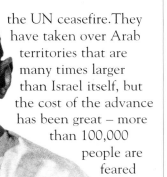
Israel's General Dayan

Surrealist master Magritte dead

Ceci n'est pas une pipe.

15 AUGUST

Belgian artist René Magritte died today aged 69. He belonged to the Surrealist school of painters whose art challenges our ideas about reality. His work explored the gap between actual objects and their images. The message under this painting reads, "This is not a pipe", because it is only the *image* of a pipe!

Revolutionary hero killed

10 OCTOBER

Ernesto "Ché" Guevara, the revolutionary hero of Cuba, who helped Fidel Castro to overthrow the Batista regime, has been shot by the Bolivian army. He left Cuba two years ago to spread the revolution to other parts of the world. In Bolivia, Ché planned a peasant uprising but the army cornered and killed him as well as his band of guerrillas in the jungle yesterday.

JULY–DECEMBER

JUL In Africa, European and US citizens flee Biafra as Nigerian troops step up their attack on the breakaway eastern region.

JUL The latest Beatles album, *Sergeant Pepper's Lonely Hearts Club Band,* is a hit worldwide.

SEP A lightweight aluminium baby buggy is designed in the UK by Owen Finlay Maclaren.

BEATLES ALBUM SERGEANT PEPPER

JUL Race riots break out in dozens of US cities. Two people have died and thousands have been reported injured.

AUG The Beatles' manager Brian Epstein is found dead after taking an overdose.

SEP UK, France, and West Germany sign an agreement to co-operate on an "Airbus" airliner.

AUG 175,000 Arab refugees are repatriated to occupied land in the Middle East in a scheme agreed by Israel and Jordan.

JUL US singer for peace Joan Baez is arrested at an anti-Vietnam war protest in California, USA.

OCT US biochemist Casimir Funk, the inventor of the now widely used term "vitamin", dies aged 83.

CHRISTIAAN BARNARD

DEC Australia's prime minister, Harold Holt, drowns while swimming near his holiday home in Portsea, Victoria.

DEC US actor Dustin Hoffman stars in the film *The Graduate* about a young man alienated from society.

DEC The first heart transplant is successfully performed by Dr Christiaan Barnard in South Africa.

1951 FIRST COLOUR TV
BROADCAST IN USA

1953 MILLIONS WATCH CORONATION
OF BRITAIN'S ELIZABETH II LIVE ON TV

1962 THE FIRST TV SATELLITE,
TELSTAR 1, IS LAUNCHED IN USA

PEYTON PLACE

THE TELEVISION AGE

HERMANN MUNSTER

"IF YOU LET A TV through your door," warned a British newspaper in 1950, "life will never be the same." By that year, there were around 7.5 million TV sets in American homes alone. But the advent of television changed things in ways that few could have foreseen. In 1962, during the Cuban Missile Crisis, US president John F Kennedy broadcast an ultimatum to the USSR on TV. That same year, the first TV space satellite was launched. Marshall McLuhan, whose writing on mass communications caused extensive debate, wrote that the new electronic communications were turning the world into a kind of "global village". Television offered new possibilities for education and entertainment. Soap operas, situation comedies, and chat shows increased viewing figures.

Soap operas

"Soaps" were domestic TV serials, long-running, usually broadcast during the daytime and often sponsored by soap manufacturers. Some soaps were so popular that viewers thought of the characters as real people, identifying strongly with their fictional problems.

For all the family

Two very successful comedy horror shows originated in the United States in the 1960s. *The Addams Family* and *The Munsters* were the adventures of two very strange families.

World wildlife

TV brought the world into the living room, and few subjects lent themselves better to this treatment than wildlife. One of the most fascinating series of the 1960s was *The Undersea World of Jacques Cousteau*, in which the French marine expert revealed the mysteries of the oceans.

JACQUES COUSTEAU

Television style

MAHOGANY TABLE SET, 1939

FREE-STANDING CABINET MODEL, 1956

PLASTIC PORTABLE TELEVISION, 1966

SPACEAGE GLOBE SET, 1970

JOHNNY CARSON HOSTS *THE TONIGHT SHOW*

Chat shows

Chat shows, on which a regular host interviewed a selection of celebrity guests, became popular the world over. Few hosts were as successful as the *Tonight Show's* Johnny Carson. Carson took over the show in 1962 from Jack Paar, and moved it to Hollywood in 1971 to be nearer even more glamorous guests. Carson himself was always introduced by the memorable catch phrase "Heeeeeeeeere's Johnny".

1966 FOOTBALL WORLD CUP FINAL IN
UK IS WATCHED BY 600 MILLION

1969 FOUR NATIONS TIE FOR TOP SPOT IN
POPULAR EUROVISION SONG CONTEST

1969 US MOON LANDING IS SEEN
LIVE ON TV ALL OVER THE WORLD

Televised sport

Television could be used to communicate images and information much faster than cinema news reels. When the Olympic Games were broadcast live from Tokyo in 1964, television viewers all over the world were able to experience the excitement of the events at first hand.

TOKYO OLYMPICS 1964

BIG BIRD

Television award for outstanding cartoon

In 1959 US animators Bill Hanna and Joseph Barbera won the first ever Emmy Award for Outstanding Achievement in Children's Programming. The sought-after statuette was awarded for their *Huckleberry Hound Show* (1958–62). One of the show's characters was Yogi Bear, a lovable character who always got into trouble with the park ranger for stealing the picnics from visitors to the fictional Jellystone Park.

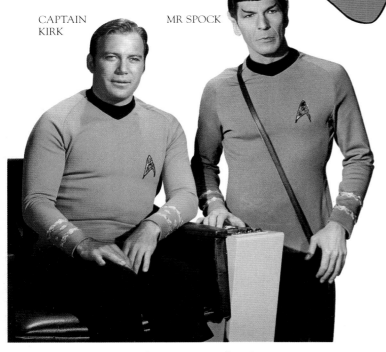

CAPTAIN KIRK

MR SPOCK

Where no man has gone before...

"Space: the final frontier...." The first series of *Star Trek* was created by former pilot and policeman Gene Roddenberry. Launched in 1966, the Starship *Enterprise* was staffed by interplanetary characters led by Captain James Kirk and his semi-alien first officer Mr Spock. Devoted fans called Trekkies helped to turn *Star Trek* into one of the most popular TV shows.

Sesame Street

Funded by the non-profit-making Children's Television Workshop in the United States, *Sesame Street* was launched in 1969. The aim of the daily hour-long shows was to educate pre-school children in deprived areas. The show's stars were a mixture of humans and bizarre characters like Big Bird, a 2-m (7-ft) high canary, Kermit the Frog, and Cookie Monster. The show helped children with their letters, numbers and social skills.

1968

A scene from Stanley Kubrick's 2001: A Space Odyssey

Trudeau is new Canadian leader

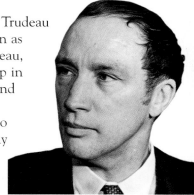

21 APRIL

Liberal Party politician Pierre Trudeau today succeeded Lester Pearson as Canada's prime minister. Trudeau, a 48-year-old bachelor, grew up in Montreal and speaks French and English, Canada's two native languages. He will now have to deal with the demands of many French speakers to turn their province of Quebec into an independent country.

A journey into deep space

4 APRIL

US director Stanley Kubrick has released a remarkable science fiction movie, *2001: A Space Odyssey*. Visually stunning, the film features vast spaceships floating on dreamlike journeys through deep space. It explores both the origins and the future of humankind through the eyes of an astronaut searching for the secrets of the universe. But film audiences must be prepared to be mystified. "The feel of the experience is the important thing", says Kubrick. "Those who won't believe their eyes won't be able to appreciate this film."

King dies, but dream lives on

9 APRIL

Five days ago, US black civil rights hero Dr Martin Luther King was shot dead by an unknown assassin in Memphis. More than 150,000 people attended the funeral of this brilliant speaker in his home town of Atlanta, Georgia, today. In his famous Washington speech of 1963, King declared that he had a dream that one day all Americans would live as equals. This has started to come true.

Mourners at the funeral of Martin Luther King

JANUARY–APRIL

World Events	**JAN** The Czechoslovak Communist Party chooses a new "liberal" leader in 46-year-old Alexander Dubcek.	**FEB** The North Koreans refuse to release the US spy ship *Pueblo*, captured last month within their boundaries.	**MAR** Soviet cosmonaut and first man in space, Yuri Gagarin, is killed in a jet aeroplane crash outside Moscow at the age of 34.	**APR** Thousands riot in West Germany following the attempted murder of left-wing student leader Rudi Dutschke.
Entertainment	**JAN** In London, UK, fans flock to The Beatles' new venture – an Apple clothes boutique.	**FEB** French skier Jean-Claude Killy wins three golds at the winter Olympics in Grenoble.	**APR** In the USA, the Oscar ceremony is postponed for 48 hours in memory of Martin Luther King.	**APR** US millionaire oil tycoon Robert McCullough buys London Bridge for a bargain £1 million.
Innovations	**JAN** In South Africa, Dr Christiaan Barnard performs a second heart transplant. SKIER JEAN-CLAUDE KILLY	**FEB** The UK Royal Navy's first *Polaris* missile is tested successfully in the Atlantic.	**MAR** In the USA, Lockheed presents the world's largest aircraft to date, the *Galaxy*. LONDON BRIDGE IN ARIZONA, USA	**APR** Five and ten pence coins are introduced to the UK in preparation for decimalization.

1968

Paris students riot

Student demonstrations bring Paris to a complete halt

7 MAY

For two days the streets of Paris, France, have been the scene of violent clashes between up to 30,000 students and riot police. Trouble has been brewing since the end of March, when six students were arrested after a large demonstration against the US involvement in the Vietnam War. Yesterday nearly 1,000 men and women were injured as the protesters fought with bricks and paving stones. Today, at the Arc de Triomphe, a huge crowd sang the communist anthem, the *Internationale*, and the riots seem likely to continue.

Student leader Daniel Cohn-Bendit

Another Kennedy gunned down

6 JUNE

The world was stunned today as a second member of the Kennedy family was gunned down in the United States. Senator Robert Kennedy, younger brother of President John F Kennedy, who was assassinated in 1963, had recently joined the race for the presidency. Last night he was at the Ambassador Hotel in Los Angeles in order to thank campaigners for his recent victory in the California primary election. As he was leaving, an Arab gunman fired five shots at him. Senator Kennedy died from his wounds this morning, only 25 hours after being shot. He would probably have been elected as the next United States president.

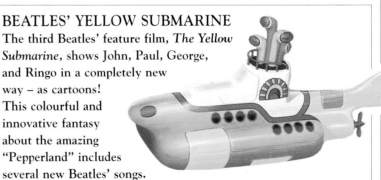

Bobby Kennedy on the campaign trail

BEATLES' YELLOW SUBMARINE

The third Beatles' feature film, *The Yellow Submarine*, shows John, Paul, George, and Ringo in a completely new way – as cartoons! This colourful and innovative fantasy about the amazing "Pepperland" includes several new Beatles' songs.

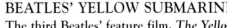

MAY–AUGUST

MAY US and North Vietnamese diplomats meet in Paris, France to discuss the setting-up of talks to end the war in Vietnam.

JUN Helen Keller, US author and worldwide campaigner for handicapped people, dies aged 88.

MAY The UK's first successful heart transplant operation is performed at a hospital in London.

PIONEER HELEN KELLER

JUN James Earl Ray, wanted by the FBI in the USA for the murder of Dr Martin Luther King, is arrested in London, UK.

JUN In New York, US "pop" artist Andy Warhol is shot and seriously injured by writer Valerie Solanas.

JUN In the USA, Roy Jacuzzi markets the first whirlpool baths called Jacuzzi Roman Baths.

JUL In three capitals – London, Moscow, and Washington – 36 nations sign a nuclear non-proliferation treaty.

JUL Australian Rod Laver wins the first Wimbledon open championships, collecting his third Wimbledon title.

JUL German nuclear physicist and winner of the Nobel Prize for Physics Otto Hahn dies aged 89.

TENNIS STAR ROD LAVER

AUG Pope John Paul arrives in Colombia for the first visit by a pope to Latin America.

AUG South African cricketer Colin Bland is refused UK entry because of his Rhodesian passport.

AUG A Channel hovercraft service opens between Dover in the UK and Boulogne in France.

1968

Czechs under siege

Czech prime minister Alexander Dubcek

22 AUGUST

The "Prague Spring" of freedom is abruptly turning into a dark, troubled winter as 600,000 Warsaw Pact troops pour into Czechoslovakia. Under Alexander Dubcek, the government has been trying to gain independence within Soviet-dominated eastern Europe. Dubcek's aim is to run the country on the principle of "socialism with a human face", rather than the oppressive form of communism imposed by the Soviet Union. This would mean greater freedom of speech and a more liberal government than in other parts of the Soviet empire. The Dubcek government had believed that the Soviets would not use force to stop the changes. Now they know better, as unarmed Czech youths try to resist the tanks.

Bob Beamon shatters the long jump record at the Mexico Olympics

Beamon leaps into record books

17 OCTOBER

Experts have long been debating whether the thin air in Mexico City, which lies about 2,134 m (7,000 ft) above sea level, would affect performances at this year's Olympics. Now the debate will get even hotter. Despite the location, Bob Beamon of the United States has just won the gold medal in the long jump with an amazing leap of 8.9 m (29.2 ft). This jump beats the world record by almost 0.6 m (2 ft).

Tanks roll through the streets of Prague

World Events

SEP In Iran, at least 11,000 people are reported to have died in a series of earthquakes lasting two days.

OCT Jackie Kennedy, widow of assassinated US president John F Kennedy, marries Greek business executive Aristotle Onassis.

OCT During their medal ceremony at the Mexico Olympics, US athletes Tommy Smith and John Carlos give the "Black Power" salute.

NOV Republican Richard Nixon narrowly beats Democrat Hubert Humphrey in the US elections to become the 37th president.

Entertainment

SEP The cast of the musical *Hair* are the first to appear naked on a stage in the UK.

OCT At the Olympic Games in Mexico, US athlete Al Oerter wins his fourth gold in the discus event.

NOV UK writer Enid Blyton, creator of the children's characters the "Famous Five", dies aged 71.

DEC US writer John Steinbeck, winner of the Nobel Prize for Literature in 1962, dies aged 66.

Innovations

SEP Over 500 UK women have tried the new epidural anaesthesia in childbirth.

JACKIE KENNEDY MARRIES ONASSIS

OCT The USA launches *Apollo 7*, the first manned *Apollo* craft, to prepare for a Moon landing.

NOV The UK's *Queen Elizabeth*, the world's largest ocean liner, completes her final passenger voyage.

NIXON IS ELECTED US PRESIDENT

DEC US spacecraft *Apollo 8* is launched in the USA, en route for a manned lunar orbit.

1969

Israel's new PM

Israel's first woman prime minister

7 MARCH

The Israeli Labour Party has elected Golda Meir as the new prime minister to succeed Levi Eshkol. Golde Meir, now 70, was born in the Ukraine. She worked as a teacher in the United States before emigrating to Palestine in 1921. In 1948, on the eve of Israel's independence, she raised $50 million in the US for defence funds.

Lennon and Yoko Ono protest in comfort

25 MARCH

Five days ago in Gibraltar, John Lennon of The Beatles married Yoko Ono. For their honeymoon, this unconventional pair have taken up residence in a large double bed in the presidential suite of the Hilton Hotel, Amsterdam. They plan to stay there for seven full days as a protest against war. The world's media has immediately converged on the "Bed-In", where John and Yoko sit in their pyjamas surrounded by placards reading "Bed Peace" and "Hair Peace". One cynical reporter has called it "the most self-indulgent demonstration of all time".

John Lennon and Yoko Ono during their "Bed-In"

Supersonic *Concorde* takes off

9 APRIL

In 1962 Britain and France agreed to develop the supersonic airliner, *Concorde*.

Earlier this year, prototype 001 of the aircraft took off in France, and today *Concorde* 002 took to the air from the UK, for a maiden flight of 21 minutes. Around

£360 million has already been invested in this project, but there is still a long way to go. Today the plane reached only 325 km/h (203 mph), and it will not be in service until 1974 at the earliest. The two countries hope eventually to sell over 400 of them, making £4,000 million by the 1980s.

JANUARY–APRIL

JAN Violence erupts in Derry, Northern Ireland, between Catholic and Protestant communities.

JAN Sir Learie Constantine, the West Indies cricketer, becomes the UK's first black life peer.

JAN In the USA, NASA chooses Neil Armstrong and Edwin "Buzz" Aldrin for the first Moon landing.

NORTHERN IRISH DEMONSTRATIONS

JAN In Prague, Jan Palach dies after setting fire to himself in protest against the Soviet invasion.

MAR Paul McCartney of UK pop group The Beatles marries US photographer Linda Eastman.

FEB Human eggs are fertilized in a test tube for the first time at Cambridge University, UK.

FEB In Cairo, Yassir Arafat, a dynamic resistance leader, is appointed head of the Palestine Liberation Organization (PLO).

APR US actress Katherine Hepburn wins a record third Best Actress Oscar for her role in *The Lion in Winter*.

MAR US spacecraft *Apollo 9* splashes down safely in the Pacific after the first test of the lunar module.

PLO LEADER YASSIR ARAFAT

APR French president Charles de Gaulle resigns at the age of 78, after losing a constitutional referendum.

APR UK sailor Robin Knox-Johnston, wins the single-handed round-the-world yacht race.

APR UK engineers Booker and McConnell set up a prize fund for UK and Commonwealth fiction.

PEACE AND PROTEST

"SOMETHING'S HAPPENING HERE," sang US rock group Buffalo Springfield in 1967, "what it is ain't exactly clear...." As the Swinging Sixties wore on, something *was* happening among young people throughout the world. They were losing faith in how the older generation were running the world. In particular, they were unhappy with the United States' involvement in the Vietnam War. Thousands joined protest marches and demonstrations chanting the slogan "make love, not war". Others decided to opt out of society altogether by living in communes where less value was given to money and possessions. Many pop stars shared the new ideals. Two songs by John Lennon of The Beatles summed up the message: *All You Need Is Love* (1967) and *Give Peace a Chance* (1969).

US OLYMPIC ATHLETES, 1968

Flower power

California in the United States was the birthplace of the "Flower Children" who believed the key to life was in nature. When the Soviets invaded Czechoslovakia in 1968, Prague students put flowers in their gun barrels as a peaceful protest.

Black power

Black Americans were unhappy with the unequal treatment they received in society. Two young US athletes, Tommie Smith and John Carlos, shocked the world in 1968 by giving the "Black Power" salute at the Mexico Olympics as a sign of black pride.

Woodstock music festival

The biggest event of the flower power era was the Woodstock Music and Arts Fair. Held on farmland outside New York in the United States in August 1969, the music festival drew an audience of nearly half a million young people, united in their love of music and their desire for world peace.

BOB DYLAN

Music and flower power went hand in hand

Songs of protest

Music was at the forefront of the protest movements around the world. In the United States singer-songwriters like Bob Dylan and Joan Baez wrote powerful anti-war songs. Dylan's *Blowin' in the Wind* combined the spiritual and political ideas of the peace movement and became an anthem for the anti-war generation.

STUDENTS RIOT IN PARIS

At the barricades

In May 1968 French students rioted on the streets of Paris when their demonstrations for educational and social reforms ended in violent clashes with the police. Days of street-fighting followed between the authorities and the revolutionary students. Around ten million French workers went out on strike to support the students, virtually bringing France to a standstill. Eventually the French president, General De Gaulle, was forced to grant the students reforms and to promise the workers better wages.

1969 US FILM *EASY RIDER* SYMBOLIZES
ALTERNATIVE YOUTH CULTURE

1969 HUGE PEACE AND MUSIC
FESTIVAL AT WOODSTOCK, USA

1969 BIGGEST EVER ANTI-VIETNAM
WAR DEMO IN WASHINGTON, USA

Psychedelic art

The hippy drug culture inspired a whole new style of art described as psychedelic. The artists used bright, swirling patterns and lurid colours. Innovative musicians like Jimi Hendrix and Joni Mitchell promoted the art form by using psychedelic images and hand-drawn graphics on their album covers, and hundreds of posters, T-shirts, and underground magazines also featured this new kind of way-out hippy expression.

The lure of the East

Many young people looked to the East, and the religions of Hinduism and Buddhism which renounce worldly goods, to make sense of the world. Many set off on the "hippy trail" across India to Katmandu in search of enlightenment. Even The Beatles visited India to find a guru.

THE BEATLES
WITH THE
MAHARISHI

Hippies

The first hippies made their home in San Francisco, USA. They were easy-going, long-haired, and brightly dressed. According to the US hippy guru Dr Timothy Leary, their goal was to turn on (take mind-expanding drugs), tune in (to the life energies they found inside themselves) and drop out (of the rat-race of everyday life).

Long "Afro" hair

Afghan coat

Strings of beads

Long, loose tunic

Flared trousers

Embroidered shoulder bag

Sandals

1969

Man on the Moon

21 JULY
Today, a man walked on the Moon for the very first time. With the words, "That's one small step for man, one giant leap for mankind", US astronaut Neil Armstrong stepped onto the Moon and into history. As he left the lunar module, he was watched on television by nearly 600 million people

around the world. Armstrong was joined by "Buzz" Aldrin, and the two delighted their TV audience by making big kangaroo bounds in the Moon's low gravity. They carried out experiments for two hours before returning to *Apollo 11*'s landing craft.

British troops in Derry

Buzz Aldrin steps onto the Moon

Troops into Ireland

15 AUGUST
After a week of furious street-fighting between groups of Protestants and Catholics, the British government has sent troops into Derry, Northern Ireland. More troops will almost certainly be deployed in trouble-torn Belfast as well. While many people greeted the move with relief, the Irish government and many Catholics in the

north have condemned it. The army chief in Northern Ireland has been instructed to "take all necessary steps, acting impartially between citizen and citizen". The British government hopes to limit their intervention and withdraw the troops when law and order is restored.

LONG AND SHORT OF IT
At the end of a decade that has seen ever-rising hemlines, the mini has been replaced on the catwalks. The latest new trend in the boutiques is the maxi-skirt, which reaches right down to the floor. And for women who do not want their hemlines to plunge too low, there is also the fashionable midi-skirt, which hovers just below the knee.

MAY–AUGUST

World Events

JUN Over 1,000 civilians are detained in Czechoslovakia, following two days of arrests.

JUN US President Nixon suggests that US, Allied, and North Vietnamese troops withdraw from South Vietnam.

JUN In Spain, General Franco closes the land frontier with Gibraltar in an attempt to cripple the UK colony.

JUN In the UK, Conservative politician Enoch Powell calls for the repatriation of black immigrants.

Entertainment

MAY The UK's Graham Hill wins the Monaco grand prix for a record fifth time.

JUN US actress and singer Judy Garland, who played Dorothy in *The Wizard of Oz*, dies aged 47.

JUN Brazilian soccer star Pelé, considered the greatest footballer of the age, scores his 1,000th goal.

JUL The Rolling Stones play a free concert in London, UK, in memory of drowned guitarist Brian Jones.

GARLAND AND HER DAUGHTER

Innovations

MAY Soviet probe *Venera 5* sends back data about Venus before crashing on the planet.

MAY The manned US *Apollo 10* orbits the Moon, as a rehearsal for the planned Moon landing in July.

JUN High-grade crude oil is found on the borders of the UK and Norwegian sectors of the North Sea.

SOCCER STAR PELÉ

JUL The US space probe *Mariner 6* sends back the first close-up pictures of the surface of the planet Mars.

1969

Woodstock festival attracts thousands

17 AUGUST

In the United States, the world's biggest peace and rock festival has just ended near the village of Woodstock in upstate New York. Nearly 500,000 fans braved the rain to enjoy three days of inspired music from Jimi Hendrix, Janis Joplin, Joan Baez, Joe Cocker, Santana, The Who, and many more. The poor sanitation and overstretched catering facilities did not deter the happy masses, and the atmosphere remained

Rock groups perform in front of the vast Woodstock crowd

positive and peaceful. Many are looking on the warm spirit of co-operation seen at Woodstock as a vibrant symbol of the anti-war generation. It marks a fitting end to a decade of protest, peace, and love.

Old guns Newman and Redford

Robert Redford as the Kid

Paul Newman as Butch Cassidy

23 SEPTEMBER

Two of Hollywood's biggest stars, Paul Newman and Robert Redford, have teamed up in a new film. They play the title roles in *Butch Cassidy and the Sundance Kid*, a comical Western based on the lives of a pair of legendary, laid-back outlaws who led the "Hole in the Wall Gang" in the last days of the old West.

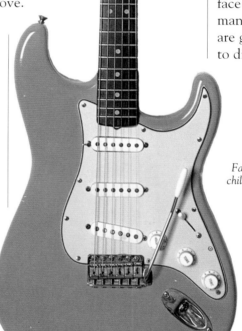

No Red Cross help for Biafra

21 OCTOBER

While civil war rages in Nigeria, 300,000 innocent refugees in the rebel republic of Biafra are facing starvation. In August, the Nigerian government stopped Red Cross night flights carrying relief aid, claiming that the Biafran rebels used them as a cover to deliver arms. A US adviser warns, "We have to face it that many people are going to die."

Famished children in Biafra

SEPTEMBER–DECEMBER

SEP In Czechoslovakia, the Communist Party expels former leader Alexander Dubcek from its praesidium, or ruling body.

OCT Jack Kerouac, the US novelist, Beat poet, and author of *On the Road*, dies at the age of 47.

OCT In the UK, the P&O ferry line announces that after 130 years it will cease passenger services to India.

GEORGES POMPIDOU

SEP North Vietnamese president Ho Chi Minh dies aged 79, while the war against the USA and South Vietnam continues.

NOV South African rugby team the Springboks begin a UK tour, sparking anti-apartheid protests.

OCT Supersonic *Concorde 001* breaks the sound barrier, to the joy of new French President Pompidou.

SEP In Libya, a group of revolutionary army officers, led by Muammar Gadhafi, seize power while King Idris is in Turkey.

DEC US actress Barbra Streisand stars in the smash hit musical *Hello Dolly* directed by Gene Kelly.

NOV In Australia, the world's longest straight-track railway is opened, from Ooldea to Nurina.

CHANCELLOR BRANDT

OCT In Germany, Willy Brandt becomes chancellor, the first Social Democrat to be elected for 39 years.

DEC The Nobel Prize for Literature is awarded to Irish poet and playwright Samuel Beckett.

DEC An Asian influenza epidemic sweeps the UK, and hundreds of people die.

1970

First jumbo jet lands at Heathrow

22 JANUARY

A new era in jet travel from continent to continent dawned today when a giant Boeing 747 aeroplane arrived at Heathrow Airport in London, Britain, from New York in the United States.

Weighing 356 tonnes and carrying 362 passengers, the jet has rapidly acquired the nickname "jumbo". The world's biggest airliner arrived at Heathrow three hours late, however, after experiencing engine problems in New York.

Apollo 13 splashes down in Pacific

17 APRIL

After a 90-hour ordeal in space, the astronauts on the *Apollo 13* spacecraft have safely returned to Earth. *Apollo 13* was crippled by an explosion in its service module early in its mission. The three astronauts on board are reported to be fit and well.

Apollo 13 being retrieved from the ocean

Hussein and Arafat sign truce

King Hussein and Yassir Arafat shake hands

27 SEPTEMBER

King Hussein of Jordan and Yassir Arafat, leader of the Palestinian Liberation Organization (PLO), have signed a truce to end the war in Jordan. The Palestinian guerrillas had earlier seized control of the north of Jordan and the approaches to the capital, Amman. But, after ten days of fierce fighting with the Jordanian army, the Palestinians were driven out of their strongholds. Recent mass hijackings of Western airliners by Palestinian terrorists ended earlier this month with three aircraft being blown up at Dawson's Field in the Jordanian desert.

JANUARY–DECEMBER

	World Events	Entertainment	Innovations
World Events	**MAY** National guardsmen shoot dead four anti-war demonstrators at Kent State University, USA.	**OCT** After the death of Gamal Abdel Nasser, Anwar Sadat, who is expected to take a more moderate line, becomes president of Egypt.	**NOV** Charles de Gaulle, leader of the Free French in World War II and president of France 1958–69, dies aged 79.	**NOV** 150,000 people are feared dead after a typhoon and tidal wave devastate east Pakistan; other countries send aid.

World Events
MAY National guardsmen shoot dead four anti-war demonstrators at Kent State University, USA.
OCT After the death of Gamal Abdel Nasser, Anwar Sadat, who is expected to take a more moderate line, becomes president of Egypt.
NOV Charles de Gaulle, leader of the Free French in World War II and president of France 1958–69, dies aged 79.
NOV 150,000 people are feared dead after a typhoon and tidal wave devastate east Pakistan; other countries send aid.

Entertainment
APR Paul McCartney issues a writ in the UK to dissolve "the business…The Beatles and Co". **JIMI HENDRIX**
SEP A few days after performing at a festival, superstar guitarist Jimi Hendrix, aged 27, dies from a drug overdose.
SEP Australian Margaret Court wins the "Grand Slam", taking all four major world tennis tournaments.
NOV Cinemas in Paris, France, close for one day as a sign of respect for General Charles de Gaulle.

CHARLES DE GAULLE

Innovations
JUL The first pacemaker driven by a nuclear battery is used at the National Heart Hospital, UK.
OCT UK company British Petroleum (BP) announces the first major oil find in the UK sector of the North Sea.
NOV The supersonic airliner *Concorde* travels at twice the speed of sound for the first time.
DEC The Soviet probe *Venera 7* becomes the first spacecraft to land on the planet Venus.

1971

HOT PANTS

Legs are bared again this summer as hot pants hit the high streets. The tight-fitting shorts are often worn with platform shoes or boots and come in a variety of materials. However, not everyone approves of the new style – hot pants have even been blamed for several traffic accidents!

Idi Amin takes president's oath

20 FEBRUARY

Idi Amin, the former army boxing champion who seized power in Uganda less than a month ago, has declared himself president. Amin, who has the full support of the army, has banned all political activities and elections for five years.

Aswan High Dam is opened

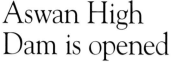

15 JANUARY

Soviet leader Podgorny joined President Sadat of Egypt at today's official opening of the Aswan High Dam on the northern shore of Lake Nasser. The project has taken 11 years and more than $1 billion to complete, with the Soviet Union providing substantial loans. The huge dam will provide Egypt with an all-year-round supply of water for irrigation and electricity.

Idi Amin, president of Uganda

New Disney magic

1 OCTOBER

Nearly 10,000 visitors converged on Orlando, Florida in the United States, today as the gates of the Magic Kingdom at Walt Disney World opened for the first time. Walt Disney picked the site and unveiled the plans shortly before he died in 1966. He had been encouraged to build another Magic Kingdom after the success of Disneyland, California. There are seven different lands inside the Florida park, all based on favourite Disney themes. Each ride and show has been specially designed by the Disney "imagineers" and has its own storyline. Construction of the site began in 1969, and altogether it has taken 9,000 workers and more than $400 million to build the Magic Kingdom, the Seven Seas Lagoon, two golf courses, and two resorts. The formal dedication of Disney World will take place on 25 October with Walt Disney's brother, Roy, officiating.

Fairy castle in Disney World

JANUARY–DECEMBER

FEB It is goodbye to pounds, shillings, and pence as the UK introduces decimal currency, confusing many people.

MAY Rolling Stone Mick Jagger marries Bianca Perez Morena de Macias in France.

APR Three USSR cosmonauts are found dead in their spacecraft after visiting *Salyut 1* space station.

LUNAR ROVING VEHICLE – THE "MOON BUGGY"

APR Nineteen-year-old Jean-Claude "Baby Doc" Duvalier succeeds his father "Papa Doc" as president of Haiti.

JUL US singer and trumpeter Louis Armstrong, famous for his jazz solos, dies aged 71.

JUL David Scott and James Irwin are the first astronauts to drive on the Moon.

JUN The *New York Times* prints secret Pentagon papers that reveal US government deception in the Vietnam War.

AUG UK yachtsman Chay Blyth completes the first solo voyage around the world in a westerly direction.

JUL The first combined heart and lung transplant is performed in a South African hospital.

ROD STEWART

DEC Pakistan surrenders to India after a two-week war and east Pakistan becomes the state of Bangladesh.

OCT Scottish singer Rod Stewart tops the albums and singles charts in both the USA and UK.

NOV US space probe *Mariner 9* transmits photos of the planet Mars back to Earth.

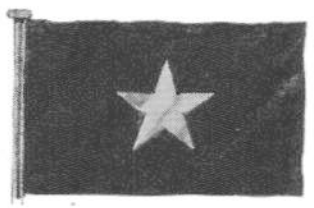

1957 THE VIETCONG REBEL AGAINST SOUTH VIETNAMESE GOVERNMENT

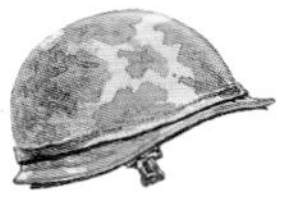

1965 US SENDS IN FIRST GROUND COMBAT TROOPS AS WAR ESCALATES

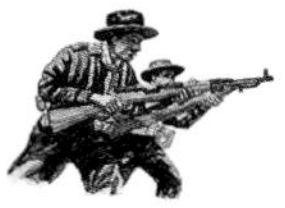

1968 VIETCONG LAUNCH MAJOR NEW YEAR OFFENSIVE

WAR IN VIETNAM

FOLLOWING THE DIVIDE OF VIETNAM in 1954, communists in South Vietnam began to rebel against a non-communist government. North Vietnam, intent on reunifying the country, provided back-up and supplies to the communist rebels, known as the Vietcong. The United States supported South Vietnam by sending money and military advisers. In 1965 the first US troops arrived in South Vietnam to be joined by soldiers from Australia, New Zealand, South Korea, Thailand, and the Philippines. For the United States it proved a costly, unpopular, and futile war. The last US troops left in 1973, but fighting continued until South Vietnam's defeat in 1975.

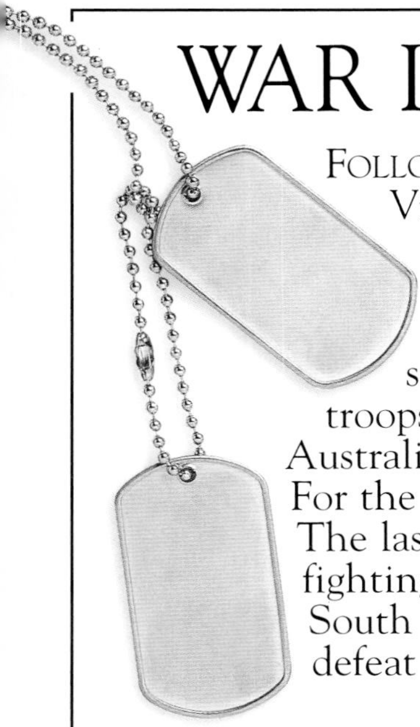

US SOLDIERS' IDENTITY TAGS

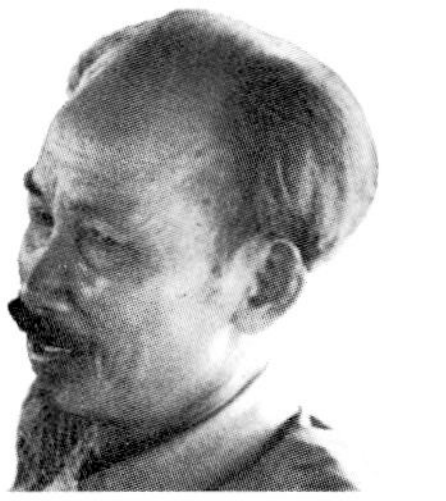

Ho Chi Minh

Communist leader Ho Chi Minh became North Vietnam's first president in 1954. He led the fight against South Vietnam until his death in 1969.

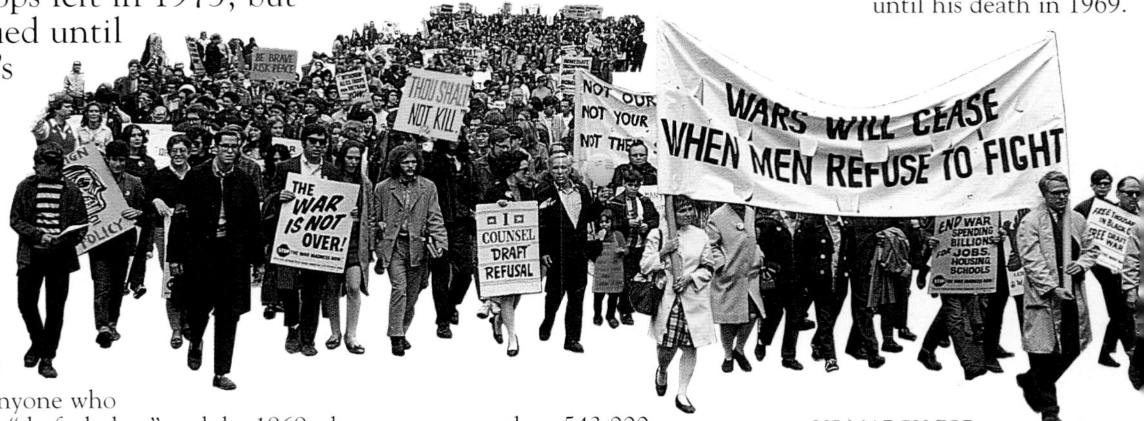

US MARCH FOR PEACE IN VIETNAM

Voices of protest

The conflict in Vietnam escalated into full-scale war in 1965 and thousands of US soldiers were sent to fight. Anyone who refused to enlist was labelled a "draft dodger" and, by 1969, there were more than 543,000 US troops in Vietnam. As fighting intensified and casualties rose, anti-war feeling grew and thousands of people took part in peace rallies, protesting against the United States' involvement in the war. One peaceful demonstration at the Pentagon ended in clashes between protesters and armed soldiers, and more than 250 arrests.

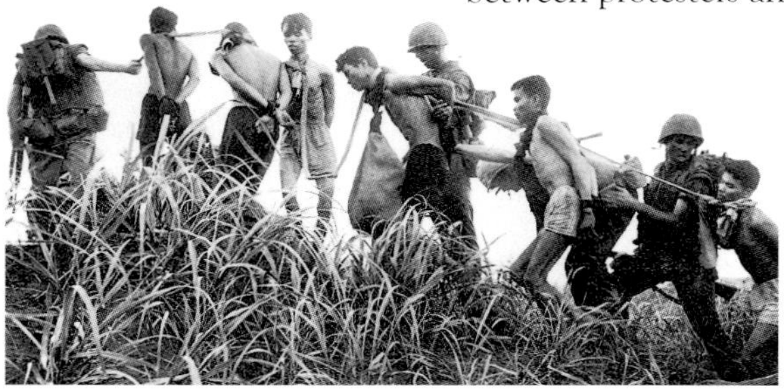

Capturing prisoners

As fighting in Vietnam spread, there were many casualties and prisoners taken on both sides. Despite the huge firepower and technological might of the United States, victory proved elusive. The Vietcong had a genius for guerrilla warfare, and could hide for days on end in the jungle.

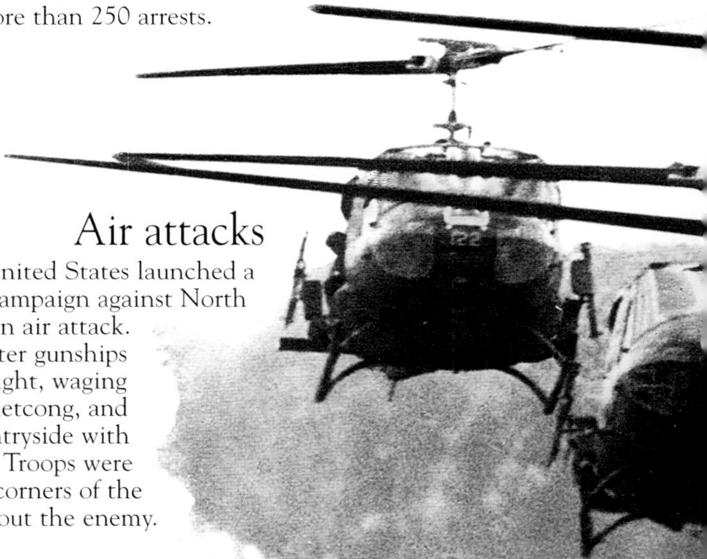

Air attacks

In 1966 the United States launched a massive bombing campaign against North Vietnam with an air attack. Fleets of helicopter gunships continued the fight, waging war against the Vietcong, and spraying the countryside with machine gun fire. Troops were landed in remote corners of the jungle to search out the enemy.

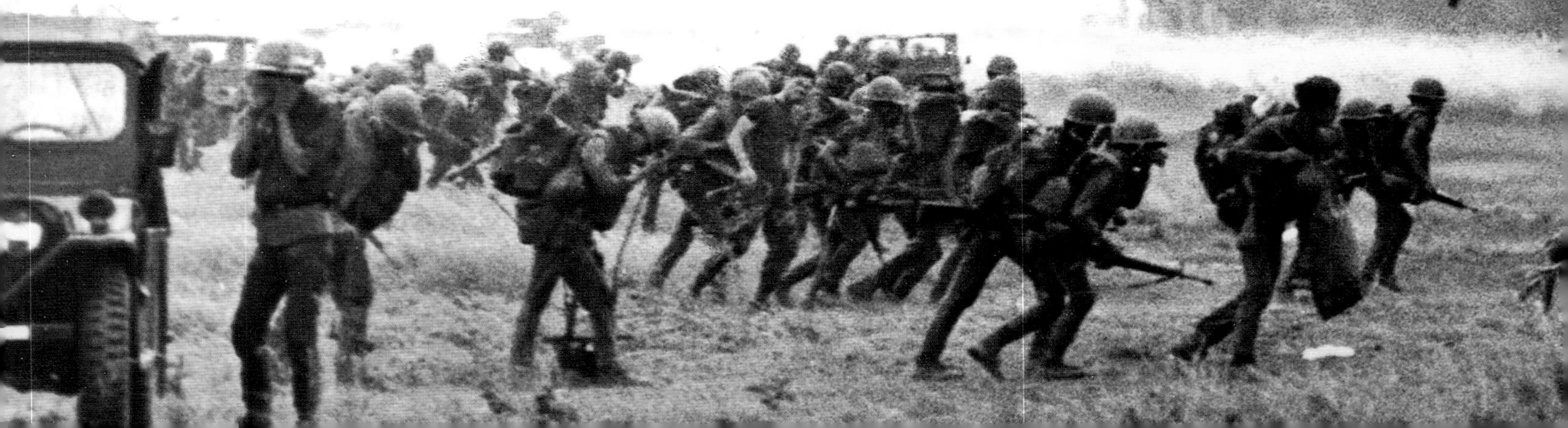

1973 CEASEFIRE AGREEMENT
SIGNED IN PARIS

1973 LAST US TROOPS
WITHDRAW FROM VIETNAM

1975 WAR ENDS AS SOUTH
VIETNAM SURRENDERS

The Tet offensive

In January 1968 at the start of Tet, the Vietnamese New Year, the Vietcong launched a series of attacks on Saigon and other cities in South Vietnam. The US and South Vietnamese forces were taken completely by surprise as they thought the end of the war was in sight. Fierce and bloody street fighting followed, with huge numbers of casualties and terrified civilians fleeing their homes in search of safety. The offensive was finally quashed but it proved that the war was far from over.

CIVILIANS CARRY A WHITE FLAG
AS THEY SEEK US PROTECTION

Vietnam on film

Over the years many films have been made about the Vietnam War. One of the most memorable of these is *Platoon*, which was written and directed by US Vietnam veteran Oliver Stone in 1986.

Coming home

From July 1969 onwards US troops were gradually withdrawn from Vietnam by order of the new president, Richard Nixon. He initiated a policy called "Vietnamization", which meant leaving the South Vietnamese to do their own fighting. The last US ground troops left for home in April 1973, after the signing of a ceasefire agreement in Paris, France, earlier in the year. It was not the end of the war, however, and fighting continued.

Effects of war

The long-term effects of the war on the South Vietnamese were incalculable. Huge numbers were killed in the fighting and bombing, and about half of the population (ten million people) became refugees. The economy, which depended on the export of timber, rubber, and rice, was ruined after the devastation of the countryside by the widespread spraying of toxic herbicides such as "Agent Orange".

1972

Bloody Sunday in Ireland

30 JANUARY
The long and troubled history of Northern Ireland entered a new phase today as 10,000 demonstrators, defying a government ban on marches, paraded through the streets of Derry. The demonstrators were protesting against the policy of internment without trial. An estimated 600 suspected IRA members are being held by the British government in special internment camps. The marchers were confronted by British troops behind army barricades and violence erupted, with rioters hurling stones over the barbed wire. The troops retaliated with rubber bullets, tear gas, and water cannons before opening fire on the crowd. Thirteen unarmed Catholic men and youths were killed, and a further 17 were wounded.

The road to peace

21 FEBRUARY
US president Richard Nixon has arrived in China for a series of historic meetings with Chairman Mao Zedong and Prime Minister Chou En-lai. For 20 years relations between the two countries have been icy, with the United States refusing to acknowledge the communist People's Republic of China, recognizing instead Chiang Kai-shek's nationalist regime of Taiwan as China's true government. China, in turn, claimed that the United States was "the most ferocious enemy of the people throughout the world". If the talks go well, they could eventually lead to trade agreements between the two countries. President Nixon is urging China to join the United States in a "long march together" on different roads to world peace.

Donny's a big hit

17 JUNE
"Osmania" is sweeping the world as US singer Donny Osmond tops the charts with *Puppy Love*, his eighth hit single. Donny has already released four gold albums.

Richard Nixon on the Great Wall of China

World Events	**MAR** Direct rule is imposed on Northern Ireland by the UK government.	**APR** President Nixon steps up the US bombing of Hanoi after communist troops invade South Vietnam.	**MAY** The former UK colony of Ceylon changes its name to Sri Lanka, which means "Resplendent Land".	**JUN** The Duke of Windsor, who abdicated from the UK throne in 1936, is buried at Frogmore in the UK.
Entertainment	**FEB** The US musical film *Cabaret*, starring Liza Minnelli, wins seven Oscars.	**MAR** Marlon Brando stars in *The Godfather*, Francis Ford Coppola's film about the Mafia in the US.	**APR** The Tate Gallery in London, UK, buys Carl André's "bricks" sculpture, *Equivalent 8*.	**MAY** The UK's Jockey Club allows women jockeys to compete in horse racing for the first time.
Innovations	**JAN** The first kidney and pancreatic tissue transplant is carried out in London, UK.	**MAR** The US *Pioneer 10* spacecraft blasts off for Jupiter, powered by four nuclear generators.	**MAR** The first video cassette recorder for professional use is introduced in Japan by Sony.	**APR** US *Apollo 16* astronauts drive on the Moon in a special Lunar Roving Vehicle (LRV).

LIZA MINNELLI

THE DUKE OF WINDSOR'S FUNERAL

1972

Ground troops leave Vietnam

12 AUGUST

The last American ground combat unit has packed up and left the giant air base at Da Nang, more than eight years after the first US marines landed in South Vietnam. The United States' role in the ground war is now at an end. It is the final stage of President Nixon's policy of "Vietnamization" – bringing the troops home and leaving South Vietnam to fight the communists of North Vietnam by itself. The USA's role in the war continues, however, with giant *B-52* bombers carrying out the heaviest raids yet on communist supply routes, while the North Vietnam army steadily advances towards Saigon in the South.

STEPPING OUT

With outrageous soles and skyscraper heels, platform shoes are the height of fashion this year. The shoes are all the rage among the young, who are following in the footsteps of their glam rock idols such as David Bowie and Gary Glitter.

Olympic nightmare

5 SEPTEMBER

At dawn today the Munich Olympics fell victim to one of the worst terrorist attacks in the history of the modern Olympic movement. A group of Palestinian guerrillas scaled the fence surrounding the Olympic village and stormed the building housing the Israeli team, killing two Israeli team members and taking nine hostages. An amazing 12,000 police officers surrounded the village as the terrorists demanded the release of 200 Palestinians held in Israeli jails and their own safe passage out of Germany. Negotiations followed, with West German chancellor Willy Brandt flying in to take charge. Finally, agreement was reached to fly the terrorists with their hostages to Egypt, and they were lifted by helicopter from the village to a military airport. As the first terrorists crossed the tarmac, police marksmen opened fire in a rescue attempt that went tragically wrong. In the gun battle that followed, all nine hostages died as well as five terrorists, and one policeman.

Hooded terrorist looks out from the building housing the Israeli team

JULY–DECEMBER

AUG Uganda's dictator Idi Amin announces that 50,000 Asians with UK passports are to be expelled.

JUL Eddy Merckx of Belgium wins his fourth Tour de France cycling race.

JUL The first cable television programme is aired in the UK by Greenwich Cablevision.

MARK SPITZ

OCT The USA and the USSR sign a Strategic Arms Limitation Treaty (SALT) to reduce the number of missiles.

SEP US swimmer Mark Spitz wins a record seven gold medals at the Olympics.

JUL In the US the first female FBI agents, a former marine and a former nun, are sworn in.

NOV Republican candidate Richard Nixon wins a second term as president of the USA in a landslide election victory.

SEP Bobby Fischer beats Boris Spassky of the USSR to become the first world chess champion from the USA.

OCT Credit cards are introduced in the UK for the first time.

RICHARD LEAKEY AND HIS FINDS

NOV UK scientist Richard Leakey displays a 2.6 million-year-old human skull, found near Lake Rudolf, Kenya.

SEP Soviet gymnast Olga Korbut captivates crowds at the Munich Olympics.

NOV *Pong*, the world's first computer game, is launched in a bar in the USA.

1973

Vietnam peace treaty signed

Vietnam peace talks

27 JANUARY

A peace treaty to end the war in Vietnam has, at last, been agreed in Paris, France. Once a ceasefire is declared and the fighting stops, a multinational force will be drafted in to monitor the truce. Within two months all the military prisoners will be released and all United States troops and advisers removed. President Nixon told the American people the treaty will "bring peace with honour", and the chief negotiator for North Vietnam, Le Duc Tho, declared that "right has triumphed over wrong".

Art world mourns Picasso

8 APRIL

Pablo Picasso died today, aged 91, after suffering a heart attack at his château in Mougins, France. Born in Malaga, Spain, he moved to Paris as a young man and spent most of his life in France. Regarded by many as the greatest artist of the 20th century, he helped to change the course of modern art through his endless experiments with different styles, including Cubism, neo-Classicism, and Surrealism. His energy for work was legendary. It is estimated that during his long life he produced about 140,000 paintings and drawings, and 100,000 engravings. Other works by him included collages and ceramics.

Ceasefire at Wounded Knee

8 MAY

After 70 days, the "Battle of Wounded Knee" in South Dakota, United States, has ended, with native American activists reaching agreement with the government. The conflict began when 200 members of the militant American Indian Movement seized Wounded Knee on the Sioux Oglala Reservation. Fighting resulted in two deaths, several injuries, and about 300 arrests. The Sioux Indians were protesting against broken treaties.

Sioux Indian at Wounded Knee

Tallest tower

Sears Tower

4 MAY

Sears Tower in Chicago, United States, has been officially recognized as the world's tallest skyscraper. At a height of 443 m (1,453 ft), its 110 storeys will provide office space for more than 16,500 people. The building has been specially designed to withstand strong winds.

JANUARY–JUNE

World Events	**JAN** The Helgafell volcano in Iceland erupts after lying dormant for nearly 5,000 years.	**JAN** The UK, Ireland, and Denmark are accepted as members of the European Economic Community (EEC).	**FEB** The London Stock Exchange, UK, admits women to the trading floor for the first time after years of campaigning.	**APR** Four senior White House officials are forced to resign after being implicated in the US Watergate scandal.
Entertainment	**FEB** *Joseph and the Technicolour Dreamcoat* musical opens in the UK.	**MAR** Sir Noël Coward, popular UK's actor and playwright, dies aged 73.	**MAR** US actor Marlon Brando protests at Hollywood's treatment of native Americans.	**JUN** Tennis stars boycott Wimbledon, UK, over the suspension of a Yugoslav player.
Innovations	**JAN** Scientists discover that Saturn's rings are made of solid material.	**APR** The 411-m (1,350-ft) tall World Trade Center in New York, USA, is officially opened.	**APR** *Pioneer 11* is launched from Cape Kennedy in Florida, USA, on a trip to Jupiter.	**MAY** *Skylab*, the USA's first orbiting space station, blasts off from Cape Canaveral.

HELGAFELL VOLCANO ERUPTS IN ICELAND

THE WATERGATE INQUIRY

1973

Kung fu star bows out

20 JULY

Bruce Lee, actor and martial arts expert, has died in Hong Kong from cerebral oedema at the age of 32. Lee, who first became a cult figure in the 1960s when he appeared in an American TV series *The Green Hornet*, later shot to international fame in the kung fu film *Fists of Fury*

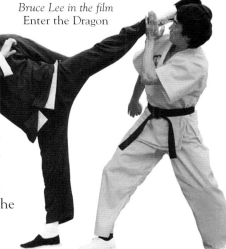

Bruce Lee in the film Enter the Dragon

in 1971. Lee's latest film *Enter the Dragon* has sparked worldwide interest in the martial arts. During one fight scene, he performed a flying kick so fast that it had to be shot in slow motion.

MOUNTAIN BIKE
A Californian cycling club has adapted standard road bikes for riding canyon slopes. With extra gears, thicker tyres, and a lightweight frame the new mountain bikes can deal with all types of difficult terrain.

War in Middle East

17 OCTOBER
The Middle East is witnessing some of the fiercest battles between the Arabs and the Israelis since World War II.

The conflict began eleven days ago on Yom Kippur, the holiest day in the Jewish calendar, when Egyptian troops launched a surprise attack on Israel across the Suez Canal. At the same time, Syria invaded the Israeli-occupied Golan Heights, rapidly capturing Mount Hebron. Israel, at first caught unprepared, fought back and regained territory, before advancing into Syria and across the Suez Canal into Egypt. The world superpowers have stepped in, with the USSR providing arms for the Arabs and the United States backing Israel.

Things hot up in Chile

11 SEPTEMBER
Right-wing opponents have assassinated President Allende of Chile and overthrown the socialist government in a military coup. Led by General Augusto Pinochet, the military attacked the presidential palace with rockets, bombs, and tanks. The president held out for over two hours, supported by the presidential guard and civilian police. More than 2,500 people have been killed in the fierce fighting. Right-wing opposition to President Allende has been gathering strength since he took office in 1970.

The military attack the presidential palace

JULY–DECEMBER

JUL A ransom is demanded for Paul Getty III, the teenage grandson of oil tycoon Paul Getty, when he is kidnapped in the USA.

JUL England beats Australia in the final of the first women's cricket world cup, scoring 279 runs for 3 wickets.

ELTON JOHN

SEP The world's largest airport opens in Texas, USA, covering 7,082 hectares (17,500 acres).

OCT War in the Middle East stops after Egypt, Israel, and Syria accept a UN call for a ceasefire.

SEP UK singer and songwriter Elton John has a number one hit single with *Goodbye Yellow Brick Road*.

OCT The Bosphorus suspension bridge, linking Europe and Asia, is opened.

DEC Paul Getty III is freed in Italy after his right ear is sent through the post with a ransom demand.

SEP UK racing driver Jackie Stewart retires with a record 27 grand prix wins.

OCT The Sydney Opera House is officially opened in Australia.

SYDNEY OPERA HOUSE

DEC The UK goes on a "three-day week" as industry grinds to a halt, paralysed by rail, mine, and power station disputes.

OCT The first UK legal commercial radio station, LBC, is launched.

DEC Two US *Skylab* astronauts make a record seven-hour space walk.

1974

Happy days mania

Henry Winkler as the Fonz

11 JANUARY

A new sitcom *Happy Days* starts tonight on ABC TV in the United States. Following the fortunes of a group of 1950s high school kids in Milwaukee, the show's star is a character called Arthur Fonzarelli, played by Henry Winkler. "The Fonz" wears a black leather jacket and is always surrounded by girls. He is so cool that he can even turn on a jukebox by simply clicking his fingers! Television critics are predicting a big hit.

NIKE TRAINER

The latest training shoes are light and comfortable and are selling like hot cakes. Some of the most exciting designs come from a new American company called Nike. This Waffle trainer, an instant bestseller, has a revolutionary sole which was developed by pouring rubber into a kitchen waffle iron.

Record home run for Aaron

8 APRIL

In a match against the LA Dodgers today, Henry Louis "Hank" Aaron hit his 715th home run, breaking the record held for 39 years by the legendary Babe Ruth. Born in Alabama, United States, Aaron was one of the first black players to enter major league baseball. Nicknamed the "Hammer", he began playing for the Atlanta Braves in 1954. Some commentators have described him as the greatest natural right-handed hitter of all time. Governor Jimmy Carter presented Aaron with a licence plate marked "HLA715" to commemorate his score.

Skylab splashes down in Pacific

8 FEBRUARY

United States astronauts Lt Col Gerald Carr, Lt Col William Pogue, and Dr Edward Gibson have splashed down safely in the Pacific Ocean after setting a new record in the history of manned space flight. They have spent 84 days in orbit on board the United States' first space station, *Skylab*, which was launched in May 1973. It has been occupied so far by three different crews, who conducted a variety of medical and scientific experiments. *Skylab* is now empty but will continue orbiting the Earth.

World Events	**FEB** UK train robber Ronnie Biggs is arrested in Brazil after eight-and-a-half years on the run.	**FEB** Soviet author Alexander Solzhenitsyn is exiled after publication of the book *The Gulag Archipelago* which is critical of the USSR.	**FEB** Prime minister Edward Heath calls a general election in the UK after coal-miners vote for an all-out national strike.	**MAY** India carries out its first underground nuclear test, becoming the sixth nation to possess an atom bomb.
Entertainment	**JAN** For the first time in the UK, professional football is played on Sundays.	**APR** The film *The Sting*, starring Paul Newman and Robert Redford, wins seven Academy Awards in the US.	**MAY** Shedding clothes is the latest craze as "streakers" run naked on campuses, at sporting events, and even at the Oscars!	**JUN** Soviet dancer, Mikhail Baryshnikov, aged 26, defects from the Bolshoi ballet company while on tour in Canada.
Innovations	**JAN** A US company develops the airbag, a new safety device for cars.	**ALEXANDER SOLZHENITSYN** / **MAR** US space probe *Mariner 10* takes the first close-up pictures of the surface of the planet Mercury.	**JUN** Bar codes are first introduced on products for sale at the Marsh Supermarket in Troy, Ohio, USA.	**A STREAKER** / **JUN** Scientists warn that the chlorofluorocarbons in aerosols may be damaging the ozone layer.

A STREAKER

1974

Patty Hearst joins captors

15 APRIL

United States newspaper heiress Patty Hearst, who was kidnapped in February by an extremist left-wing group called the Symbionese Liberation Army, has been involved in an armed bank raid in San Francisco with her captors. The FBI has issued a warrant for the arrest of the gang, including Hearst. Hearst's parents met a ransom demand but, instead of getting their daughter back, they received a taped message saying she had "chosen to stay and fight".

Scandal and corruption in US

8 AUGUST

Richard Nixon, facing impeachment by Congress for refusing to hand over taped conversations with his aides, has announced his resignation. It is the first time in the history of the United States that a president has relinquished office. It is also the final chapter of the "Watergate" scandal which began in June 1972, when five burglars were caught planting bugging devices in the Democrats' election campaign headquarters in the Watergate complex in Washington DC. The scandal has rocked the Republican party to its roots, revealing a saga of dirty tricks, cover-ups, and corruption that have implicated the president himself.

Pandas get new home

14 SEPTEMBER

Two giant pandas, given to former Conservative prime minister Edward Heath on his visit to the People's Republic of China, arrived today at their new home at Britain's zoo in Regent's Park, London. Ching Ching, meaning "crystal bright", and Chia Chia, "most excellent", were both born in 1972. In return for the two giant pandas, the zoo has sent two white rhinoceroses, Nykasi and Mungo, to China.

Chia Chia and Ching Ching get acquainted

JULY–DECEMBER

JUL Isabelita Perón becomes president of Argentina, after the death of her husband, Juan Domingo Perón.

JUL US tennis players Chris Evert and Jimmy Connors win the Wimbledon singles titles in the UK.

SEP A US astronomer discovers the 13th moon of Jupiter and names it *Leda*.

FIRST BLACK MODEL ON VOGUE COVER

SEP Emperor of Ethiopia, Haile Selassie, is overthrown and Ethiopia is declared a socialist state.

AUG Beverly Johnson becomes the first black model to appear on the front cover of *Vogue* magazine.

SEP First transmission of Ceefax Teletext, a television information service, takes place in the UK.

NOV UK police hunt Lord Lucan who disappeared after his children's nanny was found battered to death.

AUG A 13-year-old Egyptian schoolgirl Abla Khairi becomes the youngest person to swim the Channel.

OCT David Kunst, from the USA, is the first man to have walked around the world.

NOV IRA terrorists blow up two pubs in Birmingham, UK, killing 17 people and injuring 120.

NOV Teen group the Bay City Rollers are the latest pop sensation worldwide.

BAY CITY ROLLERS

DEC The Altair 880, the first personal computer (PC), is launched in the USA.

1970 FIRST WOMEN MADE
GENERALS IN THE US ARMY

1975 JUNKO TABEI OF JAPAN IS THE
FIRST WOMAN TO SCALE MT EVEREST

1977 FIRST FEMALE JOCKEY
RIDES IN THE UK GRAND NATIONAL

THE FEMINIST FIGHT

AT THE BEGINNING OF the 20th century, early feminists made giant strides along the road to equality. In many countries they won the right to vote and succeeded in opening up employment opportunities, improving education for girls, and reforming certain laws. During the late 1960s and 1970s, however, a new women's liberation movement emerged. It was inspired by student protests all around the world and by the civil rights campaigns in the United States. More than a century after the first women's rights meetings, a newly politicized generation of women began to wonder how much progress had in fact been made. Women felt they were still fighting discrimination in a male-dominated world, where men continued to hold most of the positions of power, while women provided most of the labour.

Spreading the news

New magazines produced by women for women, such as the UK magazine *Spare Rib*, were launched in the early 1970s. These magazines broke new ground with regular columns on law, sex, health, work, and the arts, instead of the traditional diet of knitting patterns and recipes. Unlike the underground press, they were professionally produced, and aimed to reach women in every walk of life.

Leading the movement

US writer Betty Friedan is often regarded as the mother of the modern women's movement. In 1963 she wrote *The Feminine Mystique* in which she argued that women were discouraged from seeking careers outside of the home. In 1969 she founded the National Organization of Women (NOW), a US pressure group. The group organized a strike to campaign for abortion on demand, 24-hour childcare centres, and equal opportunities in employment and education.

PROTESTORS CARRYING
SYMBOLIC CROSS

First voices of feminism

During World War II women worked in industry and agriculture. But when the men came home at the end of the war women had to give up their jobs and return to their traditional roles as wives and mothers. Against this background, in 1949, French philosopher and feminist Simone de Beauvoir wrote her ground-breaking book *The Second Sex*. Causing shock and outrage in many quarters, de Beauvoir argued that women had been conditioned by social tradition to occupy a secondary place in relation to men.

SIMONE DE BEAUVOIR

Too much to bear

On International Women's Day in 1971 a huge Women's Liberation March took place in London, England. It was the biggest women's rally in Britain since the suffragettes won the vote for women at the beginning of the century. Some of the marchers carried a cross made out of a female tailor's dummy draped in chains. Symbols of women's domestic enslavement – washing, a shopping bag, and an apron – dangled from the crossbar. A petition was presented to the prime minister demanding equal education, job opportunities, and equal pay, as well as free childcare, contraception, and abortion on demand.

A global movement

The women's movement has flourished in many countries all over the world for more than 150 years. New Zealand became the first country to grant national women's suffrage in 1893, while women in Switzerland had to wait another 78 years until they were granted the vote in 1971. More recently, feminists have campaigned on issues like childcare, equal education, and pay and job opportunities, aiming to change people's attitudes as well as the law.

Women in an age of change

Women's liberation in the United States grew out of the campaigns of the 1960s when thousands of students protested against the war in Vietnam and joined the fight for civil rights and racial equality. Many women realized that there was another struggle closer at hand – to liberate themselves from oppression by men. Women's groups sprang up all over the country, generating a tide of sisterly solidarity. At the 1968 Miss America Pageant in Atlantic City, feminists staged their first public protest and dumped bras and girdles into a "freedom trash bucket". The media described the event as demonstrators "burning their bras". This misleading catchphrase was used repeatedly to stereotype feminists and dismiss their campaigns.

Statue of Liberty

Freedom of dress

When Ayatollah Khomeini returned to Iran in 1979, he imposed strict laws in the name of Islam which often affected the lives of women. For example, western-style dress was forbidden and women were forced to wear a head-to-toe robe called a "chador". Many Iranian women objected to this legislation and marched through the streets of Teheran chanting "freedom not the chador", demanding the right to dress as they pleased.

Towards greater equality

Women's groups have helped to re-assess and redefine the traditional roles of men and women in the 20th century. Despite the achievements of the women's liberation movement of the 1970s, there is still a long way to go, with few women in top jobs or positions of power. The burden of childcare has remained largely on female shoulders, with many working mothers forced to opt for low-paid, part-time jobs.

YOUNG FEMINIST
CAMPAIGNS FOR
EQUAL RIGHTS

1975

Saigon falls as Americans withdraw

30 APRIL

The war in Vietnam finally ended today, two years after US forces left the area. South Vietnam surrendered as the communist North Vietnamese troops and tanks took control of the capital, Saigon, which has already been renamed Ho Chi Minh City. The last of the United States troops have left the country, airlifted to safety by helicopters. They left behind them scenes of panic as thousands of the South Vietnamese, fearful of the new communist regime, try to escape by boat and plane.

The killing fields

Khmer Rouge soldiers

15 JUNE

Cambodia, already devastated by a war that killed a quarter of a million people, is now facing another terrible human tragedy. According to reports from refugees who have managed to slip across the border into Thailand, the new communist Khmer Rouge government, led by Pol Pot, has embarked on a regime of unparalleled brutality. Since the Khmer Rouge took control only two months ago, thousands of people have been executed or worked to death. Everyone has to dress alike, and the government has forbidden the practice of any religion. Cambodians are being driven out into the countryside to till the soil with their bare hands, or to take the place of water buffalo pulling ploughs. They are starving, with only a daily cup of rice to eat.

SOLAR POWER BOAT
New alternative sources of energy, like solar power, are constantly being put to new uses. This boat, *Solar Craft 1*, built by A T Freeman, in Britain, UK, was first put through its paces in February.

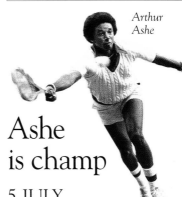

Arthur Ashe

Ashe is champ

5 JULY

Arthur Ashe, who started his tennis career playing in the segregated parks of Richmond, Virginia, today became the first black men's champion at the Wimbledon lawn tennis tournament in London, UK. He beat the favourite, fellow American Jimmy Connors, in a thrilling four-set final.

JANUARY–APRIL

World Events	**FEB** Turkish Cypriot leader Rauf Denktash declares Turkish Cyprus independent.	**FEB** Margaret Thatcher wins leadership of the Conservative Party and is the first woman to lead a political party in the UK.	**FEB** In Katmandu, Nepal, 29-year-old King Birendra is crowned as the world's only Hindu and absolute monarch.	**MAR** In Riyadh, Saudi Arabia, King Faisal is assassinated by his mentally deranged nephew, who is later beheaded.
Entertainment	**MAR** In the UK, 85-year-old actor Charlie Chaplin is knighted by Queen Elizabeth.	**APR** Anatoly Karpov of the USSR becomes the youngest ever world chess champion, aged 23.	**APR** The musical *A Chorus Line*, by Kleban and Hamlish, is first performed in the USA.	**APR** US born music-hall singer and star of the Folies Bergères, Josephine Baker, dies aged 69.
Innovations	**JAN** The UK abandons the project to connect England and France with a sea tunnel.	**FEB** UK Sir John Huxley, who made important contributions to biology, especially in genetics, dies aged 87.	**FEB** The UK government approves a plan for two new nuclear power stations.	**APR** Nineteen-year-old Bill Gates forms Microsoft with his friend Paul Allen, in the USA.

ANATOLY KARPOV

A CHORUS LINE

1975

Clay army found

11 JULY

A huge army of 6,000 life-sized terracotta warriors has been unearthed by Chinese archaeologists near the ancient capital of Xian. The army was first discovered by peasants digging for water. With their chariots, spears, and horses, the figures are drawn up rank by rank in battle formation. After more than 2,000 years they are still guarding the tomb of the first Qin emperor, who died in 206 BC. Qin Shi Huangdi unified the country and the name "China" is taken from his name. Under his rule, thousands of people died building the Great Wall of China. Workers who helped build his tomb were walled up inside to keep it secret.

Astronauts meet cosmonauts

17 JULY

While United States and Soviet missiles remain poised for mutual self-destruction on Earth, a historic encounter between the two superpowers has taken place in space. The US *Apollo* and the Soviet *Soyuz* spacecraft docked 225 km (140 miles) above the Atlantic ocean. Astronaut Tom Stafford and cosmonaut Alexei Leono shook hands through the hatches in the first international meeting to be held in space.

Hunting down the Jackal

29 JULY

As the hunt continues for the international terrorist and hit man Ilich Ramirex Sanchez evidence is mounting that the Soviet Union's KGB has been involved in his activities. Sanchez is better known by his nickname, Carlos the Jackal. This comes from his ability to carry out successful hits and then vanish into the shadows.

MAY–AUGUST

JUN In Uganda, a tribunal finds UK author Dennis Hills guilty of "treason" for criticizing the dictator Idi Amin.

MAY US singer Frank Sinatra wins damages from the UK's BBC over a programme linking him to the Mafia.

MAY Japanese climber Junko Tabei becomes the first woman to scale Mount Everest in the Himalayas.

JUNKO TABEI

JUN In Egypt, the Suez Canal re-opens to international maritime traffic for the first time in eight years.

MAY The UK's leading woman sculptor, Barbara Hepworth, dies in a fire at her studio at St Ives in Cornwall.

JUN In London, UK, a session of the House of Commons is broadcast live on the radio for the first time.

JUN Indian prime minister Mrs Indira Gandhi is barred from public office for six years after revelations of electoral corruption.

JUN Brazilian football hero Pelé signs a $7 million three-year contract with the New York Cosmos in the USA.

JUN The UK's first North Sea oil flows ashore from a tanker to a British Petroleum refinery in Kent.

JOHN WALKER

JUL Yitzhak Rabin arrives in Bonn on the first ever visit by an Israeli premier to West Germany.

JUN New Zealand athlete John Walker runs the mile in a record-breaking 3 minutes 49.4 seconds.

OCT Soviet probes *Venera 9* and *Venera 10* transmit the first pictures from the surface of the planet Venus.

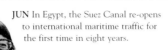

1975

New reign in Spain

22 NOVEMBER

Don Juan Carlos Borbon y Borbon today became the first king of Spain since his grandfather Alfonso XIII went into exile in 1931. He succeeds General Franco, who ruled Spain with a rod of iron from the end of the civil war in 1939 until his death two days ago.

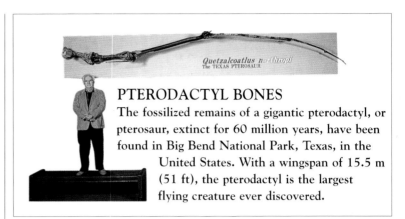

PTERODACTYL BONES

The fossilized remains of a gigantic pterodactyl, or pterosaur, extinct for 60 million years, have been found in Big Bend National Park, Texas, in the United States. With a wingspan of 15.5 m (51 ft), the pterodactyl is the largest flying creature ever discovered.

Civil war in Angola

24 NOVEMBER

Only two weeks after Angola gained independence from Portugal it is being torn apart by a devastating civil war. At least 40,000 people have been killed and a million more have been made homeless. Several groups are vying for control of the country, each receiving support from major world powers. The Marxist Popular Movement for the Liberation of Angola (MPLA) is receiving military aid from the Soviet Union and Cuba, while the United States is supporting two non-Marxist movements. South Africa is backing yet another faction.

Video boosts sales of Queen's *Bohemian Rhapsody* record

20 DECEMBER

It took six months for British group Queen to perfect their new album *A Night at the Opera*, in one of the most expensive recording sessions in the history of rock 'n' roll. The result is that *Bohemian Rhapsody*, the seven-minute single from the album, shot to the top of the UK charts and is still riding high three weeks later. It is split into two parts – or movements – and uses state of the art technology as well as snatches of classical opera. Queen has also made a special video to promote *Bohemian Rhapsody*, and this is no doubt helping to boost sales.

SEPTEMBER–DECEMBER

World Events	**SEP** Fighting between Christians and Muslims tears apart the Lebanese capital of Beirut.	**OCT** The Soviet dissident and active human rights campaigner Dr Andrei Sakharov wins the Nobel Prize for Peace.	**NOV** The Australian left-wing Labour prime minister Gough Whitlam is dismissed, causing a constitutional crisis.	**DEC** Armed South Moluccan terrorists surrender after a 15-day siege of the Indonesian consulate in Holland.
Entertainment	**SEP** Czech tennis player Martina Navratilova defects to the USA.	**OCT** UK climbers Dougal Haston and Doug Scott conquer the southwest face of Everest.	**OCT** Austrian racing driver Niki Lauda becomes world motor racing champion.	**DEC** Rod Stewart, lead singer of UK group The Faces, announces he is leaving the group to form his own band.
Innovations	**OCT** Human remains 3.75 million years old are discovered in Tanzania. **ANDREI SAKHAROV**	**NOV** UK director Ken Russell's *Lisztomania* is the first feature film in Dolby stereo.	**NOV** The UK's first underwater pipeline for North Sea oil is opened. **NIKI LAUDA**	**DEC** UK pilot Yvonne Pope is the first woman to captain a jet airline.

1976

New air supersonic super-service

21 JANUARY

A regular supersonic passenger service across the Atlantic ocean was launched today when an Air France *Concorde* airliner made its first commercial flight from Paris, France to Rio de Janeiro in Brazil. With a cruising speed of 2,338 km/h (1,461 mph) the supersonic turbojet can cross the Atlantic in just three hours.

Soweto uprising

16 JUNE

The black township of Soweto, a sprawling suburb of Johannesburg in South Africa, is today witnessing scenes of horrifying violence. There is serious rioting and looting, and at least 50 people have been killed and hundreds more wounded. The violent and bloody scenes came after white riot police fired live ammunition into a 10,000-strong group of marching school children who were protesting against the segregated education system. Last year the South African government issued a decree proclaiming that black secondary school academic subjects must be taught in the Afrikaans language. This sparked a wave of strikes, marches, and demonstrations culminating in today's events. For most black people, Afrikaans, a form of Dutch, is the hated language of white oppression.

Hostages freed after intrepid raid at Uganda's Entebbe airport

Hostages celebrate freedom

4 JULY

Israeli commandos carried out a daring rescue mission at Entebbe airport in Uganda last night, freeing more than 100 hostages held by pro-Palestinian terrorists. In a 35-minute battle, 20 Ugandan soldiers, all seven hijackers, three hostages, and one Israeli soldier were killed.

A bus set on fire during the riot

JAN Chou En-Lai, prime minister of China and second-in-command to Chairman Mao since 1949, dies in Peking aged 78.

JAN The UK's richest author and "queen of crime fiction" Agatha Christie dies aged 85.

FEB Soviet officials admit transmitting microwaves at the US embassy in Moscow.

KONICA AUTO-FOCUS CAMERA

MAR US newspaper heiress Patty Hearst is found guilty of assisting in an armed robbery with her radical leftist kidnappers.

APR German-born artist Max Ernst, leading member of the Surrealist group, dies aged 85.

MAR Japanese company Konica launches the first auto-focus camera.

MAR Isabelita Perón, president of Argentina since her husband's death in 1974, is deposed in a bloodless coup by military leaders.

MAY Boxer Muhammad Ali knocks out Richard Dunn in Germany to retain his world heavyweight title.

APR Australian scientist Dr Gerald Shannon develops a bionic artificial arm with a strong hand grip.

APR The US billionaire recluse Howard Hughes dies after suffering a stroke aboard his private jet.

JUN Jockey Lester Piggott wins the Derby at Epsom in the UK, for a record seventh time.

HOWARD HUGHES

JUN In Colorado, USA, the first women enter the formerly male-only Air Force Academy.

1976

Nadia leaps into record books

31 JULY

A tiny gymnast from Romania has stolen the show at the Olympic Games in Montreal after scoring the first perfect "10" in gymnastic history. Her name is Nadia Comaneci and she is only 14 years old. She was awarded maximum points for her dazzling vaults, leaps, and twists on the asymmetric bars in the team competition. She repeated the feat five times, winning three gold medals.

Nadia Comaneci wins five golds

Probe sends pictures of planet Mars

20 JULY

Is there really life on Mars – and if so what does it look like? We might just find out after the US *Viking 1* spacecraft made a perfect landing on the Martian sand dunes today, sending back the first close-up pictures of a barren surface littered with rocks and boulders. The $500 million probe, which will soon be joined by *Viking 2*, will also report on the planet's weather conditions. More importantly, it will carry out specially designed experiments on the soil that are aimed at discovering any signs of plant or animal life.

China mourns Chairman Mao

9 SEPTEMBER

Chairman Mao Zedong, leader of the People's Republic of China and its 800 million people since 1949, has died aged 82, after suffering a series of strokes. Wreaths have already been placed on the Revolutionary Martyrs Monument in the Square of Heavenly Peace, Beijing. Many thousands of mourners are expected to file past his body, which will be preserved and is to lie in state in a transparent crystal sarcophagus. Who will succeed him is not so clear. A power struggle between rival factions within the Chinese Communist Party seems unavoidable. The party has already split into two main groups – on the left, the "radical Maoists" led by the late leader's widow Chiang Chin, and, on the right, the "moderate communists" led by Deng Xiaoping.

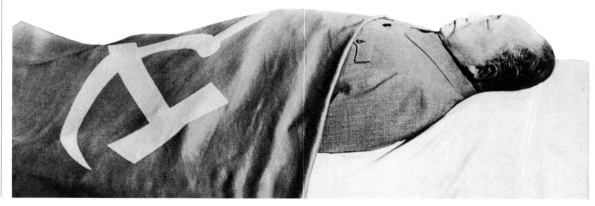

JULY–DECEMBER

World Events	**JUL** An accident at a chemical plant near Milan, Italy, releases a huge cloud of poisonous gas.	**AUG** A women's peace movement is launched in Northern Ireland at a rally of 20,000 Protestants and Roman Catholics.	**OCT** In China, Mao's widow and three other people are arrested for plotting to overthrow the government.	**NOV** A major earthquake strikes eastern Turkey, devastating 80 villages and killing 3,000 people.
Entertainment	**JUL** In the UK, 20-year-old Swedish tennis player Björn Borg becomes Wimbledon champion.	**AUG** Austrian-born film director Fritz Lang, who made *Metropolis*, *M*, and *The Big Heat*, dies aged 86.	**NOV** *Rocky*, a film about a boxer, written by and starring Sylvester Stallone, is a big hit in the USA.	**DEC** UK composer Benjamin Britten, the first musician to be created a life peer, dies aged 65.
Innovations	**AUG** Left-handed cheque books are issued for the first time by a bank in the UK.	**AUG** After nine years' work, biologists in the USA have sucessfully created the first artificial functioning gene.	**SEP** Percy Shaw, the UK inventor of "cat's-eyes", which transformed road safety, dies aged 86.	**OCT** The £16 million National Theatre in London in the UK, is officially opened, three years late.

BJÖRN BORG

ROCKY

1977

Arts Centre opens

31 JANUARY

France acquired a new landmark and tourist attraction today – the hi-tech Pompidou National Centre for Art and Culture in the Beaubourg district of Paris. Designed by Italian and British architects Renzo Piano and Richard Rogers, the six-storey glass building proudly displays its structural supports on the outside as well as its brightly painted ducts, tubes, water pipes, and escalators. Reactions to the unorthodox new building are predictably mixed.

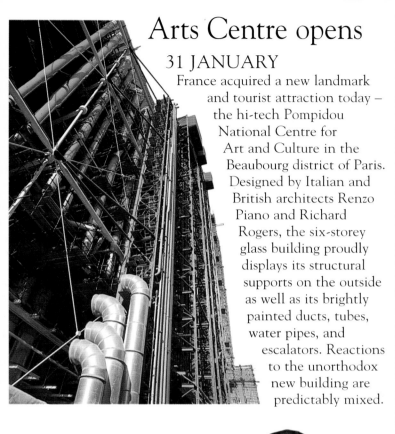

Collision leads to disaster on runway

27 MARCH

Two jumbo jets collided on the runway at Tenerife airport in the Canary Islands tonight, killing 574 people, most of them holiday-makers from the United States and Europe. It is the worst disaster in the history of aviation. The accident happened when a Pan Am jet turned onto the runway just as another plane, belonging to Dutch airline KLM, was about to take off. Both the aircrafts had been diverted from Las Palmas airport because of a bomb explosion there. As they collided, the two giant jets burst into flames and all 348 passengers on board the KLM plane died. Miraculously, there are at least 70 survivors who managed to escape from the burning wreckage of the Pan Am jet, and they are being treated for burns in hospital. Radio and television stations are putting out emergency appeals for more medical staff in order to cope with the crisis. What caused the accident is not yet known.

MORE THAN A PUPPET

Jim Henson's favourite puppets have swept to international stardom with their own TV series, *The Muppet Show*. Real-life celebrities are clamouring to be invited on the show, which has won top television awards in many countries round the world.

JANUARY–APRIL

JAN Convicted killer Gary Gilmore becomes the first person to be sentenced to be executed in the USA in ten years.

JAN TV series *Roots*, by black American Alex Haley, attracts record audiences in the USA.

JAN UK inventor Clive Sinclair introduces a £175 5-cm (2-in) screen television.

POPULAR TV SERIES ROOTS

JAN Charter 77, calling for civil rights for all citizens, is signed by more than 240 scholars in communist Czechoslovakia.

FEB UK punk rock group the Sex Pistols is fired by their record company EMI.

FEB In the USA, the space shuttle makes its maiden flight on top of a Boeing 747.

JAN Georgia-born ex-peanut farmer Jimmy Carter, the Democrat candidate, is inaugurated as the new president of the USA.

APR Red Rum is the first horse to win the UK's Grand National race three times.

APR US company Polaroid demonstrates a new home movies system, *Polavision*.

THE INAUGURATION OF PRESIDENT CARTER

FEB Ugandan archbishop Janani Luwum is murdered in the latest wave of killings by President Idi Amin's troops.

MAY Punk music is the latest youth sensation around the world.

APR Quadrophonic broadcasts are started on BBC radio in the UK.

1977

Star Wars is box office blockbuster

25 MAY

Star Wars, a new science fiction film directed by George Lucas, is an epic tale of good versus evil. Using state-of-the-art technology, including a new computer-assisted camera system, the film is full of spectacular visual and sound effects and is already being billed as this summer's box office hit. Like all good fairy stories, *Star Wars* has handsome heroes, a princess in distress, an evil emperor, and courageous knights. It also stars two comic robots called R2D2 and C-3PO.

The robot R2D2

HYDROTHERMAL VENTS

Scientists were amazed to find the first hydrothermal vents on the seabed of the Pacific this year. The vents spew mineral-rich, warm water which allows animal life, such as bacteria and clams, to flourish.

Maiden voyage

12 AUGUST

The first manned free-flight test of the space shuttle, orbiter *Enterprise*, took place successfully today at Edwards Air Force Base in California, United States. After it had separated from the Boeing *747* "taxi" jet at a height of 6,950 m (22,802 ft), astronauts Fred Haise and C. Gordon Fullerton flew the 76.2-tonne glider around a U-shaped course, before making a perfect landing on the dry lake runway. During the flight, which lasted 5 minutes 23 seconds, the orbiter performed as well as wind-tunnel tests had predicted. The crew commented on its surprisingly quick responses and said that it handled like a fighter aircraft. The test series is designed to assess the craft's performance in the lower atmosphere. It will be concluded with four more free-flight tests before the orbiter is taken to the Marshall Space Flight Center at Huntsville, Alabama, for structural tests.

The orbiter Enterprise *about to split from the Boeing* 747

MAY–AUGUST

World Events	**MAY** Menachem Begin, former leader of a Jewish terror group, is elected Israeli prime minister.	**MAY** Yomo Kenyatta, president of Kenya, bans big game hunting in an effort to conserve the country's wildlife.	**JUN** Silver Jubilee celebrations are held all over the UK to mark 25 years of Queen Elizabeth II's reign.	**JUN** In Spain's first election for 41 years, Adolfo Suarez, leader of the Democratic Centre coalition, is elected president.
Entertainment	**MAY** The Paris to Istanbul *Orient Express* makes its final journey after 94 years service.	**MAY** Eleven-year-old Nigel Short of the UK is the youngest competitor in a national chess championship.	**AUG** UK cricketer Geoff Boycott scores his one hundredth century in a cricket match.	**AUG** US comic actor Groucho Marx, famous for his crouching walk, waggling eyebrows, and cigar, dies aged 86.
Innovations	**MAY** The world's largest particle accelerator is opened in Switzerland.	**JUN** The 1,300-km (808-mile) Transalaska pipeline system begins transporting oil across Alaska, USA.	**AUG** The Soviet ship *Arktika* is the first surface vessel ever to reach the North Pole.	**AUG** US space probes *Voyager 1* and *2* are launched on journeys to Jupiter and Saturn.

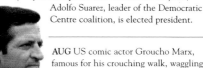
THE ORIENT EXPRESS

ADOLFO SUAREZ

1977

"The King" is dead

Elvis Presley dies in Memphis

16 AUGUST

Elvis Presley, the king of rock 'n' roll, has died at Memphis Baptist Memorial Hospital, USA, aged 42. His health had been deteriorating for some years and he was vastly overweight. For some time there have been persistent rumours of drug abuse. Thousands of distraught fans have gathered outside the star's mansion, Graceland, to say goodbye. Elvis first gyrated his way to the top with *Heartbreak Hotel* in 1956. He went on to sell a total of more than 500 million records during his long career.

Biko killed

12 SEPTEMBER

Steve Biko, the South African black leader, has died of brain injuries in a prison hospital in Pretoria. After being arrested last month, Biko was held in a police cell in Port Elizabeth. For five days he was kept naked in leg irons and handcuffs and interrogated. A struggle allegedly took place when his manacles were removed. Biko was later found dying in his cell.

Boat people flee Vietnam

3 DECEMBER

Thousands of desperate refugees are fleeing to escape the communist regime that has taken over in South Vietnam. They are taking to the open sea in small, unsafe boats in the hope of reaching a country where they can live.

Bokassa on his golden coronation throne

Crowned in glory

4 DECEMBER

Jean Bedel Bokassa, president of the Central African Republic, today realized his ambitions when he was crowned emperor to the sound of tribal drums and Mozart. The former sergeant in France's colonial army, who took office in 1966, spared no expense for the ceremony. Altogether, the celebrations cost about $30 million and were paid for by French president Giscard d'Estaing. The new emperor wore an elaborately embroidered coronation uniform, and rode in a coach pulled by specially imported horses.

SEPTEMBER–DECEMBER

SEP The USA and Panama sign the Panama Canal Treaty, in which they agree that the canal zone will return to Panama in 1999.

SEP Japanese baseball player Sadaharu Oh beats US Hank Aaron's major league record of 715 home runs.

SEP Freddie Laker's cut-price *Skytrain* service from London to New York is launched.

JOHN TRAVOLTA DOLL

OCT Hostages are rescued by German commandos from a jet hijacked by Palestinian terrorists at Mogadishu airport in Somalia.

DEC John Travolta stars in the film *Saturday Night Fever* and the Bee Gees' soundtrack popularizes disco music.

OCT Supersonic airliner *Concorde* makes its first flight from Toulouse, France, to New York, USA.

NOV President Sadat of Egypt visits Israel and addresses the Knesset, the Israeli parliament.

DEC Paul McCartney's new group Wings tops the charts with the hit single *Mull of Kintyre*.

DEC Soviet spacecraft *Soyuz 26* docks with *Salyut 6*, the orbiting research space station.

CHARLIE CHAPLIN

DEC Israeli leader Menachem Begin declares that Israel is ready to return Sinai to Egypt.

DEC UK comic genius Charlie Chaplin dies at his home in Switzerland, aged 88.

DEC Heathrow Airport in the UK is the first airport to be connected to a city rail system.

SOUNDS OF THE SEVENTIES

WHILE HEAVY METAL AND STADIUM BANDS took off in the United States, elsewhere around the world pop music exploded in many different directions. Glam rock provided welcome relief from serious progressive rock, and set the scene for the fashionable New Romantics of the Eighties. Punk thumbed its nose at disco and produced a generation of successful new wave bands that made pop music with attitude. On both sides of the Atlantic records were beginning to sell in their millions, with the result that some of the Seventies rock stars became super-rich. A new wealthy pop aristocracy was born.

Abba win Eurovision

Abba won the Eurovision Song Contest for Sweden in 1974. Their song *Waterloo* became the first of many million-selling records, making them the decade's most successful group. Their music was streamlined yet catchy, as was their name, an acronym of the band members' initials – Agnetha, Benny, Bjorn, and Anni-Frid.

First family of pop

The Jackson Five shot to stardom in 1970, having been spotted and signed up the year before at a concert in their home town of Gary, Indiana, in the United States. The Five were all brothers – Michael, aged 11, Marlon 13, Jermaine 16, Toriano 17, and Sigmund 19. Being a family business, they were managed by their father, Joe. In 1970 they released three albums which all entered the US top ten. The Jackson Five's fame lasted throughout the Seventies with a string of successful singles, albums, and concerts. They were even turned into a cartoon series!

THE JACKSON FIVE

BOB MARLEY

Reggae superstar

With their ground-breaking 1972 album, *Catch a Fire*, Bob Marley and the Wailers brought reggae out of the ghettos and introduced it to a worldwide audience. Formed in 1964, the Wailin' Wailers was made up of Marley, Peter Tosh, and Bunny Livingston. The group signed to Island Records in 1972 and was renamed Bob Marley and the Wailers. After the group split up Bob Marley went on to achieve a dazzling solo career. Sadly, this was cut short in 1981, when he died of cancer. As a tribute to the superstar, his birthday was made a national holiday in Jamaica.

Rock and Rollers

Tartan scarves acquired a new street cred during the mid-1970s thanks to a Scottish group called the Bay City Rollers. Wearing head-to-toe tartan and calf-length trousers, their carefully calculated image caused mass hysteria among teenagers on both sides of the Atlantic.

BAY CITY ROLLER'S PLATFORM SHOE

Thick sole

King of Glam

Glam rock swept the British pop scene in the early Seventies, paving the way for superstars like Queen and Elton John. Unlike progressive rock, the music was accessible and uncomplicated. The outfits, on the other hand, were extraordinary, with spectacular platform shoes, outrageous flares, and glitter galore. David Bowie put on his make-up, dyed his hair, and reinvented himself as the hero of his 1972 *Ziggy Stardust* album.

DAVID BOWIE AS ZIGGY STARDUST

1975 ROCK GROUP QUEEN
MAKE THE FIRST POP VIDEO

1977 THE SEX PISTOLS INTRODUCE
THE WORLD TO PUNK

1979 SONY LAUNCHES THE
WALKMAN PERSONAL STEREO

Pioneers of electronic pop

Kraftwerk were an avant-garde German group who experimented with synthetic electronic sounds to produce international hits like *Autobahn* in 1975, and *Man Machine* in 1978. They had a huge influence on the birth of techno and house music in Britain. Their single, *Computer World* (1981), concentrated on micro-technology, using sounds from a pocket calculator and bleeps from a home computer game.

COLLECTOR'S
PUNK RECORD

Johnny Rotten

Punk rock

The Sex Pistols' lead singer Johnny Rotten could not sing, but he was very good at swearing and hurling abuse at his fans. Strangely enough, audiences loved it and the group became an instant role model for a new generation of British teenagers hungry for rebellion and something new. The first single, *Anarchy in the UK*, entered the UK top 50 at the end of 1976. The sleeve of *God Save The Queen*, their 1977 best-selling single, showed the Queen with a safety-pin through her nose.

Punk badges

JOHN TRAVOLTA IN
SATURDAY NIGHT FEVER

Trademark golden medallion

The disco era

An actor called John Travolta put on his dancing shoes in 1977 and leaped into the lead of *Saturday Night Fever*, a film about a New York disco. With a throbbing soundtrack by the Bee Gees, it set feet tapping all around the world. A new disco craze was born, and teenagers everywhere copied the steps, leaps, and twirls they saw on the screen. The film became a box-office smash and one of the most successful films about popular music ever made. The album sold over 30 million copies worldwide, making it the best-selling soundtrack ever. Seven of the songs topped the singles charts – an all-time record!

White satin flared trousers

Takeaway tunes

Music was available at the flick of a wrist during the 1970s with this circular wrist radio from Japan. Known as a "toot-a-loop" or a "sing-o-ring", this fun radio could be placed on a table, stuck on a wall, or made into a bracelet. This forerunner to the personal walkman was all the rage among teenagers, particularly in the United States.

New wave

Post-punk groups, like the Jam, the Police, and U2 moved into the mainstream. Blondie, a successful punk group in the mid-1970s, shot to international fame in 1978 with the album *Parallel Lines* which mixed pop and disco.

1978

Cleaning the oil-polluted coastlines of Brittany

Sea turns black

16 MARCH

The world's worst oil spill to date occurred today when the super-tanker *Amoco Cadiz*, carrying 1.3 million barrels of crude oil, ran aground on rocks off the coast of Brittany in France causing untold damage. Battered by Atlantic waves, the ship broke in two, spewing its entire cargo into the ocean. Using chemical anti-pollution sprays, a fleet of vessels has been fighting to control a huge oil slick that is slithering towards the Channel Islands. The spill has already blanketed 113 km (70 miles) of French coastline with a thick, black slime. This catastrophe is likely to have a devastating effect on the local fishing industry and on tourism in the region. It will also cause incalculable harm to local birds and other wildlife in what is France's largest bird sanctuary.

GARFIELD

A comic strip by Jim Davis about a fat orange cat called Garfield has gained an enormous following this year. It was launched in June and the strip now runs in more than 40 newspapers in the United States.

Test-tube baby

25 JULY

The world's first "test-tube" baby Louise Brown was delivered today by caesarean section at Oldham Hospital in Britain. She was conceived by using a revolutionary new technique called "in vitro", which is Latin for "in glass". One of her mother's eggs was fertilized in a test-tube. The embryo was planted back in the womb to grow normally.

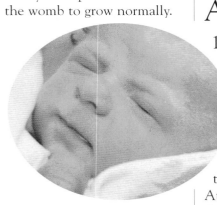

Louise, the first test-tube baby

A lot of hot air

17 AUGUST

Intrepid travellers Ben Abruzzo, Larry Newman, and Max Anderson have successfully arrived in Normandy, France. The three left US soil six days ago, in their attempt to cross the Atlantic in a specially designed hot air balloon.

JANUARY–JUNE

World Events	**JAN** Newspaper editor Donald Woods escapes from South Africa by swimming across the Tele River.	**JAN** Sweden becomes the first country in the world to ban aerosol sprays because of the damage they cause to the environment.	**MAR** Israeli troops attack Palestinian camps in southern Lebanon as an act of revenge for a terrorist attack.	**MAY** The ex-prime minister of Italy, Aldo Moro, is murdered by Red Brigade kidnappers in Rome.
Entertainment	**JAN** The Bee Gees' soundtrack to hit film *Saturday Night Fever* tops the charts worldwide.	**MAY** After being stolen, Charlie Chaplin's coffin is found buried 16 km (10 miles) from its original grave in Switzerland.	**JUN** Yachtswoman Naomi James completes a solo world voyage in a record-breaking 117 days.	**JUN** John Travolta and Olivia Newton-John star in the film of the 1950s musical *Grease*.
Innovations	**FEB** Human-like footprints made 3.6 million years ago are found in Tanzania.	**AEROSOL CAN** **APR** A Swiss manufacturer invents and produces a magnetic phonecard for use in a hotel in Paris, France.	**MAY** A Japanese explorer completes the first ever solo trek to the North Pole.	**ALDO MORO** **JUN** Speak and Spell, a speech synthesizer for use as a learning aid, is developed in the USA.

1978

Year of three Popes

Pope John Paul II is the youngest Pope this century

16 OCTOBER
The Vatican today announced that a Polish priest, Karol Wojtyla, is the successor to Pope John Paul I who died of a heart attack just 34 days after his inauguration. The first non-Italian Pope for over 400 years, Karol Wojtyla is to take on the name John Paul II as a mark of respect. John Paul II is the third Pope in what has been an eventful year for the Roman Catholic Church.

Little red book

29 OCTOBER
The *People's Daily*, the official Chinese Communist Party paper, has denounced the late Chairman Mao's "Little Red Book". This "Bible of Chinese communism" contains Mao Zedong's thoughts on a range of subjects. For many years it has been obligatory for everyone in China to carry a copy. Mao's "Little Red Book" has been translated into 80 different languages and has become one of the world's best-selling titles.

Cyanide surprise at Jonestown

29 NOVEMBER

The deadly cocktail

One of the strangest and saddest instances of mass suicide has taken place deep in the jungles of Guyana in a commune known as Jonestown. The bodies of more than 900 members of the People's Temple, an American religious cult, have been found following a bizarre suicide ritual to prove their "loyalty" to the cult's leader, the Reverend Jim Jones. The cult members had all drunk a fruit drink laced with cyanide, some willingly, some at gunpoint. Parents fed the poison to their children before drinking it themselves. The Reverend Jim Jones witnessed the carnage before shooting himself.

Super movie!

15 DECEMBER
Superman, alias Clark Kent, zooms on to the silver screen with spectacular special effects this winter in one of the most expensive movies ever made. The superhero from the planet Krypton embarks on an endless fight against the forces of evil in Metropolis. Directed by Richard Donner, the all-star cast includes Christopher Reeve.

JULY–DECEMBER

SEP Egyptian President Sadat and Israeli Prime Minister Begin sign a peace treaty at Camp David, Maryland, USA.

JUL Swedish tennis player Björn Borg wins his third consecutive men's singles title at Wimbledon, UK.

OCT The World Health Organization (WHO) announces that smallpox has finally been eradicated worldwide.

BJÖRN BORG

SEP Bulgarian defector Georgi Markov dies after a stranger jabs him with the tip of a poisoned umbrella in London, UK.

JUL Blue cartoon characters called the Smurfs top the European pop charts with their single *The Smurf Song*.

NOV Two Soviet cosmonauts spend 140 days and 14 hours in space, setting a space endurance record.

DEC Golda Meir, the first woman prime minister of Israel, dies aged 80 after suffering from leukaemia for 12 years.

SEP An eclipse of the Moon is seen by 3,000 Grateful Dead rock fans at the pyramids of Giza in Egypt.

NOV Public toilets for dogs open in Paris, France, complete with posts for dogs to cock their legs against.

GOLDA MEIR

DEC Mass protests in Iran call for the abdication of the shah and an end to the military government.

OCT Sid Vicious of the Sex Pistols is charged with murdering his girlfriend Nancy Spungen.

DEC Laser-activated videodiscs are launched by Philips/MCA in Atlanta, Georgia, USA.

1979

Shah of Iran sent into exile

16 JANUARY

There was celebration in the streets and dancing on the rooftops in Teheran today as news spread that the shah of Iran had finally fled the country. His departure comes after months of mass demonstrations against his regime and its modernizing programme, which many saw as an attempt to "Westernize" the country. Opposition has been spearheaded by supporters of Ayatollah Khomeini, the fundamentalist religious leader who is living in exile in Paris, France. There have been many deaths and bloody clashes since the shah sought to regain control by imposing martial law just over four months ago. Today, as cars hooted and soldiers waved flowers instead of guns, the mob toppled and smashed statues of the shah and his father, who seized the throne in 1925.

RUBIK'S CUBE
A plastic puzzle made out of 27 small, brightly coloured cubes is a top seller worldwide. Its inventor, a Hungarian lecturer in architectural design, Professor Erno Rubik, is now a multi-millionaire.

Subway angels

13 FEBRUARY

A 250-strong flock of civilian "Guardian Angel" vigilantes is currently patrolling the New York subway in the United States in an effort to combat soaring crime. Police officials are taking a strictly neutral stance. The organization's founder Curtis Sliwa hopes to extend the scheme.

Egypt and Israel sign peace treaty

26 MARCH

After last year's Camp David agreements, which set the scene for a settlement in the Middle East, President Sadat of Egypt and Prime Minister Begin of Israel this evening signed a peace treaty at the White House in Washington DC. But while a beaming US president Jimmy Carter announced "peace has come", Arab protestors could be heard denouncing Sadat as a traitor.

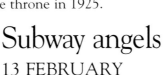

The accord is widely regarded in the Arab world as a total sell-out on the question of Palestinian autonomy. It seems likely that Egypt will be expelled from the Arab League in retaliation for signing the treaty, which indeed leaves many issues unsettled. Problems such as the status of Jerusalem and the Sinai Peninsula, and the future of the Israeli-occupied West Bank are not resolved by the peace accord.

JANUARY–MARCH

World Events	**JAN** Pol Pot's Khmer Rouge regime in Cambodia is overthrown as Vietnamese troops invade.	**JAN** The UK endures a winter of discontent as strikes against a government-imposed 5% pay increase limit cause industrial chaos.	**FEB** The Ayatollah Khomeini victoriously returns to Iran from Paris, France, after 14 years in exile.	**MAR** Idi Amin flees Kampala in the face of the forces of the Tanzanian-backed Uganda Liberation Front.
Entertainment	**FEB** Ex-Sex Pistols member Sid Vicious dies of a heroin overdose in New York, USA.	**FEB** US's Neil Armstrong breaks five world records by soaring to 15,240 m (50,000 ft) in 12 mins in a Learjet.	**FEB** Jean Renoir, French film director and son of the artist, dies aged 86 in Beverly Hills, USA.	**MAR** US film star Lee Marvin's ex-girlfriend sues him in a palimony suit for over $1 million.
Innovations	**JAN** A digital recording is made by Vienna Philharmonic Orchestra in Austria.	**FEB** A system for transmitting text between computers, called teletext, is introduced in the USA by IBM.	**MAR** US spacecraft *Voyager 1* sends back pictures showing that the planet Jupiter has rings.	**MAR** A gardening programme is the first made-for-video pre-recorded tape in the UK.

SID VICIOUS

JUPITER

1979

Technicians wear protective clothing

Three Mile nuclear leak

30 MARCH

Two days after the worst nuclear accident in the history of the United States, a new threat hangs over the Three Mile Island power plant in Pennsylvania. It is feared that a bubble of radioactive hydrogen inside the crippled reactor might explode, releasing large amounts of radiation into the atmosphere. It is also still possible that a complete meltdown might occur. Experts are claiming that the situation is being brought under control and that only a small amount of radiation has escaped so far. However, the inside of the reactor is highly contaminated and is still too hot to approach. A general evacuation of the area is not thought necessary at present although state governor Richard Thornburgh has advised that children and pregnant women should leave. The cause of the accident is not clear but the finger of suspicion points at a fatal combination of faulty equipment and human error. It seems that an automatic valve controlling the flow of cooling water in the core of the plant's Unit 2 reactor failed to function correctly. A series of mistakes compounded the fault and, by the time that technicians realized what was happening, the fuel rods were beginning to melt, releasing harmful radioactive gases.

Mass graves

2 APRIL

Chilling evidence just discovered in the northeast of Cambodia points to mass murders carried out by the former Khmer Rouge regime of Pol Pot. A lake has been discovered to contain 2,000 skeletons and bones and skulls have also been found in shallow graves.

Britain gets first woman PM

4 MAY

A triumphant 53-year-old Margaret Thatcher promised a complete transformation of the British economic and industrial climate after becoming the country's first female prime minister today. The Conservatives swept to victory with 44 per cent of the vote and a 43-seat majority.

APRIL–JUNE

APR Following a referendum, Iran is declared an Islamic republic by the Ayatollah Khomeini.

APR Woody Allen's film *Manhattan*, starring Allen and Diane Keaton is released in the USA.

APR British Rail opens the first Intercity 125 high-speed train service from London to Bristol.

APR Zulfikar Ali Bhutto, the deposed premier of Pakistan, is hanged for conspiracy to murder a political opponent.

MAY The film *Alien* opens in the USA with the slogan "In space, no-one can hear you scream".

ALIEN

MAY UK singer Elton John becomes the first rock star from the West to tour the USSR.

JUN Black leader Bishop Abel Muzorewa is appointed prime minister of Zimbabwe, formerly called Rhodesia.

JUN US film star John Wayne (real name Marion Morrison, nicknamed "Duke") dies aged 72.

MAY The worst air crash in US history occurs when 273 people die in a *DC-10* in Chicago.

JOHN WAYNE

JUN US president Jimmy Carter and Soviet Premier Leonid Brezhnev sign SALT II treaty limiting nuclear weapons.

JUN World heavyweight boxing champion Muhammad Ali announces he is to retire.

JUN The first Euro-MPs are elected to the European parliament in Strasbourg, France.

1979

Music to your ears, anywhere!

1 JULY

A tiny but revolutionary new stereo system has just been launched in Japan. It is called the Sony Walkman and costs Y33,000 ($165). With the help of lightweight plastic earphones, the Walkman enables you to listen to music wherever you are and whatever you are doing, even when out walking. There are plans to introduce it in the the rest of the world, using the names "Soundabout" and "Stowaway". Sony's competitors, however, doubt whether the "personal stereo" will ever catch on.

Nicaraguan victory

17 JULY

Nicaraguan dictator General Anastasio Somoza Debayle finally gave in to Sandinista rebels today and fled to the United States. True to style, he took with him an estimated $20 million from the treasury. It is the end of a cruel and corrupt dynasty that has lined its pockets and murdered political opponents since it came to power in 1933. The regime received strong backing from the United States, with $14 million of military aid being supplied between 1975 and 1978. The Sandinista rebels, named after General Augusto Sandino, the revolutionary leader killed in 1934, are forming a provisional coalition government. The new government faces enormous problems, however, in a country crippled by the devastation of civil war and bankrupted by foreign debt.

Nicaraguan victory poster

Mountbatten murdered

27 AUGUST

Lord Mountbatten, cousin of Queen Elizabeth II of Britain and the last viceroy of India, has been killed by an IRA bomb. The latest victim of the IRA's campaign to drive Britain out of Northern Ireland, Mountbatten was on holiday in a small fishing village on the west coast of Ireland, where he spent every summer. As he set out from the harbour for a day's fishing, a huge explosion ripped through his boat. His grandson and a friend were also killed.

JULY–SEPTEMBER

World Events	**JUL** Ahmed Ben Bella, hero of Algerian independence, is freed after 14 years' imprisonment.	**JUL** Islamic leader Ayatollah Khomeini bans the broadcast of pop music in Iran, arguing that it corrupts young people.	**JUL** Although he has effectively been in power since 1968, Saddam Hussein officially becomes president of Iraq.	**AUG** Khmer Rouge leader Pol Pot is sentenced to death for the genocide of the Cambodian people.
Entertainment	**JUL** Spinach-eating cartoon character Popeye the Sailorman celebrates his 50th birthday.	**JUL** UK runner Sebastian Coe sets two new world records for the 800 m and the mile in Oslo, Norway.	**AUG** Eighteen sailors die as Atlantic storms sink 25 Fastnet international race yachts off the coast of Ireland.	**AUG** UK runner Sebastian Coe sets another world record, winning the 1,500 m in 3 min 32.1 secs.
Innovations	**JUL** The first air-cushioned trainer is developed, based on the landing gear of lunar modules. **POPEYE**	**AUG** Two Soviet cosmonauts return to Earth after spending a record 175 days in space orbiting the planet.	**SEP** The Prestel information service in the UK is inaugurated by the national postal service.	**SEP** Two families cross from East to West Germany in a hot air balloon made out of curtains and sheets.

SADDAM HUSSEIN

1979

US hostages held at embassy

4 NOVEMBER

The United States embassy in Teheran, the capital of Iran, has been stormed and is now being occupied by followers of the Ayatollah Khomeini. Nearly 100 embassy staff and US marines have been taken hostage. Thousands of demonstrators have gathered outside, chanting anti-American slogans and waving placards.

Blindfolded American hostages

Mother Teresa wins Nobel Peace Prize

10 DECEMBER

This year's Nobel Peace Prize has been awarded to Mother Teresa, the 69-year-old Catholic nun who has worked tirelessly with the suffering and dying. "Personally I am unworthy," she said. "I accept in the name of the poor." She founded the Order of the Missionaries of Charity in India in 1950. It now has 700 shelters and clinics worldwide, including children's homes and soup kitchens.

USSR invades Afghanistan

27 DECEMBER

The Soviet Union is today maintaining that it was asked to send "urgent political, moral, military, and economic assistance" to neighbouring Afghanistan as months of civil war in the country intensified. Yesterday they began airlifting troops, while motorized rifle divisions moved in from the north, accompanied by squadrons of Soviet fighters. In the capital Kabul, Soviet forces have already overthrown President Amin and installed a puppet government. Most of the country, however, still remains in the hands of fundamentalist Muslim guerrillas, the Mujahideen, who have been waging a holy war against the Kabul government.

OCTOBER–DECEMBER

NOV It is revealed in the UK that the queen's art adviser Sir Anthony Blunt had been a spy for the USSR.

NOV Anti-US demonstrators storm the US embassy and raid other US buildings in Islamabad, Pakistan.

NOV Saudi Arabian troops storm the Great Mosque at Mecca, which had been occupied by Shi'ite Muslims.

DEC An agreement signed in the UK ends white minority rule in Rhodesia, which becomes Zimbabwe.

OCT Greta Waitz of Norway wins the New York marathon in the USA and sets a new women's record.

NOV Cameras are used to prove that Australian cricket player Jeff Thomson is the fastest test bowler.

NOV Cult television series *Star Trek* moves to the big screen in hit film *Star Trek – The Movie*.

DEC Box office hit *Kramer vs Kramer*, starring Dustin Hoffman, brings divorce to the screen.

ANTHONY BLUNT

OCT The Nobel Prize for Medicine is awarded to Godfrey Hounsfield, UK inventor of the CAT body scanner.

OCT Sir Barnes Neville Wallis, UK inventor of World War II "bouncing bombs", dies aged 92.

NOV UK engineers invent a catalytic convertor to reduce pollution caused by car exhaust fumes.

KRAMER VS KRAMER

DEC The first ever flat-screened pocket television is patented by Japanese company Matsushita.

THE MICROCHIP AGE

IN 1971 THE WORLD'S FIRST MICROPROCESSOR was developed. Microprocessors contain all the main components of a computer on a single chip. This meant that electronic equipment became smaller and cheaper. Early computers filled entire rooms and were used almost exclusively by large corporations. The microchip meant that computers could fit neatly onto desktops, in the office or at home. Machines and factories became automated, with powerful microprocessors providing the brains. Robots produced cars, trains could drive themselves, and automatic washing machines offered separate programmes for woollens or whites. Cheap, mass-produced electronic gadgets transformed everyday life too. Calculators, for example, became ever smaller, finally shrinking to the size of a credit card.

MICROCHIP ON A THUMBNAIL

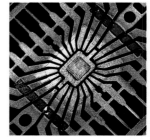

Magic microchip

Microchips are made of tiny pieces of silicon, often no bigger than a baby's fingernail. Each chip contains thousands of electronic components that are built up, layer by layer, to form an integrated circuit.

Circuit board

Electronic equipment contains a number of different microchips. The chips perform specific functions to do with storing, organizing, or processing data. Each chip is sealed into its own protective case with metal "legs", or contacts, that slot into a flat plastic plate called a circuit board. This is printed with metal lines that connect all the electronic components together to make the equipment work.

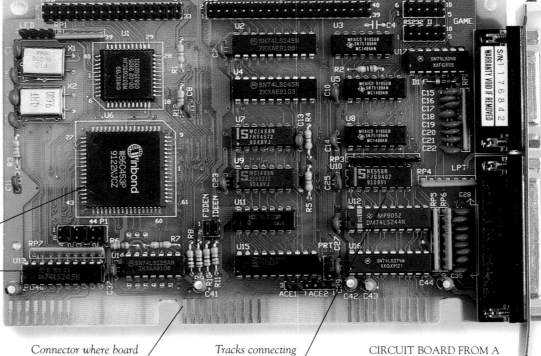

Communications chip

Logic chip

Connector where board plugs into computer

Tracks connecting components

CIRCUIT BOARD FROM A PERSONAL COMPUTER

Home computing

IBM (International Business Machines) launched its first personal computer in 1981. Built around the latest Intel microprocessor, it was operated by a brand new system called MS-DOS, which was soon used by most personal computers. The more expensive model was twice as fast as its rivals and could store much more data.

Inventing the Apple

The Apple Computer Company, founded in California in the United States, by Steve Jobs and Steve Wozniak, made history by introducing people with no special knowledge of programming or electronics to personal computing. The Apple II, launched in 1977, was the first "user-friendly" computer made specifically for the mass market. Other early microcomputers were often sold in kit form, but this came fully assembled with built-in keyboard, sound, colour graphics, and optional floppy disk drive at a cost of $1,298.

Portable video

Home movies were transformed during the 1980s by the camcorder, a portable video camera that recorded pictures and sounds electronically on magnetic tape. You could watch the results immediately on television. Camcorders gradually became cheaper, easier to use, and smaller.

Moving pictures

The introduction of sound cards, colour graphics, and a new system of storing digital data on compact disc revolutionized the personal computer's capabilities during the 1980s. With the latest generation of microprocessor chips supplying the power, an operator could choose images, text, and sounds to create their own stories, games, and cartoons, interacting with what was happening on screen.

Light-emitting diode (LED) display

SINCLAIR EXECUTIVE CALCULATOR

Pocket power

Simple pocket calculators were launched in the early 1970s and could be used to add, subtract, multiply, and divide. More complex calculators followed, with lots of extra functions for carrying out complicated scientific calculations, such as sines and cosines.

Card calculator

The smallest electronic calculators needed very little power. They used small, round, long-lasting batteries. Some calculators needed no batteries at all, like the solar-powered calculator above, which is no bigger than a credit card. It has special light-sensitive cells that turn light into electricity.

Control keys

Video games take off

Atari's *Space Invaders* (above) was one of the first TV-based video games to bring the thrills of the arcade into the home. Developments in chip technology during the 1980s led to increasingly sophisticated, high-speed games. With one tiny integrated circuit, the games became smaller, cheaper, and more exciting – Nintendo's Game Boy™ (below) provided full-sized fun in a pocket-sized package.

Add it up

Unlike the first electronic calculator, which was as big as a cash register, the Sinclair Executive calculator fitted easily into a shirt pocket. It was only 1 cm (0.39 in) thick and 12 cm (4.7 in) long, had a 7,000 transistor integrated circuit, and a wafer-thin battery. Launched in the 1970s at a price of £70, it was very expensive. However, it was one of the first everyday gadgets to make use of chip technology.

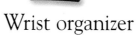

Wrist organizer

The arrival of the wristwatch calculator in the late 1970s meant that organizing life became easier than ever before. This super-efficient personal organizer can be used as a diary to store appointments, memos, and messages in its memory. It can also automatically sort telephone and fax numbers into name order, and is even able to tell the time around the world.

1980

All that glitters

28 JANUARY

Within weeks of finding a gold nugget deep in the Amazon jungle of Brazil, 10,000 gold-diggers have arrived, armed with picks and shovels, to move mountains of earth. What will happen to the ecosystem of the rainforest, however, remains to be seen.

Rescue bid fails

25 APRIL

An attempt to rescue the 53 diplomatic hostages from the United States being held in the American embassy in Teheran, the capital of Iran, ended in tragedy early this morning. Eight members of the United States' military expedition, codenamed "Operation Eagle Claw", died when a helicopter collided with a tanker aircraft on the ground in the remote Iranian desert. Ironically, when the accident occurred the rescue bid had been called off due to equipment failure, and the military expedition was actually withdrawing. US President Carter appeared grim-faced on breakfast television to tell a shocked nation, "The responsibility is purely my own". Meanwhile, the Iranians are celebrating the failure of the rescue bid with a rally in front of the occupied American embassy.

Molten lava spews from the volcano's mouth

Day becomes night in US state

18 MAY

After lying dormant for more than 120 years the Mount St Helens volcano, in Washington state, USA, erupted in spectacular fashion this morning. It had been rumbling ominously for two months and emitting ash and smoke for two weeks. The explosion, which measured 4.1 on the Richter Scale, blew the top off the 2,949-m (9,675-ft) peak. Spewing earth and ash into the air, the eruption turned day into night for most of the area and caused several floods and mud slides. At least eight people are feared dead, and property damage is estimated to be as much as $2.7 billion.

JANUARY–JUNE

World Events

JAN Dr Andrei Sakharov, the USSR's most prominent dissident, is arrested and exiled.

JAN The Islamic Conference, meeting in Islamabad, condemns the Soviet invasion of Afghanistan.

MAR More than 100 people die when a North Sea oil platform used as a floating hotel collapses in stormy weather.

MAR In El Salvador, 20 people are killed and 200 wounded at a mass for assassinated archbishop Oscar Romero.

Entertainment

JAN Pink Floyd's album *The Wall* tops the charts worldwide.

PINK FLOYD'S *THE WALL*

JAN Nigel Short from the UK becomes the youngest world chess master, aged 14.

APR French philosopher Jean-Paul Sartre, who refused the Nobel Prize for Literature, dies aged 74.

APR Sir Alfred Hitchcock, UK film director of *The Birds* and *Psycho*, dies aged 80.

Innovations

FEB *Solar Max*, the first satellite to study solar flares, is launched.

APR Cosmonauts Leonid Popov and Valery Ryumin reach *Salyut-6* space station.

JUN The *Pioneer Venus 1* space probe finds mountains higher than Everest on Venus.

ALFRED HITCHCOCK

JUN An electronic "eye" is first used in tennis at the UK Wimbledon championships.

1980

Abadan on fire as war hots up

23 SEPTEMBER

At dawn today, after months of tense border clashes, Iraqi troops launched an all-out attack against western Iran. Iraqi president Saddam Hussein's sights appear to be set on Iran's oil-rich province of Khuzistan and the Shatt al-Arab waterway. The world's largest oil refinery, at Abadan, is now blazing after being bombarded by Iraqi artillery and bombs. Other targets, further north, have also been attacked by the Iraqi army. The rest of the world is watching with concern as the Iran-Iraq war hots up, although the United States and the Soviet Union made it clear last night that they intend to remain strictly neutral. There appears to be no prospect of oil shortages at the moment as stocks in the West are high.

Actor lands star role in USA

4 NOVEMBER

The Republican candidate Ronald Wilson Reagan today won a landslide victory in the United States' presidential elections. At the age of 69, Reagan is the oldest person ever elected to the nation's highest office. The former wartime movie star will replace the Democrat incumbent, peanut farmer Jimmy Carter. Reagan was first elected to public office in 1966 as governor of the state of California.

IN-LINE SKATING

A new craze is sweeping across the United States this year. The latest skates, known as rollerblades, were developed by two US ice-hockey players, Scott and Brennan Olson. Based on a classic ice-hockey design, they are smooth and lightweight, making them fast.

Who shot J R?

19 NOVEMBER

After eight nail-biting months, the suspense is over. Tonight's episode finally reveals who shot J R Ewing, the baddie everybody loves to hate, in the top television soap *Dallas*.

JULY–DECEMBER

AUG Eighty-four people are killed and hundreds injured by a bomb blast in a railway station in Bologna, Italy.

JUL Swedish tennis player Björn Borg wins his fifth consecutive Wimbledon singles title.

SEP The world's longest tunnel is opened, through the St Gotthard, a mountain in the Swiss Alps.

REINHOLD MESSNER

SEP Polish workers, having won the right to organize trade unions, set up a central organization, Solidarity.

AUG Italian Reinhold Messner climbs the 8,847.7-m (29,027-ft) high Mount Everest on his own.

SEP Japanese newspaper *Asahi Shimbun* uses new computer technology to create its pages.

SEP The deposed dictator of Nicaragua Anastasio Somoza Debayle is assassinated on the streets of Asuncion, Paraguay.

SEP The *Les Misérables* musical is first performed at the Palais des Sports, France.

OCT Cosmonauts Popov and Ryumin set a new space endurance record on *Salyut-6*.

FANS MOURN JOHN LENNON

OCT Two big earthquakes measuring 7.3 on the Richter Scale destroy the city of El Asnam in Algeria.

DEC Ex-Beatle John Lennon is shot dead in New York, USA.

NOV *Voyager 1* sends back pictures that show Saturn has at least 100 rings.

1981

Yellow ribbons for US hostages

20 JANUARY

The United States is today celebrating the release of the last 52 hostages held in Iran by followers of Ayatollah Khomeini. Yellow ribbons, the American symbol of homecoming, are being worn by people throughout the country. The freed hostages spent a total of 444 days in captivity. As a final snub to President Carter, who tried and failed to rescue the hostages, their release was timed to coincide with Ronald Reagan's inauguration.

Election paints France red

10 MAY

Red flags are fluttering and crowds are dancing throughout France to celebrate socialist leader François Mitterrand's election victory. The new president won 52 per cent of the vote, ending 23 years of right-wing government. He promises a programme of nationalization, taxes on wealth, and an end to unemployment.

Pope wounded

13 MAY

Pope John Paul II has been rushed to hospital after being shot and seriously wounded as he blessed a 20,000 crowd from an open-topped vehicle in St Peter's Square, Rome. A lone gunman opened fire, hitting the Pope four times and injuring two women. Twenty-three-year-old Armenian Mehmet Agca, the would-be assassin, was arrested immediately. He was already wanted by Turkish police after escaping from a jail where he was being held for the murder of a newspaper editor. Agca is claiming that he planned to murder the Pope in protest at Soviet action in Afghanistan and the involvement of the Soviet Union in El Salvador. Some people, however, think there was another motive involving eastern European communist governments angry at papal support for the Solidarity trade union in Poland. Surgeons have already operated on the Pope, removing all four bullets. They are predicting that the Pope will make a full recovery.

JANUARY–JUNE

World Events	**FEB** Gro Harlem Brundtland becomes Norway's first woman prime minister.	**MAR** Solidarity trade union stages a national strike in Poland in protest at police treatment of union activists.	**MAR** US president Ronald Reagan, aged 70, is wounded in an assassination attempt in Washington, USA.	**APR** IRA prisoner Bobby Sands, who has been on hunger strike for 42 days, wins a Northern Ireland by-election.
Entertainment	**MAR** In the first London Marathon 80% of the 6,700 runners finish the UK course.	**MAY** Jamaican reggae superstar Bob Marley dies of cancer in Miami, USA, aged 36.	**MAY** UK group Adam and the Ants top the charts with hit single *Stand and Deliver*.	**MAY** A new musical by Andrew Lloyd Webber called *Cats* opens in London, UK.
Innovations	**JAN** US astronomers discover a star 100 times brighter than the Sun.	**APR** The US space shuttle *Columbia*, the world's first reusable spacecraft, blasts off.	**JUN** The Stealth fighter plane, the Lockheed *F-117*, makes its maiden flight in the USA.	**JUN** The world's first test-tube twins are born in Melbourne, Australia.

REUSABLE SPACE SHUTTLE TAKES OFF

ADAM AND THE ANTS

1981

The Prince and Princess of Wales leave St Paul's in a horse-drawn carriage

Fairytale royal wedding

29 JULY

By royal proclamation, today was a special national holiday in Britain. London came to a standstill and street parties were held across the country as Prince Charles, the queen's eldest son, married 20-year-old Lady Diana Spencer in St Paul's Cathedral. A total of 2,500 guests attended the ceremony, including heads of state from all over the world. Cheering crowds lined the streets to catch a glimpse of the couple as they drove back to Buckingham Palace. The bride's exquisite dress, designed by the Emmanuels of London, was made of ivory pure silk taffeta and old lace. It was embroidered with tiny mother-of-pearl sequins and had a spectacular 7.6-m (25-ft) train. It is estimated that about 700 million people worldwide watched the wedding on television.

Sadat shot in raid

6 OCTOBER

President Anwar Sadat of Egypt was today shot dead during a military parade in Cairo. The assassination of the Nobel Peace Prize winner happened as all eyes were fixed on a fly-past by air force jets overhead. Four men dressed in army uniforms jumped out of an armoured vehicle, hurling grenades and spraying automatic gunfire at the rostrum on which the president was sitting. Sadat was hit by five bullets and collapsed in a pool of blood. In the fierce gun battle that followed, one of the assassins was shot dead. The rest of the conspirators were finally arrested. Five other people attending the parade also lost their lives in the shoot-out, and a number of other bystanders were wounded. The vice-president Hosni Mubarak has acted swiftly to take control of the country. A state of emergency has been declared and troops and riot police are out in force on the streets of Cairo. Those who are responsible for ordering the murder are not yet known. Sadat had many enemies in the Arab world after signing a peace accord with Israel and it seems likely that he was killed by members of an extremist Islamic group, such as the Muslim Brotherhood. World leaders have tonight been paying tribute to the Egyptian leader who worked so hard for peace in the Middle East.

TGV TRAIN IN FRANCE

The first "Trains à Grande Vitesse" (high-speed trains) have gone into service between Paris and Lyon in France. The TGV requires specially built tracks with steeply banked curves to reach maximum speeds of up to 300 km/h (188 mph).

JULY–DECEMBER

AUG Iran goes into mourning after both the president and prime minister are assassinated in a bomb blast.

SEP French president François Mitterrand abolishes the guillotine which made its debut in the French Revolution.

NOV Egypt's parliament selects Hosni Mubarak as president after the assassination of president Anwar Sadat.

DEC Strikes continue in spite of the arrest of at least 14,000 trade union activists after martial law is imposed in Poland.

AUG Music Television (MTV) begins broadcasting to people across the USA.

MTV MUSIC CHANNEL

AUG UK runner Steve Ovett clips 0.13 secs off the world mile record.

AUG UK runner Sebastian Coe reclaims the world mile record with a time of 3 min 47.53 secs.

DEC UK batsman Geoff Boycott beats Sir Gary Sobers' record of 8,032 runs in test cricket.

AUG US space probe *Voyager 2* arrives at Saturn after a four-year journey.

AUG US company IBM launches its new "personal computer" (PC).

SEP Sandra Day O'Connor is the first woman judge on the US Supreme Court.

HOSNI MUBARAK

NOV US space shuttle *Columbia* is the first shuttle to be launched twice.

DECADE OF DESIGN

THE EIGHTIES SAW AN EXPLOSION OF INTEREST in style and design. Architects and designers belonging to the Post-Modernist movement rejected the order of previous decades and introduced a kaleidoscope of colours, ornaments, and styles dating back to different periods in history. Others went back to basics, using industrial materials like steel scaffolding and factory flooring to produce revolutionary buildings and interiors. A new generation of young, upwardly mobile professionals, nicknamed "Yuppies", adopted the latest styles. Mobile phones, bottled mineral water, and designer labels became status symbols in a money-obsessed decade.

Bags of style

Famous French names had dominated the exclusive world of haute couture for decades. They now began appearing on new ranges of ready-to-wear clothes, perfume, and accessories that were sold worldwide.

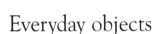

Everyday objects

The design of everyday useful objects such as lamps, torches, and calculators acquired a new importance during the Eighties. It was no longer enough that objects were functional – they also had to look good. The bulb of this pocket torch, designed by BIB Consultants for Duracell in 1982, lights up when the top is swivelled open.

Heat-proof foam handle

Swatch watch

The cheap, plastic Swatch watch, launched in 1983, came in a wide range of designs which made it an instant fashion accessory. This transparent Swatch has become a collector's item.

Whistling bird spout

Alessi kettle

Tableware and household design became more decorative and ornamental during the Eighties after the plain practicality of previous decades. This was due partly to new developments in computer-controlled machines that could now produce the kind of detail that had only been possible by hand in the past. Architect Michael Graves designed this steam kettle for Alessi in 1986.

Ornamental studs

Hi-tech skyscraper

One of the most famous examples of hi-tech architecture, the Hong Kong and Shanghai Bank, was completed in 1986. Designed as a pre-fabricated kit by the British architect Sir Norman Foster, the 47-storey high building is supported from the outside by a giant skeleton of steel columns and trusses. Its parts were made in 80 different countries and fitted together on site.

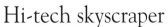

Battery

Radio in a bag

Designed by Daniel Weil in 1981, the Bag Radio questioned the idea that electronic components should be hidden away neatly. Like many of the most exciting designs of the decade, it made people look at ordinary objects in new ways.

Speaker

Graphic design

Graphic design grew up during the Eighties due largely to advances in microchip technology. Dazzling new tricks with images and text became possible as pages began to be designed on computer screen. *The Face* magazine broke new ground with its innovative layout and style. Launched in 1980 as a music monthly, it reflected the mood of the times and appealed to a wide readership.

Japanese designer

Parisian fashion houses were stormed during the early Eighties by Japanese designers using new fabrics, textures, and shapes to challenge the traditional concepts of Western haute couture. Colour was played down, with designer Kei Kawakubo saying she used "shades of black". A label on some of Yohji Yamamoto's designs stated, "There is nothing so boring as a neat and tidy look."

Memphis style

Although it was based in Milan, Italy, the Memphis Group, founded in 1981 by architect and designer Ettore Sottsass, was named after the home of rock 'n' roll in Memphis, United States. Like rock 'n' roll, it challenged convention and broke the rules, taking different elements from different cultures to invent something new. The group produced avant-garde furniture, fabric, and ceramics that helped change the face of design in the Eighties.

CARLTON ROOM DIVIDER

Designer diary

The Filofax™ was based on a classic design that dated back to World War I. During the Eighties it took on a new lease of life and became the essential accessory for people who wanted to organize their lives efficiently. In fact, it became known as the "personal organizer". The design was simple – a small ring-binder, with wallet compartments inside the covers, and loose-leaf diary pages that could be changed every year. The organizer also contained blank pages for notes and memos.

Unconventional angles

Brightly coloured drawers

Sloping shelves

All-round design

French designer Philippe Starck was very popular in the 1980s. He re-invented the shapes of everyday objects, such as ashtrays, juicers, toothbrushes, and furniture. He also designed cafe and hotel interiors, including the Royalton Hotel in New York, United States, shown above.

1982

Argie-bargie!

14 JUNE

After almost two-and-a-half months of fierce fighting, the Argentine forces that invaded the Falkland Islands in the south Pacific have today surrendered to British troops. The white flag was raised in the capital Port Stanley after fierce fighting at Tumbledown Mountain, Wireless Ridge, and Mount Londgon. The commander of the British land forces, Major-General Jeremy Moore, announced that "the Falkland Islands are once more under the government desired by the inhabitants." The Falkland Islands have been controlled by Britain since 1833 but have long been claimed by the Argentines, who call the islands the Malvinas. While crowds in London cheer a jubilant British prime minister, Margaret Thatcher, it seems likely that Argentine president General Leopoldo Galtieri will be forced to resign. At least 255 Britons and 700 Argentines were killed in the fighting. Many were victims of the deadly long-range Exocet missile, which has opened a new chapter in maritime warfare.

Israel drives PLO out of Beirut

30 AUGUST

After more than 12 years, the Palestinian Liberation Organization (PLO) has been forced to abandon its powerbase in Beirut, Lebanon, driven out by a massive Israeli bombardment that started in early June. PLO guerrilla bases in Lebanon were bombed before a force of 20,000 Israeli soldiers advanced across the border towards the city of Beirut. An international peacekeeping force has arrived to ensure the safe evacuation of PLO fighters to Arab countries. Today their leader Yassir Arafat left the shattered Lebanese capital to set up a new PLO headquarters in Tunisia.

Argentine soldiers

TRIVIAL PURSUIT
A new brain-teasing board game has turned trivia into serious business. Trivial Pursuit was invented by three young Canadians and is expected to be a big hit. Players chase each other round the board answering questions divided into different subject categories.

JANUARY–JUNE

World Events

JAN Seventy-eight people die when a Boeing 737 crashes into a bridge in Washington state, USA.

MAR Nicaragua's Sandinista government declares a state of emergency because of fears of a US-inspired attack.

JUN King Khaled of Saudi Arabia dies aged 69 and is succeeded by his brother Prince Fahd.

JUN General Galtieri is ousted as president of Argentina and stripped of his post of commander-in-chief of the army.

Entertainment

FEB Thelonius Monk, a popular jazz pianist from the USA, dies aged 64.

MAR Fifteen UK cricketers are condemned for embarking on a rebel tour of South Africa.

MAR UK film *Chariots of Fire*, directed by David Puttnam, wins a US Academy Award for best film.

MAY Argentine footballer Diego Maradona is bought by Barcelona for a record £5 million.

Innovations

FEB Kodak launches a new "wind-on" camera with disc film worldwide.

KODAK DISC FILM AND CAMERA

MAR Unmanned Soviet space probe *Venera 13* lands on Venus after a four-month flight.

MAR US space shuttle *Columbia* is launched on its third mission from Cape Canaveral, Florida, USA.

CHARIOTS OF FIRE

MAR US company Proctor & Gamble develops the first liquid detergent for washing machines.

1982

Ancient wreck raised from ocean

11 OCTOBER

A piece of English history was raised from the seabed today when the wreck of the *Mary Rose* was slowly freed from the thick mud off the coast of Portsmouth. King Henry VIII's 700-tonne flagship foundered and sank in the Solent in 1545 on her way to a sea battle with the French. Many relics of

The Mary Rose

Tudor England have already been recovered from the wreck, including the bones of 120 of the 715 men who drowned when the ship sank.

First artificial heart

2 DECEMBER

The first operation to implant an artificial heart in a human being has been successfully carried out at the University of Utah Medical Center in the United States. The lucky recipient was 61-year-old Barney Clark, a retired dentist from Seattle, who had been suffering from heart failure and was close to death. His new mechanical heart is made of plastic and metal and is called Jarvik-7 after its inventor, Robert Jarvik. The operation took seven-and-a-half hours and the patient is said to be doing well.

The Jarvik-7 artificial heart

Vietnam victims remembered

13 NOVEMBER

In a moving ceremony, the Vietnam Veterans Memorial in Washington DC was today dedicated as a permanent tribute to the Americans who lost their lives in the Vietnam War. Made of grey granite and designed by Yale University architecture student Maya Yang Lin, the monument is inscribed with the names of more than 58,000 dead.

JULY–DECEMBER

JUL The Reverend Sun Myung Moon presides over the simultaneous marriage of 2,075 couples in New York, USA.

JUL Italy wins the football World Cup in Spain, beating West Germany in the final.

MOONIES' MASS WEDDING

AUG Coca Cola Company launches a new Diet Coke soft drink in the USA.

SEP Palestinian refugees are massacred by Lebanese Christian militia in refugee camps in Beirut, Lebanon.

AUG The US's Ashby Harper becomes the oldest person to swim the Channel, aged 65.

OCT Japanese company Sony launches the Watchman, a TV with a 5 cm (2 in) screen.

OCT Spain's socialist party sweeps to victory in the general election and 40-year-old Felipe Gonzales becomes prime minister.

DEC Michael Jackson releases his critically acclaimed album *Thriller*, which tops the charts worldwide.

OCT The Experimental Prototype Community of Tomorrow Center (EPCOT) opens in Florida, USA.

EPCOT CENTER OPENS

NOV Soviet premier Leonid Brezhnev dies after a heart attack aged 75, and is succeeded by Yuri Andropov.

DEC Steven Spielberg's latest movie *ET* is a massive box-office hit around the world.

DEC *Time* magazine in the US votes Pac-Man, a computer character, its "Man of the Year".

1983

"Star Wars"

23 MARCH

In a speech televised across the United States, President Reagan tonight proposed a revolutionary new defence system dubbed "Star Wars". Using the most sophisticated technology, and based both on land and in space, it will protect America from Soviet attack.

Diversion at Mount Etna

KING KONG IS 50!

Residents of the United States' most famous city were taken by surprise when a strange figure appeared on top of New York's Empire State Building this year. King Kong is back in the shape of a giant 25-m (82-ft) tall gorilla balloon to celebrate the 50th anniversary of his first film.

14 MAY

People in the Sicilian towns of Nicolosi and Belpasso are today heaving a huge sigh of relief. Their homes have been saved from being engulfed in a torrent of molten lava from Mount Etna. The volcano has been erupting for the last few weeks, sending a steady stream of red-hot debris down the mountain. Experts have managed to divert the flow by using a massive explosive charge which created an artificial avalanche. This is sending the lava flow into a special channel dug by bulldozers. Rising 3,390 m (11,122 ft) over Sicily, Mount Etna is the highest and most active volcano in the whole of Europe, with 135 recorded eruptions to date.

JANUARY–JUNE

World Events	FEB Police suspect arson when 68 people die in Australia's worst ever bush fires.	MAY US President Reagan backs the Contra rebels fighting to overthrow the Marxist Sandinista government in Nicaragua.	MAY Diaries allegedly written by Adolf Hitler are discovered to be fakes by experts in Germany.	JUN Thousands of people in Chile take part in nationwide protests against the rule of dictator General Pinochet.
Entertainment	FEB An unknown Mozart symphony is discovered in Denmark.	FEB The £10 million race horse Shergar is kidnapped from a stud farm in Ireland.	APR The film ET wins four Oscars in Los Angeles, USA, after breaking all box-office records.	MAY Veteran UK pop star Cliff Richard celebrates his 25th anniversary in show business.
Innovations	JAN A dinosaur is named Baryonyx walkeri after its clawbone is found in the UK.	PRESERVED BARYONYX	FEB The Thames Flood Barrier in London, UK, is raised for the first time to protect the city from flooding.	MAR The first compact disc players go on sale in UK, France, West Germany, and Holland.	DR SALLY RIDE	JUN Dr Sally Ride becomes the first US spacewoman in space shuttle Challenger.

PRESERVED BARYONYX

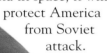

DR SALLY RIDE

1983

In the pink

21 MAY

American artists Christo and Jeanne-Claude have begun to dismantle their latest installation, *Surrounded Islands*. There have been mixed reactions to this version of Monet's *Water Lilies*. Eleven islands in Biscayne Bay, Miami, United States, were surrounded with 603,850 m² (6,500,000 ft²) of shiny, pink fabric.

Soviets shoot down Flight 007

31 AUGUST

All 269 people on board a routine Korean Air Lines flight from New York, United States, to Seoul, South Korea, have died after the plane was shot down by a Soviet fighter plane off the coast of Siberia. How the aircraft strayed into restricted Soviet airspace is, at the moment, a tragic mystery. Soviet authorities are claiming that the airliner was on a US spying mission.

US invade Grenada

25 OCTOBER

The Cold War came to the Caribbean today as the United States flexed its muscles and invaded Grenada, which for the past four years has been supported by the Soviet Union. The action is being widely deplored as a violation of international law. President Reagan has justified the invasion on the grounds of protecting American citizens living in Grenada. Unrest had swept the island after the Grenada prime minister Maurice Bishop was murdered in a Marxist coup.

Solidarity and peace

10 DECEMBER

Lech Walesa, leader of Poland's outlawed trade union Solidarity, was today awarded the Nobel Peace Prize. He received the award for his "massive personal effort" in the fight for Polish workers' rights to a free trade union – often in the face of brutal and violent opposition by the communist authorities.

JULY–DECEMBER

JUL General Jaruzelski lifts martial law in Poland after 19 months, although anti-socialist activity will still be crushed.

JUL In Sri Lanka more than 100 people are killed in racial violence between the Sinhalese and Tamils.

AUG Philippines opposition leader Benigno Aquino is assassinated as he returns home from three years' exile in the USA.

DEC Raul Alfonsin is inaugurated as president of Argentina, restoring democracy after eight years of military rule.

AUG Wham!, who already have three UK hit singles, storm the album charts with *Fantastic*.

AUG Athletes from 159 nations take part in the first athletics world championships in Finland.

SEP Alan Bond's *Australia II* wins the America's Cup yachting trophy – the USA has held the trophy for 132 years.

OCT UK racing driver Richard Noble sets a land-speed record of 1,013 km/h (633 mph) in his jet car *Thrust 2*.

AUG US space shuttle *Challenger* is launched again with a crew that includes the first US black astronaut.

WHAM!

OCT Astronomers use the world's largest telescope in the Caucasus Mountains to spot Halley's Comet.

NOV Two Soviet cosmonauts arrive home after five months on board *Salyut-7* space station.

AUSTRALIA II

NOV An Australian woman becomes the first to give birth after receiving a donated egg.

1984

Killer virus identified

23 APRIL

The discovery of the virus that causes AIDS (Acquired Immune Deficiency Syndrome) has just been announced in Washington DC by the US health and human services secretary, Margaret Heckler. A team of scientists – led by Dr Robert Gallo of the National Cancer Institute – have identified the virus as HTLV-3 (human T-cell lymphotropic virus). The announcement is, however, being bitterly contested by French scientists who claim they discovered the virus last year. Despite the scientific row, it is clear that the rate of infection of the deadly disease is of epidemic proportions.

India's Golden Temple attacked

6 JUNE

The Golden Temple at Amritsar, the holiest of Sikh shrines, was today stormed by Indian troops in an assault codenamed "Operation Blue Star". This comes four days after the famous temple in the Punjab was seized and occupied by militant Sikh extremists demanding their own state of Khalistan. Resistance to the attack was ferocious and the Sikhs, who are a warrior sect, well prepared. They fought from strong fortifications and a network of tunnels and manholes. As the battle raged on, the Indian authorities sent in tanks and commandos, with strict instructions not to damage the golden-domed temple. Altogether, 90 soldiers and 712 extremists have died, including Sikh leader Sant Jarnail Singh Bhindranwale.

The sacred temple

GEORGE IS THE BOY
Britain's latest pop idol is Boy George, the lead singer of Culture Club. His make-up, hair, and frocks have aided the group's success.

JANUARY–JUNE

World Events	**FEB** International peace-keeping force withdraws from Lebanon, leaving Beirut to the local militias.	**FEB** In the USSR Konstantin Chernenko is named new Soviet party chief after the death of Yuri Andropov.	**MAR** As many as 1,000 people are feared dead after a week of religious rioting in northern Nigeria.	**MAY** The USSR announces that it will boycott the US Los Angeles Olympics due to security concerns.
Entertainment	**JAN** Johnny Weissmuller, swimming champion and star of *Tarzan* movies, dies aged 79.	**FEB** "Gender-bending" is the latest trend as stars dress in the fashions of the opposite sex.	**FEB** UK ice skaters Jayne Torvill and Christopher Dean win an Olympic gold medal in Yugoslavia.	**APR** South African runner Zola Budd is granted UK citizenship so that she can compete in the Olympics.
Innovations	**FEB** US astronaut Brian McCandless makes the first untethered space walk. **US ASTRONAUT**	**APR** US astronauts from the space shuttle *Challenger* successfully replace a control box in a satellite.	**APR** The first baby to have started life as a frozen embryo is born in Melbourne, Australia.	**MAY** The first domestic robot is manufactured in the US and advertised in a New York paper.

TORVILL AND DEAN

1984

Indira Gandhi killed

31 OCTOBER

Mrs Indira Gandhi, 66-year-old prime minister of India, was today ambushed and assassinated by two of her own Sikh bodyguards as she walked in the garden of her New Delhi home. She was shot ten times. It is clear that the murder was carried out in revenge for the storming of the Sikhs' holiest shrine, the Golden Temple at Amritsar, earlier in the year. Mrs Gandhi's 40-year-old son Rajiv has already been sworn in as the new prime minister.

Bishop Tutu wins Nobel Peace Prize

10 DECEMBER

Anglican bishop of Johannesburg Desmond Tutu today accepted the Nobel Peace Prize for his non-violent struggle against apartheid. "I have just got to believe God is around," he said. "If He is not, we in South Africa have had it."

Desmond Tutu

John Torrington, naval petty officer

Ice-men found

26 SEPTEMBER

The bodies of three English sailors have been discovered on Canada's Beechey Island, perfectly preserved by Arctic permafrost for 139 years. Scientists have even been able to carry out autopsies on the sailors' internal organs. The sailors died on an ill-fated expedition led by Sir John Franklin in 1845 to find the northwest passage from the Atlantic to the Pacific.

Bhopal nightmare

8 DECEMBER

At least 2,000 people have died in the Indian city of Bhopal after the worst industrial disaster in history. Five days ago, a leak from the chemical factory owned by the US-based Union Carbide corporation discharged a cloud of toxic methyl isocyanate gas. Hundreds of people were suffocated in their beds as the deadly vapour enveloped the city. Thousands more have been blinded and injured.

JULY–DECEMBER

JUL A former Nigerian transport minister is found kidnapped and drugged in a crate at Stansted Airport in the UK.

SEP After two years of negotiations, agreement is reached for the UK to return Hong Kong to China in 1997.

OCT Four people die when an IRA bomb explodes during the UK's Conservative Party conference.

NOV Republican Ronald Reagan wins a second term in the presidential election in the USA.

JUL This summer's box-office hit in the USA is the special effects extravaganza *Ghostbusters*.

JUL James F Fixx, the US man who popularized jogging, dies of a heart attack while out jogging.

AUG US athlete Carl Lewis wins gold medals in two sprints, the sprint relay, and the long jump at the Olympics.

DEC The Band Aid single *Do They Know It's Christmas?* raises £8 million in the UK for famine relief in Africa.

JUL In the UK's City of London the new hi-tech Lloyds Building, designed by Richard Rogers, is finished.

GHOSTBUSTERS

JUL Soviet cosmonaut Svetlana Savitskaya becomes the first woman to walk in space.

SEP The British Museum examines the body of a prehistoric man discovered in a peat bog in Cheshire, UK.

CARL LEWIS

OCT Three Soviet cosmonauts return to Earth after setting a new space endurance record of 238 days.

FEED THE WORLD

IN OCTOBER 1984, harrowing pictures of the Ethiopian famine were shown on British television. Bob Geldof, lead singer of the Boomtown Rats band, could not get the images of starving people out of his mind and decided to do something about it. Band Aid was born. Geldof persuaded more than 40 musicians and a recording company to donate their services in recording a charity single, *Do They Know it's Christmas?/Feed the World*. It raised £8 million and became Britain's biggest-selling single ever. Rock stars in the United States followed suit, forming USA For Africa. Their record *We Are the World* was a huge hit worldwide. Geldof and other musicians still felt more could be done and set about organizing a huge transatlantic fundraising concert called Live Aid.

THE BEST-SELLING BAND AID SINGLE

Worldwide live

At midday on Saturday 13 July 1985, Status Quo sang *Rocking All Over The World* to a crowd of 72,000 at Wembley Stadium in London, Britain. It was the launch of Live Aid, a non-stop rock marathon, held simultaneously in London and Philadelphia, United States, and viewed worldwide by 1.5 billion people. The superstars included Queen, Elton John, and Paul McCartney.

Famine in Ethiopia

Years of drought in Ethiopia and Sudan had left more than 150 million people facing starvation. The rain had not fallen since 1981 and crops had failed. Millions of people were forced to leave their homes in search of food. The UN called it "the greatest natural disaster faced by man".

BOB GELDOF IN ETHIOPIA

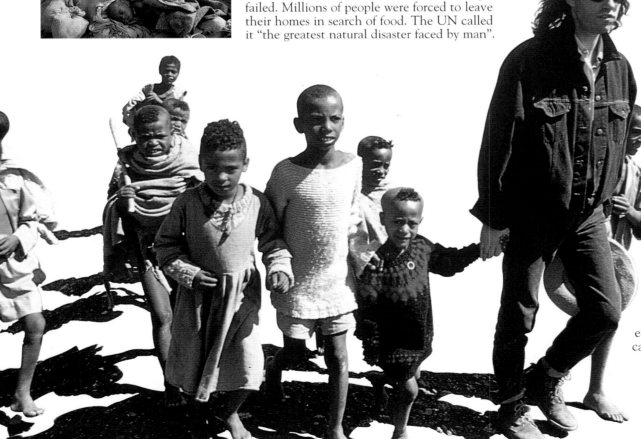

Geldof's visit

Bob Geldof flew to Ethiopia in January 1985 to find out how best to use the money raised by Band Aid. He visited feeding camps in Tigre, and refugee camps in the Sudan. He was horrified by what he saw. Starving people walked hundreds of miles for the chance of receiving some meagre emergency relief. At one camp he counted 15 bags of flour that had to be shared between 27,000 people. Starving babies with swollen stomachs were too hungry to cry, and dying people curled up like stones on the hard ground.

1985 WE ARE THE WORLD
RELEASED BY USA FOR AFRICA

1985 LIVE AID CONCERTS
BEAMED TO 1.5 BILLION PEOPLE

1985 CONCERTS RAISE £40
MILLION FOR RELIEF EFFORT

Bob takes a bow

Live Aid was such a success that no-one
left Wembley Stadium before the end of
the concert. For the finale, the entire
cast lined up on stage to sing *Do They
Know It's Christmas?*, led by Bob Geldof.
The audience joined in, filling the
stadium with sound.

LIVE AID
CONCERT TICKETS

Live from Philadelphia

A crowd of 90,000 people roared as the Live Aid concert began
at noon in the JFK Stadium at Philadelphia, in the United
States. Across the Atlantic, at Wembley, the stars had already
been on stage for five hours. Live pictures beamed via satellite
were shown on huge screens to link the two concerts taking place
simultaneously, 3,000 miles apart. The performers in Philadelphia
included Bob Dylan, Mick Jagger, Madonna, Eric Clapton, and
Tina Turner. The longest concert in the history of rock 'n' roll
lasted for 16 hours. As the finale was reached in Philadelphia,
it was already the next day at Wembley.

Special delivery

Thousands of tonnes of food were transported by
Band Aid on specially chartered ships and planes
from the United Kingdom to Africa, but that was
not the end of the story. There was no point in
sending desperately needed famine relief halfway
across the world if the sacks of food then lay rotting
at the dockside while people starved. Band Aid solved
this by buying its own fleet of vehicles that could take
food directly from the ports to the refugee camps.

Life-saving biscuits

Famine relief usually consisted of grain
and basic foodstuffs, but the Band Aid
team discovered that there was an
urgent need for something more
nutritious if children's lives were to
be saved. As a result, tonnes of high-
energy biscuits and milk powder
were shipped over to Ethiopia.

Medical aid

As well as food and long-term aid, such as seeds, tools,
and tractors, urgent medical help was vital if lives were
to be saved in the appalling conditions of the refugee
camps in Ethiopia and the Sudan. People were dying in
their thousands, not only from hunger, but also from disease. Band
Aid sent tonnes of medical supplies, including vitamins, to tackle
the crisis. One particular shipment contained 40,000 vitamin A
tablets, which helped to prevent blindness in starving children.

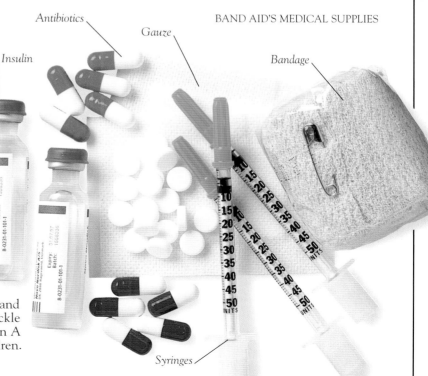

Antibiotics

Gauze

BAND AID'S MEDICAL SUPPLIES

Insulin

Bandage

Syringes

1985

New way to get around!

10 JANUARY

The electronics genius Sir Clive Sinclair has unveiled his answer to Britain's traffic problems. Known as the C5, it is a lightweight, single-seat, battery- and pedal-powered tricycle. It can travel up to 32 km (20 miles) before the battery needs to be recharged. Sir Clive predicts that, by the end of the century, "the petrol engine will be a thing of the past". However, critics are describing the C5 as little more than a toy.

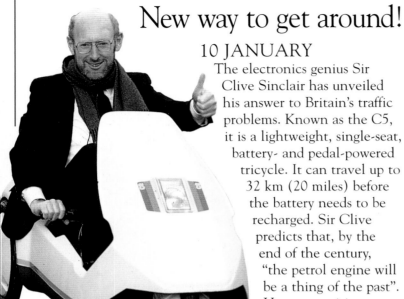
Clive Sinclair in his C5

Pandemonium at Heysel Stadium

29 MAY

The football world is in shock tonight after tragedy struck a European Cup Final match at Belgium's Heysel Stadium. It is believed that 41 Italian and Belgian supporters died, and a further 350 were injured as British football hooligans went on the rampage. A wall and safety fence collapsed as Liverpool FC fans charged towards supporters of the Juventus team. In the ensuing panic, many of the victims were trampled or crushed to death. As a priest gave the last rites to the dying, the fighting continued with missiles being hurled through the air. British football hooligans have become a cause for growing concern and there are calls for British teams to be banned from Europe.

Armed hijackers guard jet at airport

30 JUNE

Seventeen days after their TWA flight from Athens, Greece, to Rome in Italy was hijacked by Islamic Jihad terrorists, 39 tired US hostages were released today in Beirut, Lebanon. The hijackers, who flown to a US base in West Germany where they will be reunited with their families. Meanwhile, the hijackers are still guarding the TWA jet at Beirut Airport. One of the hijackers has bragged to the waiting journalists of "the

Hijackers in the cockpit

were demanding the release of Palestinians from Israeli jails, beat up some of their hostages. One passenger, US navy diver Robert Stethem, was brutally murdered. The freed hostages were driven in a Red Cross convoy to Damascus, Syria, before being ability of the oppressed to control America". Although both the United States and Israel are insisting that no deal has been struck with the terrorists, it appears that their demands have been met, and tomorrow 700 prisoners will be released in Israel.

JANUARY–JUNE

World Events	**FEB** Gibraltar's frontier with Spain re-opens after 16 years. Spain had tried to force the UK to transfer sovereignty.	**MAR** PM Thatcher claims a victory as the National Union of Miners ends its year-long strike in the UK.	**MAR** Fifty-four-year-old Mikhail Gorbachev succeeds as leader of the USSR after the death of Konstantin Chernenko.	**MAY** Many countries send aid as thousands of people die after a cyclone and tidal wave batter the coast of Bangladesh.
Entertainment	**MAR** South African-born UK barefoot runner Zola Budd wins a cross-country race in Portugal.	**APR** Australian media tycoon Rupert Murdoch buys 50% of the Twentieth Century Fox Film Corporation.	**APR** UK pop group Wham! performs in front of an audience of 10,000 in China.	**JUN** UK boxer Barry McGuigan becomes WBA featherweight boxing champion.
Innovations	**JAN** The first UK mobile telephones are introduced by Racal-Vodaphone and Cellnet. **MOBILE PHONE**	**FEB** *Concorde*'s first commercial flight from the UK, to Sydney, Australia, takes 17 hours 3 mins 45 secs.	**JUN** US space shuttle *Discovery* blasts off with Prince Sultan, the first Arab astronaut, on board. **PRINCE SULTAN**	**JUN** The Sir Isaac Newton Telescope, located on the Canary Islands, is inaugurated.

1985

Wreck of the *Titanic* found

3 SEPTEMBER

The wreck of the *Titanic*, the luxury liner that sank on its maiden voyage in April 1912, has finally been found. It was located 640 km (400 miles) south of Newfoundland by a joint French-American expedition.

Town drowns in Colombian mud

13 NOVEMBER

A large area of Colombia has been declared a disaster zone tonight after a long-dormant volcano, 129 km (81 miles) west of Bogotá, erupted violently for the first time since 1845. The Nevado del Ruiz volcano spewed huge quantities of rocks, ash, mud, and water over nearby towns, and it is thought that up to 20,000 people may have died. Worst hit is the town of Armero which has virtually disappeared under a stream of hot mud. Clouds of ash and smoke from the volcano are being carried by the wind up to 480 km (300 miles) away. It is being described as one of the most destructive volcanic eruptions in history.

Superpowers talk

21 NOVEMBER

The United States president Ronald Reagan flew home today after a highly successful series of summit meetings in Geneva with Soviet premier Mikhail Gorbachev. The two leaders spent a record six hours together in private sessions, with only interpreters present. Despite differences about the United States "Star Wars" space defence programme, agreement was reached to begin negotiations on strategic nuclear arms control and human rights. Both men appeared to be delighted with the progress of the Swiss talks and the course seems set for a new era of co-operation between the world's two giant superpowers.

Gorbachev and Reagan reach agreement at talks

NEW POP SENSATION

Madonna Louise Veronica Ciccone has had a string of hit singles this year on both sides of the Atlantic. In April she embarked on her first tour, playing to 355,000 fans in 27 US cities. Madonna has also received favourable reviews for her first acting role in the film *Desperately Seeking Susan*, as well as appearing on the cover of *Time* magazine.

JULY–DECEMBER

JUL Greenpeace peace protest ship *Rainbow Warrior* is sunk by two explosions in Auckland Harbour, New Zealand.

JUL A transatlantic Live Aid concert, at Wembley Stadium in the UK and JFK Stadium in USA, raises £40 million.

JUL European Space Agency's (ESA) launches a *Giotto* spacecraft, which aims to intercept Halley's Comet.

BORIS BECKER

JUL South African president P W Botha imposes a state of emergency in black townships after unrest leaves 500 dead.

JUL The unseeded West German tennis player, 17-year-old Boris Becker, wins the UK's Wimbledon men's title.

JUL *Challenger*, the USA's 50th manned space flight and the 19th space shuttle, is launched.

SEP An earthquake that measures 8.5 on the Richter Scale devastates Mexico City, killing nearly 2,000 people.

JUL UK runner Steve Cram wins the "Dream Mile" in Oslo, Norway, taking more than a second off the world record.

SEP Switzerland becomes the first country to make lead-free catalytic convertors compulsory.

ROCK HUDSON

OCT The Australian government gives back Ayers Rock (Uluru) in the Northern Territory to the Aboriginals.

OCT US film star Rock Hudson dies after a year-long battle against AIDS, aged 59.

NOV Halley's Comet reappears in the skies for the first time in 75 years.

1986

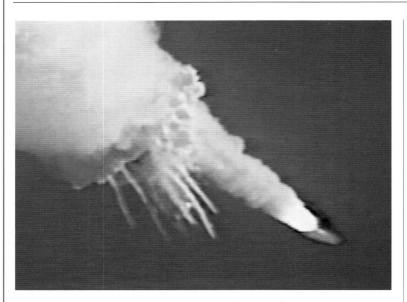

Shuttle explodes

DISPOSABLE CAMERA

The disposable camera, the ultimate holiday accessory, was launched this year. Introduced by Japanese company Fuji, the camera consists of a 24-shot colour film in a cardboard box with lens and shutter. When finished, the whole camera is sent for processing.

28 JANUARY

The United States is in shock today after the worst accident in space history. As thousands of spectators gathered at Cape Canaveral, and millions more watched on television, the space shuttle *Challenger* exploded into a massive fireball, killing all seven astronauts on board. After several delays because of bad weather, the launch seemed routine until disaster struck just 73 seconds after lift-off. Among the dead is Christa McAuliffe, a schoolteacher from New Hampshire, who had been chosen to be the first "citizen in space".

Aquino triumphs in Philippines

25 FEBRUARY

Philippines dictator Ferdinand Marcos has been ousted from power by Corazon Aquino. The coup comes after a campaign of disobedience. As Aquino supporters stormed the presidential palace, the president and his family escaped to safety in the United States. They leave behind them the trappings of a lavish lifestyle, including 1,060 pairs of shoes owned by the president's wife.

Corazon Aquino

The return of Halley's Comet

14 MARCH

Several spacecraft from around the world has been heading for Halley's Comet, which is only visible once every 75 years. However, it was revealed today that *Giotto*, launched by the European Space Agency (ESA), has had the closest encounter. Named after the famous Italian artist who painted Halley's Comet as the Star of Bethlehem, the *Giotto* is travelling at 68 km (42 miles) per second. It has passed within 544 km (340 miles) of the comet. Data sent back to Earth suggest that the nucleus of the comet, which is streaking through the skies in its orbit of the Sun, is one of the darkest bodies of the solar system.

JANUARY–JUNE

World Events	JAN Spain and Portugal become the eleventh and twelfth members of the European Community.	FEB After 29 years the Duvalier dictatorship in Haiti ends as "Baby Doc", the son of "Papa Doc", flees to France.	APR The USA launches air strikes against Libya in retaliation for acts of terrorism aimed at US citizens.	JUN One thousand black activists are arrested in South Africa after President Botha announces a state of emergency.
Entertainment	MAR US film star and tough guy James Cagney dies at the age of 86.	APR US actor Clint Eastwood wins a landslide victory to become mayor of Carmel town.	MAY US film *Top Gun* is a huge box-office hit with Tom Cruise starring as a gung-ho pilot.	JUN For the first time yellow balls are used at the UK's Wimbledon lawn tennis championships.
Innovations	JAN US space probe *Voyager 2* discovers that Uranus has 15 moons.	FEB The USSR launches a new orbiting space station called *Mir*, which means "peace".	MAY All new telephones in the UK are to have push buttons instead of old-fashioned dials.	JUN The "Mexican wave" is invented in the opening game of the World Cup when Mexico beat Belgium 2–1.

"BABY DOC" DUVALIER

TOM CRUISE

1986

Nuclear disaster at Chernobyl

30 APRIL

The Soviet Union today revealed that a major nuclear accident has taken place at the Chernobyl power plant in the Ukraine. It could well be the worst civil nuclear catastrophe ever. An explosion ripped through one of the reactors four days ago, releasing huge amounts of radiation into the atmosphere. Poor safety controls, human error, and lack of containment buildings turned the accident into

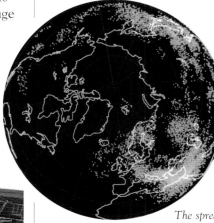
The spread of radiation

a disaster of gigantic proportions. One of the reactors is still blazing, making any attempt to plug the leak and halt the damage impossible. The other three reactors at Chernobyl have been shut down. Thirty-one people have died so far, and about 15,000 people have been evacuated from the immediate vicinity, which is already highly contaminated. At present, the global implications of the toxic meltdown and radiation leak can only be guessed at.

A handy victory for Argentina

29 JUNE

A victorious Argentine team claimed the World Cup in Mexico today after beating West Germany 3–2 in a bad-tempered final. Argentina's triumphant captain, Diego Maradona, will be remembered for the fisted goal that helped beat England in

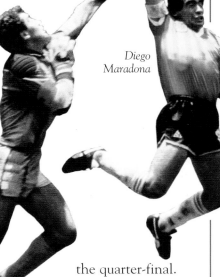
Diego Maradona

the quarter-final. He later called it "the hand of God". Superstar Maradona also scored the two goals that beat Belgium in the semi-final.

JULY–DECEMBER

JUL The USA holds lavish celebrations for the Statue of Liberty's 100th birthday, after a $70 million restoration.

JUL Greg LeMond is the first cyclist from the USA to win the 4,023-km (2,500-mile) Tour de France race.

JUL An underwater robot takes pictures of the inside of the wreck of the *Titanic*, which sank in 1912.

STATUE OF LIBERTY

SEP Desmond Tutu is enthroned as the first ever black archbishop of the city of Cape Town in South Africa.

OCT *Phantom of the Opera*, the musical by Andrew Lloyd-Webber and Charles Hart, opens in the UK.

SEP Japanese car manufacturer Nissan opens a new assembly plant in northeast England, UK.

OCT President Shimon Peres hands over premiership of Israel to his coalition partner Yitzhak Shamir.

NOV 20-year-old Mike Tyson from the USA becomes the youngest-ever world heavyweight boxing champion.

DEC Surgeons in the UK perform the world's first triple heart, lungs, and liver transplant.

NOV The River Rhine in Europe is polluted with toxic liquid pesticides after a blaze at a chemical plant in Basle, Switzerland.

DEC Oprah Winfrey becomes ratings champion of daytime television with her US talk show.

DEC Experimental aircraft *Voyager 4* completes the first flight around the world without refuelling.

OPRAH WINFREY

THE FIGHT FOR THE PLANET

AS THE THREAT OF NUCLEAR WAR waned in the late Eighties, a new battle to save the Earth began. Long-term exploitation of the planet by a fast-growing human population had carried on unchecked for generations. As a result many precious natural resources, such as tropical rainforests, had already been destroyed, and many more, such as the ozone layer that protects living things from ultra-violet radiation, were at risk. The climate itself was threatened because the indiscriminate burning of oil and fossils, mainly by motor cars and industry, had dramatically increased levels of carbon dioxide and other poisonous gases in the air, causing the "greenhouse effect". Global warming was the inevitable result. Most scientists believe that the average world temperature would rise by 4°C (7.2°F) by the end of the 21st century.

Smoke-filled skies

Most air pollution comes from the chimneys of coal-fired power stations and factories that emit sulphur dioxide and nitrogen oxides. These pollutants combine with the atmosphere to create acid rain, which damages forests, plants, and crops, and contaminates lakes and rivers.

Rainforest destruction

About half of the world's original tropical rainforest has been destroyed and, with it, countless unique species of insects and plants. During the Eighties, the rate of destruction almost doubled. An estimated 160,000 sq km (63,000 sq miles) of rainforest disappeared each year, because of slash-and-burn methods of farming, logging, and mining. Vast tracts of Central and South America were also cleared and burned for cattle ranching.

ANTI-NUCLEAR
DISPOSAL SIGNS

Forest devastation caused by slash-and-burn farming techniques

AMAZON WASTELAND

Nuclear testing

The nuclear arms race involved the constant development of deadly atomic and thermonuclear weapons. Test explosions were carried out in remote areas, under the ground, or under the sea. With the end of the Cold War the superpowers agreed to dismantle nuclear stockpiles and to ban nuclear testing.

Calibrated sight

Trigger

Nuclear protest

Anti-nuclear protestors and pressure groups, such as Greenpeace, helped to focus world attention on the threat posed by nuclear weapons and the dangers of the nuclear power industry, with its highly toxic waste. The protestors' fears were confirmed in 1986 when a massive explosion at the Chernobyl power plant, in the Soviet Union, resulted in the worst nuclear accident ever, causing the contamination of vast areas of eastern Europe and Scandinavia.

Weapon of death

For 300 years whales have been hunted for food or to provide oil. The right whale was almost hunted to extinction in the late 1800s, and the number of sperm whales has been severely affected. But it was not until 1860, when the harpoon gun was invented, that it became easier to catch some of the faster whales. In the 1920s, the Norwegians revolutionized whaling by introducing a modern harpoon with a deadly explosive tip.

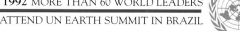

Ivory trade

During the Seventies, the numbers of elephants in Africa dwindled from 1.3 million to 609,000. Most of the elephants were slaughtered and left to rot by poachers in search of the "white gold", or ivory, of their tusks. When, in 1989, the African elephant was listed in the Convention on International Trade in Endangered Species (CITES), more than 115 countries agreed to stop trading in ivory.

Recycling

During the Eighties there was a new-found concern about the planet's fragile state and its dwindling resources, particularly in the rich industrialized nations. People realized that caring for the environment began at home and they started to recycle wastepaper, bottles, and cans. As consumers, they also began to realize the power of their purses, opting for new planet-friendly goods that did not damage the environment, such as environmentally-friendly washing-up liquid.

Hole in the ozone layer

Each spring since the 1970s, a hole in the ozone layer has opened over Antarctica, allowing in harmful ultra-violet rays from the Sun. Elsewhere, this protective layer is thinning as it is eroded by manufactured gases called chlorofluorocarbons (CFCs), which are used in aerosols and refrigerators. CFCs take about eight years to reach the stratosphere, where they can survive for a century. The Montreal Protocol to protect the ozone layer was signed in 1987 and aims to cut CFC production by 50 per cent by 1999.

Violet and pink areas show the severe depletion in the ozone layer

Taking action

In October 1983, six hundred Greenpeace activists clad in "death" suits lay down as if dead in London, Britain, to protest against the Sellafield nuclear reprocessing plant, THORP, in Cumbria, and the radioactive discharges it would cause.

Barbs open on impact to anchor the harpoon in the whale's flesh

HARPOON GUN

Muzzle

Grenade-loaded tip explodes inside the whale

Swivelling muzzle support

Fast and deadly

By the beginning of this century, steam-powered ships enabled whalers to hunt the fin whale and the blue whale in the most remote waters in the world. There were about 250,000 blue whales in the Antarctic when the first whaling fleets arrived. Now there are probably only a few hundred left. Huge modern factory ships were built that could process the dead whales at sea, rather than towing them back to shore. Whale populations plummeted and, in 1986, the International Whaling Commisssion (IWC) introduced a temporary ban on commercial whaling.

1987

Pilot meets red-faced Russians!

28 MAY

Strollers in Moscow's Red Square were amazed when a small Cessna four-seater light aircraft appeared from

Rust lands in Red Square

nowhere, swooped over the Kremlin and St Basil's Cathedral, and landed on an upward slope near the huge Kremlin Wall. A young man stepped out of the cockpit and proceeded to sign autographs. Nineteen-year-old West German Mathias Rust had succeeded in dodging the combined might of the Soviet military authorities, flying single-handed through heavily defended airspace. Previously, he had only 24 hours' flying time to his credit.

Wrong way North!

7 JULY

"God Bless Ollie" T-shirts are selling like hot cakes and telegrams of support are pouring in after Lt-Col Oliver North defended himself to the US Congress about his part in the "Irangate" arms for hostages scandal. The much-decorated marine officer, who has been nicknamed the president's "swashbuckler-in-chief", was dismissed from the National Security Council at the end of last year. The scandal concerns $30-million profit made from the sale of arms to Iran in exchange for US hostages. The money was transferred to Contra rebels fighting the Sandinista government in Nicaragua.

JANUARY–JUNE

World Events	**JAN** The archbishop of Canterbury's envoy and negotiator Terry Waite is kidnapped in Lebanon.	**FEB** Charles Haughey is elected prime minister (Taoiseach) of the Republic of Ireland for the third time.	**MAR** 189 people die when the 8,078-tonne car ferry *Herald of Free Enterprise* sinks off the coast of Zeebrugge in Belgium.	**JUN** Fifteen people die when a car bomb planted by Basque separatist group ETA explodes in Barcelona, Spain.
Entertainment	**FEB** US pop artist Andy Warhol dies during an operation, aged 55.	**APR** The duchess of Windsor's jewels are sold in Geneva, Switzerland, for £31,380,197.	**JUN** US actor and dancer Fred Astaire (born Frederick Austerlitz) dies in his Hollywood home at the age of 88.	**JUN** New Zealand's All Blacks win the first rugby world cup, beating France 29–9 in the final.
Innovations	**FEB** Supernova 1987A, the first exploding star visible to the naked eye, is spotted.	**FEB** The new European Airbus *320*, built jointly by France, Germany, Spain, and the UK, is launched.	**MAR** The DAT (Digital Audio Tape) recorder is launched by Sony in Japan for professional use only.	**MAR** "Ecu" coins are struck in Belgium on the 30th anniversary of the European Community.

TERRY WAITE

ZEEBRUGGE DISASTER

1987

Stock markets crash

19 OCTOBER

Dealers are dubbing it "Black Monday" as stock market shares plummet all round the world. Wall Street has had its worst day ever, with the Dow Jones Industrial Average plunging 508 points from 2,246.73 to 1,738.41. It is the end of the "bull market" of the last five years, which has seen a 350 per cent rise in average share prices. Analysts are pointing to the appalling state of the US economy as one of the major factors. The economic boom of the 1980s appears to be at an end.

FIRST SOLAR-POWERED CAR RACE

It took General Motors' *Sunraycer* six days to win the first solar-powered car race, held in Australia this November. There were 22 entries in the 3,218-km (2,011-mile) Pentax World Solar Challenge.

High price for floral tribute

11 NOVEMBER

The 1980s have seen the prices of Impressionist and Post-Impressionist paintings go through the roof, and a new record was set today in New York. Australian tycoon Alan Bond has bought Van Gogh's *Irises* for a staggering $53.9 million at Sotheby's United States auction house. Earlier in the year Yasuda Fire and Marine, a Japanese insurance firm, bought one of Van Gogh's most famous paintings, *Sunflowers*, at an auction held in Britain for a breathtaking £24.75 million.

Irises by Vincent Van Gogh

Mafia on trial

16 DECEMBER

After two years the marathon trial of Sicily's Mafia, held in a special bombproof courthouse, reached its climax today. The 338 Mafiosi were sentenced to a total of 2,665 years in prison for crimes including extortion and murder.

JULY–DECEMBER

JUL Former Nazi SS officer Klaus Barbie, the "Butcher of Lyon", is found guilty of wartime atrocities and is imprisoned for life.

JUL The UK's Richard Branson and Norwegian Per Lindstrand cross the Atlantic ocean in a hot-air balloon.

JUL The USSR launches an 18-tonne space platform, *Cosmos 1870*, into orbit.

WHITNEY HOUSTON

JUL The Greek government declares a national state of emergency when a heatwave claims over 700 lives.

AUG Whitney Houston's album *I Wanna Dance with Somebody* enters the US charts at number one.

NOV Construction work is started on the Channel Tunnel between France and the UK.

OCT A "Great Storm" sweeps across the Atlantic and destructive hurricane-force winds hit the UK.

AUG Tom McLean from the UK rows across the Atlantic ocean in a record-breaking 54 days 23 hours.

NOV A talking watch, which answers when asked the time, is launched by Citizen in Japan.

STORM DAMAGE IN THE UK

NOV An IRA bomb explodes at a parade in Enniskillen, Northern Ireland, killing 11 people.

AUG Lynne Cox from the USA swims across the Bering Straits from the USA to the USSR.

DEC Soviet cosmonaut Yuri Romananko returns to Earth after a record 326 days in space.

1988

Happy birthday Australia!

26 JANUARY

Sydney Harbour is teeming today as Australia celebrates the 200th anniversary of the arrival of the first settlers from Britain. Sailing ships from all over the world are joining in, and a special fleet of 160 tall ships has

Sydney Harbour

re-enacted the anchoring of the first fleet in 1788. Other birthday events include the arrival in Adelaide of ten camels, which have trekked 3,426 km (2,141 miles) across Australia from Darwin to commemorate the part that their ancestors played in opening up the heart of the continent. Britain presented the country with a sailing ship. Aboriginal people, however, have declared it a "year of mourning", throwing wreaths into Botany Bay, where Captain Cook, the first European to discover the continent, landed in 1770.

Longest tunnel in the world

13 MARCH

The Seikan tunnel, linking the islands of Honshu and Hokkaido in Japan, was officially opened today by the Japanese minister of transport who described the tunnel as "a technical achievement without parallel in the world". It is the last stage in a project to link the four islands of Japan by train, something which has inspired many Japanese engineers for decades. Covering a distance of 53.85 km (33.46 miles), it is not only the longest tunnel in the world, it is also the most expensive. The total cost spiralled from an original estimate of $783 million in 1971 to $6.5 billion, largely because of the extreme difficulty of tunnelling through unstable and porous rock. It was drilled more than 91.4 m (300 ft) under the seabed, reaching a maximum depth of 240 m (787 ft).

The Seikan tunnel

Hannibal's trek

19 APRIL

Two elephants have just arrived in Turin, Italy, after a trip organized by English cricketer and fundraiser, Ian Botham, retraced Hannibal's famous journey across the Alps from France. It took them 21 days to complete the 805-km (503-mile) trek.

STEALTH BOMBER
The United States' Pentagon has released the first pictures of the *F-117A* Stealth jet fighter, the revolutionary aircraft that has been operational since 1983 and that is invisible to radar. The prototype of the *B-2* Stealth bomber, which is designed to absorb radar, was also unveiled.

JANUARY–APRIL

World Events	**JAN** Defiant Palestinians take part in an intifada, or uprising, against occupying Israeli forces in Gaza.	**FEB** Archbishop Desmond Tutu is arrested in South Africa for defying a law banning protests outside parliament.	**MAR** In an act widely condemned, three members of the Irish Republican Army are shot dead by UK soldiers in Gibraltar.	**APR** The National People's Congress in China votes to allow capitalist-style enterprise to set up in the communist country.
Entertainment	**FEB** Comic Relief Day in the UK raises £7 million for charity.	**FEB** UK ski-jumper Eddie "The Eagle" Edwards comes last at the Calgary Olympics.	**FEB** At the winter Olympics, Pirmin Zurbriggen of Switzerland wins the men's downhill ski event.	**APR** Bernado Bertolucci's film *The Last Emperor* wins nine Oscars, the most for a single film for 27 years.
Innovations	**JAN** A $10 plastic polymer banknote is issued by the Reserve Bank of Australia.	**JAN** Japan's new magnetic levitation train, the *Maglev*, reaches speeds of 257.48 km/h (160.92 mph).	**FEB** UK archaeologists discover the grave of Boadicea, warrior queen of ancient Britain, under a train station.	**APR** The 12.87-km (8.04-miles) Great Seto Bridge, connecting two of Japan's islands, is opened.

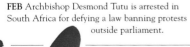

EDDIE "THE EAGLE"

THE LAST EMPEROR

1988

160 die on *Piper Alpha* platform

6 JULY
At least 160 people have been killed and dozens more injured after a huge explosion at the 34,544-tonne North Sea oil platform *Piper Alpha*, off the coast of Scotland. Those who survived the original blast were forced to jump 61 m (200 ft) into the sea, which was covered with burning oil, in a desperate attempt to escape. Emergency services are fighting the inferno and helicopters are scanning the area for survivors. First reports suggest the disaster was caused by a faulty safety valve that allowed the build-up of inflammable gas.

Fatal flooding in Bangladesh

4 SEPTEMBER
Bangladesh has once again been hit by a catastrophic natural disaster as floods sweep two-thirds of the country. The capital, Dacca, is under water, 25 million people have been left homeless, and at least 1,000 people have lost their lives. A quarter of the year's crops have been destroyed, which will surely mean desperate food shortages. The international airport has been closed and road and railways are submerged, making rescue work difficult and preventing a co-ordinated relief programme. Bangladesh's information minister, Mahabur Rahmanthe, has appealed for helicopters to provide emergency aid. He said, "No other country in the region has suffered so much damage from natural calamity." The tragedy comes less than a month after 700 people died when the country was hit by a monsoon.

Turin Shroud declared fake

13 OCTOBER
The famous Turin Shroud, believed to have been used to wrap the body of Christ and revered by Catholics for centuries as one of the most sacred holy relics, has been declared a fake. Extensive carbon-dating tests carried out at Oxford University in Britain and elsewhere, have proved that the linen actually dates from between 1260 and 1390. However, scientists cannot understand how a length of material more than 600 years old came to be imprinted with the blood-stained image of a crucified man.

MAY–AUGUST

MAY Socialist leader François Mitterrand is re-elected president of France for a second term, taking 54% of the popular vote.

MAY US president Ronald Reagan pays his first visit to the USSR for talks with Soviet premier Mikhail Gorbachev.

AUG In Rangoon, Burma, the president Sein Lwin resigns after huge anti-government demonstrations and rioting.

AUG Pakistan's military ruler President Zia ul-Haq is killed when his plane explodes in mid-air.

JUN *Who Framed Roger Rabbit?*, a US film mixing live action and animation, is a box-office hit.

JUN 80,000 people celebrate Nelson Mandela's 70th birthday at a huge concert in the UK.

JUL Top-earning pop star Michael Jackson "moonwalks" his way to Europe at the start of a world tour.

AUG Legendary Italian racing car magnate Enzo Ferrari dies aged 90, he had retired in 1977.

NELSON MANDELA CONCERT

JUN Personal TV sets for airline passengers are introduced by Northwest Airlines in the USA.

JUL In the UK, automatic cameras are introduced to catch motorists jumping traffic lights.

AUG In Japan, Sony launch the first video walkman which combines a colour TV and video recorder.

FERRARI LOGO

AUG An Afghan-Soviet space mission blasts off for the orbiting Soviet space station *Mir*.

1988

First female Islamic PM

1 DECEMBER

Benazir Bhutto today became prime minister of Pakistan. Two weeks ago her People's Party won the country's first democratic election in 11 years. She is the first woman prime minister in an Islamic country.

BUNGEE JUMPING

People have been flocking to jump off the Kawarau Suspension Bridge. This first permanent bungee jumping site in Queenstown, New Zealand, was opened this year. Bungee jumping is now one of the most popular dangerous sports.

Devastation strikes Armenia

7 DECEMBER

A huge international relief effort is being mounted after a major earthquake struck Armenia, in the southern part of the Soviet Union earlier today, killing an estimated 100,000 people. Nearly half a million people have been left homeless, with temperatures dropping below freezing point and rescue work proving difficult in the mountainous and isolated countryside. The epicentre of the earthquake, near the Turkish border, measured 6.9 on the Richter Scale. It is by far the worst quake the region has ever known, with the town of Spitak, which had a population of 50,000, being completely destroyed. More than three-quarters of the apartment blocks in the city of Leninakan, which has a population of more than 300,000, collapsed, burying many alive in the rubble. Soviet premier Mikhail Gorbachev has cut short his trip to the United States to visit the devastated area.

Jet explodes over Lockerbie

22 DECEMBER

The Scottish town of Lockerbie is this morning coming to terms with the tragic events of last night. A Pan Am jumbo jet exploded over the town, killing all 259 passengers on board and at least 11 people on the ground. The airliner was on its way from Frankfurt, Germany, to New York in the United States when it suddenly broke up in mid-air, scattering wreckage far and wide. It has now emerged that United States embassies received a warning that a Pan Am flight would be a target for a terrorist bomb.

SEPTEMBER–DECEMBER

	World Events		
World Events	SEP Hundreds of thousands are left homeless in Mexico after a hurricane strikes.	NOV George Bush, the current US vice-president, wins the presidential election for the Republican Party.	DEC Thirty-six people die and 100 are injured when a packed commuter train crashes into another train in the UK.	DEC Palestinian Liberation Organization chairman Yassir Arafat renounces terrorism and recognizes Israeli rights.
Entertainment	SEP US sprinter Florence Griffith-Joyner (nicknamed Flo-Jo) wins three gold medals at the Seoul Olympics.	SEP Canadian sprinter Ben Johnson is stripped of the 100 m Olympic gold medal he won at Seoul after failing a drugs test.	DEC UK academic Dr Stephen Hawking has an unlikely bestseller with his book A Brief History of Time.	DEC US rock star Roy Orbison, nicknamed the "Big O", dies after suffering a heart attack, aged 52.
Innovations	SEP The Australian Telescope, the largest in the southern hemisphere, is inaugurated.	NOV The first unmanned Soviet space shuttle Buran ("Snowstorm") orbits the Earth twice in a flight of 3 hours 25 mins.	DEC Transatlantic optical fibre cable capable to carrying 40,000 simultaneous telephone calls becomes operational.	DEC Soviet cosmonauts Vladimir Titov and Musa Manarov set a new space endurance record of over a year.

GEORGE BUSH

YASSIR ARAFAT

1989

Sun sets on Hirohito reign

7 JANUARY

Michinomiya Hirohito, emperor of Japan for 62 years, has died. At 87 years old, he was the oldest reigning monarch in the world. His death brings to an end the era in Japan known as Showa, which means "enlightened peace". His long reign saw Japan develop into one of the most powerful economies in the world, after surviving defeat in World War II. In 1945, Hirohito admitted to his shattered nation that the emperor is not a god incarnate. Crown Prince Akihito, Hirohito's 55-year-old son, automatically became emperor at the moment his father died.

Democracy protests crushed in Tiananmen Square

9 JUNE

Hundreds of demonstrators have been killed and thousands badly injured after the Chinese People's Liberation Army mounted a sudden and savage crackdown in Beijing this week. Troops advanced on Tiananmen Square, where almost half a million students and pro-democracy activists were denouncing the communist regime and demanding freedom of speech and other basic human rights. Some of the demonstrators have been on hunger strike since 13 May. A "Statue of Democracy and Freedom", modelled on the Statue of Liberty, had been unveiled. As the huge armoured tanks moved in, one demonstrator single-handedly stopped the advance before being pulled away. In the massacre that followed, soldiers fired indiscriminately as the protestors fought back. A similar crackdown is now taking place all over China, with hundreds of so-called "counter-revolutionaries" being rounded up and put on trial in people's courts. World leaders are condemning the horrific actions of the Chinese government.

Protestors in Tiananmen Square

A lone protestor stops the tanks from advancing. His bravery is admired throughout the world

---

JANUARY–APRIL

FEB After a ten-year occupation, the last Soviet troops withdraw from Afghanistan in central Asia.

JAN The world famous Surrealist painter Salvador Dali dies at the age of 84 in Figueras, Spain.

JAN The world's first holographic postage stamps are issued by the Austrian postal service.

SALMAN RUSHDIE

FEB The Iranian Ayatollah Khomeini calls for the death of UK writer Salman Rushdie for blaspheming against Islam.

FEB US boxer Mike Tyson retains the world heavyweight title after beating UK boxer Frank Bruno.

FEB Rupert Murdoch's £25 million *Sky* television satellite network is launched across Europe.

MAR Oil tanker *Exxon Valdez* runs aground in Alaska, USA, spilling millions of litres of crude oil into Prince William Sound.

FEB *The Joshua Tree* by Irish rock group U2 becomes the first million-selling CD.

FEB Soviet space probe *Phobos* orbits Mars and sends back pictures of its moon.

EXXON VALDEZ

APR Ninety-four people are crushed to death and 170 are injured at Hillsborough Stadium in Sheffield, UK, during a football match.

MAR Dustin Hoffman wins an Oscar for his portrayal of autism in US film *Rain Man*.

APR Researchers in Toronto, Canada, identify the gene responsible for cystic fibrosis.

1989

Revolution remembered

14 JULY

Celebrations to mark the 200th anniversary of the French Revolution reached a climax in Paris today. More than 5,000 soldiers and 300 armoured vehicles took part in a huge Bastille Day parade down the Champs Elysée, with a flyover by 250 planes and helicopters. This was followed by a spectacular international pageant.

Dictator dies in disgrace

28 SEPTEMBER

Former dictator of the Philippines, Ferdinand Marcos, has died in Hawaii, aged 72.

He spent the last three years of his life in exile fighting charges of embezzlement, after fleeing the country he had defrauded of billions of dollars in 1986. He is survived by his wife Imelda, a former beauty queen, whose 1,060 pairs of shoes became a symbol of their lavish and corrupt regime.

THE LOUVRE PYRAMID

A controversial glass and steel pyramid, designed by American architect I M Pei, has taken shape in the Cour Napoléon at the Louvre museum in Paris, France. Qualified climbers will do the cleaning.

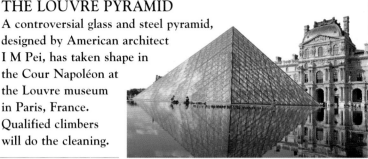

The earth moves in San Francisco

17 OCTOBER

A devastating earthquake today struck San Francisco, killing an estimated 90 people and causing billions of dollars worth of damage. The tremor, which erupted along the San Andreas Fault, lasted 15 seconds and measured 6.9 on the Richter Scale. Badly hit by the quake was the double-decker Interstate 880 highway which collapsed, crushing vehicles travelling on the lower road.

MAY–AUGUST

World Events	**MAY** The Czechoslovakian dissident Vaclav Havel is freed after four months in jail for inciting unrest.	**JUN** Iranian fundamentalist religious leader Ayatollah Khomeini dies in the capital Teheran aged 87.	**JUN** The Solidarity trade union achieves a landslide victory in elections to the parliament in Poland.	**JUL** South African president P W Botha makes a historic visit to Nelson Mandela, the jailed leader of the ANC.
Entertainment	**JUN** UK rock group Pink Floyd stage a spectacular £2 million show in the USSR.	**JUL** Prince's soundtrack album for the hit film *Batman* tops the music charts all around the world.	**JUL** London theatres dim their lights when the legendary UK actor Lord Laurence Olivier dies aged 82.	**JUL** US cyclist Greg LeMond wins the Tour de France in Paris, with an average speed of 54.4 km/h (34 mph).
Innovations	**MAY** NASA's *Magellan* space probe blasts off from the USA on its way to Venus.	**JUL** The large electron positron collider (LEP) is inaugurated at the CERN research centre in Switzerland.	**AUG** NASA's *Voyager 2* space probe sends back stunning pictures of Neptune's moon Triton.	**AUG** The first newspapers to be printed with non-rub ink are distributed by Associated Newspapers in the UK.

MOURNING THE AYATOLLAH

LAURENCE OLIVIER

1989

Gateway to the West is opened

10 NOVEMBER
Hundreds of thousands of East Berliners are flooding to the West after the hated Berlin Wall, which has divided the city for 28 years and has come to symbolize the Cold War, was finally opened. At the stroke of midnight, checkpoints were opened and swarms of people climbed up and over the wall, while others danced and celebrated on top. East German bulldozers are today opening new crossing-points.

Batman's sinister new look

31 DECEMBER
Comic book hero Batman celebrates his 50th birthday this year but he is still waging war on that arch-criminal, the Joker. His latest film, released by Warner Bros, puts a sinister new spin on the familiar story of good versus evil and has been an instant box-office hit. Starring Michael Keaton and Jack Nicholson, *Batman* has broken all box- office records in the United States and a sequel is planned.

Tyranny and terror end in Romania

31 DECEMBER
Romanians are tonight celebrating not only New Year's Eve but the sudden end of Nicolae Ceausescu's 24-year tyranny and rule of terror. A small protest in Timisoara two weeks ago escalated into full-scale and bloody civil war, with the army giving crucial support to the protesters. The dictator and his wife Elena were executed by firing squad on Christmas day after being found guilty of "crimes against the people" and an alleged 60,000 deaths. The Communist Party was abolished yesterday and free elections are planned.

Romanians celebrate a bright future

SEPTEMBER–DECEMBER

OCT In South Africa eight jailed nationalists, including anti-apartheid campaigner Walter Sisulu, are freed.

SEP Famous US song writer Irving Berlin, whose songs include *White Christmas*, dies aged 101.

OCT Archaeologists discover the remains of Shakespeare's Globe Theatre in London, UK.

WALTER SISULU

OCT A new Hungarian republic is declared, with a constitution that allows multi-party democracy.

OCT The Nobel Peace Prize is awarded to the Dalai Lama, the exiled spiritual leader of Tibet.

OCT A worldwide ban on trading in ivory is agreed at a convention in Switzerland.

OCT East German leader Erich Honecker is ousted by his own Communist Party and is replaced by Egon Krenz.

NOV Rudolf Nureyev dances with the Soviet Kirov Ballet for the first time since he defected to the West in 1961.

OCT NASA's space probe *Galileo* blasts off from Cape Canaveral, USA, at the start of a six-year journey to Jupiter.

ERICH HONECKER

DEC Czechoslovakia's Vaclav Havel is elected as the country's first non-communist president for 41 years.

NOV Romanian gymnast and Olympic gold medallist Nadia Comaneci seeks political asylum in Hungary.

DEC The 16,300-km (10,188-mile) national highway round the coast of Australia is completed after 15 years.

THE END OF THE COLD WAR

AFTER THE SOVIET UNION exploded its first atom bomb in 1949, the two world superpowers, the Soviet Union and the United States, began a nuclear arms race, known as the Cold War, that continued for over 40 years. Relations between the superpowers only began to improve when Mikhail Gorbachev came to power in the Soviet Union. In 1987, Gorbachev and US president Ronald Reagan agreed to dismantle their missiles. By the end of the decade, the Soviet Union had withdrawn its troops from Afghanistan and had begun to reduce its military force in eastern Europe. At home, Gorbachev and his policies of reform were not so popular and led, ultimately, to the break-up of the Soviet Union.

Soviet propaganda

During the Cold War both the Soviet Union and the United States used propaganda including films, books, magazines, and posters to discredit one another and to fuel public fear. This 1952 anti-US cartoon appeared in a Soviet magazine and satirized the United States' use of nerve gas. It shows huge rockets firing diseases such as typhus and cholera.

The arms race

By the end of the Cold War each side had enough nuclear weapons to destroy the world many times over. The first hydrogen bomb, tested in 1952, was as powerful as all the bombs dropped on Germany and Japan during World War II. During the following decades, nuclear bombs dropped by aircraft were joined by unmanned intercontinental ballistic missiles (ICBMs), multiple warhead missiles (MIRVs), and ground-hugging cruise missiles.

The fall of the Berlin Wall

In 1989, as Hungary transformed itself from a communist state into a multi-party democracy and opened its borders, the first East Germans were able to escape from communist oppression to a new life in the West. Meanwhile, there were mass demonstrations in cities all over East Germany and the hard-line communist government resigned. An estimated one million protestors marched through the streets of east Berlin. In November, bulldozers moved in and the Berlin Wall was torn down. For the first time since 1961, when the Wall was built, east Berliners could pass freely into west Berlin. In the following weeks hundreds of thousands of people poured across the border.

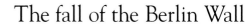

Crowds gather as the Berlin Wall is torn down

Toppling communism

In 1989 the Iron Curtain that divided Europe for more than forty years was lifted. National, ethnic, and religious unrest, suppressed for decades, erupted in the Soviet Union. People took to the streets, demanding freedom. The Baltic republics of Lithuania, Latvia, and Estonia led the way, declaring independence from Moscow. Pro-freedom movements also gathered force in the Soviet satellite states in eastern Europe. By the end of the year communism had been toppled in Hungary, Czechoslovakia, East Germany, Bulgaria, and Romania.

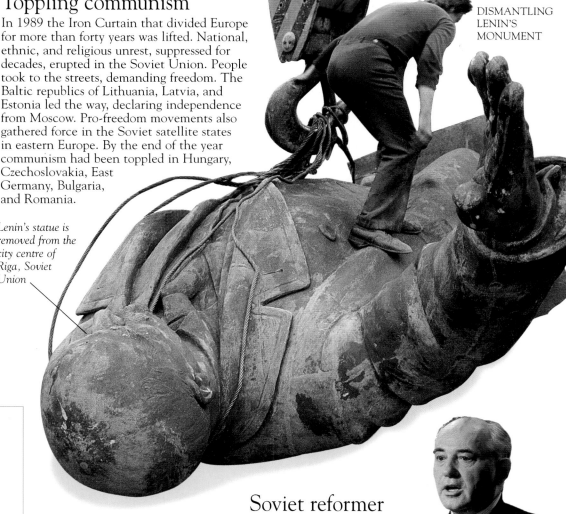

DISMANTLING LENIN'S MONUMENT

Lenin's statue is removed from the city centre of Riga, Soviet Union

Film mirrors life

Stanley Kubrick made *Dr Strangelove* as early as 1963, a year after Soviet missile bases had been installed in Cuba and the world had teetered on the brink of nuclear war. The film satirizes the insane logic of the nuclear arms race and the doctrine of deterrence known as Mutually Assured Destruction (MAD).

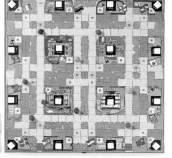

Only a game?

Suspicion thrived during the nuclear arms race, with espionage playing a vital role. Spies were used to find out what the other side was doing – and to catch enemy agents at home. If caught, they were often executed or jailed. This *Spy Ring* game (1965) is set in the fictional city of Espiona and players must gather as many secrets as they can.

Soviet reformer

Mikhail Gorbachev was 54 when he became secretary general of the Soviet Communist Party in 1985. His task was daunting – an economy bankrupted by the nuclear arms race and a government riddled with corruption. He embarked on a programme of reforms, launching a new era of freedom in the Soviet Union. He promised "perestroika", a major reconstruction of the Soviet state, and "glasnost", a new policy of openness. Within months of taking office, he was proposing drastic reductions in nuclear arms.

Food queues

Although Gorbachev won instant popularity in the West for his nuclear arms agreement, domestic politics proved more problematic. His programme of economic reforms made the price of bread, meat, and some other products rocket. There was an immediate increase in food shortages and a fall in living standards.

March for peace

Growing revolt against the communist government in Poland gave birth to the independent trade union, Solidarity, in 1980. Led by Lech Walesa, an electrician, it had huge popular support, organizing a series of workers' strikes, and bringing the country to a standstill. In 1981, the government banned Solidarity, which led to a decade of confrontation until 1989 when the ban was lifted. As the Soviet Union disintegrated, Solidarity swept to power, and in 1990 Lech Walesa was elected president.

279

1990

Mandela's first taste of freedom

11 FEBRUARY
After 27 years in prison, South African black leader Nelson Mandela is at last a free man. His release comes just one week after President F W de Klerk lifted the ban on the African National Congress (ANC), an organization that has led the black struggle against apartheid. A jubilant crowd of 2,000 supporters greeted Mandela as he left Victor Verster prison, and another 50,000 waited to welcome him in Cape Town. The campaign to free Nelson Mandela has been very much at the centre of the anti-apartheid movement and Mandela paid tribute to everyone involved in the campaign. He also made clear his continued support for the ANC and his commitment to the fight against apartheid in South Africa.

MUTANT TURTLES
Turtle-mania has taken off with the arrival of a film starring the *Teenage Mutant Ninja Turtles* cartoon heroes. The four turtles enjoy eating pizza and fighting crime.

A jubilant Nelson Mandela

NASA keeps an eye on the stars

Hubble Space Telescope

24 APRIL
NASA's long-awaited $1.5 million, 12.5-tonne Hubble Space Telescope today finally blasted off from Cape Canaveral in the United States on board the space shuttle *Discovery*. Tomorrow, with the help of a 15-m (49-ft) mechanical arm, it will be put into orbit 595 km (372 miles) above the Earth. Named after US astronomer Edwin Hubble, the telescope will probe the furthest reaches of the universe and has been described as the greatest advance in astronomy since Galileo.

JANUARY–APRIL

World Events	**JAN** In Panama, General Noriega surrenders to US authorities and is charged with drug trafficking.	**FEB** The central committee of the USSR Communist Party votes to end the party's monopoly on power.	**FEB** The Sandinista government in Nicaragua concedes victory in an election to a US-backed coalition.	**MAR** In the Australian general election, the ruling Labour Party, which is led by Bob Hawke, is returned for a fourth term.
Entertainment	**JAN** US boy band New Kids On The Block top the pop charts on both sides of the Atlantic.	**JAN** US tennis player John McEnroe is kicked out of the Australian Open contest for bad behaviour.	**JAN** A UK man is fined for refusing to remove a 8-m (26-ft) high fibreglass shark from the roof of his house.	**FEB** New Zealander Richard Hadlee becomes the first cricketer to take an incredible 400 test wickets.
Innovations	**JAN** US shuttle astronauts rescue a damaged space lab and bring it to Earth.	**JAN** A worldwide ban on ivory trading comes into effect to protect elephants from dying out.	**JAN** Japan launches the first space probe to be sent to the Moon for 14 years.	**APR** Four asteroids discovered in 1982 and 1983 are named after Sixties' pop group The Beatles.

GENERAL NORIEGA

SHARK ADDITION TO HOUSE IN THE UK

1990

Double murder shocks the world

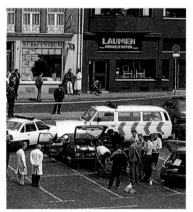

28 MAY
The Irish Republican Army (IRA) has admitted responsibility for the murder of two Australian lawyers in the Dutch town of Roermond. The two men were mistaken for British servicemen and were gunned down in the main square as they got out of their British-registered cars to take photographs.

BSE leads to worldwide beef ban

31 MAY
France has today followed Austria, West Germany, the Soviet Union, and 14 other nations in banning all imports of beef and live cattle from Britain. This follows public fears that BSE (bovine spongiform encephalopathy), or "mad cow disease", which has spread rapidly through British cattle, can be passed on in a deadly form to humans.

Saddam's sick show

Saddam Hussein with a young hostage

Hussein offered a formal peace treaty to Iraq's arch-enemy Iran in order to concentrate his forces against the international troops that are gathering in Saudi Arabia, which borders Kuwait.

23 AUGUST
Iraqi leader Saddam Hussein continues to thumb his nose at Western powers after invading and annexing the tiny oil-rich Gulf state of Kuwait earlier this month. Today he paraded American and British hostages on television in a grotesque attempt to reassure the world of their well-being. Hundreds of Westerners were taken from Kuwait and detained in Baghdad, the Iraqi capital, after the invasion. They are being held as pawns, their lives in immediate danger if the West takes any military action against Iraq in retaliation for the invasion of Kuwait. Last week, after ten years of conflict, Saddam

Iraqi man shows his support for Saddam Hussein

MAY–AUGUST

MAY Anti-communist demonstrations disrupt the USSR's May Day parade that is held each year in Moscow.

MAY Ion Iliescu and the National Salvation Front triumph in the first free elections to be held in Romania since 1937.

JUN In Algeria, the fundamentalist Islamic Salvation Front wins control of municipal and provincial assemblies.

AUG After holding them for seven days, Saddam Hussein of Iraq frees all Western women and children hostages.

JUL Czech-born US tennis player Martina Navratilova wins a record ninth Wimbledon singles' title.

JUL In the soccer World Cup West Germany beat Argentina 1–0 in the final in Italy.

JUL Opera tenors José Carreras, Placido Domingo, and Luciano Pavarotti sing together in Italy.

JUL UK rock group Pink Floyd perform a free, open-air version of *The Wall* in Berlin, Germany.

MAY Robert Maxwell's new newspaper *The European* is launched throughout Europe.

WEST GERMANY WIN THE WORLD CUP

MAY Home-produced beef is banned in UK schools as concern over BSE grows.

JUN Disney's *Dick Tracy*, the first film to be made in digital sound, is released in the USA.

PERFORMANCE OF THE WALL IN BERLIN

JUL Japanese company Sony produce the revolutionary Data Discman, an electronic book.

1990

Germany reunited

3 OCTOBER

Bells are pealing and flags are flying as the people of East and West Germany are reunited after 45 years of division. Germany was divided in two in 1949. Although reunification seemed inevitable after the collapse of the Soviet Union, the pace of change has been amazing. An economic integration between the two countries has already taken place and NATO membership for a unified Germany guaranteed. However, whether a relatively wealthy West Germany will be able to afford to absorb the bankrupt East Germany remains to be seen.

New Irish president

7 NOVEMBER

Leaders of the main political parties in the Republic of Ireland are in a state of shock after 46-year-old Mary Robinson, standing as an independent candidate, is elected president. A lawyer and civil rights campaigner, she is the first woman to hold the office. She says she will speak up for society's disadvantaged.

Akihito tries out heavenly throne

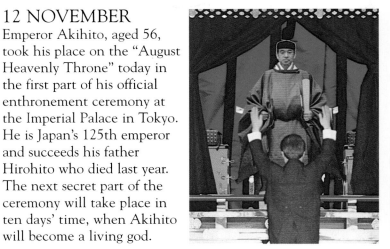

12 NOVEMBER

Emperor Akihito, aged 56, took his place on the "August Heavenly Throne" today in the first part of his official enthronement ceremony at the Imperial Palace in Tokyo. He is Japan's 125th emperor and succeeds his father Hirohito who died last year. The next secret part of the ceremony will take place in ten days' time, when Akihito will become a living god.

Poles get to go to the polls

9 DECEMBER

In the wake of the collapse of communism in Eastern bloc countries, shipyard worker Lech Walesa today won a historic landslide presidential election victory in Poland.

Ten years ago he spearheaded resistance to the communist regime by forming Solidarity, a free trade union, in Gdansk. He gained a huge following and has long been regarded as the country's natural leader.

SEPTEMBER–DECEMBER

	World Events			
World Events	**NOV** John Major becomes the new UK prime minister after Margaret Thatcher is forced to resign.	**NOV** The United Nations sets a deadline for Iraq to withdraw its troops from Kuwait before force is used.	**DEC** UK and French tunnellers break through and shake hands 30 m (98 ft) under the Channel after three years of digging.	**DEC** Socialist Party leader Slobodan Milosovic is elected president in Serbia's first free elections for 50 years.
Entertainment	**NOV** Record-breaking UK cricketer Sir Leonard Hutton dies aged 74.	**NOV** Child actor Macauley Culkin stars in US box office smash hit comedy film *Home Alone*.	**NOV** Best-selling UK author Roald Dahl, famous for his children's stories, dies aged 74.	**DEC** Mexican writer Octavio Paz is named winner of the Nobel Prize for Literature.
Innovations	**SEP** The Pope consecrates the world's biggest church on the Ivory Coast.	**OCT** European space probe *Ulysses* blasts off from the USA on a five-year journey to the Sun.	**NOV** Swiss solar car *Spirit of Biel* wins the world solar challenge in Australia.	**DEC** Toyohiro Akiyama from Japan is the first fare-paying passenger in space.

MACAULEY CULKIN
IN *HOME ALONE*

CHANNEL TUNNEL
BREAKTHROUGH

1991

Dust settles in desert

28 FEBRUARY
The war in the Gulf is today at an end and Kuwait has been liberated. After a month of intensive air attacks against Iraq, the huge international forces that had gathered in Saudi Arabia crossed the border into Iraq and Kuwait to begin a four-day land battle to force the Iraqi army to flee the small Gulf kingdom. The people of Kuwait are now celebrating their liberation after nearly seven months of brutal Iraqi occupation. The capital Kuwait City is left without power, however, and the sun is blotted out by thick black smoke pouring from burning oil wells set on fire by Iraqi soldiers as they were forced to retreat.

Kuwaiti children greet their liberators

Famine hits and Sudan starves

30 MARCH
Relief workers are working round the clock as famine sweeps a huge area of the Sudan, putting an estimated seven million lives at risk.

Nobody knows how many people have died since the harvest failed last November. Tragically, the catastrophe was foreseen by aid agencies but Sudan's military regime rejected offers of help.

KARAOKE FOR KIDS
Tape recorders are now being designed specially for children. This one comes complete with a microphone so that children can have a crack at karaoke.

JANUARY–APRIL

JAN Abu Iyad (Salah Khalaf), the deputy leader of the Palestinian Liberation Organization, is assassinated.

JAN Richard Branson and Per Lindstrand cross the Pacific in a hot-air balloon.

FEB Soviet space station *Salyut 7* re-enters the Earth's atmosphere and crash lands.

COLIN POWELL AND NORMAN SCHWARZKOPF

FEB US generals Powell and Schwarzkopf lead troops in Operation *Desert Storm* to liberate Kuwait from Iraq.

FEB UK prima ballerina Dame Margot Fonteyn dies in Panama aged 71.

FEB Helen Sharman is chosen to be the first UK citizen to go into space.

MAR Prime Minister Guilio Andreotti announces that Italy's 49th postwar government is to resign.

MAR Kevin Costner's US film *Dances With Wolves* wins seven Acadamy Awards.

MAR US fast-food chain McDonald's launches a new low-fat hamburger called the McLean.

FIRST WOMEN'S RUGBY WORLD CUP

APR European Community foreign ministers meet in Strasbourg, France, and agree to end sanctions against South Africa.

APR The USA wins the first women's rugby world cup in the UK.

MAR Soviet space station *Mir* comes within 19 km (12 miles) of colliding with a cargo craft.

1991

Cyclone devastates Bangladesh

3 MAY

At least 125,000 people have died and ten million are homeless after a 233 km/h (145 mph) cyclone hit Bangladesh three days ago. The low-lying area around the delta of the Ganges river, home to millions of subsistence farmers, has been completely devastated by the disaster. Each day more corpses are washed ashore and the beaches of Chittagong, the main port in the Bay of Bengal, are littered with swollen and decomposing corpses.

Hostage released after 1,934 days

8 AUGUST

British journalist John McCarthy received an ecstatic welcome when he arrived home today after being held hostage in Lebanon by Islamic Jihad for five years and three months. With him he brings a letter from his captors to UN secretary general Javier Pérez de Cuellar, and the news that fellow American and British hostages are in good shape.

Yeltsin to the rescue

21 AUGUST

A dramatic coup mounted in Moscow by communist hardliners two days ago has failed. It was a last desperate attempt to reassert the power of the Communist Party and to topple Soviet premier Mikhail Gorbachev, who was placed under house arrest in the Crimea. Hero of the day was the president of the Russian Republic Boris Yeltsin, who rallied huge popular support after climbing on a tank near the Russian parliament to denounce the coup.

A Soviet army lieutenant holds the white flag of surrender

MAY–AUGUST

World Events	**MAY** More than 60 people die in street battles in South Africa's black townships.	**MAY** Indian prime minister Rajiv Gandhi is assassinated by a suicide bomber during a national election rally near Madras.	**JUN** Slovenia and Croatia declare independence from the communist Yugoslavian federation of republics.	**JUN** Sixty-year-old Boris Yeltsin wins Russia's first free elections, defeating official communist candidates.
Entertainment	**MAY** Sweden wins the Eurovision Song Contest in Rome, Italy.	**MAY** A pop concert in the UK raises £57 million in aid of Kurdish refugees.	**JUN** *Terminator 2: Judgment Day*, starring Arnold Schwarzenegger and with new special effects, is a smash hit in the USA.	**AUG** At the Tokyo athletics championships in Japan, US long-jumper Mike Powell sets a new world record of 8.95 m (29.36 ft).
Innovations	**MAY** Sony demonstrate the digital sound of the mini disc in Japan.	**JUN** A treaty declares Antarctica to be a "continent for peace and science".	**JUL** Thousands of people arrive in Hawaii, USA, to watch a total solar eclipse which lasts for four minutes.	**JUL** The European Remote Sensing satellite (ERS-1), Europe's first environmental satellite, goes into orbit.

RAJIV GANDHI'S FUNERAL

TERMINATOR 2: JUDGMENT DAY

1991

Soviet Union crumbles

31 AUGUST
Soviet premier Mikhail Gorbachev, badly betrayed by some of his closest allies in the failed coup two weeks ago, is struggling to hold on to power in Moscow. Fourteen leading communists have been charged with treason and await trial in prison. They include his deputy Gennady Yanayev, KGB chief Vladimir Kryuchkov, and defence minister Dmitri Yazov. Meanwhile, seven republics, including Russia and the Ukraine, have joined the three Baltic states of Lithuania, Estonia, and Latvia in declaring independence.

Yeltsin declares Russia's independence

Dubrovnik under Serb siege

26 OCTOBER
Croatian towns along the Adriatic coast are being heavily bombarded by the Serb-dominated Yugoslav army. The army moved into Croatia four months ago after the republic, together with Slovenia, declared independence from the communist Yugoslav federation. Black smoke is rising from Dubrovnik, the "pearl of the Adriatic", which has been shelled mercilessly and is now completely besieged. Designated a "world heritage site", its unique Venetian architecture and baroque churches are at risk, as are its 50,000 inhabitants, who have been without electricity or water for weeks. A naval blockade is now preventing any supplies from getting through. With ancient ethnic hatreds boiling over, it seems increasingly likely that a bitter war will engulf the whole region.

SEPTEMBER–DECEMBER

OCT Burmese opposition leader Aung Suu Kyi, who is under house arrest, is awarded the Nobel Peace Prize.

SEP Exiled Soviet Nobel prize winner Alexander Solzhenitsyn is officially cleared of treason in the USSR.

SEP *The Big Issue*, a new magazine sold by homeless people in aid of the homeless, goes on sale in London, UK.

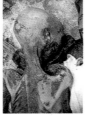

TYROLEAN HUNTER

NOV UK publishing tycoon Robert Maxwell falls off his yacht and drowns near the Canary Islands.

OCT Canadian singer Bryan Adams has a record-breaking hit with the song *Everything I Do, I Do It For You*.

SEP The almost-intact body of a 4,000-year old prehistoric hunter is found in the Tyrolean Alps, Austria.

DEC European Community heads of government meet in Maastricht, Holland, to agree a treaty on closer economic union.

NOV UK rock star Freddie Mercury, the lead singer of popular group Queen, dies of AIDS in London aged 45.

SEP Eight people are sealed inside the giant *Biosphere II* greenhouse in the USA for a two-year experiment.

FREDDIE MERCURY

DEC Mikhail Gorbachev resigns as premier of the USSR, which is replaced by a Russian Federation.

DEC Fifteen-year-old Judit Polgar from Hungary becomes the world's youngest ever chess grandmaster.

OCT A joint UK-Australian team makes the first flight over Mount Everest in a hot-air balloon.

1992

Croatian soldier burns Serbian flag

Independence recognized

15 JANUARY

Slovenia and Croatia, who simultaneously declared independence from Yugoslavia in June last year, have both won recognition from the European Community. The Yugoslav federation once consisted of six republics but is now disintegrating. Macedonia also declared independence last September and it seems likely that the ethnically mixed republic of Bosnia and Hercegovina will follow suit. There has been much fighting between the Serb-dominated federal army and the breakaway republics.

Race riots rock LA

2 MAY

The United States city of Los Angeles is today recovering after the worst race riots this century left 58 people dead and thousands injured. Simmering racial tensions exploded when, despite video evidence, an all-white jury acquitted four white policemen of savagely beating Rodney King, a young black motorist. The black community was stunned by the verdict and two days of violence followed, with an orgy of looting, murder, and rioting throughout the mainly black neighbourhood of South Central. Several whites and Koreans have been beaten to death, and hundreds of buildings were set on fire. The army has been called in and 5,000 soldiers and marines are now on standby just outside the city. A dusk-to-dawn curfew has also been introduced.

VATICAN ADMITS GALILEO RIGHT

After 359 years the Vatican has finally admitted formally that the great 17th-century Italian astronomer Galileo Galilei was right when he argued that the Earth orbits the Sun. In 1633, Galileo was forced to renounce his doctrine by the Inquisition.

Soldiers look on as rioters burn down shops

World Events

JAN Boutros Boutros Ghali of Egypt takes over the post of secretary general of the United Nations.

APR Betty Boothroyd is the first ever woman to become speaker of the UK's House of Commons.

JUN In a national referendum, Danish voters reject the Maastricht Treaty by voting against closer European political union.

JUN A steel corset is tightened around the Leaning Tower of Pisa in Italy, which is slowly sinking each year.

Entertainment

JAN Paul Simon becomes the first US star to perform in sanction-free South Africa.

FEB Film star Elizabeth Taylor celebrates her 60th birthday at Sleeping Beauty's Castle in Disneyland, USA.

APR Costing £6.4 million, the massive Euro Disney amusement park opens on the outskirts of Paris, France.

MAY Legendary film star Marlene Dietrich dies in her apartment in Paris, France, aged 91.

Innovations

JAN Japan launches a 285-tonne ship, *Yamoto One*, run on superconducting magnets.

BETTY BOOTHROYD

FEB On the 517th birthday of its namesake, the computer virus Michelangelo infects IBM computers.

FEB The USA and the UK promise to phase out CFCs by 1995 – five years earlier than planned.

THE LEANING TOWER OF PISA

MAR Russian cosmonaut Sergei Krikalyev returns to Earth after ten months in the *Mir* space station.

1992

Earth summit opens

3 JUNE
Representatives of 178 governments around the world have arrived in Rio de Janeiro, Brazil, for the opening of the United Nations Conference on Environment and Development. It is the largest United Nations conference ever held, reflecting the growing concern worldwide for "green" issues. A special "Tree of Life" will be on display, covered in leaf-shaped pledges from people all round the world who have promised to take action personally.

Celebrations in Rio as the summit opens

Monetary crisis causes chaos

16 SEPTEMBER
Shock waves shot through the world's money markets today after Britain withdrew from the Exchange Rate Mechanism (ERM). The ERM links the currencies of 12 European countries. It was created to stabilize exchange rates in preparation for a European central bank and a single currency.

Britain's withdrawal has caused a rift with Germany, whose economic policies are being blamed.

A right royal "Annus horribilis"

9 DECEMBER
After months of mounting rumours Buckingham Palace, the home of the British royal family, today announced that the Prince and Princess of Wales are to separate after 11 years of marriage. In a year of two royal separations and a divorce, as well as a damaging fire at Windsor Castle, it is no wonder that the queen is describing 1992 as an "Annus horribilis" for the royals.

Horrors of Serbian death camps

15 AUGUST
Horrifying television pictures of Serbian prison camps have caused shock and outrage. They show starving and emaciated victims of "ethnic cleansing", a policy that has been used extensively since the Yugoslav civil war erupted. Most of the death camps are in the ethnically diverse republic of Bosnia. Huge numbers of innocent civilians have been rounded up and forcibly moved from their homes as ethnic groups attempt to "cleanse" areas of people from different origin.

Charles and Diana split up

JULY–DECEMBER

OCT Huge demonstrations are held in Germany protesting against the extreme racist violence sweeping the country.

OCT Demonstrations are held all over Latin America to mark the 500th anniversary of the arrival of Christopher Columbus.

NOV Democrat candidate 46-year-old Bill Clinton of Arkansas is elected to be the 42nd president of the USA.

DEC A devastating earthquake in Indonesia kills 1,500 people and leaves many more homeless.

JUL 10,000 competitors from 172 countries take part in the Barcelona Olympics in Spain.

OCT Poet and dramatist Derek Walcott becomes the first Caribbean writer to win the Nobel Prize for Literature.

OCT US country artist Garth Brooks has a record four albums in the US top 20 chart at the same time.

OCT Agatha Christie's West End hit show *The Mousetrap* celebrates its 40th anniversary in London, UK.

JUL *Columbia* lands after the longest-ever US shuttle mission, lasting a total of 14 days.

POET AND DRAMATIST DEREK WALCOTT

SEP Twelve European countries agree to an unconditional ban on dumping waste at sea.

OCT The hole in the ozone layer stretches over the coast of South America for the first time.

BILL AND HILLARY CLINTON

DEC Virtual reality is developed by the US Spectrum Holobyte company as a 3-D video game.

1993

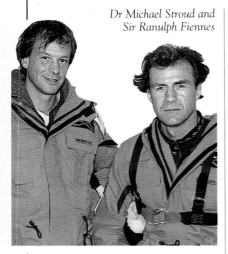

Dr Michael Stroud and Sir Ranulph Fiennes

Ice walk ends

12 FEBRUARY

British explorers Sir Ranulph Fiennes and Dr Michael Stroud have today completed the first unsupported crossing of the Antarctic ice shelf. Their epic 2,164-km (1,352-mile) journey started last November. They used cross-country skis and sleds to carry food and equipment, sometimes walking up to 13 hours a day across the frozen wastes. The last stage of their record-breaking trek had to be abandoned, however, because Fiennes and Stroud were suffering from frostbite, infected feet, severe weight loss, and equipment failure. The Antarctic walk was undertaken to raise money for a number of charities.

Trade Center blast

26 FEBRUARY

New York ground to a halt at lunchtime today after a bomb exploded in the underground car park beneath the twin towers of the World Trade Center. Five people were killed and hundreds more are injured. Smoke billowed up to the 96th floor of the 110-storey skyscraper as firefighters struggled for two hours to bring the blaze under control. Some people had to be rescued by helicopter from the top of the building. This is the first time there has been a terrorist bombing attack on American soil and it has shocked the whole nation. Police suspect the device was planted by Muslim fundamentalists angry at the United States' policy in the Middle East. It is fortunate that so few lost their lives in the explosion. At least 55,000 people work in the Trade Center, which also attracts 80,000 visitors daily.

HAPPY BIRTHDAY HARLEY!

It is 90 years since the first Harley-Davidson "hog" was made and as part of the celebrations the world's biggest Harley has been built. Weighing 4 tonnes, the Harley seats six and boasts an on-board jacuzzi.

JANUARY–JUNE

World Events	**MAR** Chinese president Jiang Zemin amends the constitution to include a "socialist market economy".	**APR** Chris Hani, black rights hero and head of the Communist Party in South Africa, is assassinated outside his Johannesburg home.	**APR** Eighty-five members of a cult in the USA die in a self-inflicted blaze after a 51-day siege of their Waco compound.	**APR** UN sanctions against Serbia come into force after the Bosnian-Serb parliament rejects a peace plan.
Entertainment	**APR** The UK's Grand National horse race is declared null and void after three false starts.	**APR** A record 79-day circumnavigation of the globe in a catamaran is completed by French yachtsman Bruno Peyron.	**JUN** Steven Spielberg's hit US dinosaur film *Jurassic Park* takes $81.7 million at the box office in its first week.	**JUN** Australian Damian Taylor beats seven women to win Queensland's Miss Wintersun Queen contest.
Innovations	**JAN** Two astronauts make a record 5-hour space walk from the US space shuttle *Endeavour*.	**JAN** Norwegian Erling Kagge is the first person to complete a solo trek on foot to the South Pole.	**MAR** Barbara Harmer from the UK becomes *Concorde's* first woman pilot on a British Airways flight.	**MAY** The first long-lasting perfume, *Shiseido* Eau de Cologne, is launched in Japan; it takes nine hours to fade.

BRUNO PEYRON

JURASSIC PARK

1993

Arafat and Rabin shake hands with Clinton looking on

Yeltsin sends in the tanks

4 OCTOBER

Moscow's besieged parliament is pockmarked with tank shells and blackened with smoke after the Russian army moved in to crush a rebellion organized by die-hard communists against President Boris Yeltsin. Fierce fighting raged inside the building before the rebellion leaders were forced to surrender.

The Russian parliament blackened by smoke

Rabin and Arafat sign peace accord

13 SEPTEMBER

Israeli prime minister Yitzhak Rabin hesitated for a split second before shaking hands with Yassir Arafat, the leader of the Palestinian Liberation Organization (PLO). This historic moment in the long, troubled search for peace in the Middle East took place outside the White House in Washington DC with United States president Bill Clinton looking on. The handshake cements an agreement signed by Israel and the PLO which will immediately give limited self-rule to Palestinians living in Gaza, Jericho, and some parts of the West Bank. Israel will withdraw its forces from Gaza and Jericho in December and the territories will be run by a Palestinian Council to be elected next July. A permanent peace accord is, of course, the ultimate goal, but already extremists on both sides are condemning the agreement and threatening renewed violence. It seems likely that more blood will be spilt in the troubled Middle East.

The road to peace in Ireland

15 DECEMBER

A historic declaration setting out principles for peace talks on Northern Ireland was signed today by British and Irish prime ministers, John Major and Albert Reynolds. It paves the way for Sinn Féin, the political wing of the Irish Republican Army (IRA), to join talks about the future of Northern Ireland.

Young boy on the divided streets of Belfast

JULY–DECEMBER

OCT The Nobel Peace Prize is awarded jointly to ANC president Nelson Mandela and South African president F W de Klerk.

OCT Benazir Bhutto, who was ousted from power three years ago, is sworn in as prime minister of Pakistan for a second term.

NOV The Maastricht Treaty finally comes into force and the European Community is renamed the European Union.

DEC Aboriginals in Australia win the right to claim land lost to European colonizers more than 200 years ago.

AUG Jacqui Mofokeng is the first black woman ever to be crowned Miss South Africa.

SEP US rapper Snoop Doggy Dogg is arrested on a murder charge at the MTV Music Awards.

SEP Nourredine Morceli from Algeria sets a new world record for running the mile.

SEP International Olympic Committee awards the year 2000 games to Australia.

AUG The Grand Hassan II Mosque in Morocco, which has a 175-m (574-ft) minaret, is dedicated.

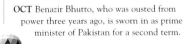

BIOSPHERE

SEP Eight people emerge at the end of a two-year US experiment living in a self-sufficient "Biosphere".

DEC The first voice-operated TV/radio remote control is launched worldwide.

ABORIGINALS WIN LAND RIGHTS

DEC The first passenger trains travel through the Channel Tunnel.

1978 THE FIRST PHONE CARD IS INTRODUCED IN PARIS, FRANCE

1979 THE WORLD'S FIRST SATELLITE PHONE IS LAUNCHED

1985 MOBILE PHONES ARE LAUNCHED IN EUROPE

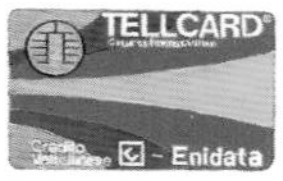

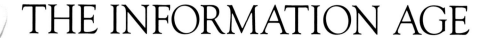

THE INFORMATION AGE

TECHNOLOGY HAS REVOLUTIONIZED every aspect of life in the Nineties. Home computers, videophones, virtual reality, and robots with artificial intelligence were once science-fiction, but are now a reality. Mobile phones, fax machines, and electronic mail enable us to keep in touch wherever we are. At the cutting edge of the information revolution, the "world wide web" acts as a global encyclopedia, allowing people from all over the world to send information and tap into information resources. Huge quantities of facts and figures are shifted around the planet in seconds, turning the world into a technological "global village".

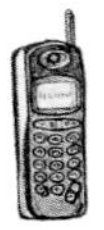

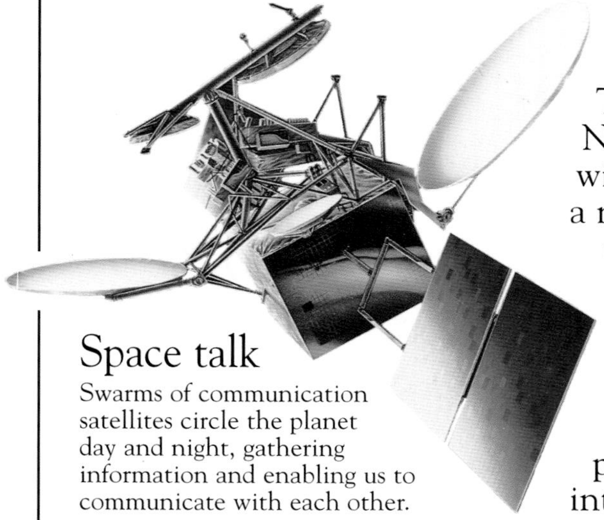

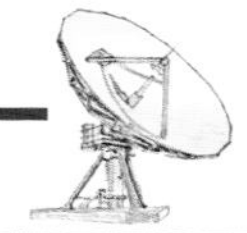

Space talk

Swarms of communication satellites circle the planet day and night, gathering information and enabling us to communicate with each other.

Electronic money

The introduction of an experimental "smartcard" may eventually lead to a cashless society. The card has a tiny microchip embedded in its plastic surface which stores money electronically, making notes and coins redundant.

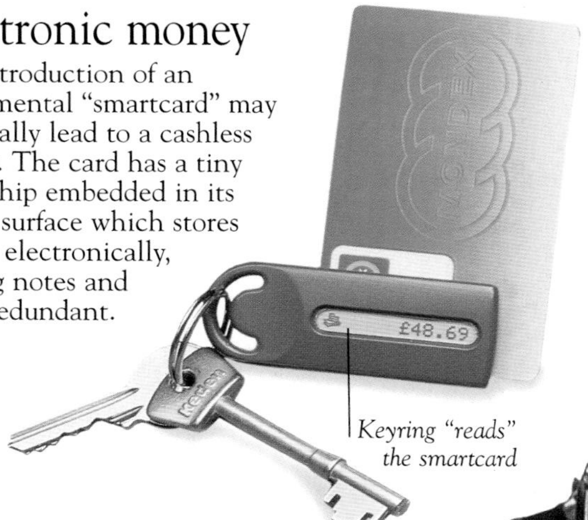

Keyring "reads" the smartcard

Computer design

Using the latest microchips, industry can accurately design and plan buildings, cars, and machine parts using computers. Computer-aided design (CAD) has become increasingly flexible and sophisticated. This screen display shows the pressures exerted on parts of a jet engine used in aviation.

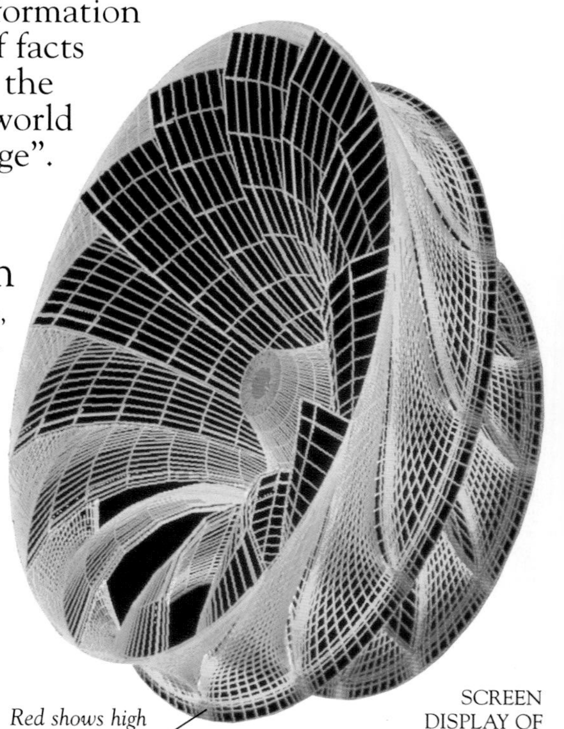

Red shows high pressure areas

SCREEN DISPLAY OF A JET ENGINE

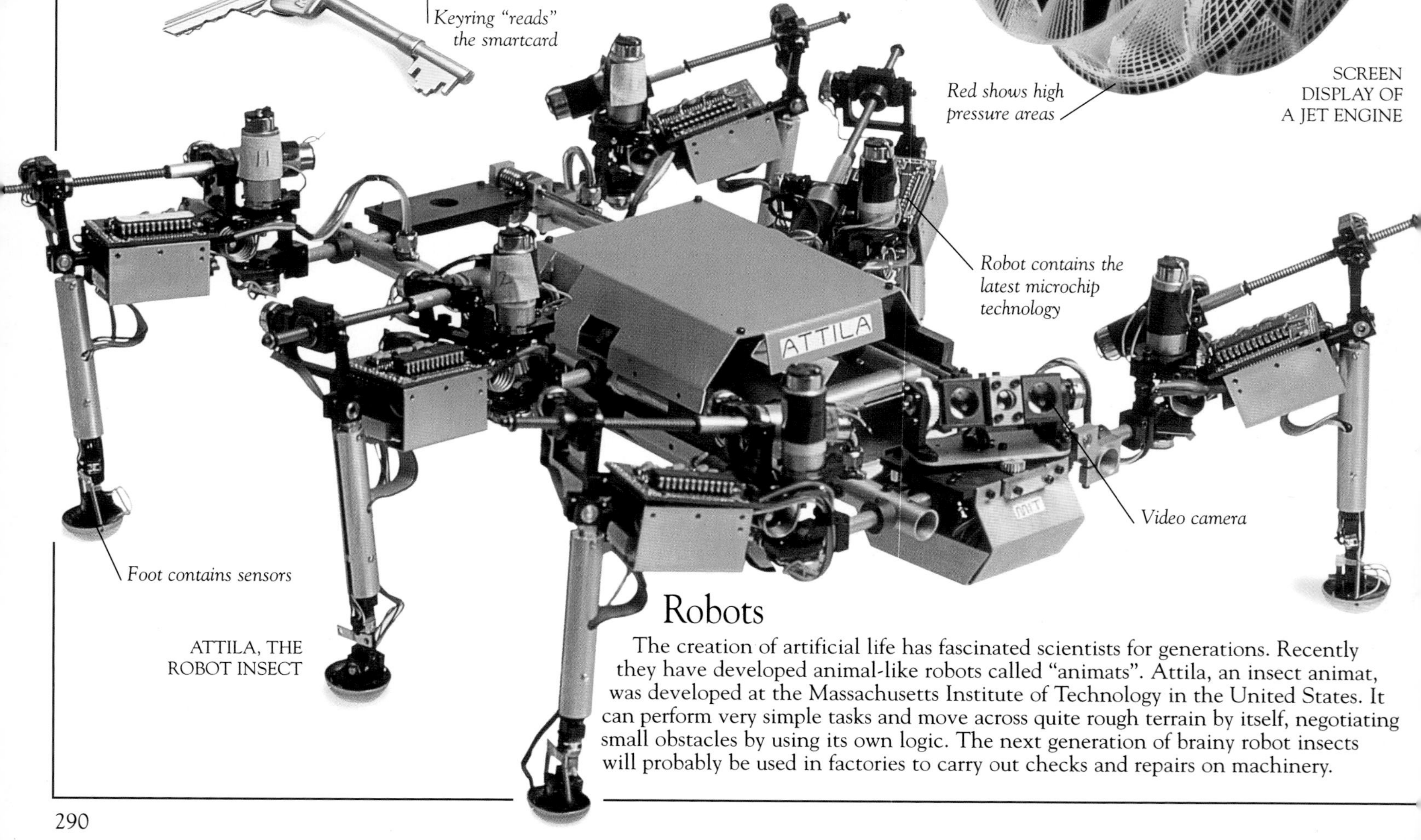

Robot contains the latest microchip technology

Video camera

Foot contains sensors

ATTILA, THE ROBOT INSECT

Robots

The creation of artificial life has fascinated scientists for generations. Recently they have developed animal-like robots called "animats". Attila, an insect animat, was developed at the Massachusetts Institute of Technology in the United States. It can perform very simple tasks and move across quite rough terrain by itself, negotiating small obstacles by using its own logic. The next generation of brainy robot insects will probably be used in factories to carry out checks and repairs on machinery.

Computer-sensitive

Scientists have developed a new electronic "NOSE" (Neotronics Olfactory Sensing Equipment) which uses tiny sensors fitted to a silicon chip to imitate the workings of a human nose. It is independent, objective, and never catches a cold. It can distinguish a good wine from a fake and might eventually replace humans in testing food, drinks, and fragrances.

NEOTRONICS OLFACTORY SENSING EQUIPMENT ("NOSE")

Polymer sensor to detect odours

Techno-movie

The smash hit of 1996, *Toy Story*, was the first film to be created entirely on computer. Made by Pixar Animation Studios, it used the latest technical wizardry to create amazing effects and realistic detail. Despite being computer-generated heroes, Woody and Buzz Lightyear delighted the most cynical of movie-goers, becoming the year's most sought-after Christmas toys.

VIRTUAL REALITY SET

Player wears head set

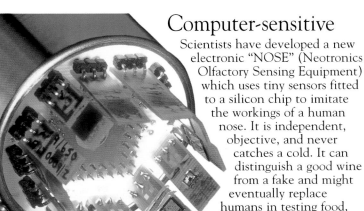

A VIRTUAL VIEW OF THE IMAGINARY 3-D *CITY OF GIOTTO*, BASED ON GIOTTO'S 14-CENTURY PAINTINGS

Data glove

Virtual reality

Special headsets and gloves whisk players off to another world in the latest virtual reality computer games. The headset contains two miniature television screens for 3-D stereo vision, and headphones for stereo sound. It also contains a sensor that allows the computer to calculate the direction of sight and what the player can see. The "data glove" and joystick allow the player to control the game. However, virtual reality is not only being used for exciting computer games. "Virtual tourism" will soon enable you to travel the world without leaving your home, and medical and military uses are being researched and developed.

1994

Carnage in Sarajevo central market

5 FEBRUARY

A deadly attack on the central market in Sarajevo, Bosnia, has left 68 innocent civilians dead and nearly 200 others seriously wounded. A single mortar bomb landed without warning in the middle of the busy market, crowded with weekend shoppers queuing for food. The UN peacekeeping forces in Bosnia, who were sent into the region in 1992 in an attempt to stop the civil war, will not say where the bomb came from. The citizens of Sarajevo, however, are in little doubt that the attack was launched by Serb troops who have taken control of the hills overlooking the city. World leaders are condemning the massacre but have not yet decided how to respond. There is still much disagreement about the role of the United Nations and NATO in the area. The United States see the Serbs as the aggressors and want to arm the Muslims. Other nations argue that guns will only aggravate the problem.

Devastation in Sarajevo's market

Children at a refugee camp near Goma, on the border between Rwanda and Zaire

War in Rwanda

22 APRIL

The long-running ethnic conflict between Tutsi rebels and the Hutu government in the central African republic of Rwanda has erupted into violence on an unprecedented scale. The crisis was triggered two weeks ago by the death in a plane crash of the Rwandan president Juvenal Habyarimana, who had recently reached agreement with the Tutsi-led Rwandan Patriotic Front. It is believed that his plane was shot down. Since then violent fighting between Tutsi and the Hutu has turned the country into a bloodbath. According to the Red Cross, at least 100,000 people have died so far. As hundreds of thousands of people flee the fighting, makeshift refugee camps have been set up in a desperate attempt to cope with the humanitarian crisis. However, relief agencies and charities are finding it hard to get food and supplies through to the camps, and every day hundreds of refugees are dying from cholera.

JANUARY–JUNE

World Events	**FEB** India's legendary "Bandit Queen" Phoolan Devi, heroine for many low-caste Indians, is released from prison.	**MAR** Right-wing media baron Sivio Berlusconi and his Forza Italia party wins the Italian general election.	**MAY** ANC leader Nelson Mandela is elected as the first black president of South Africa.	**MAY** Russian dissident novelist Alexander Solzhenitsyn returns to his homeland after 20 years spent in exile in the USA.
Entertainment	**FEB** Norwegian speed skater Johann Koss sets three world records at the Olympics.	**APR** Twenty-seven-year-old US rock star Kurt Cobain, of Nirvana, kills himself with a shotgun at his Seattle home.	**MAY** US film *Pulp Fiction*, directed by Quentin Tarantino, wins the an award at the Cannes Film Festival.	**JUN** UK rock singer George Michael loses a lengthy legal battle with his record company, Sony.
Innovations	**FEB** An interactive television system allows US viewers to find out more about what is on.	**MAR** Mercedez-Benz and Swatch unveil their new bubble car, the Swatchmobile, planned for 1997.	**MAR** In Germany, the new *Eurofighter 200* makes a successful first test flight.	**MAY** The Channel Tunnel linking France and the UK is officially inaugurated.

JOHANN KOSS

PRESIDENT NELSON MANDELA

1994

Wacko Jacko ties the knot

26 MAY

It is official, Michael Jackson and Lisa Marie Presley, daughter of Elvis, did indeed get married today – despite denials from both of them. The distinctly low-key, top-secret event took place well away from the glare of the cameras in the Dominican Republic. Lacking the glitter of many of his performances, Jackson was dressed in black, wore a plaster across his nose, and said "Why not?" instead of "I do".

Michael Jackson and Lisa Marie Presley

O J Simpson – a fallen hero

17 JUNE

Former American football hero and film star Orenthal James Simpson gave himself up to police today after a dramatic car chase through Los Angeles County, watched by millions on television. Fleets of news helicopters captured the scene live as "O J", driven in a white Ford Bronco, tried to shake off the massed strength of California's highway patrol. Earlier in the day Simpson had failed to appear in court to be formally charged with the murder of his wife, Nicole Brown Simpson, and her friend Ronald Goldman.

RIDE WITH A VIEW
A gigantic rollercoaster, the tallest in the world, has been unveiled in Blackpool, England. It has a record incline of 65 degrees, which churns stomachs nicely as the carriages hurtle down at 135 km/h (85 mph).

Troops sent into Chechenia

11 DECEMBER

Russian tanks and artillery today crossed the border into Chechenia after a two-week bombing campaign failed to subdue the breakaway republic, which is demanding independence from the Russian Federation. In the capital, Grozny, the Chechen leader, General Dzhokar Dudayev, remains defiant, surviving an attempt to topple him by Russian-backed opponents of his rule. His troops are fierce fighters, with a long history of guerrilla warfare. The Russian army, however, is not the force it once was and morale is low.

Russian troops enter Chechenia

JULY–DECEMBER

JUL President Kim Il Sung of North Korea, the century's longest-ruling dictator, dies after a heart attack aged 82.

JUL Brazil wins the soccer world cup in the USA, after beating Italy in an exciting penalty shoot-out.

JUL Gigantic fireballs are produced in space when 21 fragments of a comet crash into the planet Jupiter.

BRAZIL WIN WORLD CUP

JUL The United Nations authorizes a US-led invasion of Haiti to drive out the military government and restore President Aristide.

AUG The World Series is cancelled as major league baseball players in the USA strike over salary capping.

SEP US astronaut Col Mark Lee makes the first untethered space walk for a decade, using a jet pack.

SEP More than 900 people die when roll-on, roll-off ferry *Estonia* sinks in heavy weather in the Baltic Sea.

NOV Boxer George Foreman, aged 47, beats Michael Moorer, aged 27, to win a world heavyweight title.

SEP Kansai International Airport, built on a specially created artificial island, is opened in Japan.

KANSAI AIRPORT

AUG The IRA announces a ceasefire, paving the way for political settlement in the Northern Ireland conflict.

DEC UK writer John Osborne, famous for the "kitchen sink" play *Look Back In Anger*, dies aged 65.

DEC Clear pictures of galaxies in their infancies, taken by Hubble Space Telescope, are published.

ENDING APARTHEID

IN APRIL 1994 THE NEW RAINBOW FLAG of South Africa was raised and the new anthem "Nkosi Sikelele Afrika" ("God Bless Africa") sung, when African National Congress (ANC) leader Nelson Mandela was elected president of South Africa. The election marked the end of a long and painful struggle by black South Africans to free themselves from white rule. For more than three centuries, the country had been dominated by a white minority and, from 1948, a rigid and brutal policy had segregated the people according to race. Black people, denied the vote, had been forced to live in appalling poverty in special areas called homelands.

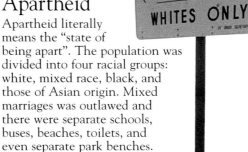

Sign indicates a "whites only" area

Apartheid

Apartheid literally means the "state of being apart". The population was divided into four racial groups: white, mixed race, black, and those of Asian origin. Mixed marriages was outlawed and there were separate schools, buses, beaches, toilets, and even separate park benches.

Mandela's release

Nelson Mandela was leader of the banned ANC in the Sixties, and helped to found its armed wing, "Umkonto was Sizwe" ("Spear of the Nation"). In 1963 he was sentenced to life imprisonment because of his political activities. Throughout his 27 years of imprisonment, Mandela came to symbolize the struggle against apartheid and, on his release in 1990, he pledged to continue the long fight. As ANC leader in the Nineties, Mandela became South Africa's first black president.

MANDELA VISITS HIS PRISON CELL AFTER HIS RELEASE

Pass book

Fires rage in a black township

The long road to equality

In December 1991 delegates from all major South African organizations, with the exception of far-right groups, took part in the Convention for a Democratic South Africa to begin working towards a transitional, multi-racial government and a new constitution that would extend political rights to everyone. However, negotiations were long and difficult and political violence once again flared up in the black townships.

End of apartheid laws

By 1990 international pressure and social unrest compelled the government to repeal discriminatory laws. Within two years, huge progress had been made and most apartheid regulations had been abolished. Laws that classified people by race and created separate public facilities were swept away, and black people were finally able to travel freely within their own country, without carrying the hated pass book.

Economic sanctions

Worldwide concern about the abuse of human rights in South Africa grew dramatically during the 1980s as the regime suppressed political protest with increasing brutality. In 1986 economic sanctions were imposed on South Africa by the United States and the European Community. The resulting isolation caused severe damage to the economy in South Africa.

Diamonds are one of South Africa's main exports

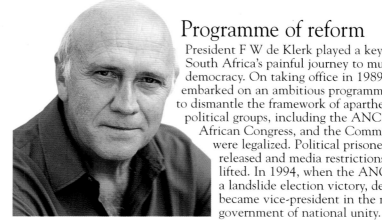

Programme of reform

President F W de Klerk played a key role in South Africa's painful journey to multi-party democracy. On taking office in 1989 he embarked on an ambitious programme of reform to dismantle the framework of apartheid. Banned political groups, including the ANC, the Pan African Congress, and the Communist Party, were legalized. Political prisoners were released and media restrictions were lifted. In 1994, when the ANC won a landslide election victory, de Klerk became vice-president in the new government of national unity.

A new future

Economic, sporting, and cultural sanctions were dropped after the end of apartheid, and South Africa finally emerged from international isolation. The legacy of 350 years of white domination, however, has left deep and bitter internal scars that will take years to heal. In 1996 black children were finally integrated into white schools, with armed guards employed in the beginning to secure their safety. In the same year the government set up a commission chaired by Archbishop Desmond Tutu to investigate the crimes of apartheid.

BLACK AND WHITE CHILDREN STUDYING TOGETHER

Popular opposition

Over the years popular protest against apartheid became increasingly militant. It was backed by a campaign of violence waged by banned opposition groups. Many opposition campaigners were imprisoned and tortured by the police but this did little to deter the protesters.

South Africans queue to vote

Electoral queues

The queues stretched for miles outside polling stations as 16 million black people, together with over 9 million whites, Asians, and people of mixed race, took part in South Africa's first free election in April 1994. The voting lasted four days and was closely monitored by international observers. The ANC won a landslide victory and Nelson Mandela became the country's first black president. Posts were found in the government for leaders of the other parties to ensure that all have a say in the new South Africa.

295

1995

Kobe devastated

17 JANUARY

As many as 2,700 people are feared dead after a huge earthquake hit Kobe, a busy port in western Japan at the heart of an important industrial area, early this morning. It measured 7.2 on the Richter Scale and is the worst earthquake to hit Japan since Tokyo was devastated in 1923. More than 1,100 buildings, many of them supposedly earthquake-proof, crashed to the ground as people lay sleeping in

their beds, and whole areas of the city have been reduced to rubble. Overhead motorways and railways collapsed, sending early-morning commuters plunging to their deaths. Fires are still raging out of control all over the city, fed by fractured gas pipes, while firefighters are facing an impossible task battling with broken water mains and blocked roads. The authorities appear to be in a state of shock after the disaster, with hundreds of thousands of people homeless in near freezing temperatures.

The federal building in Oklahoma

Blast in the heart of America

21 APRIL

Flags are flying at half mast throughout the United States after the worst terrorist outrage the nation has ever known. More than 100 people, including 15 children, were killed in Oklahoma City two days ago when a huge car bomb exploded outside a federal building, tearing a gaping hole in its side. The FBI have today arrested a key suspect, 27-year-old Timothy McVeigh, a former soldier with far-right political views and links with paramilitary "patriotic" militia groups. The nation is deeply shocked that a citizen of the United States could be responsible for such an outrage.

Peace celebrated

Peace lanterns in Hiroshima

6 AUGUST

It is exactly 50 years since the first atomic bomb was dropped on Hiroshima in Japan. Today 60,000 people commemorated the dead with a minute's silence in the Peace Park.

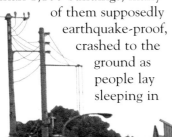

JANUARY– JUNE

World Events	**MAR** The Tokyo subway in Japan is paralysed by a deadly sarin nerve gas attack that kills ten people.	**MAY** Millions of people around the world celebrate the 50th anniversary of the Allies' Victory in Europe (VE) day.	**JUN** Newly elected French president Jacques Chirac announces the resumption of nuclear testing in the Pacific.	**JUN** After massive environmental protest, Shell UK abandons plans to dump an old oil platform in the North Sea.
Entertainment	**MAR** Paul McCartney announces that The Beatles will release a new record.	**MAY** *Superman* star Christopher Reeve is paralysed after falling off a horse in Virginia, USA.	**JUN** South Africa wins the rugby world cup, beating New Zealand 15–12 in the final.	**JUN** Disney's *Pocahontas* is launched with the biggest-ever premiere in New York, USA.
Innovations	**JAN** Astronomers in Hawaii find a galaxy 15 billion light years away from Earth.	**FEB** Space shuttle *Discovery* crew member Michael Foale becomes the first Briton to walk in space.	**FEB** Scientists reveal that a huge iceberg has broken away from the continent of Antarctica.	**MAR** Russian cosmonaut Valeri Polyakov lands after spending a record 438 days in space.

BEATLES' RECORD

SOUTH AFRICA WINS WORLD CUP

1995

Israeli premier assassinated

4 NOVEMBER

Israeli prime minister Yitzhak Rabin was assassinated tonight, only minutes after he addressed a "Peace Yes, Violence No" rally held in Tel Aviv. It had been called to stem the tide of right-wing resentment at the concessions made to Palestinians over self-rule. A lone gunman pushed through the security men surrounding Rabin as he left the speakers' platform and shot him twice at close range. The prime minister was taken to Ichilov hospital for emergency surgery but died one hour later, The killer, 25-year-old law student Yigal Amir, was arrested by security forces immediately. He said, "I acted alone on God's orders and I have no regrets." World leaders have been paying tribute to Rabin who worked so hard for peace in the troubled Middle East.

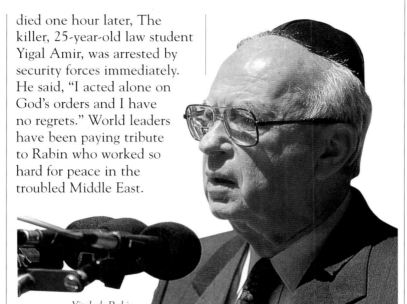
Yitzhak Rabin

GAME TECHNOLOGY
Huge leaps in technology have meant that games programmes are becoming increasingly sophisticated all the time. The Sony Playstation games console has been a top seller this year and is operated through a television screen.

Nigerian writer executed

11 NOVEMBER

Despite international appeals for clemency, the distinguished dissident writer Ken Saro-Wiwa has been executed by Nigeria's military dictatorship. Eight other environmental campaigners died with him, after being convicted of murder at a military tribunal. Saro-Wiwa led a movement against the pollution of Nigeria by oil companies.

Peace plan for Bosnia

21 NOVEMBER

After three weeks of talks in Dayton, Ohio, chaired by United States negotiator Richard Holbrook, an agreement has been struck that will hopefully bring peace to war-torn Bosnia. Slobodan Milosevic of Serbia, Franjo Tudjman of Croatia, and Alija Izetbegovic from Bosnia approved the plan that will create a unified country divided along racial lines. NATO troops will be sent in to enforce the agreement.

JULY–DECEMBER

AUG US satellites and spy planes spot mass graves in the Bosnian town of Srebrenica, giving evidence of genocide in the war.

JUL Legendary Argentine racing driver Juan Manuel Fangio dies in Buenos Aires aged 84.

AUG Analysis of fossils found in Spain prove humans reached Europe earlier than thought.

O J SIMPSON IS CLEARED

OCT A US jury of ten women and two men find O J Simpson not guilty of the murders of his wife Nicole and her friend.

SEP In Hollywood, USA, *Home Alone* star Macaulay Culkin sacks his father as manager.

AUG Antarctic survey reveals that the fall in ozone levels is detectable in summer as well as spring.

OCT Louis Farrakhan, leader of the Nation of Islam in the USA, leads 400,000 black men on a march through Washington DC.

OCT Seamus Heaney, a 57-year-old poet from Ireland, is awarded the Nobel Prize for Literature.

SEP France explodes a nuclear bomb in an underground test at Mururoa Atoll in the Pacific.

DEC UK trader Nick Leeson is given a six-and-a-half year jail sentence in Singapore after the collapse of Barings Bank.

NOV French film director Louis Malle, whose films include *Au Revoir Les Enfants*, dies aged 63.

NICK LEESON

NOV In Egypt, the tomb of the legendary Queen Nefertiti opens to visitors for the first time.

MUSIC IN THE NINETIES

THE MUSIC SCENE of the 1990s has exploded with a wealth of new talent. In Britain the success of new bands has generated a wave of excitement that is comparable to the mass hysteria of the Swinging Sixties. CD sales have risen throughout the decade, and even established artists are experiencing new-found fame with the release of remixed, remastered, and unplugged versions of old favourites. The music technology revolution has brought about huge advances in high-quality digital sound with the launch of new systems such as the mini disc and the digital compact cassette.

ICE-T

Country sounds

The country music boom in the United States has become a multi-billion dollar industry with *Rolling Stone* rock magazine dubbing it America's "new gold rush". Garth Brooks has spearheaded the boom with his soft, mellow rockabilly sound. His record sales have even outstripped those of global superstars such as Michael Jackson and Irish group U2.

GARTH BROOKS

Rap it up!

A truly radical musical movement, rap music has its roots in the urban street culture of young black Americans. Hard-hitting, and often controversial, rap artists such as Snoop Doggy Dog and Ice-T have popularized the music, establishing a global market.

Teenage idols

Certain to get teenage pulses racing, singing and dancing "boy bands" have dominated pop charts in the 1990s. When British group Take That split up in 1995 helplines were set up to console the thousands of grieving fans. Countless batches of manufactured teen idols have since found success, such as the Backstreet Boys from the United States and Irish group Boyzone. All-girl bands are also getting their share of the pop glory. Raunchy queens of pop the Spice Girls have sold over five million copies of their debut album worldwide since they first burst on to the pop scene in 1996 with their cry of "Girl power!"

Dance music

The repetitive bass-lines and drum beats of Nineties dance music has spawned a rave "club culture" with DJs elevated to the status of pop stars. The computer-generated music achieves its appeal through its wide spectrum of sounds ranging from garage and house to techno and jungle. Ravers love to dance till they drop, have a rest, and then come back for more.

TAKE THAT PERFORM ONE OF THEIR MANY TOP TEN HITS

1994 THE FIRST MTV EUROPE
MUSIC AWARDS ARE HELD

1995 INTRODUCTION OF CRIMINAL
JUSTICE ACT THREATENS UK RAVERS

1996 THE BAND R.E.M. SIGN A $50
MILLION CONTRACT WITH SONY

SHABBA RANKS

Independence

The diversity of popular music in the 1990s is in part due to the rise of the independent record label. Small independent labels, sometimes called "indies" are often more willing to take a chance on signing an unknown or controversial band or singer than a large multinational record company.

LIAM GALLAGHER OF OASIS

Rise of ragga

Ragga is part of the extended musical family that includes both reggae and rap. Made with digital instruments, its roots stretch back to Jamaica. Outspoken Ragga superstar Shabba Ranks has had several hit records worldwide.

BJÖRK

The invasion of Brit Pop

Pop music in Britain exploded with new vitality and talent in the Nineties. Labelled "Brit Pop" by the media, major names include Kula Shaker, Pulp, Blur, and Oasis. The British renaissance was recognized in 1996 by US magazine *Newsweek* when it described London as "the coolest city in the world".

Grunge

Firmly rooted in punk, the Grunge scene emerged in Seattle, USA, in the early Nineties. Disaffected youth readily responded, adopting a uniform of ripped jeans, flannel shirts, and knit stocking hats. Seattle's leading grunge group, Nirvana, became worldwide icons with their 1991 monster success *Nevermind*, which topped the album charts and went on to gross $50 million.

Female artists top the charts

The Nineties has witnessed a huge increase in the number of hit singles by solo female artists, from the powerful ballads of Alanis Morrisette and Sheryl Crow to the unique country sounds of kd lang. The decade has also seen the rise of Icelandic singer Björk from cult indie singer to international star.

KURT COBAIN OF NIRVANA

1996

Evil visits school

13 MARCH

Horror came to a small Scottish town yesterday morning when 16 children and their teacher were massacred in the gym of the Dunblane Primary School. Five more children and another teacher were seriously injured. The attacker, local man Thomas Hamilton, finally turned a gun on himself. A misfit, Hamilton had been sacked from the scout movement, banned from running boys' clubs, and had already been investigated by the police. Legally, however, he was allowed to own the four handguns and the 105 rounds of ammunition he used to kill his victims and himself. It took him four minutes. As the world tries to come to terms with the horrific events, demands are already being made in Britain for a complete ban on handguns. The school's headteacher has spoken bravely about the tragedy. "Evil visited us yesterday," he said, "and why we will never know."

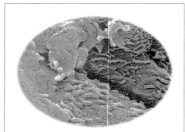

LIFE ON MARS
NASA scientists in the USA have revealed evidence that a primitive life form might have existed more than three billion years ago on Mars. They have discovered possible fossil remains in a meteorite that arrived from the red planet 13,000 years ago and was found in Antarctica in 1984.

Taliban take Afghan capital

27 SEPTEMBER

After fierce fighting between rival guerrilla factions in Afghanistan's long-running civil war, Taliban Islamic fundamentalists today took control of the capital Kabul. They have now declared Afghanistan a completely Islamic country. Taliban are enforcing strict laws wherever they seize control. All women have been ordered to wear a full veil and cover their faces in public. Breaking the dress code can lead to a beating with a stick as punishment.

An Afghan woman with face covered

JANUARY–JUNE

World Events	**JAN** The Tamil Tigers, who are fighting for a separate Tamil state within Sri Lanka, bomb the capital.	**FEB** The 17-month-old IRA ceasefire comes to an end when a massive bomb explodes in London's Docklands in the UK.	**MAR** After four decades of one-party rule, Lee Teng-Hui scores a victory in Taiwan's first democratic presidential elections.	**APR** Lone gunman Martin Bryant is arrested after massacring at least 34 people at Port Arthur on the Australian island of Tasmania.
Entertainment	**FEB** Keiki, the whale star of US film *Free Willy*, may be released into the wild.	**FEB** World chess champion Gary Kasparov beats the top chess computer Deep Blue in the USA.	**FEB** Michael Jackson's performance at the UK's Brit Awards is disrupted by Jarvis Cocker of pop group Pulp.	**JUN** Germany beats the Czech Republic with a "golden goal" in extra time to win the European Cup, held in the UK.
Innovations	**FEB** A $442 million US satellite breaks away from a shuttle and is lost.	**MAR** In Scotland scientists announce that they have just succeeded in cloning two sheep.	**MAR** At Stonehenge, UK, carbon-dating of bone suggest that the monument may be older than previously thought.	**APR** The World Health Organization (WHO) announces the invention of a birth-control injection for men.

DOCKLANDS BOMB DAMAGE

LEE TENG-HUI

1996

The wrong cab!

21 OCTOBER

Wallace and Gromit's big adventure in New York in the United States ended happily today when they were reunited with their creator, Nick Park. The Oscar-winning British animator had accidentally left the original models of the world-famous characters in a taxi two days ago.

Wallace and Gromit

Miss-take?

23 NOVEMBER

Irene Skliva was crowned Miss World today in the annual beauty contest which, for the first time, took place in India. It caused widespread protest throughout the country from both women's groups and Hindu extremists. Security was tightened when a number of protesters threatened to commit suicide at the event in Bangalore.

Rwandans flee ethnic war

16 NOVEMBER

In the last two days an estimated 400,000 Hutu refugees, who fled Rwanda in 1994, have left their camps in east Zaire and are heading for their homes. The exodus comes after extremist Hutu militiamen, who had held them captive, were overrun in a surprise attack by Tutsi rebel forces, backed by the Rwandan government.

Serbs protest at fixed elections

31 DECEMBER

The Serbian capital Belgrade has ground to a halt as mass protest swells and threatens to destabilize Slobodan Milosevic's government. Thousands of riot police have been drafted in. Daily protests began over a month ago when opposition victories in the municipal elections were not recognized and then declared invalid by Milosevic. Last week Serb police and government supporters attacked protestors and one man is believed to have died from the injuries he received. Morale among the protesters remains high, however, and opposition leaders look set to continue the fight well into the new year.

JULY–DECEMBER

JUL In the second round of voting Boris Yeltsin is re-elected president of Russia despite continuing ill health.

JUL Cinema audiences in the USA flock to see *Independence Day* which opens, appropriately, on 4 July.

INDEPENDENCE DAY

NOV French marine biologists find the remains of Alexandria which sank beneath the Mediterranean in AD 335.

JUL A Boeing 747 jumbo jet, TWA Flight 800, explodes shortly after take-off from New York, USA, killing 228 people.

JUL Eleven thousand athletes from 197 nations take part in the Olympic Games in Atlanta, Georgia, USA.

NOV The *Global Surveyor* spacecraft sets off from Cape Canaveral, USA, on a mission to the planet Mars.

DEC US ambassador to the United Nations Madeleine Albright becomes the first woman US secretary of state.

AUG An exact replica of Shakespeare's Globe Theatre is opened on the site of the original in London, UK.

NOV The Russian *Mars-96* spacecraft falls back to Earth after two days in space, crashing in the Pacific ocean.

MADELEINE ALBRIGHT

DEC Several hundred people are taken hostage by a Marxist group at the Japanese embassy in Lima, Peru.

DEC All-female UK group the Spice Girls are the latest pop sensation, topping charts worldwide.

DEC A US satellite finds evidence of a frozen lake in a crater on the dark side of the Moon.

A NEW MILLENNIUM

AS THE TWENTIETH CENTURY draws to a close, millennium fever has swept the globe. In some countries, such as the Arab states, Israel, and Japan, where other calendars are used, it is, of course, something of a non-event. Iran has even banned millennium celebrations altogether. But, for much of the world, plans are on course and a bewildering array of millennium projects are being hatched. However, with an estimated population of 6.5 billion people and a growing environmental awareness, scientists are already beginning to grapple with potential problems in the 21st century.

THE SITE OF CERN

Fuel of the future

Scientific fact and fiction merged at the end of 1995 when the first complete atoms of anti-matter were created at Switzerland's European Laboratory for Particle Physics (known as CERN). Anti-matter releases enormous bursts of energy, making it a potential fuel source.

It's a wind-up!

This clockwork radio, designed by British inventor Trevor Baylis, offers a simple solution to an old problem. It does not need batteries or electricity and is therefore ideal for use in remote areas with no electricity supply in developing countries.

Hotel is shaped like a sail

Aerodynamic hotel

The world's tallest hotel is taking shape in the Arab sheikdom of Dubai. It is the centrepiece of a huge new beach resort complex which will incorporate marina, waterpark, and sports and conference centres. The 321-m (1,053-ft) high hotel has 56 storeys and three basements below sea level. Designed in an aerodynamic sail shape, it is located on its own artificial island, which is linked to the mainland by a road bridge.

MODEL OF DUBAI HOTEL

Under construction

After more than 100 years, the gigantic, Neo-Gothic Sagrada Familia church in Barcelona, Spain, is still a building-site. Although construction began in 1882, it remains a shell. The designer, the famous Catalan architect Antonio Gaudí, who died in 1926, predicted it would take two centuries to complete. Even uncompleted, the church is a magnificent architectural achievement.

Airport on an island

A special artificial island 4.5 km (2.8 miles) long and 2.5 km (1.5 miles) wide was built in Osaka Bay to house Japan's new Kansai International Airport. It is connected to the overcrowded mainland by a six-lane highway and a railway. The vast steel and glass terminal was designed to withstand both earthquakes and typhoons.

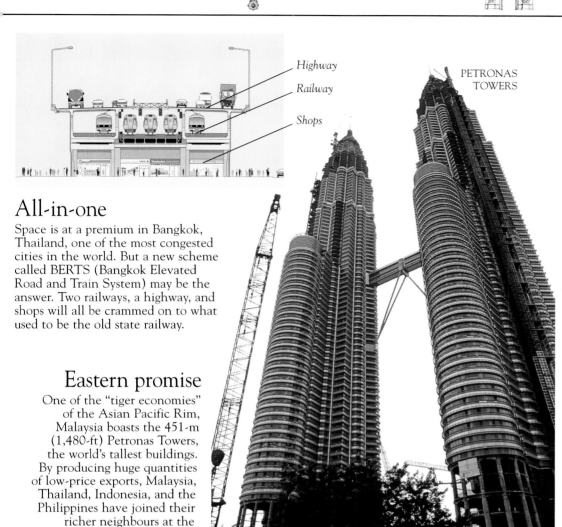

Highway

Railway

Shops

PETRONAS TOWERS

AN ARTIST'S IMPRESSION OF *ALPHA*

All-in-one

Space is at a premium in Bangkok, Thailand, one of the most congested cities in the world. But a new scheme called BERTS (Bangkok Elevated Road and Train System) may be the answer. Two railways, a highway, and shops will all be crammed on to what used to be the old state railway.

Eastern promise

One of the "tiger economies" of the Asian Pacific Rim, Malaysia boasts the 451-m (1,480-ft) Petronas Towers, the world's tallest buildings. By producing huge quantities of low-price exports, Malaysia, Thailand, Indonesia, and the Philippines have joined their richer neighbours at the hub of world trade.

New space age

Work is starting on a new International Space Station (ISS), codenamed *Alpha*, which will provide a permanent orbiting research complex in the unique, nearly zero-gravity environment of space. In a new spirit of international co-operation, the project is jointly financed and organized by Russia, Japan, Europe, and the United States. The station will take 44 assembly flights to build and is due for completion in 2002.

CONCEPT 2096

Car date 2096

Concept 2096, designed to celebrate 100 years of the British motor industry, shows what cars might look like in the new millennium. It is computer-controlled and will reach speeds of 483 km/h (302 mph), with no driver, no steering wheel, and no brakes. It can also change shape and colour.

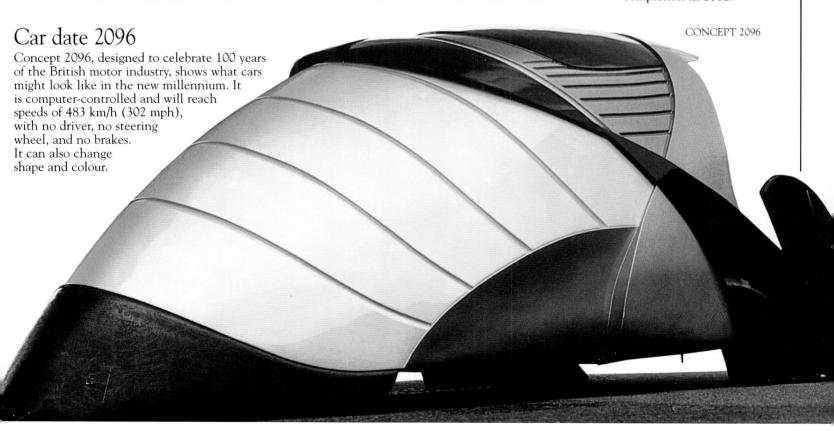

HOLLYWOOD SUPERSTARS

1900–1909	1910–1919	1920–1929	1930–1939	1940–1949

G M ANDERSON ("BRONCO BILLY")

An unsuccessful vaudeville actor, Anderson made his name in the first western, *The Great Train Robbery*, in 1903. He made nearly 400 films in his career.

LINDA AVISON

US actress Linda Avison was the first wife of the renowned film director D W Griffith appearing in several of his "shorts" before taking early retirement.

HOBART BOSWORTH

Former producer and stage actor, Bosworth made his silent screen debut in 1909 after losing his voice. He appeared as a cowboy in *In the Sultan's Power*.

FLORENCE LAWRENCE

US leading lady of the silent screen, Lawrence made her career as the "Biograph Girl", named after the company for whom she worked.

CHARLIE CHAPLIN

A legend in his lifetime, the British-born mime artist found fame in the United States. He was best known for his role as "the Tramp" which captured the hearts of US audiences after he appeared in 1914.

WILLIAM S HART

A solemn-faced hero of many silent westerns, such as *Blue Blazes Rawden*, Hart became one of the key performers of the 1920s.

MARY PICKFORD

Nicknamed "the world's sweetheart", Pickford co-founded United Artists with her husband Douglas Fairbanks Senior, Charlie Chaplin, and D W Griffith.

LILLIAN GISH

Gish appeared in films from 1912. The US actress gave a memorable performance in *Broken Blossoms* in 1918.

DOUGLAS FAIRBANKS SENIOR

A swashbuckling star of the silent screen, Fairbanks Snr produced many of his own comedy and drama films.

RUDOLPH VALENTINO

Having gained acclaim for *The Sheik* in 1921, an early and untimely death incited female suicides. His funeral was a national event.

BUSTER KEATON

Although a great clown of the silent era, Keaton was rarely seen smiling. His best-known films include *The Navigator* and *The General*.

LAUREL AND HARDY

British-born Stan Laurel teamed up with his large American partner Oliver Hardy in 1926. Arguably the finest screen comedy duo, their first success was in *The Battle of the Century*.

CLARA BOW

US leading lady, Bow was the "It" girl of the 1920s, so-called after her role in the film of that name in 1927.

JAMES CAGNEY

A former vaudeville song-and-dance man, Cagney had his first screen success in 1931 with *Public Enemy*.

FRED ASTAIRE AND GINGER ROGERS

Assuredly cinema's most remarkable singing and dancing duo, Astaire and Rogers' most popular films include *Top Hat, Swing Time* and *Shall We Dance?*

SPENCER TRACY

A supremely cinematic actor, Tracy's rugged features initially placed him in gangster roles, but he went on to play tough but kind, and intelligent men.

GRETA GARBO

Hollywood brought goddess status to this Swedish actress. In 1936 she was nominated for an Oscar for her performance in *Camille*.

CLARK GABLE

"The King of Hollywood" is best known for his part as Rhett Butler in *Gone With The Wind*, which he played opposite Vivien Leigh.

BETTE DAVIS

Beautiful big-eyed Davis won an Oscar for *Jezebel* in 1938 and was an Oscar nominee for *Little Foxes* and *The Letter* in the 1940s.

HUMPHREY BOGART

Bogart starred in film noir of the 1940s such as *The Maltese Falcon*. His other classic roles were in *The Big Sleep* and *Casablanca*.

INGRID BERGMAN

Gifted Swedish actress Bergman made her greatest films in Hollywood in the 1940s and won an Oscar for her part in *Gaslight* in 1944.

CARY GRANT

British-born Grant epitomized the debonair hero and was unsurpassed in 1940s light comedy.

KATHERINE HEPBURN

A dominant and enduring star actress, Hepburn was one of the most talented interpreters of emancipated females roles. She is unique in having won four Oscars.

1950–1959	1960–1969	1970–1979	1980–1989	1990–1997

MARLON BRANDO

Brando played a wide range of parts and was nominated for several Oscars. His part in *The Wild One* made him popular as a teen idol.

PAUL NEWMAN

Newman has had a long, distinguished career. His films of the 1960s include *The Hustler* and *The Prize*.

JANE FONDA

Former model and political activist, Fonda was first awarded an Oscar for *Klute* in 1971, and later in 1978 for the film *Coming Home*.

CLINT EASTWOOD

A success as Dirty Harry in 1971, Eastwood is also known for his spaghetti westerns and in the 1990s was the Oscar-winning director of *The Unforgiven*.

ROBERT DE NIRO

One of the century's greatest screen actors, De Niro won an Oscar for *Raging Bull* in 1980, a part for which he had to gain 25 kg (55 lb) in weight.

KEVIN COSTNER

As well as achieving success as an actor, Costner was an Oscar-winning director in 1990 with *Dances With Wolves* and the producer of *Waterworld* in 1995.

MARILYN MONROE

The number one US leading lady, Monroe's career took off in 1953 with a run of hits including *How To Marry A Millionaire* and *Gentlemen Prefer Blondes*.

SEAN CONNERY

Smooth Scotsman Connery shot to fame with his role as James Bond in *Dr No* in 1962. He still plays gruff, indomitable leading men.

AL PACINO

A New York-born Sicilian, Pacino made his mark in 1972 in *The Godfather*, a thrilling mafia saga of epic proportions. He starred in two *Godfather* sequels.

MERYL STREEP

US actress Streep can speak with many accents. She won an Oscar for *Sophie's Choice* in 1982 and has been nominated for others.

JODIE FOSTER

A talented child actress, Foster has matured to play demanding roles like FBI agent Starling in *Silence of the Lambs* in 1991, for which she won an Oscar.

JAMES DEAN

A tragic car crash ended teen idol Dean's promising career. He had already been nominated for Oscars for *East of Eden* and *Giant*.

ELIZABETH TAYLOR

Known as much for the number of husbands she has had as for her acting, one of Taylor's most famous roles was in *Cleopatra* in 1963.

HARRISON FORD

After initial success with *Star Wars* in 1977, Ford has had a varied and award-studded career. He made *The Fugitive* in 1993.

JOHN TRAVOLTA

US dancing and singing star, Travolta rocked to fame in the 1970s in *Saturday Night Fever* and the ever-popular *Grease*.

BRAD PITT

Teen heartthrob Pitt shot to stardom in *A River Runs Through It* in 1992 and has gone on to play a key role in *Legends of the Fall*.

SIDNEY POITIER

A handsome and successful leading actor, Poitier won an Oscar for *Lilies of the Field* in 1963 and has helped to promote racial equality.

JULIE CHRISTIE

British actress Christie won an Oscar for her role in *Darling* in 1965 and made *Dr Zhivago* in the same year.

ROBERT REDFORD

Blond and good-looking, Redford appeared in many films during the 1970s and 1980s. Also a fine director, he won an Oscar for *Ordinary People* in 1980.

ARNOLD SCHWARZENEGGER

Former body-builder and winner of Mr Universe, "Arnie" became a huge box office star with a string of hits after *Terminator* in 1984.

TOM CRUISE

Cruise's career was launched in 1985 with *Top Gun* and he is now one of the hottest properties in Hollywood. He was an Oscar nominee for *Born On The Fourth of July*.

DENZEL WASHINGTON

US actor Washington's popular performances in the 1990s include *Philadelphia*, *Devil in a Blue Dress*, and the biographical *Malcolm X*.

TOM HANKS

After several low-key parts in the 1980s, Hanks won Oscars in 1994 and 1995 for *Philadelphia* and *Forrest Gump* and is now one of the leading US actors.

DORIS DAY

A vivacious dance-band singer, Day was an instant success with a unique brand of innocent sex comedy. *Calamity Jane* was one of her most popular films.

SCIENTISTS AND INVENTORS

1900–1909	1910–1919	1920–1929	1930–1939	1940–1949

WRIGHT BROTHERS

US brothers Orville and Wilbur Wright built and, in 1903, flew the first successful powered aeroplane. They were self-taught aeronauts, and the *Flyer* was driven by a lightweight petrol engine, flying a distance of 800 m (2,625 ft).

GEORGE EASTMAN

Photography was difficult and time-consuming until Eastman introduced the public to the lightweight roll-film Brownie camera.

GUGLIELMO MARCONI

In 1895, Italian scientist Marconi invented radio communication. Six years later, he succeeded in sending the first radio signals across the Atlantic.

LUMIÈRE BROTHERS

The Lumière brothers invented the first practical film projector. In 1904, they marketed colour plates capable of producing a colour transparency.

LEO BAEKELAND

In 1909, Belgian chemist Baekeland developed the first synthetic plastic. Known as Bakelite, it was used to make all kinds of things from jugs to radio sets.

MARY PHELPS JACOB

When Jacob designed the first bra it consisted of two handkerchiefs with straps, intended to flatter the bust.

HENRY FORD

US car manufacturer Ford pioneered mass production with the invention of the moving assembly line.

MARIE CURIE

Curie pioneered research into radioactivity with the discovery of the elements polonium and radium.

ALBERT EINSTEIN

In 1916, Albert Einstein revolutionized the laws of physics with the formulation of the special and general theories of relativity.

HARRY BREARLEY

Brearley mixed steel and chromium to produce an alloy that did not rust. The result was stainless steel.

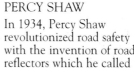

ALEXANDER FLEMING

Fleming accidentally discovered penicillin in 1928. The first samples of the antibiotic drug were used on wounded soldiers in World War II.

CLARENCE BIRDSEYE

In 1925, US entrepreneur Birdseye revolutionized the food industry with the development of a method used for quick-freezing pre-cooked foods.

ROBERT GODDARD

In 1926, Goddard launched the first liquid-fuelled rocket. Although it only rose 56 m (184 ft), it had far-reaching effects on the future of space exploration.

BALZER VON PLATEN & CARL MUNTERS

In 1922, von Platen and Munters invented the electric refrigerator in Sweden. They called it the "D fridge" and it was marketed by Electrolux.

PERCY SHAW

In 1934, Percy Shaw revolutionized road safety with the invention of road reflectors which he called "cat's-eyes". They have since saved countless lives.

CHESTER CARLSON

US lawyer Chester Carlson invented the photocopier in 1938. The first practical machines for office use went on sale in 1960.

OTTO HAHN & LISE MEITNER

Physicists Hahn and Meitner conducted research into radioactive methods leading to the discovery of nuclear fission in 1939.

JOHN LOGIE BAIRD

The first demonstration of television was given by Baird in 1928. Eight years later, he conducted the first high-definition television broadcast in colour.

WILLIAM SHOCKLEY

The invention of transistors in 1947 by Shockley and his team of scientists led to the development of microchips and compact electronic machines.

FRANK WHITTLE

Whittle built a prototype jet engine in 1937 that was first used in aircraft in 1941, becoming the forerunner of the modern jet engine.

IGOR SIKORSKY

Sikorsky developed the first practical helicopter, with a single rotor to give enough lifting power. Many modern helicopters are of this type.

ENRICO FERMI

Fermi built the first nuclear reactor whilst conducting research into producing controlled and self-sustaining nuclear fission.

1950–1959	1960–1969	1970–1979	1980–1989	1990–1997

1950–1959

EDWARD JONAS SALK
US physician Salk was the first person to develop an oral vaccine against the crippling and infectious children's disease, polio.

FRANCIS T BACON
From 1932 to the 1950s, Bacon and his team of scientists worked on creating the first practical hydrogen-oxygen fuel cell.

ROSALIND FRANKLIN
UK chemist Franklin conducted x-ray investigations of DNA which led to the discovery of their structure in 1953.

CHRISTOPHER COCKERELL
When Cockerell invented the hovercraft in 1955 the UK government were so impressed they placed it on the top secret list!

1960–1969

ROY JACUZZI
Jacuzzi invented the first fully integrated whirlpool bath in 1968. Since then, the Jacuzzi has remained a popular form of relaxation.

JANE GOODALL
Through many years of observation, UK scientist Goodall uncovered the amazing similarities between chimpanzees and humans.

THEODORE MAIMAN
Maiman built the first working laser beam. Today, the laser has all kinds of uses, from bar code reading to delicate surgery.

CHRISTIAAN BARNARD
South African cardiologist Barnard performed the first human heart transplant on a patient with heart disease.

DENNIS GABOR
Gabor pioneered holography in 1948, but the technique was not of any practical use until the invention of the laser during the 1960s.

1970–1979

GODFREY HOUNSFIELD
Hounsfield invented a computerized tomography (CT) scanner in 1972. It used low-intensity x-rays to produce diagnostic pictures.

CLIVE SINCLAIR
Sinclair developed miniature electronic goods, including the first pocket calculator. In 1985, he launched the C5, the world's first electric car.

JAMES E LOVELOCK
In his Gaia theory, Lovelock claims that the Earth and all life on it are linked as if they are a single living thing.

ABDUS SALAM
Pakistani scientist Salam was the first person from his country to win a Nobel Prize for his theory of the electroweak force.

1980–1989

JOHN WARNOCK & PAUL BRAINERD
Warnock and Brainerd invented desktop publishing (DTP) software, enabling editors to create books and magazines on a computer.

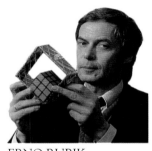

ALEC JEFFREYS
Jeffreys revealed that our unique DNA profiles can be used for identification purposes and therefore aid forensic scientists in the task of solving crimes.

ERNO RUBIK
Hungarian Professor Rubik launched his maddening Rubik's Cube in 1980. The puzzle looked easy, but it had to be solved by the correct combination.

ROLAND MORENO
In 1981, Moreno invented a credit card with its own memory, by embedding it with a computer chip. Smart card-holders use the card to balance their bank accounts.

JOHN SANFORD
Sanford devised the gene gun in 1987. Geneticists use this instrument to introduce new genetic material into cells in order to change the structure of the cells.

1990–1997

TREVOR BAYLIS
Baylis invented a clockwork radio capable of generating its own power supply. The radio was specially designed for use in communities in Africa that lack electricity.

DR ROBERT WILLIAMS
Dr Williams, director of the Space Telescope Science Institute, confirmed the existence of black holes while working with NASA's Hubble Space Telescope.

DR ALAN ROBERTS
In 1994, Dr Roberts of the Bio-Materials Research Unit in the UK, invented a powerful superglue capable of closing severe wounds without the risk of infection.

DANIEL COHEN
In 1993, genetic expert Professor Cohen led a team of researchers that generated the first physical mapping of all 24 human chromosomes, known as the genome.

SPORT STARS

1900–1909	1910–1919	1920–1929	1930–1939	1940–1949

CHARLOTTE COOPER

UK tennis player Charlotte Cooper became the first ever woman Olympic champion at the Paris Games in 1900.

RAY EWRY

The legendary US athlete Ray Ewry won an incredible ten Olympic gold medals between 1900 and 1908. He demolished all opposition in the standing long jump, the standing high jump and the standing triple jump – events that are not contested today.

PRINCE BORGHESE

After a gruelling 62 days at the wheel, Prince Borghese of Italy won the 12,872-km (8,045-mile) Peking to Paris motor race in 1907.

DR WG GRACE

W G Grace dominated English cricket for over four decades. He scored 54,211 runs and took 2,809 wickets.

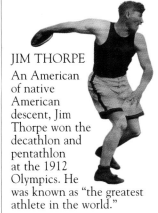

JIM THORPE

An American of native American descent, Jim Thorpe won the decathlon and pentathlon at the 1912 Olympics. He was known as "the greatest athlete in the world."

SUZANNE LENGLEN

Twenty-year-old French tennis star Suzanne Lenglen was the first non-English speaking singles champion at Wimbledon, in 1919. She won the title six times in all.

HANNES KOLEHMAINEN

"Flying Finn" Kolehmainen won the Olympic 5,000 m, 10,000 m, and the 8,000 m cross country in 1912.

JACK DEMPSEY

US Jack Dempsey, "The Manassa Mauler", became a national hero in 1919 after winning the heavyweight world boxing championship.

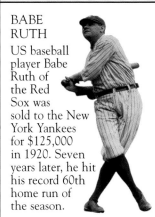

BABE RUTH

US baseball player Babe Ruth of the Red Sox was sold to the New York Yankees for $125,000 in 1920. Seven years later, he hit his record 60th home run of the season.

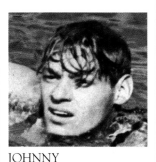

JOHNNY WEISSMULLER

Austrian-born American Johnny Weissmuller was the first man to swim 100 m in less than a minute. He won five Olympic medals.

DIXIE DEAN

At the age of only 21, the UK footballer Dixie Dean, playing for Everton, scored a record sixtieth league goal in a total of 39 matches.

PAAVO NURMI

One of the famous "Flying Finns", Nurmi won nine Olympic golds altogether, five at the 1924 Paris Games in France. He broke the 1,500 m and 5,000 m records on the same afternoon.

GORDON RICHARDS

Champion UK flat-racing jockey, the legendary Gordon Richards, galloped into the record books in 1933 with more than 246 winners in one season.

DONALD BRADMAN

The most prolific batsman ever, Australian cricketer Donald Bradman set a test match record on 12 July 1930, with a score of 334 runs in Leeds, UK.

JESSE OWENS

Black US athlete Jesse Owens set an amazing six world records in a single afternoon in Michigan, USA. He then went on to win four gold medals at the 1936 Berlin Olympics.

FRED PERRY

Former world table tennis champion, UK's Fred Perry won the US Open tennis championship in 1933, 1934, and 1936. He won the Australian Open in 1934, and Wimbledon in 1934, 1935, and 1936.

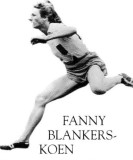

FANNY BLANKERS-KOEN

Nicknamed "The Flying Dutchwoman", Blankers-Koen won the 100 m, the 200 m, the 80 m hurdles, and the sprint relay at the 1948 Olympics in London.

MALCOLM CAMPBELL

UK racing driver Sir Malcolm Campbell broke world speed records on both land and water. He reached 480 km/h (300 mph) in his car, *Bluebell*.

GORDIE HOWE

Canadian ice hockey professional Gordie Howe played for the Detroit Red Wings. He scored 1,071 goals in his 32-year career.

JOE LOUIS

The "Brown Bomber" Joe Lewis, the first black world heavyweight champion since 1915, successfully defended his title 25 times.

1950–1959	1960–1969	1970–1979	1980–1989	1990–1997

JUAN MANUEL FANGIO

Argentine motor racing driver Fangio won a record five world championships in the 1950s, driving for Alfa Romeo, Ferrari, Maserati, and Mercedes-Benz.

EMIL ZÁTOPEK

Czech long-distance runner Emil Zátopek won the 5,000 m, the 10,000 m, and the marathon at the 1952 Helsinki Olympics. His wife Dana won the javelin event.

ROGER BANNISTER

In 1954, UK runner Roger Bannister was the first man to run a mile in under four minutes. He ran the distance in an incredible 3 minutes, 59.4 seconds.

LARISSA LATYNINA

One of the first great Soviet gymnasts, Larissa Latynina won a record 18 Olympic medals between 1956 and 1964 – nine gold, five silver, and four bronze.

ABEBE BIKILA

Ethiopian barefoot runner Abebe Bikila, know as "the metronome on legs", won the Olympic marathon in 1960, and again in 1964.

DAWN FRASER

The Australian swimmer Dawn Fraser won the 100 m freestyle gold medal in three successive Olympic Games – 1956, 1960 and 1964.

MUHAMMAD ALI

World heavyweight boxing champion Cassius Clay changed his name to Muhammad Ali after converting to Islam.

BOB BEAMON

In the thin air of Mexico City, US long-jumper Bob Beamon cleared an historic 8.90 m (29.19 ft) at the 1968 Olympic Games. It was a record that remained unbeaten for more than 25 years.

EDSON ARANTES DO NASCIMENTO PELÉ

The incomparable Brazilian football player Pelé was only 17 years old when he played in his first World Cup.

OLGA KORBUT

The tiny Soviet gymnast Olga Korbut captivated the crowds and won two gold medals – for floor exercise and beam events – at the Munich Olympics in 1972.

LESTER PIGGOTT

Winner of some 5,200 races in Britain and overseas, this jockey has dominated racing, winning the Derby 9 times.

NIJINSKY

In 1970 Nijinsky, a three-year-old horse ridden by Lester Piggott, won the UK Triple Crown – the Derby, 2,000 Guineas, and St Leger.

JACK NICKLAUS

US golfer Jack Nicklaus is one of the sport's greatest players. He was the first person to win five different major titles at least twice.

ZOLA BUDD

In 1985, the South African-born barefoot distance runner Zola Budd set a new 5,000 m world record of 14 mins 48.07 sec.

DIEGO MARADONA

Barcelona paid a record £5 million for Argentine footballer Maradona in 1982. He led Argentina to World Cup victory in 1986.

JOE MONTANA

Inspirational American footballer Joe Montana led his team, the San Fransisco 49ers, to victory in four Super Bowls in the 1980s.

JAYNE TORVIL & CHRISOPHER DEAN

UK skaters Torvil and Dean won the world ice-dancing championships in four successive years. In the 1984 competition, they won an amazing 29 perfect sixes.

YAPING DENG

Chinese table tennis ace Yaping Deng became world champion in 1991. She won both the singles and doubles title at the 1992 Barcelona Olympic Games.

MARTINA NAVRATILOVA

Czech-born tennis player Navratilova, who defected to the US in 1975, won her record ninth Wimbledon singles title in 1991.

MICHAEL JOHNSON

The US sprint superstar Michael Johnson was 200 m world champion in 1991 and 1993, and the 400 m world champion in 1993 and 1995. At the 1996 Olympics in Atlanta, USA, he became the first person ever to win both the 200 m and the 400 m events.

MIGUEL INDURAIN

The legendary Miguel Indurain, a cyclist from the Basque country, won the Tour de France for a record fifth time in 1995.

BRIAN LARA

In 1995, West Indian left-handed batsman Brian Lara beat Garfield Sobers's 1958 record by scoring 375 runs not out against England.

WORLD LEADERS

1900–1909	1910–1919	1920–1929	1930–1939	1940–1949

KAISER WILHELM II

Ruler of Germany between 1888 and 1918, Wilhelm II pursued a vigorous policy of expansion in Central Europe. He fled to Holland following defeat in WWI.

TSAR NICHOLAS II

Nicholas II of Russia clung onto power from 1894 until the 1917 revolution, when he was forced to abdicate. He was executed in 1918.

EMMELINE PANKHURST

Leading UK suffragette Mrs Emmeline Pankhurst fought for women's voting rights, which were finally granted in 1918.

SUN YAT-SEN

The most important figure in the Chinese nationalist revolution, Sun Yat-Sen was elected president of the new republic in 1911.

LEON TROTSKY

Russian revolutionary Leon Trotsky was a leader of the 1917 Bolshevik victory. He was later exiled by Stalin.

WOODROW WILSON

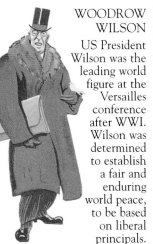

US President Wilson was the leading world figure at the Versailles conference after WWI. Wilson was determined to establish a fair and enduring world peace, to be based on liberal principals.

VLADIMIR LENIN

Vladimir Ilyich Lenin, founder of the Communist party in Russia, became the first premier of the USSR.

ROSA LUXEMBURG

Polish-born Luxemburg was a brilliant speaker and writer. She helped to found the communist "Spartacists", leading an uprising in Berlin in 1919 which failed and resulted in her death.

MUSTAPHA KEMAL

Mustapha Kemal was called Ataturk, meaning "Father of the Turks", after establishing a Turkish republic in 1923.

ÉAMON DE VALERA

Irish politician de Valera was president of Sinn Féin until 1926, and a leading figure in Ireland's fight for independence from the UK.

CHIANG KAI-SHEK

General Chiang Kai-Shek was president of the Chinese Republic from 1928 to 1949, after he led the Chinese nationalist Kuomintang forces to victory over the warlords of north China.

AUGUSTO SANDINO

Nicaraguan rebel leader General Sandino waged a guerrilla war against US-backed government troops.

EMPEROR HIROHITO

Hirohito ruled as emperor of Japan for 63 years. His reign became known as *Showa* – Enlightened Peace.

MAHATMA GANDHI

Admired by all, Gandhi was at the forefront of the fight to free India from British rule by non-violent means.

JOSEPH STALIN

Stalin's reign of terror as dictator of the USSR lasted from 1929 to 1953. Millions of peasants died, opposed to his collective farming laws.

RAS TAFARI HAILLE SELASSIE

Ras (Duke) Tafari took the name Haille Selassie, "Power of the Trinity", when he became emperor of Ethiopia in 1931.

BENITO MUSSOLINI

Italian fascist dictator Mussolini ruled Italy from 1922 for 21 years as *Il Duce* – The Leader. He tried to create an Italian empire.

GENERAL FRANCO

Franco's nationalist forces defeated the republicans in the Spanish Civil War. He ruled as dictator from 1939.

GENERAL DE GAULLE

De Gaulle fled Nazi-occupied France in 1940, and founded the Free French Movement. He was made president of France after liberation in 1944, and later became president of the Fifth Republic.

ADOLF HITLER

German dictator Adolf Hitler, known as the Führer, was responsible for the Holocaust, when millions of Jews were exterminated.

JAWAHARLAL NEHRU

After playing a key role in negotiating independence, Jawaharlal Nehru became India's first prime minister.

WINSTON CHURCHILL

A statesman and writer, Churchill was at the height of his power as UK prime minister during WWII.

1950–1959	1960–1969	1970–1979	1980–1989	1990–1997

KONRAD ADENAUER
At 73, Adenauer became the first chancellor after WWII of the newly-created West German Republic.

DALAI LAMA
Traditionally a spiritual leader, the Dalai Lama also ruled over Tibet until the 1950s. The 14th Lama, he was forced to flee Tibet after the Chinese invasion.

HO CHI MINH
Communist revolutionary Ho Chi Minh became president of North Vietnam after defeating the French.

COLONEL NASSER
After leading the revolt against King Faruk, Nasser became prime minister of the new republic of Egypt.

JOHN F KENNEDY
At 43, Kennedy became the youngest US president. He was greatly mourned after his assassination in 1963.

JOMO KENYATTA
Nationalist leader Kenyatta became the first president of Kenya after his country gained independence.

MARTIN LUTHER KING
A Nobel Peace Prize winner, King was the leading figure of the non-violent civil rights movement in the US.

GOLDA MEIR
A member of the Mapai Labour Party, 70-year-old Golda Meir became prime minister of Israel in 1969.

MARGARET THATCHER
A Conservative Party leader, Thatcher became the UK's first woman prime minister, and held office for 11 years.

INDIRA GANDHI
The first woman prime minister of India, Indira Gandhi was assassinated in 1984 by her bodyguards.

AYATOLLAH KHOMEINI
Islamic fundamentalist Khomeini inspired the 1979 revolution that created the Islamic Republic of Iran.

POPE JOHN PAUL II
Polish-born Karol Jozef Wojtyla took the name John Paul II when he became Pope in 1978.

HELMUT KOHL
Elected as chancellor of West Germany in 1982, Kohl played a major role in the unification of Germany.

MIKHAIL GORBACHEV
Soviet premier Gorbachev won the Nobel Peace Prize for his role in ending the Cold War and aiding peace.

LECH WALESA
Lech Walesa became leader of the banned Polish trade union, Solidarity. He was elected president in 1990.

VACLAV HAVEL
Czech playwright Havel set up the civil rights group Charter 77. He was elected Czech president in 1989.

BENAZIR BHUTTO
Benazir Bhutto was elected prime minister of Pakistan in 1988, the first woman to head an Islamic nation.

AUNG SAN SUU KYI
1991 Nobel Peace prize-winner for trying to restore democracy to Burma, she is currently under house arrest.

YITZHAK RABIN
Israeli prime minister Rabin made a huge contribution to Middle East peace talks. He was assassinated in 1995.

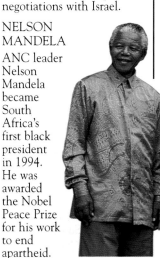

YASSIR ARAFAT
PLO leader Yassir Arafat won international support for his efforts in the peace negotiations with Israel.

NELSON MANDELA
ANC leader Nelson Mandela became South Africa's first black president in 1994. He was awarded the Nobel Peace Prize for his work to end apartheid.

311

MUSIC-MAKERS

| 1900–1909 | 1910–1919 | 1920–1929 | 1930–1939 | 1940–1949 |

SCOTT JOPLIN

Joplin was known as the "King of Ragtime" in the United States, particularly for his *Maple Leaf Rag*.

MARIE LLOYD

Music hall star Marie Lloyd first appeared on the UK stage at the age of only 15 and became best known for slightly saucy songs like *A Little of What You Fancy*. She was very popular with a large following.

DAME NELLIE MELBA

A hugely popular soprano, Nellie Melba took her name from her birthplace – Melbourne in Australia.

ENRICO CARUSO

The "greatest tenor of modern times", this Italian was one of the first opera singers to record extensively.

QUAKER CITY FOUR

The most famous barbershop quartet of all time, this US group achieved immortality with the song *Sweet Adeline*.

DIXIELAND JAZZ BAND

This US quintet of white musicians were the first jazz band to make records. Their top hits include *Tiger Rag*.

SOPHIE TUCKER

Sophie Tucker, known as "the last of the red-hot mamas", was a US ragtime singer with a raucous style.

IRVING BERLIN

One of the USA's most successful popular song-writers, Berlin could neither read or compose music.

AL JOLSON

US vaudeville entertainer Al Jolson starred and sang in the first-ever talking picture, *The Jazz Singer*.

EDWARD ELGAR

One of the UK's favourite composers, Elgar won worldwide recognition with *The Enigma Variations*.

JOSEPHINE BAKER

Josephine Baker moved from the USA to France where she introduced the Charleston dance wearing only a girdle of bananas.

LOUIS ARMSTRONG

A genius at improvization, the US cornet and trumpet player, known as "Satchmo", became the most famous jazz musician of all times.

PAUL ROBESON

Best remembered for his version of *Ol' Man River*, Robeson was one of the most influential US black performers of his decade.

TOMMY DORSEY

Trombone player Tommy Dorsey formed his own orchestra in the USA which became one of the most famous swing and dance bands of all time.

ELLA FITZGERALD

One of the most technically accomplished jazz singers ever, Fitzgerald's biggest hit was *A Tisket A Tasket*.

BENNY GOODMAN

Goodman was a virtuoso clarinettist who made his name as leader of his own swing band in the USA.

BING CROSBY

One of the first crooners, Crosby's recordings include *White Christmas*, which sold 30 million copies.

MAHALIA JACKSON

Jackson grew up in New Orleans in the USA and became her generation's most popular gospel singer.

JUDY GARLAND

Garland made her stage debut at the age of three. She is best remembered for *Somewhere Over the Rainbow*.

GLEN MILLER

Known for the hit tune *In the Mood*, the famous swing band leader died during World War II.

CARMEN MIRANDA

A night-club singer and recording star, the "Brazilian Bombshell" was famous for her towering fruit headdress.

BILLIE HOLIDAY

Nicknamed "Lady Day", American Billie Holiday was one of the greatest jazz vocalists ever.

FRANK SINATRA

The success of "ole blue eyes" as a US solo artist heralded a new era of teen hysteria and idol worship.

COUNT BASIE

Given the name "Count" by a radio broadcaster, Basie ranked high among US pianists and band leaders.

1950–1959	1960–1969	1970–1979	1980–1989	1990–1997

ELVIS PRESLEY

The first major rock 'n' roll star, heart-throb Elvis "The Pelvis" made fans swoon on both sides of the Atlantic with 18 US chart-toppers.

LITTLE RICHARD

With his wild piano style and sometimes manic singing style, Little Richard's first hit was *Tutti Frutti*.

DORIS DAY

Doris Day had a successful career as a singer with many international hits, including seven million-sellers.

BUDDY HOLLY

Although he died tragically young in a plane crash, rock 'n' roll giant Holly has had a huge musical influence.

RODGERS AND HAMMERSTEIN

Richard Rodgers and Oscar Hammerstein produced a string of smash-hit musicals including *Oklahoma!* and *The Sound of Music*.

THE BEATLES

The UK's "Fab Four" were the most famous pop group of the swinging Sixties. They dominated the charts throughout the world.

THE ROLLING STONES

With their rebellious image, the performances of this UK rock group were wild and exciting, making them a hit wherever they played.

JIMI HENDRIX

The legendary guitarist Jimi Hendrix died young but has been a huge influence on rock and jazz musicians.

ARETHA FRANKLIN

Aretha Franklin was the most important US female vocalist to emerge from the Sixties boom in soul music.

STEVIE WONDER

Blind from birth, Stevie Wonder was a child prodigy, playing piano and drums. He had his first hit in the USA when only 12 and went on to have a string of chart toppers throughout the decade.

T-REX

Fans fainted when UK glam-rock band and teen idols T-Rex went on tour in the early Seventies.

ABBA

Swedish Eurovision Song Contest winner Abba had their first million-selling record with *Waterloo* in 1974.

BAY CITY ROLLERS

A trend for tartan took off when this new Scottish group, aimed at teenagers, burst on to the pop scene.

BOB MARLEY

Bob Marley achieved worldwide fame and helped to popularize reggae, but his roots remained in Jamaica.

SEX PISTOLS

Founding fathers of punk rock, the Sex Pistols began performing live in the UK, causing outrage in 1975.

MADONNA

A genius for self-promotion, US star Madonna shot to fame in the mid-Eighties with hits including *Like a Virgin* and *Material Girl*.

PRINCE

Prince was one of the decade's controversial stars. His *Purple Rain* album topped the US charts for 20 weeks.

DIRE STRAITS

UK rock band Dire Straits' 1985 album *Brothers in Arms* was one of the decade's biggest sellers.

MICHAEL JACKSON

Michael Jackson achieved the status of mega-star with his 1982 album *Thriller*, which became the biggest-selling record ever.

DURAN DURAN

At the heart of the "New Romantic" backlash against punk, this UK group also appealed as teen idols.

NIRVANA

Spearheading the grunge revolution, US group Nirvana had instant success with their album *Nevermind*.

OASIS

The bad boys of Nineties rock, UK group Oasis has often been likened to The Beatles and have led the British pop revival.

TAKE THAT

Helplines for distraught teenage fans were set up when UK boy band Take That split up in 1996.

SNOOP DOGGY DOG

In 1993 US rapper Snoop Doggy Dog made history when his debut album *Doggystyle* entered the US chart at number one.

GARTH BROOKS

As a country music boom spread across the USA, Garth Brooks hit

the charts with his winning blend of soft rockabilly and old-style country tradition.

LAWBREAKERS

1900–1909	1910–1919	1920–1929	1930–1939	1940–1949

BUTCH CASSIDY
Originally named Robert LeRoy Parker, Cassidy was a cattle rustler before joining the Wild Bunch and meeting the Sundance Kid.

THE SUNDANCE KID
This outlaw, real name Harry Longabaugh, teamed up with Butch Cassidy to rob banks, trains, and mines. It is believed that they were killed in Bolivia in 1909.

GAETANO BRESCI
The assassin of the king of Italy, Umberto I, Bresci saved up his wages as a weaver in the USA so he could travel to Italy to carry out the murder in 1900.

LEON CZOLGOSZ
In 1901, US anarchist Leon Czolgosz shot the president of the USA, William McKinley. The president later died of his wounds.

MATA HARI
An exotic dancer, Mata Hari also tried to spy for both Germany and the Allies in WWI. She was finally betrayed by Germany and executed by the French in 1917.

ARNOLD ROTHSTEIN
Rothstein was responsible for fixing the 1919 baseball World Series in the USA by bribing members of the Chicago White Sox team.

OLD BLUEBEARD
Henri Desiré Landru, nicknamed "Old Bluebeard", seduced several French war widows, and swindled them out of their life savings before murdering them.

DR CRIPPEN
Dr Crippen poisoned his wife, buried her in the cellar, and ran away with his mistress. He was caught on a boat bound for Canada.

AL CAPONE
The USA's most famous mobster, Capone controlled the underworld in Chicago in the days of Prohibition.

JOHN DILLINGER
John Dillinger was leader of a gang of crooks famous for a series of armed bank robberies in the USA. He was gunned down by FBI agents in 1934.

LEOPOLD AND LOEB
The spoilt sons of US millionaires, Leopold and Loeb murdered a 14-year-old boy for fun in 1924.

SACCO AND VANZETTI
Sacco and Vanzetti killed two people in a US robbery. It was thought they were convicted because they were anarchists.

PETER KÜRTEN
Nicknamed the "Vampire of Düsseldorf", Peter Kürten was finally caught and executed in Germany for nine murders and seven attempted murders. Kürten had a passion for the taste of human blood.

BONNIE AND CLYDE
A couple of small-time hoods, Bonnie and Clyde became the USA's most notorious criminals.

LUCKY LUCIANO
Inheriting Al Capone's position as head of the US mafia, Salvatore Luciano controlled a large number of crime rackets.

BRUNO HAUPTMANN
A German carpenter, Hauptmann was convicted of the kidnapping and murder of the toddler son of US hero Charles Lindbergh.

ALBERT HOWARD FISH
One of America's worst serial killers, Fish was brought to justice in 1934. Fish cooked his victims' flesh and ate it for dinner.

GIUSEPPE ZANGARA
Zangara explained his 1933 assassination attempt on US president-elect Roosevelt by saying, "I hate all officials".

JOHN GEORGE HAIGH
Haigh believed that if he destroyed his victim's body in a vat of sulphuric acid he could escape conviction in the UK, but he was wrong.

HIRASAWA
Hirasawa tricked all 16 employees of a Japanese bank into taking cyanide. When they were nearly dead, he robbed the bank.

WONG YU
In 1947 Wong Yu invented hijacking when he staged the takeover of a flying boat and demanded a ransom.

GEORGE METESKY
Metesky terrorized New York in the USA by planting bombs around the city. However, many were duds and injuries were few.

1950–1959	1960–1969	1970–1979	1980–1989	1990–1997

JOHN CHRISTIE

Eight bodies were found in Christie's home at 10 Rillington Place in London, UK. Three bodies had been stacked in a cupboard.

NANNIE DOSS

Nannie Doss from the USA admitted to killing four of her five husbands by putting liquid rat poison in their food and drink.

THE ROSENBERGS

Julius and Ethel Rosenberg were convicted in the USA of selling atomic secrets to the Russians. They were executed for espionage.

BURGESS & MACLEAN

In 1951, warned by fellow spy Kim Philby, Guy Burgess and Donald Maclean, who had been leaking secrets to Russia, fled to Moscow.

RUTH ELLIS

The last woman to be executed in the UK, Ellis shot dead her lover outside a London pub after he ended their love affair.

BOSTON STRANGLER

Albert DeSalvo strangled 13 women in Boston, USA. He gained their confidence by claiming to be a talent scout for a model agency.

THE KRAY TWINS

Ronald and Reginald Kray controlled the underworld in the East End of London in the UK. The twins' gang was known as the "Firm".

LEE HARVEY OSWALD

Oswald was arrested for the assassination of US president John F Kennedy. His own murder, whilst in custody, was caught by TV cameras.

CHARLES MANSON

Leader of a US commune called the "Family", Manson incited his disciples to carry out murders in Hollywood.

TOM KEATING

Picture restorer Tom Keating admitted to forging the works of world-famous painters. The paintings were sold as originals.

ALBERT SPAGGIARI

Spaggiari masterminded a bank robbery in Nice, France and escaped. He got into the bank by tunnelling though the town sewers.

CARLOS THE JACKAL

An international killer, Carlos worked for a variety of terrorist groups. The world's most-wanted terrorist was finally caught in 1994.

TED BUNDY

US serial killer Ted Bundy confessed to murdering 23 women over a period between 1974 and 1978. He was executed in 1989.

MICHAEL MILKEN

Milken was nicknamed "the Hannibal Lecter of American business" after he was convicted for his insider dealing and fraud.

ISSEI SAGAWA

A Japanese student, Sagawa murdered and ate a Dutch girl while living in France. He has since published his best-selling memoirs.

PABLO ESCOBAR

Escobar was a Colombian drug baron and head of the underworld. After escaping imprisonment, Escobar was gunned down in 1993.

ROBERT MAXWELL

UK press baron Maxwell drowned in 1991, escaping being charged with stealing from his company's pension fund to pay creditors.

ANDREI CHIKATILO

A Ukrainian serial killer, Chikatilo murdered 53 women and children before being caught in 1990.

NICK LEESON

Charged with fraud, Nick Leeson was responsible for the collapse of Barings, a respected UK bank.

ABIMAEL GUZMÁN

Guzmán led the "Shining Path" guerrillas in Peru and was responsible for many acts of terrorism.

THOMAS HAMILTON

Hamilton walked into a Scottish school in 1996 and shot dead 16 young children and their teacher before shooting himself.

315

BRITISH GOVERNMENT

Britain is a constitutional monarchy. The Queen, Elizabeth II, is head of state, but real power lies with the Prime Minister, who is head of the government. He or she is the leader of the largest party in the House of Commons and governs the country with a team of ministers known as secretaries of state, each of whom controls a department of state such as the Treasury or the Home Office. The 20 or so most important ministers sit in the Cabinet, notably the Foreign Secretary, who looks after relations with other countries, the Chancellor of the Exchequer, who looks after the nation's finances, and the Home Secretary, who is responsible for law and order. A further 80 or so junior ministers assist the various secretaries of state in the running of their government departments.

Local government

- London is currently the only capital city in the world without a single local authority to speak for it. The capital is divided between 32 London boroughs and the City of London, which is the historic financial centre of the country.
- The rest of England is governed by a two-tier system of county and district councils.
- The major cities of England, plus Wales and Scotland, are all governed by unitary authorities controlling every aspect of local services.

The Royal Family

House of Hanover
Victoria   1837–1901
House of Saxe-Coburg-Gotha
Edward VII   1901–1910
House of Windsor
George V   1910–1936
Edward VIII   1936
George VI   1936–1952
Elizabeth II   1952–

In 1917, during World War I, George V became embarrassed by the royal family's German origins and changed the name of the royal family from Saxe-Coburg-Gotha to Windsor. Other members of the royal family were also forced to change to more English-sounding names. The current heir to the throne is Charles, Prince of Wales, the eldest son of Elizabeth II. His two sons, Princes William and Henry, usually known as Harry, are next in line to the throne. The Queen has three other children: Princess Anne, the Princess Royal; Prince Andrew, Duke of York; and Prince Edward.

Prime Ministers of the 20th Century

1895–1902	Lord Salisbury	Conservative
1902–1905	Arthur Balfour	Conservative
1905–1908	Sir Henry Campbell-Bannerman	Liberal
1908–1915	Herbert Asquith	Liberal
1915–1916	Herbert Asquith	Coalition
1916–1922	David Lloyd George	Coalition
1922–1923	Andrew Bonar Law	Conservative
1923–1924	Stanley Baldwin	Conservative
1924	Ramsay MacDonald	Labour
1924–1929	Stanley Baldwin	Conservative
1929–1931	Ramsay MacDonald	Labour
1931–1935	Ramsay MacDonald	National
1935–1937	Stanley Baldwin	National
1937–1940	Neville Chamberlain	National
1940–1945	Winston Churchill	Coalition
1945	Winston Churchill	Conservative
1945–1951	Clement Attlee	Labour
1951–1955	Winston Churchill	Conservative
1955–1957	Sir Anthony Eden	Conservative
1957–1963	Harold Macmillan	Conservative
1963–1964	Sir Alec Douglas-Home	Conservative
1964–1970	Harold Wilson	Labour
1970–1974	Edward Heath	Conservative
1974–1976	Harold Wilson	Labour
1976–1979	James Callaghan	Labour
1979–1990	Margaret Thatcher	Conservative
1990–1997	John Major	Conservative

The Conservative Party

The British Conservative Party is one of the oldest and most successful political parties in Europe. It began in the 1680s, when it was known as the Tory Party. During the 1830s, under the leadership of Sir Robert Peel, the party re-formed as the Conservative Party, adopting a programme of moderate social reform, a commitment to traditional institutions, and defence of the growing British Empire. In this century, the party has held power almost without a break from 1915–45, and again from 1951–64. Under Margaret Thatcher, Britain's first woman prime minister, and John Major, the Conservatives won four elections in a row from 1979–92, gaining the biggest popular vote for a political party in 1992. Today the Conservative Party is the party of private ownership and big business, and is increasingly anti-Europe.

The Labour Party

In 1900, a number of trade unions and left-wing political parties and organizations came together to form the Labour Representation Committee. Its aim was to secure parliamentary representation for the working-class. After 29 MPs were elected in the 1906 General Election, the LRC changed its name to the Labour Party. The Labour Party replaced the Liberals as the main opposition party in 1918, and formed two minority governments in 1924 and 1929–31. In 1940 the party joined in a wartime coalition led by Winston Churchill, and then secured a massive majority in the general election of 1945. Under Clement Attlee, the Labour government of 1945–51 nationalized the coal mines and railways, granted independence to India and Pakistan, and established the National Health Service. The party held power again in 1964–70, and 1974–79, but remained out of office in the 1980s. The "New Labour" party has re-defined its socialist commitment to common ownership and nationalization, and is now pro-European with moderately progressive views.

The Liberal Democrat Party

The Liberal Democrat Party began life as the pro-Protestant Whig Party of the 1680s, which re-formed as the Liberal Party in the 1860s, supporting social reform, non-conformity in religion, and Home Rule for Ireland. The Liberal Party split during WWI, and although Liberals have held office in coalition governments since then, they have not held power. They fought the 1983 and 1987 elections in alliance with the Social Democratic Party (which split from the Labour Party), after which the two parties merged to become the Liberal Democrat Party. They favour proportional representation and devolution of government to Scotland and Wales.

Ulster Unionists

Formerly part of the Conservative Party, the Ulster Unionists represent Protestant opinion in Northern Ireland and are in favour of continuing the union between Northern Ireland and Great Britain. The Ulster Unionists are the largest party in Northern Ireland, and usually return a dozen of the province's 17 MPs to Westminster.

Democratic Unionist Party

A small Protestant party, led by Reverend Ian Paisley, the DUP represents more extreme unionist views than the Ulster Unionists. The DUP draws much of its support from non-conformists and Presbyterians.

Social Democratic and Labour Party

This Northern Ireland party represents moderate nationalists who favour union with the Irish Republic. The SDLP has close links with the British Labour Party and draws much of its support from the Catholic minority in the province.

Sinn Féin

Sinn Féin ("ourselves alone") was founded in 1902 to fight for independence for Ireland, then part of Britain. It played a leading role in the Easter Rising against British rule in 1916 and continues to strongly campaign for a united Ireland.

Plaid Cymru

Established in 1925, Plaid Cymru is a Welsh nationalist party that wants independence for Wales. It first won a seat in parliament in 1966, and won four seats in 1992. Plaid Cymru draws its support from Welsh-speaking areas in the north and west of the principality.

Scottish Nationalist Party

Formed in 1928, the SNP favours independence for Scotland within a united Europe. The SNP briefly held a parliamentary seat in 1945 and again in 1967–70, but gained support during the 1970s as oil revenues flowed in from the North Sea, winning 11 seats in the 1974 election and 30% of the Scottish vote.

The House of Lords

The House of Lords is the upper house of parliament. Membership of the House of Lords is restricted to 763 hereditary peers, life peers (currently 374), 21 law lords, and 26 bishops of the Church of England. The House of Lords can amend or reject government bills, but they can be overridden by the House of Commons. The House of Lords has no power to delay a money bill, such as the annual budget set by the Chancellor of Exchequer to raise taxes for the government. When the House of Lords has finished with a bill, it is either returned to the House of Commons for them to consider any amendments, or goes to the Queen to receive the royal assent. The bill then becomes an act of parliament and therefore law.

- The Speaker of the House of Lords is the Lord Chancellor, the most senior law lord in the country. Unlike the Speaker of the House of Commons, the Lord Chancellor is a member of the government, and both speaks and votes in debates.
- The House of Lords is the final court of appeal in the British judicial system. Difficult cases are brought to the Lords, where three of the law lords hear them.

- At the beginning of the new parliamentary year in the autumn, the Queen goes to parliament to announce the government's new legislation for the year. The Queen reads her speech in the House of Lords; MPs are summoned to attend by Black Rod, an official of the Lords.
- A life peer is created a member of the Lords only as long as he or she lives; a hereditary peer passes his title down to his heir.

The Commonwealth

Britain and 50 of her former colonies are linked together as members of the Commonwealth. Most member states are either republics or have their own monarchs, but 16 countries, including Britain, Australia, Canada, New Zealand, and Jamaica, recognize Elizabeth II as head of state. Every two years the heads of Commonwealth governments meet to discuss issues of mutual interest. The Commonwealth Games take place every four years.

NATO

In 1949 Britain and other western European nations joined with Canada and the USA to form the North Atlantic Treaty Organization. NATO was set up to support western Europe against a possible military threat from the USSR. With the collapse of the USSR in 1991, NATO has lost much of its importance, although it is now discussing expansion eastwards to include former communist nations in eastern Europe.

The European Union

The European Union began life in 1957 as the European Economic Community. It has since grown from the 6 original members to 15 today, and has evolved from being a trading block into an economic union which is moving towards establishing its own single currency. Britain joined in 1973.

- The 15 member states of the EU are Britain, Ireland, Sweden, Denmark, Finland, Belgium, Netherlands, Luxembourg, Germany, Austria, France, Italy, Spain, Portugal, and Greece. Many other central European nations have applied to join.
- The European Parliament contains 626 members (MEPs) elected every five years from every member nation. Britain elects 87 MEPs – 71 from England, 8 from Scotland, and 5 from Wales, currently elected on a simple majority. The 3 MEPs from Northern Ireland are elected by proportional representation. The European Parliament meets in Strasbourg, France. It cannot make new laws, but supervises the work of the EU and approves the budget.

The House of Commons

The House of Commons consists of 659 Members of Parliament (MPs) elected from every part of the United Kingdom. To form a government, one political party usually has an absolute majority of MPs in the House of Commons. The Prime Minister leads the government and the Leader of the Opposition is the leader of the biggest opposition party. The business of the House of Commons is conducted by the Speaker of the House. In order to produce a new law, the government has to get it passed by the House of Commons. Detailed scrutiny of the law, known as a bill, is conducted in a standing committee. When the House of Commons has agreed a bill, it passes to the House of Lords.

- The Speaker of the House of Commons is elected by MPs after each general election. In 1992 Betty Boothroyd MP was elected as the first-ever woman Speaker. The Speaker does not vote and must remain above party politics.
- The Father of the House is the MP who has been a member the longest. The current Father is Sir Edward Heath, the former Conservative Prime Minister, who was first elected in 1950.

- Every five years, a general election is called to elect an entirely new House of Commons. If an MP resigns or dies between elections, a by-election is called to elect a new MP.
- Government ministers, and their "shadows" on the opposition side, are known as frontbenchers because of where they sit in the House of Commons. MPs who hold no governmental office are known as backbenchers.

BRITISH SPORT & CULTURE

Britain leads the world in many cultural areas and has set standards in the field of sport. British television programmes win many international awards, while the London theatre is still considered the most challenging anywhere in the world. The British film industry is underfunded, yet individual films are often successful – *The English Patient* won a British record of nine Oscars in 1997 – and British actors are in great demand in Hollywood, USA. Thoughout the twentieth century Britain has been at the forefront of youth culture, setting trends that have been adopted around the world, and British bands dominate rock and pop music. Britain has also produced its share of sporting heroes and sporting successes, notably in athletics and football, the world's most popular game.

The FA Cup

Date	Winners	Runners-up	Score
1977	Manchester Utd	Liverpool	2–1
1978	Ipswich Town	Arsenal	1–0
1979	Arsenal	Manchester Utd	3–2
1980	West Ham Utd	Arsenal	1–0
1981	Tottenham Hotspur	Manchester City	1–1, 3–2
1982	Tottenham Hotspur	QPR	1–1, 1–0
1983	Manchester Utd	Brighton & HA	2–2, 4–0
1984	Everton	Watford	2–0
1985	Manchester Utd	Everton	1–0
1986	Liverpool	Everton	3–1
1987	Coventry City	Tottenham H	3–2
1988	Wimbledon	Liverpool	1–0
1989	Liverpool	Everton	3–2
1990	Manchester Utd	Crystal Palace	3–3, 1–0
1991	Tottenham Hotspur	Nottingham F	2–1
1992	Liverpool	Sunderland	2–0
1993	Arsenal	Sheffield Wed	1–1, 2–1
1994	Manchester Utd	Chelsea	4–0
1995	Everton	Manchester Utd	1–0
1996	Manchester Utd	Liverpool	1–0

The Scottish FA Cup

Date	Winners	Runners-up	Score
1977	Celtic	Rangers	1–0
1978	Rangers	Aberdeen	2–1
1979	Rangers	Hiberian	0–0, 0–0, 3–2
1980	Celtic	Rangers	1–0
1981	Rangers	Dundee Utd	0–0, 4–1
1982	Aberdeen	Rangers	4–1
1983	Aberdeen	Rangers	1–0
1984	Aberdeen	Celtic	2–1
1985	Celtic	Dundee Utd	2–1
1986	Aberdeen	Hearts	3–0
1987	St Mirren	Dundee Utd	1–0
1988	Celtic	Dundee Utd	2–1
1989	Celtic	Rangers	1–0
1990	Aberdeen	Celtic	0–0
	(Aberdeen won 9–8 on penalties)		
1991	Motherwell	Dundee Utd	4–3
1992	Rangers	Airdrieonians	2–1
1993	Rangers	Aberdeen	2–1
1994	Dundee Utd	Rangers	1–0
1995	Celtic	Airdrieonians	1–0
1996	Rangers	Hearts	5–1

Football League

Since 1970, two clubs have dominated English football. Liverpool won the First Division championship no less than 11 times between 1973–91, taking the runners-up position a further seven times. The only club to match them has been Manchester United, runners-up in 1980, 1988, 1992, and 1995, and winners of the renamed Premier League four times in the last five seasons. Leeds, Everton, and Arsenal have also been consistently successful. In Scotland, the Glasgow rivals of Rangers and Celtic have dominated Scottish football, with only Aberdeen and Hearts able to challenge the dominant duo.

The World Cup

In 1966 England hosted the World Cup for the first time. They headed Group 1 against Uruguay, Mexico, and France, and then defeated Argentina 1–0 in the quarter finals. In a thrilling semi-final, the English team defeated Portugal 2–1 to face West Germany in the final at Wembley. Haller scored first for the German team, and then Geoff Hurst and Martin Peters scored to give England a 2–1 lead. Just before time, Weber scored for West Germany, forcing the game into extra time. A controversial goal by Geoff Hurst in the 100th minute was awarded to England, but the result was in no doubt when Hurst scored again to settle the match at 4–2. For the first time in 32 years, the host nation had won the World Cup.

Test match venues

Edgbaston, Birmingham: home ground of Warwickshire.
Headingley, Leeds: home ground of Yorkshire.
Lord's, north London: the home of English cricket, Lord's is owned by the MCC – the Marylebone Cricket Club – who controlled the game from 1787 until 1968 when the Cricket Council was established. Lord's is the home of Middlesex and the premier English test venue.
Old Trafford, Manchester: home ground of Lancashire.
The Oval, south London: the oldest test venue in England – the first two test matches against Australia in 1880 and 1881 were played here. Home ground of Surrey.
Trent Bridge, Nottingham: home ground to Nottingham.

Rugby grounds

Arms Park, Cardiff: national stadium of Welsh rugby.
Lansdowne Road, Dublin: home ground to Ireland.
Murrayfield, Edinburgh: home ground to Scotland.
Twickenham, Middlesex: home ground to England.

Film and music

• Only The Beatles and Elvis Presley have had 17 number one singles. Cliff Richard has had 13. No other act has had more than 10 number one singles.
• Cliff Richard has had the most top ten hits with 63 singles. Elvis Presley has had 55, Madonna, 33, Michael Jackson 29, and The Beatles 25. Madonna holds the record for the most consecutive top ten hits with 32 records. The Beatles have had 24.
• The single which stayed the longest at number one was *I Believe* by Frankie Lane, which remained at the top for 27 weeks in 1953. Second is *(Everything I Do) I Do It For You* by Bryan Adams, which spent 16 weeks at the top in 1991, followed by *Love Is All Around* by Wet Wet Wet with 15 weeks in 1994.
• Britain has won the Eurovision Song Contest four times: 1967 with *Puppet On A String*, by Sandie Shaw; 1969, with *Boom Bang-A-Bang*, by Lulu; 1976, with *Save Your Kisses For Me*, by Brotherhood of Man; and 1981, with *Making Your Mind Up*, by Bucks Fizz.

Top album of the year in the UK

Year	Artist	Album title
1970	Simon & Garfunkel	*Bridge over Troubled Water*
1971	T Rex	*Electric Warrior*
1972	Simon & Garfunkel	*Greatest Hits*
1973	Mike Oldfield	*Tubular Bells*
1974	The Carpenters	*The Singles 1969–1973*
1975	The Stylistics	*The Best of the Stylistics*
1976	Abba	*Greatest Hits*
1977	Fleetwood Mac	*Rumours*
1978	Soundtrack	*Saturday Night Fever*
1979	The Police	*Regatta de Blanc*
1980	Adam & The Ants	*Kings of the Wild Frontier*
1981	Human League	*Dare*
1982	Michael Jackson	*Thriller*
1983	Lionel Richie	*Can't Slow Down*
1984	Bruce Springsteen	*Born in the USA*
1985	Dire Straits	*Brothers in Arms*
1986	Paul Simon	*Graceland*
1987	Fleetwood Mac	*Tango in the Night*
1988	Kylie Minogue	*Kylie*
1989	Phil Collins	*…But Seriously*
1990	Madonna	*The Immaculate Collection*
1991	Simply Red	*Stars*
1992	REM	*Automatic For The People*
1993	Mariah Carey	*Music Box*
1994	Deacon Blue	*Our Town – Greatest Hits*
1995	Robson & Jerome	*Robson & Jerome*
1996	Oasis	*(What's the Story) Morning Glory?*

British television

The British Broadcasting Corporation (BBC) broadcast its first television programme in 1936, and, after a break during the war, regular services resumed in 1946. Independent commercial television began in 1955, with BBC 2 following in 1964 and Channel 4 in 1982. Channel 5 began broadcasting in 1997. The first colour broadcasts were made on BBC 2 in July 1976. The launch of the Sky TV satellite in February 1989 doubled the number of existing TV channels, although few people had the necessary dish aerials to receive the new satellite programmes. During the 1990s, new satellite and cable television companies offering dedicated sport and movie channels have massively increased the number of programmes people can watch.

• First broadcast in 1960, *Coronation Street* is the longest-running, most successful British soap opera. Set in a working-class street in Manchester, the programme regularly attracts more than 15 million viewers.
• The first *Top of the Pops* was broadcast on 1 January 1964.
• The largest TV audience of all time was for the royal wedding of Prince Charles to Lady Diana Spencer in July 1981.
• The longest-running children's programme is *Sooty*, which was first broadcast in 1952.
• The BBC's answer to Granada's *Coronation Street* – *EastEnders* is Britain's most popular TV programme with more than 18 million viewers for each episode: 30.15 million people watched the 1986 Christmas edition.
• Patrick Moore has presented the *Sky at Night* every month without a break since April 1957.

British theatres

• The Royal National Theatre occupies three modern theatres on London's South Bank and presents a mixture of classics, modern drama, and musicals.
• The Royal Shakespeare Company operates from both the Barbican Centre in the City of London and Stratford-upon-Avon, the birthplace of Shakespeare, and presents the works of Shakespeare as well as other plays.
• The Royal Court Theatre currently in London's West End is the home of modern English drama; it presented the premiere of John Osborne's *Look Back in Anger* in 1956 as well as many other plays by new writers.
• The Globe Theatre on London's South Bank is an accurate reconstruction of an Elizabethan theatre.
• The Stephen Joseph Theatre in Scarborough presents the premiere of every Alan Ayckbourn play.
• The Royal Opera House in London's Covent Garden is home to both the Royal Opera and the Royal Ballet companies.
• The Coliseum in London's West End is the home of the English National Opera.

British film studios

• Opened in 1926, Elstree Studios has made over 500 films including blockbusters such as *Stars Wars* and *Raiders of the Lost Ark*.
• Opened by the Rank Group in 1936, Pinewood Studios also produce TV commercials and pop videos.
• Shepperton Studios was bought in 1994 by UK director brothers, Tony and Ridley Scott.
• Ealing Studios is home to BBC Television and Drama and the future home of the National Television and Film School.

Festivals

• Edinburgh Festival: annual arts festival, first held in 1947
• The Eisteddfod: annual festival of Welsh culture
• Glastonbury: midsummer music and arts festival
• Gay Pride: biggest annual gay festival in Europe
• Notting Hill Carnival: Europe's biggest street carnival, held in London in August
• The Fleadh: annual festival of Irish music, held in London's Finsbury Park
• Cambridge Folk Festival: premier folk festival in England

INDEX

A

G

K

L

P Q

ACKNOWLEDGEMENTS

Dorling Kindersley would like to thank the following:

Carlton Hibbert for all his help in finishing the book
Paul Cornish at the Imperial War Museum; the Fawcett Library; Hamish MacGillivray at the London Toy and Model Museum; Nick Hill and the staff at Eden Camp Modern History Theme Museum, Malton; and the staff at Paul Smith, Covent Garden
Jacket design: Mark Haygarth
Feature illustrations and maps: David Ashby
Editorial assistance: Alison Copland, Nancy Jones, Carey Scott, Nicki Waine
Design assistance: Emma Bowden, Tony Chung, Alex Clifford, Joanne Connor, Jason Lee, Anna Martin, Iain Morris, Darren Troughton
DTP assistance: Tamsin Pender
Picture assistance: Rachel Leach, Mariana Sonnenberg
Index: Marion Dent
Specially commissioned photography: Peter Anderson, Sarah Ashun, Geoff Dann, Steve Gorton, Alex Wilson
Additional photography: M. Alexander, Geoff Brightling, Jane Burton, Martin Cameron, Peter Chadwick, Tina Chambers, Andy Crawford, Geoff Dann, Philip Dowell, Mike Dunning, Neil Fletcher, Lynton Gardiner, Philip Gatward, Steve Gorton, Peter Hayman, Colin Keates, Roland Kemp, Dave King, Liz McAulay, Robert O'Dea, Stephen Oliver, Roger Philips, Martin Plomer, Dave Rudkin, James Stevenson, Clive Streeter, Matthew Ward, Daniel Weil, Jerry Young, Michael Zabé

Picture Acknowledgements

Abbrieviations key: FJ=Front Jacket, BJ=Back Jacket, FF=Front Flap, BF=Back Flap, SP=Spine, A=Above, B=Below, C=Centre, L=Left, R-Right, T=Top and for pages 304-315: col=column

The Publisher would like to thank the following for their kind permission to reproduce the photographs:

Jacket: Allsport/Shaun Botterill: BJ/cl; Royal Pavilion, Art Gallery and Museums, Brighton: FJ/c; Casio: FJ/tcr; Jean-Loup Charmet: FJ/tcr; Corbis-Bettmann: BF/1-8, FJ/bcr, BJ/bl; Early Technology: BJ/bc; Mary Evans Picture Library: FF/b, FF/tl; Ronald Grant Archive/Columbia: BF/1-10; Kobal Collection/Warner Bros.: BJ/tr, FJ/cl; Mirror Syndication International: BJ/cr; Robert Opie Collection: FJ/tl; Rex Features: BF/1-1, FJ/cr, /© Sega Enterprises Ltd. Sp/t, FJ/tr; Science Photo Library/James King Holmes/W. Industries: BF/1-11; Frank Spooner Pictures: FJ/bc, FJ/brTeddy Bear Museum, Stratford-upon-Avon/Roland Kemp: BJ/tc; Topham Picturepoint: FJ/bl, FJ/bc

Prelims and 1900–1909: 1 Corbis-Bettmann; 2 L Science Photo Library/NASA; 3 C The Kid, Kobal Collection/First National/Charles Chaplin; 4 B National Maritime Museum; 5 BC National Motor Museum Beaulieu; 5 BCL Design Council; 5 BCR Police Academy Museum, NY; 5 BL Hulton Getty Picture Collection; 5 RBC By courtesy of BT Archives; 5 TCL Hulton Getty Picture Collection; 5 TR Liz McAulay; 6 BL Science Photo Library/Starlight; 6 LC Corbis-Bettmann; 6TL Peter Roberts Coll. c/o Neill Bruce; 6 RC Gone with the Wind, 1939, Ronald Grant Archive/Ted Turner Entertainment; 7 ABR Colorsport; 7 BC Rex Features; 7 BCL Rex Features; 7 BCR Kobal Collection; 7 BL Cleopatra, 1963, Ronald Grant Archive/Twentieth Century Fox; 7 BR Hulton Getty Picture Collection; 7 LC Rex Features; 7 RC Popperfoto; 7 TL ESA; 7 TR Brighton Museum & Art Gallery; 8 BL Sonia Halliday & Laura Lushington Photographs; 8 BR Robert Opie Collection; 8 CR Mary Evans Picture Library; 8 L Topham Picturepoint; 8 TR Mary Evans Picture Library; 9 BL Corbis-Bettmann; 9 BR Corbis-Bettmann; 9 C Mary Evans Picture Library; 9 TL Corbis-Bettmann; 9 TR Mary Evans Picture Library; 10 BL Robert Opie Collection; 10 BR Corbis-Bettmann; 10 CA The Peter Roberts Collection/c/o Neill Bruce; 10 CB The Peter Roberts Collection/c/o Neill Bruce; 10 TL Topham Picturepoint; 10 TR Corbis-Bettmann; 11 BL Visual Arts Library; 11 BR Mary Evans Picture Library; 11 TL Picasso: Harlequin & His Companion, AKG London/© Sucession Picasso/DACS 1997; 11 TR Mary Evans Picture Library; 11 CR by Jacques & Hamley Bros, UK/London Toy &Model Museum; 12 BL Mary Evans Picture Library; 12 BR Corbis-Bettmann; 12 C Hulton Getty Picture Collection; 12 TL Cooper-Hewitt, National Design Museum, Smithsonian Institution, Art Resource, NY, Gift of Margaret Carnegie Miller, 1977-111-1a/c, photo by Dave King; 12 TR Voyage dans la Lune, 1902, Kobal Collection/Melies; 13 BL Corbis-Bettmann; 13 BR Mary Evans Picture Library; 13 CL © Frederick Warne & Co., 1902, 1987; 13 CR Teddy Bear Museum, Stratford-upon-Avon/Roland Kemp; 13 TL Mary Evans Picture Library; 14 CR Hulton Getty Picture Collection; 14 TL Corbis-Bettmann; 15 CL Robert Harding Picture Library; 15 CR Corbis-Bettmann; 15 TL Robert Opie Collection; 16 BL The Granger Collection, New York; 16 BR Bridgeman Art Library London/Louvre, Paris; 16 CL Mary Evans Picture Library; 16 CR Great Train Robbery, 1903, Kobal Collection/Edison; 16 TL Hulton Getty Picture Collection; 17 BL Corbis-Bettmann; 17 CL Corbis-Bettmann; 17 CR Mary Evans Picture Library; 17 T Action Images/Presse Sportss; 18-19 CR/CL Corbis-Bettmann; 18 BL Mary Evans Picture Library; 18 BR Mary Evans Picture Library; 18 C Mary Evans Picture Library; 18 TC Mary Evans Picture Library; 18 TL Bridgeman Art Library London/Victoria & Albert Museum, London; 19 BL Mary Evans Picture Library; 19 BR Corbis-Bettmann; 19 CR Mary Evans Picture Library; 19 TR Corbis-Bettmann; 20 BL AKG London; 20 BR Mary Evans Picture Library; 20 CL Corbis-Bettmann; 20 TL Mary Evans Picture Library; 21 BL Mary Evans Picture Library; 21 BR Mary Evans Picture Library; 21 C Hulton Getty Picture Collection; 21 TL Mary Evans Picture Library; 21 TR Matisse: The Open Window, Collioure, 1905, Bridgeman Art Library London/John Hay Whitney Collection, New York/© Sucession H. Matisse/DACS 1997;
22 BC Mary Evans Picture Library; 22 CL Science & Society Picture Library; 22 TR Science & Society Picture Library; 23 BL GEC-Marconi; 23 TC Mary Evans Picture Library; 23 TL Mirror Syndication International; 23 TR British Telecommunications plc; 24 BR Mary Evans Picture Library; 24 R Corbis-Bettmann; 24 TL Topham Picturepoint; 25 BC Hulton Getty Picture Collection; 25 BL Mary Evans Picture Library; 25 CR Private Collection; 25 TC Corbis-Bettmann; 25 TL Popperfoto; 25 TR AKG London; 26 BL Corbis-Bettmann; 26 BR Hulton Getty Picture Collection; 26 CR Corbis-Bettmann; 26 TL The Granger Collection, New York; 27 BC Corbis-Bettmann; 27 BL National Park Service, Statue of Liberty National Monument; 27 CL Corbis-Bettmann; 27 TL Hulton Getty Picture Collection; 28 BR Ronald Grant Archive; 28 CR Picasso: Demoiselles d'Avignon, 1906-07, AKG London/© Succession Picasso/DACS 1997; 28 TL Popperfoto; 29 BL Popperfoto; 29 CL Hulton Getty Picture Collection; 29 CR Mary Evans Picture Library; 29 CR Mary Evans Picture Library; 29 TR Hulton Getty Picture Collection; 30 BL Mary Evans Picture Library; 30 CR Robert Opie Collection; 30 TL Hulton Getty Picture Collection; 30 TR Smithsonian Institution; 31 BL Mary Evans Picture Library; 31 BR Popperfoto; 31 CL Hulton Getty Picture Collection; 31 TL Mary Evans Picture Library; 31 TR Mary Evans Picture Library; 32-33B National Maritime Museum; 32 C Retrograph Archive Ltd; 32 CL Retrograph Archive Ltd; 32 CR Hulton Getty Picture Collection; 32 TL Mary Evans Picture Library; 32 TR Mary Evans Picture Library; 33 BR Mary Evans Picture Library; 33 CL Mary Evans Picture Library; 33 TL Robert Opie Collection; 33 TR Retrograph Archive Ltd; 34 BR Corbis-Bettmann; 34 CR Ronald Grant Archive; 34 TL Kobal Collection; 34 TR Mary Evans Picture Library; 35 BL Mary Evans Picture Library; 35 BL Mary Evans Picture Library; 35 BR Hulton Getty Picture Collection; 35 CL Corbis-Bettmann; 35 CR Tony Stone Images; 35 TR Mirror Syndication International.

1910–1919: 36 BL Hulton Getty Picture Collection; 36 BR Popperfoto; 36 CL Corbis-Bettmann; 36 TL Mary Evans Picture Library; 36 TR Corbis-Bettmann; 37 BR Corbis-Bettmann; 37 BR Mary Evans Picture Library; 37 CR Hulton Getty Picture Collection; 37 TL Hulton Getty Picture Collection; 37 TR Corbis-Bettmann; 38 BL Mary Evans Picture Library; 38 BR Corbis-Bettmann; 38 CL Mary Evans Picture Library; 38 R Tony Stone Images; 38 TL Popperfoto; 39 BL Courtesy of the Manager, National Postal Museum; 39 BR The Granger Collection, New York; 39 R Corbis-Bettmann; 39 TL AKG London/Musee du Louvre; 40 B Illustrated London News Picture Library; 40 BL Illustrated London News Picture Library; 40 CL Illustrated London News Picture Library; 41 CR Popperfoto; 41 TR Popperfoto; 42 BL Popperfoto; 42 BR Mary Evans Picture Library; 42 CL Corbis-Bettmann; 42 CR Mary Evans Picture Library; 42 TL Archive Photos; 42 TR Mary Evans Picture Library; 43 BL British Film Institute; 43 BR Illustrated London News Picture Library; 43 C Corbis-Bettmann; 43 CR Hulton Getty Picture Collection; 43 TR Hulton Getty Picture Collection; 44 B Corbis-Bettmann; 44 C Mary Evans Picture Library; 44 CL Mary Evans Picture Library; 44 TL Mary Evans Picture Library; 44 TR Mary Evans Picture Library; 45 BC Mary Evans Picture Library; 45 BR Mary Evans Picture Library; 45 C Mary Evans Picture Library; 45 CR Mary Evans Picture Library; 45 TC Mary Evans Picture Library; 45 TL Mary Evans Picture Library; 45 TR Mary Evans Picture Library; 46 BL Archive Photos; 46 CR Mary Evans Picture Library; 46 TL Mary Evans Picture Library; 46 TR Corbis-Bettmann; 47 CR Corbis-Bettmann; 47 BL Barnes Collection; 47 TL Corbis-Bettmann; 47 TR Popperfoto; 48 BR Mary Evans Picture Library; 48 CL Hulton Getty Picture Collection; 48 TR Mary Evans Picture Library; 49 BL Mary Evans Picture Library; 49 C Ronald Grant Archive; 49 CR Illustrated London News Picture Library; 49 TL David King Collection; 49 TR Mary Evans Picture Library; 51 BR Corbis-Bettmann; 51 TL Popperfoto; 52 BL Imperial War Museum, London; 52 C Topham Picturepoint; 52 CL Birth of a Nation, 1914, Ronald Grant Archive/Epic; 52 TC Mary Evans Picture Library; 53 BL Hulton Getty Picture Collection; 53 BR Mary Evans Picture Library; 53 CL Imperial War Museum; 54 BL Dada poster, 1922 by Kurt Schwitters, Vintage Magazine Co. Archive./© DACS 1997; 54 BR Ronald Grant Archive; 54 CL Hulton Getty Picture Collection; 54 TL Hulton Getty Picture Collection; 54 TR Rex Features; 55 BR Popperfoto; 55 CR Mary Evans Picture Library; 55 TR Hulton Getty Picture Collection; 56 BL AKG London; 56 BR Ronald Grant Archive; 56 CR Popperfoto; 57 BL Topham Picturepoint; 57 BR Mary Evans Picture Library; 57 CR Mary Evans Picture Library; 57 TR Hulton Getty Picture Collection; 58 CL Imperial War Museum; 58 CR Mary Evans Picture Library; 59 BL Mary Evans Picture Library; 59 BR David King Collection; 59 CR Popperfoto; 59 TL Imperial War Museum; 59 TR Hulton Getty Picture Collection; 60 BL Mary Evans Picture Library; 60 BR David King Collection; 60 CR Popperfoto; 60 TL David King Collection; 60 TR David King Collection; 61 BL David King Collection; 61 BR David King Collection; 61 C David King Collection; 61 CA David King Collection; 61 TL Jean-Loup Charmet; 62 BL AKG London; 62 BR Corbis-Bettmann; 62 CR Corbis-Bettmann; 62 TL Mary Evans Picture Library; 63 BL Tarzan, 1918, Kobal Collection; 63 BR CinePlus; 63 CR Camera Press; 63 T Illustrated London News Picture Library; 63 TR Hulton Getty Picture Collection; 64 BR Corbis-Bettmann; 64 C Corbis-Bettmann; 64 TL Mary Evans Picture Library; 65 BL Topham Picturepoint; 65 BR Carmen,Ronald Grant Archive; 65 C Paul Nash: We are making a New World, Bridgeman Art Library London/Imperial War Museum, London/Reproduced by permission of the Paul Nash Trust; 65 CR Archive Photos; 65 TL Corbis-Bettmann; 65 TR Popperfoto; 66 BL Mary Evans Picture Library; 66 BR Corbis-Bettmann; 66 CL AKG London; 66 TR Ullstein Bilderdienst; 66 TR Hulton Getty Picture Collection; 67 BL Hulton Getty Picture Collection; 67 BR Bridgeman Art Library London/National Gallery, London; 67 C Mary Evans Picture Library; 67 CL Topham Picturepoint; 67 CR Felix the Cat, Kobal Collection; 67 TR Popperfoto.

1920–1929: 68 BL Marcel Duchamps: Fountain, AKG London/© ADAGP, Paris and DACS, London 1997; 68 BL Treasure Island, 1920, Kobal Collection; 68 CR Archive Photos; 68 TL Corbis-Bettmann; 68 TR Mary Evans Picture Library; 69 BL Corbis-Bettmann; 69 BR David King Collection; 69 CR Hulton Getty Picture Collection; 70 BL Robert Opie Collection; 70 BR Mary Evans Picture Library; 70 CR Four Horsemen of the Apocalypse, 1921, Ronald Grant Archive/Metro; 70 TL The Kid, Kobal Collection/First National/Charles Chaplin; 70 TR Hulton Getty Picture Collection; 71 BL Smithsonian Institution; 71 BR Mary Evans Picture Library; 71 CL Archive Photos; 71 CR David King Collection; 71 TR Corbis-Bettmann; 72 BL Reader's Digest; 73 BR Corbis-Bettmann; 73 BR Robert Harding Picture Library; 73 C Topham Picturepoint; 73 CL Topham Picturepoint; 73 TL Nosferatu, 1922, Ronald Grant Archive/Prana-Film GMBH; 73 TL Metropolis, 1926, Kobal Collection/UFA; 73 TR Mary Evans Picture Library; 74 BL Robert Harding Picture Library; 74 BR Mary Evans Picture Library; 74 CL Popperfoto; 74 TR Griffiths Institute, Ashmolean Museum; 74 TL Mary Evans Picture Library; 75 BL Ancient Art & Architecture Collection; 75 BR Mary Evans Picture Library; 75 BR High Clere Castle; 75 CR Mary Evans Picture Library; 75 TR Robert Harding Picture Library; 75 TL Peter Clayton; 6 BL Robert Opie Collection; 76 BR National Motor Museum Beaulieu/Dave King; 76 C Topham Picturepoint; 76 CL Corbis-Bettmann; 76 CR by Meccano, UK/London Toy & Model Museum; 76 TR Archive Photos; 77 BL David King Collection; 77 BR Mary Evans Picture Library; 77 CL AKG London; 77 CR AKG London; 77 T Hulton Getty Picture Collection; 78-9 C Hulton Getty Picture Collection; 78 BR Mary Evans Picture Library; 78 TL Topham Picturepoint; 78 CL by J.A.J., Paris/London Toy & Model Museum; 78 TR Corbis-Bettmann; 78 TR Mary Evans Picture Library; 79 BL Mary Evans Picture Library; 79 BL Robert Opie Collection; 79 BR Ronald Grant Archive; 79 CR Ronald Grant Archive; 79 TL Joel Finler; 79 TR Archive Photos; 80 BC Mary Evans Picture Library; 80 C Corbis-Bettmann; 80 TL Corbis-Bettmann; 81 CL Corbis-Bettmann; 81 CR The Granger Collection, New York; 81 TC The Sheik, 1921, Ronald Grant Archive; 81 TR Hulton Getty Picture Collection; 82 BL Corbis-Bettmann; 82 BR Mary Evans Picture Library; 82 C Hulton Getty Picture Collection; 82 CL Bridgeman Art Library London/Private Collection; 82 TR Corbis-Bettmann; 83 BL Corbis-Bettmann; 83 BR Hulton Getty Picture Collection; 83 CL Corbis-Bettmann; 83 TR Corbis-Bettmann; 84 BL Corbis-Bettmann; 84 BR Topham Picturepoint; 84 C Smithsonian Institution; 84 T Hulton Getty Picture Collection; 85 BL Mary Evans Picture Library; 85 BR Bridgeman Art Library London/National Gallery, London; 85 C Mary Evans Picture Library; 85 CL Redferns/Max Jones Files; 85 TL Archive Photos; 85 TR From Winnie-the-Pooh by A.A.Milne, line illustration by E.H.Shepard copyright under the Berne Convention, reproduced by permission of Curtis Brown, London. © 1926 by E.P.Dutton, renewed 1954 by A.A.Milne. Used by permission of Dutton Children's Books, a division of Penguin Books USA Inc.; 86 BL Mary Evans Picture Library; 86 CL Corbis-Bettmann; 86 CL National Motor Museum Beaulieu; 86 CLA National Motor Museum Beaulieu; 86 CR National Motor Museum Beaulieu/Dave King; 86 TL Mary Evans Picture Library; 87 BR Mary Evans Picture Library; 87 CR Mary Evans Picture Library; 87 TL Corbis-Bettmann; 88 BL Topham Picturepoint; 88 BR Mary Evans Picture Library; 88 C Topham Picturepoint; 88 TR Illustrated London News Picture Library; 89 BL Mary Evans Picture Library; 89 BR AKG London; 89 TL Illustrated London News Picture Library; 89 TR Ronald Grant Archive; 90 BL Liz McAulay; 90 BR Knudsens Fotosenter; 90 CL Illustrated London News Picture Library; 90 CR Steamboat Willie (Mickey Mouse), 1928, Ronald Grant Archive/© Walt Disney; 90 CR Illustrated London News Picture Library; 90 T Hulton Getty Picture Collection; 91 BL Corbis-Bettmann ; 91 BR Archive Photos; 91 TL Archive Photos; 91 TR Mary Evans Picture Library; 92 BL Broadway Melody , 1929, Kobal Collection; 92 BR Chien Andalou, 1929, Kobal Collection/Bunuel-Dali; 92 CL Police Academy Museum, NY; 92 CR Robert Opie Collection; 92 TC Wings, Kobal Collection/Paramount; 92 TR Oscar® A. M. P. A. S./MOMI/Photo: Dave King; 93 BR Hulton Getty Picture Collection; 93 BR Topham Picturepoint; 93 CL Popeye, Ronald Grant Archive/Paramount; 93 CR Topham Picturepoint; 93 T Mary Evans Picture Library; 94-5 BR/BL Popperfoto; 94 BL Popperfoto; 94 CL

1950s

- **1950** Pass books become compulsory in South Africa.
- **1950** North Korea invades South Korea.

- **1952** *This is Cinerama* uses wide-screen system.
- **1952** Eva Perón, wife of Argentine president, dies.
- **1952** Crown Prince Hussein becomes king of Jordan.
- **1953** UK scientists reveal the structure of DNA.
- **1953** Miniature matchbox toy cars are an instant hit.

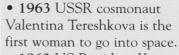

- **1953** Blue jeans become popular as leisure wear.
- **1953** New Zealander Edmund Hillary and Sherpa Tensing climb Everest.
- **1954** In the USA, a new vaccine against polio is tested.
- **1954** UK athlete Roger Bannister runs a mile in under four minutes.

1960s

- **1960** Troops kill 93 blacks in Sharpeville in South Africa.
- **1960** Sirimavo Bandaranaike of Ceylon is the world's first woman prime minister.

- **1961** Democrat John Kennedy is sworn in as US President.
- **1961** East Germans build wall to separate east and west Berlin.
- **1962** US actress and sex symbol Marilyn Monroe is found dead.
- **1962** UK group The Beatles' first hit single is *Love Me Do*.

- **1963** USSR cosmonaut Valentina Tereshkova is the first woman to go into space.
- **1963** US President Kennedy is assassinated in Dallas.
- **1964** Vidal Sassoon creates sharp new hairstyles.
- **1964** Nelson Mandela is imprisoned in South Africa.
- **1964** Kenya is made a republic.

1970s

- **1970** King Hussein of Jordan and Yassir Arafat of the PLO sign a war truce.
- **1971** A microprocessor (chip) is developed.

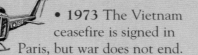

- **1973** The Vietnam ceasefire is signed in Paris, but war does not end.
- **1973** Picasso dies in France.
- **1973** President Allende of Chile is assassinated.
- **1974** President Nixon resigns.
- **1974** Altair is the first small home computer manufactured.

- **1975** The Vietnam War ends as South Vietnam surrenders.
- **1975** A terracotta army is found by Chinese archaeologists excavating tomb.
- **1975** Civil war breaks out in Angola after it gains independence.
- **1976** White police fire on children in Soweto, South Africa.

1980s

- **1980** Mount St Helens in the state of Washington, USA, erupts.
- **1980** The Iran-Iraq war escalates.
- **1981** Nobel Peace Prize winner President Sadat of Egypt is assassinated.

- **1982** The French launch their telecom minitel on-line service.
- **1983** President Reagan of the USA proposes a new defence system called "Star Wars".
- **1984** News reports of famine in Ethiopia stun people all over the world.

- **1984** Scientists warn of global warming (the greenhouse effect).
- **1984** The virus that causes AIDS is discovered.
- **1984** A chemical leak in the Indian city of Bhopal kills at least 2,000 people.
- **1985** Live Aid concert is watched by 1.5 million people.

1990s

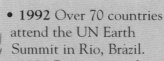

- **1990** The Hubble Space Telescope is launched from Cape Canaveral in the USA.
- **1991** Coup in the USSR topples Premier Gorbachev.

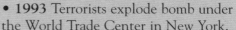
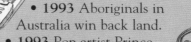

- **1992** Over 70 countries attend the UN Earth Summit in Rio, Brazil.
- **1992** Race riots rock Los Angeles in the USA.
- **1992** Personal colour videophones are introduced.
- **1992** Film of conditions in Serbian death camps cause shock and outrage worldwide.

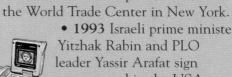

- **1993** Terrorists explode bomb under the World Trade Center in New York.
- **1993** Israeli prime minister Yitzhak Rabin and PLO leader Yassir Arafat sign peace accord in the USA.
- **1993** Aboriginals in Australia win back land.
- **1993** Pop artist Prince changes his name to a symbol.